The Limits of History

THE LIMITS OF HISTORY

Constantin Fasolt

THE UNIVERSITY OF CHICAGO PRESS
CHICAGO AND LONDON

The University of Chicago Press, Chicago 60637
The University of Chicago Press, Ltd., London
© 2004 by The University of Chicago
All rights reserved. Published 2004.
Paperback edition 2013
Printed in the United States of America

22 21 20 19 18 17 16 15 14 13   2 3 4 5 6

ISBN-13: 978-0-226-23910-1 (cloth)
ISBN-13: 978-0-226-10124-8 (paperback)
ISBN-13: 978-0-226-11564-1 (e-book)
10.7208/chicago/9780226115641.001.0001

The University of Chicago Press gratefully acknowledges the generous support of the John Simon Guggenheim Memorial Foundation toward the publication of this book.

Library of Congress Cataloging-in-Publication Data

Fasolt, Constantin, 1951–
    The limits of history / Constantin Fasolt.
        p. cm.
    Includes bibliographical references and index.
    ISBN: 0-226-23910-1 (cloth : alk. paper)
    1. History—Philosophy.   2. History—Historiography.
    3. Historiography.   4. History, Ancient—Historiography.   I. Title.
    D16.8.F328 2004
    901—dc21
                                                    2003010411

♾ This paper meets the requirements of ANSI/NISO Z39.48-1992 (Permanence of Paper).

Go, go, go, said the bird: human kind
Cannot bear very much reality.

T. S. Eliot, *Burnt Norton*

Contents

Preface ix
Acknowledgments xi
Introduction xiii

ONE
A Dangerous Form of Knowledge 3

TWO
The Subject: Hermann Conring 46

THREE
The Context: Discursus Novus 92

FOUR
The Text: Bartolus of Sassoferrato 155

FIVE
The Limits of History 219

Notes 233
Works Cited 285
Index 317

Preface

Our attitude toward the past is governed by three principles:
 1. the past is gone forever;
 2. to understand the meaning of a text, you must first put it in the context of its time and place;
 3. you cannot tell where you are going unless you know where you are coming from.

There may be more, but these are fundamental. They seem simple and obvious. So simple that they cannot be analyzed, so obvious that they are subject to no doubt. But they rest on assumptions about time and eternity, truth and meaning, freedom and responsibility that are neither simple nor obvious at all. People did not always believe them to be true. The spell they cast on our minds only began to take effect after the Middle Ages, and their ascendancy over all other forms of thought was not assured (insofar as it ever was) until history became the province of professionals. Since then they may have seemed to rule supreme. But they are no more obvious today than when they were first put in place, and they have consequences for our understanding of society, the state, and ourselves that are no longer quite so welcome as they once were.

Their truth needs to be tested.

Acknowledgments

Over the years it took me to write *The Limits of History,* I enjoyed the help and friendship of more people than I could properly acknowledge without writing another book. Some of them were close and helped me often; others were distant and helped only on occasion. Some helped because they knew me personally, others because they met me in some official capacity, and yet others did so for both reasons. They helped with knowledge and emotion, money and conversation, criticism and assent. Some even helped by helping not at all. To each and every one of them I gladly offer thanks.

I would like to mention some of them by name. To Andy Abbott, Karl Otmar Freiherr von Aretin, David Armitage, Paul Berliner, Robert Bireley, John Boyer, Tom Brady, Dipesh Chakrabarty, Laurence Dreyfus, Hermann Josef Echterhoff, Anthony Grafton, Notker Hammerstein, John Headley, Tamar Herzog, Julius Kirshner, Tony LaVopa, Erik Midelfort, the late Arnaldo Momigliano, Bob Moore, John Mundy, Frank Oakley, Peter Onuf, Hans Peterse, Tom Robisheaux, and Michael Stolleis I am grateful that they talked to me with interest, read some of what I wrote, and kept me on my intellectual toes.

My friends Bob Rosen and Zachary Schiffman did more than keep me on my toes. They read successive drafts with close attention and stopped me from publishing until the book was ready. I hope they will be pleased with the result.

To the University of Chicago, the University of Virginia, the Herzog August Bibliothek in Wolfenbüttel, the Max-Planck-Institut für Europäische Rechtsgeschichte in Frankfurt, the Institut für Europäische Geschichte in Mainz, the American Philosophical Society, the Gladys Krieble Delmas Foundation, the National Humanities Center, and the John Simon Guggenheim Memorial Foundation I am grateful for financial and institutional support. They paid me, housed me, fed me, put me in the company of like-minded people, and gave me the opportunity to read and think and write.

To the librarians and archivists of the University of Chicago, the University of Virginia, the Herzog August Bibliothek, the Newberry Library, the University of Wisconsin at Madison, the Historisches Archiv der Stadt Köln, the Niedersächsisches Staatsarchiv in Wolfenbüttel, and the National Humanities Center I am grateful for giving me books and documents to study. I am grateful to David Reis and Thomas Cornfield for helping to compile a bibliographical database and to Karen Carroll for editing an early draft.

For their gracious permission to use material in chapters 3 and 4 to which they hold the copyright, I thank the Renaissance Society of America ("Author and Authenticity in Conring's *New Discourse on the Roman-German Emperor:* A Seventeenth-Century Case Study," *Renaissance Quarterly* 54 [2001]: 188–220) and the Sixteenth Century Journal Publishers ("A Question of Right: Hermann Conring's *New Discourse on the Roman-German Emperor,*" *Sixteenth Century Journal* 28 [1997]: 739–58).

Special thanks go to Douglas Mitchell, my editor at the University of Chicago Press. I could not have wished for a more professionally supportive and intellectually engaging editor. Once he showed interest in this book, I had the wind at my back. I would also like to thank his assistant Timothy McGovern for helping to steer the book through the press, Lois Crum for her efficient copyediting, and Christine Schwab for coordinating the editing.

To these and to all other friends, colleagues, students, and institutions from whose conversation and assistance I have benefited I acknowledge my indebtedness with gratitude and pleasure.

Nick and Catherine, do you remember the Springfield Apartments? That's where most of this was written. Thanks for being there with me.

Prema, I quoted Morgenstern to you: "Lass die Moleküle rasen. . . ." Here we go, love, progress, revolution, and fire on the mountain.

Introduction

> Ob die Geschichte sich in ihrem Wesen nur durch und für die Historie offenbart oder ob die Geschichte durch die historische Vergegenständlichung nicht eher verdeckt wird, bleibt für die Geschichtswissenschaft unentscheidbar. Entschieden aber ist: in der Theorie der Geschichte waltet die Geschichte als das Unumgängliche.
>
> Heidegger, *Wissenschaft und Besinnung*

I wrote this book to make a basic point: history and politics are far more closely joined together than is commonly realized. By history I mean knowledge of the past, as well as the technique by which such knowledge is produced and the activity required to that end, especially in the forms developed by professionally trained historians. By politics I mean the actions human beings take to change their fate, especially the actions taken by human beings with the power to affect the fate of others. Put crudely, the point is that our knowledge of the past cannot be separated from the actions that we take to change our fate.

I would like to make this point for two main reasons. The first is merely to make something better known that is not clearly understood. To understand it better will entail a certain intellectual advance. If that is all I can accomplish with this book, I shall be satisfied. The second reason is to undo the ties by which history keeps human beings in bondage to themselves. Even if I can only loosen them a little bit, I shall have reached my goal.

History still serves as a bulwark against ignorance and lies. In that regard its value is utterly undiminished and will undoubtedly remain so for all time. But history used to be more than that. During the centuries between the

Renaissance and the Enlightenment, history put human beings in charge of their own affairs and gave them the liberty to differ. More than just another form of knowledge, history was a challenge thrown in the face of tradition and authority, an undertaking full of doubt and danger, a knowledge not merely considered part of a liberal education, but one that actually fostered liberty. In those days history was the stuff of revolution.

That time is gone. There is nothing revolutionary about history today, and it has very little to do with liberty. Now history teaches human beings in a school whose doors are shut. No one can seem to think of any way to open them again. History may well exercise a more seductive power over the modern mind than any other form of thought, including science and religion. Outside, the world is surging. Inside, history demands attention while liberty and progress sit well-behaved on benches and study rules and ponder theory and gather information.

History is the product of a technology. It does not simply lie around like stones or apples, ready to be picked up by anyone who pleases. It must first be produced. It is the output that results (usually in the form of books) when historians (experts in the technology) perform a certain set of operations (collecting, reading, analyzing, comparing, writing, editing, publishing) upon a certain class of objects (writings, paintings, buildings, coins, ceramics) in order to gain knowledge of the past. History takes effort. Its chief attraction consists of the enhanced control it promises to human beings over the world of self and society. That promise is why it was adopted in early modern times and why it spread. It was a prized possession for those who knew how to direct its forces against a target of their choosing in order to achieve a desirable effect. In that regard historical technology is just like any other kind of technology. And its benefits have not lost their appeal.

But now we seem no longer to have a choice. Our survival as the human beings that we have made of ourselves depends upon the smooth operation of the historical machine. The machine has grown so unwieldy that merely to prevent its creaking gears from grinding to a halt requires more energy than would be worth the effort if we could do without. It seems, however, that we can no longer do without. In that respect as well, history resembles other forms of technology. Invented more or less by chance, adopted for its stupendous benefits, it has become an indispensable necessity. History allowed us to create a new kind of humanity. Now we cannot think of any other kind. The knowledge on which we called in order to assert our freedom now limits our liberty. We are possessed by history, compelled to bail the water with a tiny bucket from the rising tide of time.

That history and politics are somehow linked together is of course a commonplace. But though the link is familiar, its nature remains obscure. Let me describe two different approaches to the matter that are both often taken and are both fundamentally misleading. One is to seek the link between history and politics in the attention historians pay to politics. History is linked to politics, some say, because politics is what history is *about*. From that perspective the link consists of the relation between a given method of examination (history) and a given subject matter to which that method is applied (politics). But that link is weak. It is as quickly broken as the historian's decision to shift attention to another subject, and as quickly reaffirmed as the historian's gaze can be turned back. It is a matter of seemingly free choice, subject to moral judgment, to censure, and to praise.

This helps us understand the energy historians have spent on deciding whether history ought to be focused on politics or not. For the most part, those who prefer to focus elsewhere seem to have won this great debate. In some places the history of politics is still extolled; more commonly it is dismissed as the history of kings and battles, redescribed as military and diplomatic history, transformed into the history of political culture, or turned inside out as the history of imperialism and colonialism. Much of it has in the process been superseded by economic, social, and cultural histories of different stripes. True, in recent decades, political history has made a reappearance on the stage. But its renewed vitality reflects, I think, more the exhaustion of alternatives than an improvement in the fate of political history itself. History no longer deals nearly as exclusively with politics as it once did, and it is not likely ever to do so again.

The link between history and politics may therefore seem to be either a vice of past historians whose overthrow deserves to be greeted with applause or (from the perspective of conservative observers) a virtue requiring reaffirmation against the corruption rampant in the discipline of history today. In neither case is it believed to be intact. Yet nothing could be further from the truth. The link between history and politics has scarcely anything to do with what history is *about*. It is alive and well and cannot be undone by changing only the subject of investigation.

A second common view of the link between history and politics rests on the elementary observation that historians are often *influenced by* politics. This, too, is utterly familiar. Regardless of the subject to which historians pay attention, they often do so in order to drive home some point they happen to be fond of for reasons that have more to do with what they want for themselves than with the truth about the past. The history that results is biased. Since biased history is universally condemned, historians worth their salt make systematic efforts to prevent politics from entering into their work. These efforts are precisely what makes them professionals. And they work better than uninitiated or suspicious minds imagine. But they disable the link between history and politics no more than does the turn from political history to other subject matters.

This is because the link does not consist of the influence that politics exercises *over* history either. On the contrary, the more clearly the biases of historians are demonstrated, and the more carefully those biases are trimmed, the more the link between history and politics is hardened. Its strength is at its peak: not where historians lean left or right in the interest of some cause, but just the opposite, where they walk on the straight and narrow path toward nothing besides real knowledge of the past. The vulgar doubts about historians' ability and willingness to resist personal biases, the image of history's waxen nose, and the postmodern critique of objectivity do not suffice to bring the link between history and politics to light. They serve much better to distract attention from its irresistible allure.

History is linked to politics by the practice of history itself. There is no need for historians to focus their attention on politics in order to establish the connection. The connection is complete the moment they turn their attention to the past. Nor do historians need to defend the interests of one or another party for history to be placed in the service of politics. They serve politics as soon as they begin to do research. Contrary to common wisdom, nothing keeps history more firmly in the grip of politics than the self-discipline with which historians devote themselves to the pursuit of historical truth. It is the pursuit of knowledge about the past as such that places them into alliance with politicians.

This is not to say that history and politics are identical. There are many other ways of taking political action than by studying history. Nor is it to say that history is only a political activity. Many things are required for the study of the past that have very little, if anything, to do with politics. But there exists a point where history and politics are indistinguishable from each other, like the area where two circles intersect or the element that enters into two different chemical compositions.

That point is relatively easy to describe in the abstract. It consists of the commitment to a certain view of human nature that has held sway since medieval ways of thought and action were shattered in early modern times. This is the view that human beings are free and independent agents with the ability to shape their fate, the obligation to act on that ability, and responsibility for the consequences. According to this view, human beings are neither governed by divine providence nor condemned to the thoughtless repetition of custom, much less compelled to obey mere animal instinct or do battle with the devil. They are in charge of their own affairs. Of course their freedom is admittedly limited by laws of physics and the particular circumstances of their time and place—those circumstances which it is the function of history to determine. But only limited, not abolished. History can therefore help one understand why human beings acted as they did; perhaps it can even explain certain historical developments in terms of cause and effect (it certainly has tried). But history can never absolve human beings from the responsibilities of freedom. On the contrary, history does nothing more effectively than to assert the liberty that is a necessary precondition for responsibility—and politics.

This sketch of the character of history may seem improbable so long as attention is focused solely on history in the sense of knowledge of the past. For history in that sense consists of *explanations* of *why* human beings behaved like this or that. In that sense history consists of an account of conditions limiting human liberty, rather than an assertion of human responsibility. But the technology by which such explanations are produced rests on the opposite assumption: that the bits and pieces historians use in order to construct their knowledge of the past are grounded in some human action taken for some freely chosen purpose—as opposed to custom, providence, or nature. Providence writes no books, custom has no intentions, and nature takes no actions; only human beings do. Providence, custom, and nature are not responsible for the evidence before the historian; human beings are. That is the historian's fundamental creed; and it is daily reaffirmed in the analysis of evidence and the reports on the results.

Historians therefore may never agree upon exactly *what* the evidence testifies. But they are certain *that* it testifies to something some human being did. This letter here? That temple there? That ancient song? None of them are there by accident, nor have they all been there from time immemorial, much less because God put them there, and certainly not solely for reasons of the sort that explain why it may rain today and shine tomorrow. They are there because *someone* wrote the letter, built the temple, sang the song, and did so at some particular time and place, for some particular purpose. That is the only reason why the letter, the temple, and the song can testify to the conditions of any particular time and place at all. Someone's *responsibility* is the chain by which the letter, the temple, and the song in front of the historian are fastened directly to the past. That chain ends in the person with the responsibility. If it did not end there, sources of information about the past would turn from evidence about the past into channels to eternity. Historians would have no way to stop at what someone did. They would have to go all the way back to natural causes, custom immemorial, or the creation of the universe. If sources could not be attributed to authors, if evidence could not be tied to some specific action taken by someone at some specific time, history would collapse into natural science, surrender to tradition and religion, or vanish in an entirely different order of reality and time.

The commitment to the principle that someone is *responsible for the evidence* is fundamental. It is also utterly independent of the subjects to which historians devote their attention and equally independent of whatever influence politics exercises over their thinking—even independent of the meaning they find in the evidence. It is inherent in the very claim that knowledge of the past must be derived from an examination of evidence. It is strengthened, not attenuated, by the degree to which historians subject partisan motivations to the discipline of knowledge. It operates with just the same efficiency in Ranke's universal history, Marx's analysis of the class struggle, and the most recent histories of sexuality. Even reviews of current postmodern theories need to assume—sometimes despite themselves—that whatever theory happens to be under examination is *someone's* theory, conveyed from someone to the examiner by some piece of writing. That is how history is linked to politics.

History therefore needs not at all to oblige its followers to render allegiance to a specific party. It rather places limits on their choice. History helps to determine what counts as politics and what does not. It makes the politics of liberty, responsibility, and progress seem natural while ruling others out as nonpolitical. It leaves much room to fight over the meaning and possibility of liberty, progress, and responsibility. But there may be no other fight in town. Someone must be responsible, and someone must be free. The past, as a familiar saying goes, is a foreign country. Historians are just as active in invading that foreign country, conquering its inhabitants, subjecting them to their discipline, and annexing their territories to the possessions of the present as any imperialist who ever sought to impose his power on colonies abroad. To call their activity a conquest is no mere figure of speech. It is a perfectly accurate description of history's political effect.

All of this, as I have said, is relatively easy to point out in the abstract. But as soon as one attempts to state it in detail, a host of difficulties blocks the way. Most of these consist of straightforward intellectual problems. By far the greatest difficulty, however, lies prior to the point where such problems could even be addressed. It arises from the very claim that the study of history is in and of itself a form of political activity. For such a claim casts doubt on a distinction that is basic not only to history, but to the economy of knowledge as a whole: the distinction between knowledge and action. That claim will therefore be resisted.

Historians stake their professional existence on the conviction that the life of action enters history only from the outside, as it were, as something extraneous to the examination of the evidence. According to that understanding, history may never be confused with politics. History is rather said to be a form of contemplation, a branch of academic life. Whatever value the study of the past possesses depends entirely on research without foregone conclusions. That is the source from which historians derive their right to have any impact on politics at all. Not by taking action, but quite the opposite: by refraining from action in order to examine the evidence. Not because they participate in politics, but because their examination of the data can change the minds of those who do.

Of course this is merely an ideal. Politics inevitably enters into the practice of the craft. History is always biased in some way. That much will be conceded. But to acknowledge bias is not to welcome it, much less to assert that history essentially coincides with politics. The opposite is true. History is theory of the past. History should tell it like it is (or was)—and if that turns out to be impossible, history should still not stoop to telling it like it is not, merely because that suits the historian or because someone in power would like to hear it told that way. The very acknowledgment of bias testifies to the strength of the conviction that history exists in separation from politics. If it were otherwise, research would be a pointless thing to do. Research is time spent away from action; archives yield evidence that all too often contradicts a given political agenda. If history served merely to elaborate a given political position, why do research at all? Why not go straight to the seats of power?

The point made here, however, is not that history is biased. The point is that history is in and of itself political. Whatever biases historians may have are personal distractions from an official theme. To make this point is to encounter something different from a straightforward intellectual problem. It is to meet with historical consciousness as such and ask why history ought to be believed if even history without bias is merely politics under a different name. That question threatens the possibility of knowing anything about the past at all.

That threat is perfectly well known. And more than just well known. It occupies the heart of the historical endeavor. It is the fear that history might offer no escape from politics. Like an ugly frog, that fear sits right in the middle of the well from which historians draw water. Nothing has shaped the destiny of history more deeply. Nothing has been a sharper spur to history than the desire to defeat that fear with knowledge. What was the point of Ranke's ringing call for history "wie es eigentlich gewesen," if not precisely to proclaim the danger that history was all too likely *not* to report what actually happened? Who has not heard that proclamation? Which historian has not tried to defend the truth about the past from politics?

There is no denying that the results have been spectacular. From Ranke down to the most recent histories of gender, memory, and consumption, even cursory observers cannot fail to be impressed by the tremendous intellectual and emotional energy with which historians have labored in order to perfect our knowledge of the past. Much the same energy has gone into the search for an adequate theory of history. From Vico's *New Science* down to the most recent issue of *History and Theory,* historians and theorists of history have looked at the standing of history in the realm of knowledge and its relationship not only to politics, but also to society and economics, the sciences, literature and linguistics, religion, art, and philosophy. For more than two centuries, historians and theorists have labored hard to show just what we know and what we can reasonably expect to know about the past in a concerted effort to shake off the fear that history might suffer from some congenital deficiency tainting its very core. That is the great enterprise in which success bestows professional distinction and public recognition, the cause in whose service different schools of history have been succeeding one another one by one. And this is doubtless how it will continue in the future.

But neither historians nor theorists have ever reached their goal. On the contrary, they have succeeded only in moving it further out of reach. As each new book that claimed to be more adequate than the last fell to the ax of criticism, the recognition dawned that *more* adequate accounts would be superfluous if *plain* adequate accounts were possible. As theorists divided into opposing schools of thought, suspicions grew that theory only heightens the fever it promises to cure. If once upon a time the search for an adequate account of the past and the search for an adequate theory of history seemed to be mutually reinforcing, they now oppose each other. Practitioners of history affect indifference to theory if not downright contempt. Theoreticians retaliate by lampooning the naïveté of practitioners. The right denounces the left for failing to distinguish knowledge from political agitation. The left accuses the right of lying about its motives. Neo-Aristotelians and poststructuralists trade insults with each other over truth and moral relativism. If the point of the endeavor once was to distinguish history from politics, it is now virtually impossible to study history at all without taking explicitly political positions. The struggle to redeem the soul of history seems to have brought about the very ruin for fear of which it was begun.

From my perspective, no other outcome ought to have been expected. If it is true that the historian's search for adequate knowledge of the past is itself a form of political activity, then the pursuit of more adequate knowledge of the past can only result in an increasing number of more or less inadequate books and articles with patently doubtful claims upon the truth and visibly political commitments. And if it is true that at the bottom of history lies a political commitment, then the attempt to gain a theoretical perspective on history can only result in tautology or absurdity. Tautology, because the theory of history must presuppose the very commitment it wishes to examine; absurdity, because it seeks to leave the ground on which alone it can exist.

Heidegger put it succinctly in the epigraph above, with more subtle overtones than English can reproduce: "It is not enough to study history in order to determine if the reality of the past reveals itself only through, and to, historical examination, or if that reality is not rather covered up by historical objectification."[1] Indeed not. Hence, the desire to criticize old works of history for their sins of omission and commission is both perpetually active and impossible to satisfy by more research. "But that much is certain: the theory of history depends on history as what it cannot do without." Which is to say, the theory of history assumes precisely that which needs to be explained. Like the Cretan who maintained that all Cretans are liars, the theorists cannot decide whether their claims are true or false; and like the lying Cretans, historians can take no comfort from the perplexity of their critics.

Whoever wants to demonstrate that history and politics are consubstantial thus faces a considerable problem. Such demonstrations cannot be expected from the study of the past, because the status of history is itself in doubt. Nor can they be expected from any theory of history, because that begs the question. Neither theory nor practice of history seem capable of an unclouded view on the commitment that makes history possible. What then? Clearly it is not enough to state that history is just one other form of politics and leave it at that. That might spare us absurdity, but it would also put an end to the pursuit of knowledge. Yet it is just as clearly not enough to continue with history as though nothing had changed. And above all it surely will not do to advance a hypothesis whose very point appears to be that it cannot be proven true.

That leaves only one possibility: to practice history for no other purpose than to experience the limits placed on our understanding of the past by the commitment at its core. The frog needs to be swallowed with the water. Emphatically not in order to reduce history to absurdity, and much less in order to abandon knowledge, but in the hope that by encountering the limits of history we may at least become aware of something that cannot possibly reveal itself so long as it is actively denied or presupposed. That is what I shall try to accomplish in this book.

The Limits of History

For me the self-conscious ego is the seat of boredom. This increasing, swelling, domineering, painful self-consciousness is the only rival of the political and social powers that run my life (business, technological-bureaucratic powers, the state). You have a great organized movement of life, and you have the single self, independently conscious, proud of its detachment and its absolute immunity, its stability and its power to remain unaffected by anything whatsoever—by the sufferings of others or by society or by politics or by external chaos. In a way it doesn't give a damn. It is asked to give a damn, and we often urge it to give a damn but the curse of noncaring lies upon this painfully free consciousness. It is free from attachment to beliefs and to other souls. Cosmologies, ethical systems? It can run through them by the dozens. For to be fully conscious of oneself as an individual is also to be separated from all else. This is Hamlet's kingdom of infinite space in a nutshell, of "words, words, words," of "Denmark's a prison."

Saul Bellow, *Humboldt's Gift*

1

A Dangerous Form of Knowledge

On its face, history looks like a very good thing. I mean history in the sense of knowledge of the past, not the past itself. Whether or not the past itself can be considered a good thing is a different matter altogether. But knowledge of the past? What could be wrong with that? Knowledge is surely worth having. The plain fact that history is knowledge is enough to draw our praise all by itself. But history is not just any kind of knowledge; it is knowledge of the best kind. It seems to hold no dangers and to entail no risks.

And what great benefits it yields! History expands our horizons beyond the narrow confines of the present. It furthers understanding across the great divides of time and space. It furnishes a point of view from which to comprehend both others and ourselves. It gives us a means of orientation. It shows us where we came from and helps us discern where we are going. It pleases us no end with its variety and teaches us by its example. History uncovers lies and exposes myths. It rehabilitates the slandered and honors the forgotten. Very good things, all of these.

The only bad thing, it would seem, is that our knowledge of the past remains so sadly incomplete. So many errors abound, so many lapses of our judgment bias our understanding; there are so many archives yet to be explored, so many truths untold, and so many people not accorded their fair place in history. No wonder that we spare no effort in the pursuit of a complete and well-documented history of everything.

All that is true. At least I believe it to be true. But it is only part of the truth. There is another side to history, not so often noted but very much in need of recognition. For history is not as innocent as it pretends to be. It sprang like Athena fully armed from the head of Zeus. It is a weapon that was invented on a battlefield, a dangerous form of knowledge that can do harm to both its subjects and its practitioners. I do not mean the harm that history does by failing to live up to the standards of fairness, thoroughness, and accuracy that are supposed to govern the historical profession and, to some extent, the modern world. Everyone knows that mendacious histories can do harm beyond mere intellectual error. But that is history at its worst. The harm I have in mind is caused by history at its best.

In this chapter I shall focus on that harm. I shall first try to identify some elementary assumptions beneath the form of knowledge we call history. I will then turn to its origins in the disintegration of medieval principles of order during the early modern phase of European history and sketch its ascendancy. After making a few disclaimers and qualifications to put a brake on possible misunderstandings, I will try to define the problem that history confronts today. And I will explain why the remainder of this book deals with Hermann Conring, a subject so narrowly defined that readers have a right to know about its connection to the limits of history.

A Brief but Doubtful Lesson

In order to perceive how any harm could come from history at its best, we need to start at the beginning. Or at least as close to the beginning as possible. We need to put aside all of the usual ideas about what history is or ought to be and take a good close look instead at the one thing that underlies all forms of history. That one thing is the distinction between past and present. This is so elementary, so necessary for the very possibility of thinking about the past at all, that it may be considered the founding principle of history.[1]

At first glance the distinction between past and present seems reasonable beyond dispute. Things obviously change. We have experience of that. Hence it seems natural to divide the world into things the way they used to be and things as they are now: past and present. This is clearly something more than just an arbitrary construct of the mind, something that we could change at will or even do without. If there were no difference between the present and the past, all things would be the same—not merely in the jocular sense of the French *plus ça change, plus c'est la même chose,* but in actual reality. Nothing could happen. Everything would simply be the way it is. There would be nothing for historians to study.

None of this is quite as certain as it seems. But let us examine it more closely before we put it to the test. For the distinction between past and present has interesting implications. For one thing, it gives historians an object to examine. That object is, of course, the past: things that were then. But the distinction between past and present does more than merely set aside a piece of reality for historical inspection. It also assigns specific characteristics to that piece of reality. Two, in particular: absence and immutability. These are perhaps the two most fundamental features of the past the way we tend to think of it. They seem to follow by definition and to apply without exception. Whatever else may be said about the past (and there is an infinite number of possibilities, on which historians never can agree), this much seems certain: all aspects of the past are gone, and none of them can be changed. Even if there were nothing else to unite historians (and chances are that there is not), historians would still at least remain united in this one respect: they study things immutable and gone.

This characterization of the object of historical investigation is of course abstract. But it is worth attention. Absence and immutability are crucial for the fascination the past exercises over the minds of those who think of it. They fill us with a sense of awe, and they confront us with the peculiar task that every living person must complete on occasion: the task of recovering something, somehow, from the silent depths of that immutable absence that is the past, so that it will not be gone forever but will remain alive in memories and images and, best of all, perhaps, scholarly knowledge. To confront that immutable absence without fear and wrest it from the darkness so that it may be exhibited to present and future generations for their appreciation and, if possible, instruction: that is the task of historians.

Since, however, no one can lay his hands on anything that is genuinely gone, the means by which historians complete their task follow with the same clarity from the distinction between past and present as do the object of history and the task of the historian. Those means consist of things existing in the present that carry traces of information about the past. Such objects may be called evidence (because they are visible present signs that testify to something in the invisible absent past), or sources (because information about the past is thought to flow from them as water flows from a spring), or primary literature (because they come first, as opposed to the secondary literature historians write based on sources), or data (because they are given, as opposed to the theories we build on them).

The difference between *evidence, sources, primary literature,* and *data* is mostly a matter of emphasis. I shall use these terms more or less interchangeably. But one thing is worth underscoring: sources need not be written. Anything—ruined buildings, sculptures, music, blooming flowers, mountain ranges, painted furniture, untied shoes, stacked cords of wood, smoothly polished stone—anything can serve as evidence so long as two conditions are fulfilled: it must be present, so that it can be examined, and it must carry information about the past, so that it can function as a source. If writings are the sources most historians prefer, then it is only because they are easier to read than bones and stones and mountain ranges. Their function is the same.

One more thing: the distinction between past and present also furnishes historians with their most basic principle of method. That principle consists of one command: thou shalt place everything in the context of its time. This keeps historians from committing anachronism. It places the past under a great taboo in order to prevent a kind of chronological pollution. No one who violates that great taboo may claim to be a true historian. The past is sacred; the present is profane. Anachronism profanes the past by mixing past and present. That is the worst offense historians qua historians can commit. All other sins can be forgiven, but not this one. Anachronism is the sin against the holy spirit of history. Show that a historian has unwittingly infected the interpretation of the past with some particle of present, and you have shown the historian not only to have failed at the task, but to have failed shamefully.

The distinction between past and present thus undergirds history as a whole. It defines the object on which historians practice their art (gone and immutable), sets them their task (learn what you can about that thing that is immutable and gone), establishes the means by which to achieve the task (sources), and lays down the method they must follow (avoid anachronism). That is why it deserves to be called the founding principle of history.

But its significance goes further than just history. In the first place, as the distinction between past and present is constitutive of the past, so it is obviously constitutive of the present. The present, by virtue of the same distinction, is that which the past is not: it is right here and now (not gone) and it can change (not immutable). It need not be reconstructed in any way; it can be felt, and it even makes its presence felt, whether we like the experience or not. There are, it seems, no sources to which we need to turn in order to experience the present. The present *is* the source; we live in it. And as the present is experienced, it changes. Indeed, it changes with every passing second because it opens to the future. There seems to be no line dividing the present from the future like that dividing the present from the past. The past is past forever, gone from the world and never to return. But the future will not be future forever. It is not gone from the world at all. It may not yet be here but it will eventually arrive. Present and future lie on the same side of the great divide between the present and the past. They belong together like freedom and changeability. They are united in opposition to the past.

The changeability of the present has disadvantages: it makes for uncertainty. Hence people worry, especially when changes strike them with unpleasant force. Often they look for guidance as to what they should be doing next. Sometimes (strangely enough) they find it in the very past whose distinction from the present is the reason they want guidance to begin with. But the changeability of the present has great advantages as well. It means that we who are presently alive are not compelled to repeat the past. Our forefathers' sins need not be visited on us. We can seek a future better than the present, and definitely better than the past. Freedom and progress depend on the distinction between past and present. The founding principle of history is therefore also a founding principle of politics.

A sovereign state is usually defined as one whose citizens are free to determine their own affairs without interference from any agency beyond its territorial borders. But freedom in space (and limits on its territorial extent) is merely one characteristic of sovereignty. Freedom in time (and limits on its temporal extent) is equally important and probably more fundamental.[2] Sovereignty and citizenship require freedom from the past at least as much as freedom from contemporary powers. No state could be sovereign if its inhabitants lacked the ability to change a course of action adopted by their forefathers in the past, or even one to which they once committed themselves. No citizen could be a full member of the community so long as she was tied to ancestral traditions with which the community might wish to break—the problem of Antigone in Sophocles' tragedy. Sovereignty and citizenship thus require not only borders in space, but also borders in time.

Borders in time are moments of foundation or conversion to mark the point where sovereignty and citizenship begin and the past leaves off. They guarantee presence to the state by setting it apart from the past. Without their assistance, the state would constantly have to look over its shoulder in order to fulfill archaic obligations. The state could not protect the freedom of its citizens or their progress into the future. Hence the simple structure of the oath that foreigners are asked to swear on the occasion of their naturalization as citizens of the United States of America (in this matter I happen to have personal experience): first they renounce "absolutely and entirely" all past obligations to foreign rulers, and then they declare "freely without any mental reservation" their willingness to defend the Constitution and laws of the United States of America against all enemies in the future.[3]

The place of history in the scheme of things thus is impossible to understand if we restrict its meaning solely to contemplation of the past. History is directly and systematically linked to citizenship, sovereignty, and the state. If history is the form in which we contemplate a past that is immutably divided from the present, then citizenship, sovereignty, and the state are the categories by which we declare our freedom to change the present into the form that we desire for the future. History and politics reinforce each other. They function as complementary elements of one overarching structure.

They are related to each other as the contemplation of something immutable and gone is related to action here and now on something changeable and present.

One can extend this line of thinking even further, because the world includes more things than those that are immutably gone and mutably present. Some things are simply immutable: exempt from time, and hence from the distinction between past and present, but not gone. Numbers and rules of logic, for example, are such things. Numbers and rules of logic are neither past nor present, and future least of all, but always and everywhere the same. Two is two, here and there and everywhere, unchanging, now and forever. "Yes" is "yes" and "no" is "no" in all corners of the universe at any time.

Others might add laws of nature (for the universe of physics) and natural laws (for the universe of morals) as further instances of things that are eternally the same. Of course such laws are notoriously difficult to establish. But even in a book of history it may be pointed out that they can be imagined and that, like numbers and rules of logic, they stand in a definite relationship to history and politics. That relationship is one of difference: unlike history and politics, laws of nature (physical) and natural laws (moral) do not obey the distinction between past and present. If history and politics complement each other within the realm of time, physics and morality do so beyond the realm of time; or so, at least, they claim. They occupy a realm where history and politics have (or are at least supposed to have) no sway. Nature endures forever.

That history keeps doing battle with science (each science, all sciences, natural, moral, political, and social) is therefore neither an accident nor a deplorable oversight soon to be corrected by an improved variety of history. Nor can it be accounted for by the distinction between particulars and general laws, much less the distinction between science and art.[4] It reflects a division of the labor of society according to the parts of time, a distinction so obvious and fundamental that its significance is easily overlooked. Historians clear a space in time so that it may be occupied by individuals no longer tied to custom and tradition. They shelter the present from the past by tending to records in libraries and archives safely removed from places where they might interfere with laws of nature, conscience, and the state. History is nonscience, nonmorality, and nonlaw. Among all modern forms of knowledge, it is the counterdiscipline par excellence. It operates behind the scenes of science and philosophy and seems exempt from the critique of reason. Its function is essential for the well-being of a modern world (any modern world). Its modern occupants could not imagine life if their present were cluttered by the laws of ancient Rome, the science of Aristotle, and the morals of Saint Augustine.

Thus the distinction between past and present leads us straight back to the conception of a morally autonomous human being taking control of his own fate by making politics and society conform to principles of nature. That human being depends for his reality on the distinction between past and present no less than history does. He differs from the past as subjects differ from objects of agency and knowledge, as reason differs from custom, and as responsible adults differ from the children they once were. Morally autonomous human beings are held accountable; children are not. Unlike people who lived in the past, the morally autonomous human being is present and alive. He may know about the past by acts of interpretation that bring the evidence to life, but he is himself impossible to know because he does all of the knowing. He is subject to laws of nature and natural laws but never to the past. He knows the past only as something with which he may part company at any time, and politics as a world by which he is bound only to the degree that he consents. He is responsible not to the past but to himself, obliged to follow no tradition, enjoying sovereignty over his own affairs.

The subject so conceived is neither a fact of nature nor a clear and distinct idea, much less a product of tradition or politics. He is a product of the same fundamental act by which the past is distinguished from the present and time from eternity. He is a correlate of the objectivity that history obtains from evidence. This individual subject, with his presence, his autonomy, his freedom from all laws except laws of conscience, laws of nature, and positive laws sanctioned by the unconstrained expression of his own free will, with his ability to transcend all circumstantial limitations and to escape from time itself in order to claim a ticket of direct admission (as it were) to eternal life—this subject is the cause that history serves.

It is scarcely an accident that *subject* is a word we use with equal facility for the subjects of a sovereign ruler (in the realm of politics), the subjects of scientific investigation (in the realm of nature), and the mind behind all thought and action—the subject behind Descartes's *cogito ergo sum*.[5] This coincidence of different meanings in one word is a sign that the subject—the self that distinguishes itself from the rest of the world and is the source of all distinctions—resides at the center of what we call the modern world. Nor is it an accident that the *subjectivity* (in the sense of uncertainty of judgment) that we attribute to history and politics stands in definite tension with the apparent stability of nature, conscience, and the state. It is an indication that history performs a special role in linking freedom to subjectivity.

History thus forms part of a coherent framework of principles and assumptions about the world and the things of which the world consists. This framework helps to organize the thought and action of modern subjects into a whole whose integrity is threatened not by the Devil whom medieval Christians feared, but by that demon of fallibility whom Descartes is justly famous for having elevated to a place of honor. This framework assigns a definite place to nature and culture, past and present, mind and matter, and grants supreme authority to conscience, sovereignty, and nature. History may be relative. But the trinity of conscience, sovereignty, and nature is absolute. Each of its three persons is fully present. And each is singular. No man or woman can have two natures, two sovereigns, or two consciences—unless they happen to be mad, disloyal, or divine.

Only one point remains in order to complete this lesson. It is that the distinction between past and present is doubtful in the extreme. No one that I have heard of has ever found a line between the present and the past. And a moment's reflection shows that none is likely ever to be found. Where could that line be drawn? A second ago? A millisecond? Last year? The birth of Christ? The creation of the universe? These are examples of some points in time where one could try to draw the line. All of them have something to recommend themselves. But only for some people and only for some time. None can claim to represent *the* line dividing the present from the past. If the present could really be divided from the past at all, it would have to be divided by as many lines as there are present moments: not one line between one present and one past, but an infinity of lines between an infinity of presents and an infinity of pasts, one for each incremental movement into the future.

This simple truth casts fundamental doubt on everything said to this point. Assume that the past is really dead and gone. How could it be recalled? By means of sources? But if the past were gone, we could not even recognize the sources as dealing with the past. If we know anything about the past at all, it is only because we have some knowledge that there exists some past of which the sources speak to us before we even start to examine them. Without such prior knowledge, the sources would speak a language as full of meaning as the wind.

Assume that the past is really immutable. How could the present change? How could one part of time keep passing if the other part stood still? Change in the present must surely change the past in ways that we may very well not understand only because we never stop to ponder them. At least the past keeps changing in extent, because the sum of all things past grows in extent with the addition of every passing second. Whether that changes only the sum total of the past (as two changes into three when one is added) but does not change the elements of which it is composed (because two can still emerge unchanged from three when one is subtracted once again) may deserve more serious consideration than we have given it. Perhaps I am mistaken, but I know of no law of nature that makes the past immutable. Nor does science seem qualified to formulate such laws. Science requires observation and experiment. But if the past is really gone, it lies beyond observation and experiment. The very reason we regard the past as immutable (its absence) makes that immutability impossible to verify. If, however, the past is present here and now in some yet-to-be-determined sense, available for observation and experiment, there seems to be no reason to assume that it can never change. In either case the immutability of the past can hardly be considered more than speculation.

And what about the requirement to place everything in the context of its time? Which context would that be? Did things get lost on cross-temporal excursions? Do they confuse the tenses? Do they require our help to find their place of origin? How could we help them if they did? There is no universal office of chronology where things that have been lost and found in time could be turned in for temporal safekeeping. There are no lines distinguishing the context of one piece of evidence from that of others with any more reliability than the reliability of the line between past and present itself. History does not fall into discrete contextual packages, each properly aligned next to the others so as to cover the entire past (without any messy overlapping, without embarrassing lacunae) and stop obediently at the line between yesterday and today. Contexts do not arrive in sizes conveniently tailored to suit the purposes of historians who wish to write the history of, say, a person's life, a country, a revolution, or an idea.[6]

The number of contexts into which things have to be placed is either infinite or one. Infinite because you might as well admit that every action ever taken, every sentence written, every word spoken, every particle of meaning, and every event at any moment in the history of the universe has its own proper context into which it would have to be placed in order to avoid anachronism. Contexts are just as infinitely divisible as reality itself—which helps us understand why the historical literature multiplies with a speed that stands in an instructive contrast to the presumed immutability of the past. Or else context is singular, numerically one, a context into which nothing needs to be placed because everything is placed in it already. In that case all contexts blend with one another straight across the boundary between the present and the past. Each subject is connected to all others in ways so fluid as to make every contextual boundary a matter (more or less) of arbitrary choice. Only the faith that some real boundary exists between the present and the past lends plausibility to the belief that historians can actually place things past into the context of "their" time and place.

The Other Side of History

Should we conclude that history is nothing but a useless waste of time? Not in the least! We rather need to recognize that knowledge of the past is merely the fruit of history, not to be confused with the tree on which it grows. The tree is the action by which the present is divided from the past. For the distinction between past and present does not exist apart from our activity. We place that distinction into the uninterrupted flow of time. We assert ourselves and thereby we transform the world. We claim a place for ourselves in the here-and-now and hold it in opposition to the there-and-then. We draw a fence around a part of reality, call that the past, and mine it for the knowledge in which historians specialize. That is the founding act of history. The tropes of metaphor, metonymy, synecdoche, and irony, whose operation in the historical imagination of the nineteenth century Hayden White described so cogently a quarter century ago, prefigure the field of history.[7] But they prefigure only what kind of history historians will write. They presuppose that there is a field. That field first needs to be created.[8]

We must therefore revise what we said about history before. We said that history was founded on the distinction between past and present. Quite so. But we failed to add that this is not a distinction given, but a distinction made. Reality may be impossible to know. (In order to avoid skeptical misinterpretations, I hasten to add that this is different from saying that reality does not exist. The opposite is closer to the truth: reality does exist, which is why it is difficult to know. The hardboiled egg is not particularly difficult to eat. But what it is? No one can tell.) But history is not the study of reality, much less the study of the reality of time. History is the study of evidence . . . and evidence is not reality. Evidence is a sign, as different from reality as letters are from meaning and as numerals are from numbers. It is not there by accident. It carries on its back the difference between the signifier and the signified and points beyond itself to something else from whence it came: the past. That is how it gives us the means to draw a line through time where none may in reality exist.

Evidence seems merely to serve historians as the source from which they draw knowledge about the past. But its function as a source is secondary. Its main function is to divide the present from the past. The absence of the signified is what historians seek to comprehend. But absence can never be experienced as such. Absence can only be discovered in the gap between the signifier and the signified. That absence is what writing marks, as a letter marks the distance that must be overcome for meaning to be communicated from one person to another. Writing results in evidence par excellence: a record carrying information about something that happened at some other place and in some other time. It lends conviction to our image of the past as dead and gone.

Historians therefore only appear to privilege written sources because they furnish more information about the past than other kinds of evidence. In truth they privilege written sources because writing is the most fundamental means so far devised by human beings to divide a live reality (embracing both past and present) into one thing that is completely dead and gone (the past) and one that lives only here and now (the present). But it is not the past that is gone; only the records are. Or more precisely, that which has been recorded in the records seems to be gone from them. Writing leads us to confuse the record with the reality, to mistake the exchange of information for understanding, and to misconstrue mere distance in space and time as an abyss—as if there could be communication if reader were not joined to writer by something above and beyond the writing. Nor is the past immutable; only the records are. Or more precisely (since records can be forged and changed beyond all recognition), only the information that was recorded in the evidence is immutable. Reality and its meaning may be in eternal flux. But letters, once written, just like words once spoken, may seem to have a significance that will remain the same until the end of time.[9]

Seen in this light, all aspects of the historical endeavor take on a different meaning. History only appears to be a form of knowledge about the past. In truth history serves to confirm a line between now and then that is not given in reality. The complementary relationship between history, politics, and nature that we evoked above goes deeper than mere agreement on dividing respective spheres of influence. History is constitutive of modern politics, constitutive of the kind of modern state that claims sovereignty for itself and the autonomy of individuals subject to nothing except their conscience and the laws of the physical universe. The prohibition on anachronism? It merely seems to be a principle of method by which historians secure the adequacy of their interpretation. In truth the prohibition on anachronism defines the purpose for which the discipline of history exists: to divide the reality of time into past and present. History enlists the desire for knowledge about the past to meet a deeper need: the need for power and independence, the need to have done with the past and to be rid of things that cannot be forgotten.

Whatever knowledge it may pick up along the way is but a means toward that end.

Once this is understood, the seemingly insoluble methodological quandaries in which history involves its practitioners can be seen for what they are: not reasons to change course, but quite the opposite, a salutary spur to keep on marching, a necessary source of the unflagging energy with which historians pursue their unacknowledged goal: dividing the present from the past forever. Here is the reason that the obvious, repeated, and inevitable failure of historians to reach their publicly stated goal (a fair, complete, and true understanding of the past) amounts to no valid argument against the utility of history at all. Historians never treat knowledge of the past simply as knowledge, no matter how good it is. They treat it as a point of departure for further expeditions. Only slackers take good books as an excuse to rest. Historians worth their salt leave them behind the very instant they are published and resume the long march to history's final destination. Historians may never cease to criticize the fruits of their own labor, to toil for the subjection of ever new areas of temporal reality to the distinction between past and present, and thereby to emancipate humanity from time.

Have previous historians fallen into anachronism? Of course they have, as all historians must. Is that a reason to turn back? Quite the opposite, it is a reason to go on. It is a signal that the line between past and present has been breached. Alarms are sounded and historians rush to the defense in order to prevent the past from making its presence felt again. Have past generations of historians ignored the history of private life, of women, children, animals, and dreams? Let us extend the range of subjects to which historians may lay claim! Have previous historians focused only on written sources? They have been insufficiently ambitious! We need to turn attention to unwritten sources, too, and place them in the same distance modeled effectively by written ones. That will be harder. But anything can with sufficient effort be pressed into service to history.

In short, there are two different sides to history. So long as history is viewed as theory of the past, the distinction between past and present looks like a fact; the past, like an object to be studied; the study of the past, like the proper task of the historian; the evidence, like the source from which historians obtain their knowledge; and the prohibition on anachronism, like the basic point of method that keeps the knowledge pure. But things look different just as soon as it is recognized that history is also a form of action. From that perspective the distinction between past and present looks like an act of self-determination by which the sovereign subject assumes her rightful place in time; the knowledge historians draw from evidence, like the means by which historians make the past lie still; and the prohibition of anachronism, like marching orders for a mission to make the world safe for autonomy.

There is a whole series of conceptual pairs on which one could rely to make the difference between the two sides of history intelligible. Just now I used the distinction between theory and practice. I could as well have called it the difference between the objective and the subjective sides of history. In its objective capacity, history represents whatever knowledge may in fact be drawn from the examination of the sources; in its subjective capacity, history underwrites the freedom of the self that is engaged in the examination. I could have used the distinction between public and private, too. In public, history consists of the pursuit of knowledge. In private, it consists of competition among historians who seek to displace rival interpretations of the past with one of their own original design.

Or take the distinction between locutionary content and illocutionary act that has in recent years been brought so fruitfully to bear upon the study of the past, and to which I shall have reason to refer on several occasions.[10] One side of history consists of things historians say about the past (locutionary content); the other side consists of what they do in saying them (illocutionary act). The former is the object to which historians draw attention; the latter is what makes them historians. Considered in terms of its locutionary form, history may well be indistinguishable from fiction. Considered in terms of illocutionary acts, however, the difference is profound. Literature transports readers elsewhere in space and time; history places them firmly here and now. Literature can take its readers away only because it claims not to deal with real persons and events, however unfounded such a claim may actually be (seeing how often fiction is thinly disguised history); history binds them to their location because it claims the opposite, regardless that this claim, too, may be entirely unfounded (seeing how often history turns out to be poorly substantiated fiction). Whoever feels uplifted by reading history does so because learning about what happened in the past is tantamount to realizing that "I am here and now." Whether the reader then goes on to criticize the past from a progressive point of view or to identify with it from a conservative position is a subordinate and secondary question. In either case history gives the reader the satisfaction of temporal self-affirmation.

Each of these pairs—the list could be extended—has something to recommend itself. But all of them agree on one central point: that there exists a difference within history itself, a difference that constitutes at one and the same time a boundary and a bond. The subjective and the objective, the theoretical and the practical, the locutionary and the illocutionary sides of history presuppose a whole. However differently they may be construed, they reinforce each other in such a way that neither could exist without its opposite. They stand in a dialectical relation.

The past, therefore, is not just to be found in sources preserved in libraries and archives, laboriously deciphered by specialists. It lives and breathes without assistance in every corner of the world, right here and now. It joins the present in one temporal order that is present but not "present," given, but not only here and now, because it contains the present together with the past. Nor does the present simply age and fade away into the past with uniformity. The ticking of the clock measures neither the speed nor the intensity with which the present shades into the past. Christ is much younger than the Grand Inquisitor, and Stalin older than Karl Marx. The past, if it is anything at all, is a dimension of the present and changes along with it. I know this is a startling thought: the past not immutable? But it may be startling only because the fascination with immutability (with death) lulls us into a trance.

Historians who limit their account of the past to things that can be stated on the basis of a complete examination of surviving records deserve every last bit of the praise that long-standing custom bestows on them for their pursuit of objectivity (if only to the necessarily limited extent that they have managed to achieve their aims). Let that be writ in stone. But the pursuit of objectivity is only half the point. Historians who miss the other half mistake the meaning of their work. They exclude the unrecordable from recognition and cut the past in two: one documented, known, and dead; the other undocumented, unknown, and undead. History then concerns itself only with the past abroad and scorns the past at home—the home from where historians take off, leaving behind what they need most for history to flourish: knowledge of self.

The Historical Revolt

These thoughts will seem unnecessary to some readers; to some they will seem worse. But they are needed to understand the condition of history today. History was not always the province of professionals. Nor was it always the traditional form of knowledge it has become. History jumped on the scene of European mental life with the force of a revolution against a specific form of governance. If it involved new knowledge about the past, it did so not simply out of intellectual curiosity, but because a definite attitude toward the past was integral to the rule of the two chief surviving representatives of so-called medieval universalism, the Roman emperor and the Roman pope (a third, the eastern Roman emperor, having conveniently been eliminated by Turks unwittingly assisting the historical revolt).[11]

These rulers claimed not only universality in space. They also claimed universality in time. Both emperor and pope insisted that they were in communion with eternity, and both sought to embody the past as though it had endured over the centuries without change. They founded their authority on a deliberate anachronism that only a modern point of view can construe as an error in historical methodology. The empire and the papacy knew the distance in time between themselves and antiquity. But they judged it with a different measure from the one historians use. To charge them with failure to understand the course of historical events, as though they were schoolboys who had not listened to their master, is misleading. They were themselves the masters. If they did not appreciate history as modern people do, and never did succeed in building modern states, it was at least in part because that was not their ambition. Anachronism was built into the foundation of their government, a source of their authority, a means enabling them to draw legitimacy from texts that dated from antiquity and bore the traces of an alien civilization.

This was the world that was turned upside down in the historical revolt. The chief protagonists of the revolt were humanists, so-called because they claimed to revive what they called *studia humanitatis* and what still underlies the disciplines we call humanities: classical grammar, poetry, rhetoric, history, and moral philosophy.[12] Humanists placed history at the service of European princes and republics seeking to emancipate themselves in fierce campaigns from the authority of pope and emperor. And though they did not succeed in removing pope or emperor completely from the stage, they did force both to change their mode of operation. In the process they ruined the foundations on which the medieval universe had rested, and they built new ones for the inhabitants of modern, territorial, sovereign states.

Humanists, of course, were not alone. No doubt the historical revolt could never have prevailed without the help of soldiers and standing armies fighting real battles with real weapons.[13] At least as indispensable were tax collectors, lawyers, bureaucrats, accountants administering state finances, and men of state conducting modern diplomacy.[14] There were Protestants and scientists who worked toward a transformation of the early modern world following paths that sometimes coincided with those traveled by humanists and sometimes diverged from them, paths that led sometimes into rebellion and sometimes only toward gradual change.[15] A good case can even be made that scholastic philosophers and theologians traveling along what they themselves already called the modern way (*via moderna*) deserve more credit for breaking the old mold than any other intellectual movement at the time.[16]

Humanists, in other words, were only one of many groups of people engaged in the historical revolt, and history was only one of the weapons in their armory. Rhetoric was more conspicuous (or shall we say more audible?) and classical philology more elementary. But humanists were indispensable to the articulation and dissemination of the new set of principles for carving the world into manageable pieces that I touched on above. And history, though not their only weapon, went deeper than any other in cutting the mind of Europe loose from its universal moorings. The Protestant Reformation, the Catholic Reformation, and the Scientific Revolution could not have happened without the efforts of humanists. Humanists oiled the machines put into motion by modern princes and republics—not to mention that they themselves served often as bureaucrats, diplomats, and soldiers.[17] They played a crucial role in handing methods of drill and self-discipline to modern armies.[18] In short, humanists represent more clearly what was entailed in the historical revolt than any other single group, if only because their way of thinking entered all of them.

The most enduring symbol of the victory that humanists won over medieval universalism is the success with which they imposed a new periodization on history. Until early modern times, Europeans had used many different ways of reckoning with the past. The one according to which the world had been ruled by four world monarchies—Babylonian, Persian, Greek, and Roman—was merely one of the most familiar. But all Christian accounts agreed on this: the most important turning point had been the advent of Christ. Hence Christian accounts agreed as well (as they still do) on reckoning time in years since the birth of Christ. That the birth of Christ coincided (more or less) with Emperor Augustus's foundation of the Roman empire, the last of the four world monarchies, merely reinforced the perception that the beginning of the Christian era had unique significance.

According to that view, the people we now call medieval were not living in the Middle Ages, much less in an age of cultural or intellectual decline, whatever their assessment of the debt they were so deeply aware of owing to Christian and Roman antiquity. They were living in the most advanced age of the world. They were in the forefront of history, face to face with the end of time. Only one other turning point was left in the remaining stretch of time, and that was the return of Christ to judge the living and the dead. There was much difference of opinion about the ways in which the world would end. There were disputes about the temporal location of the millennium and the rule of Antichrist. But none of those disputes shook the belief in the unity, singularity, and finality of the period of world history that began with the birth of Christ. Whatever happenings the future could possibly have held in store paled to insignificance compared to the two events defining the period over which pope and emperor claimed to rule: the birth of Christ and the end of time.

This was the view the humanists destroyed.[19] They never managed (because they never tried) to abolish one of the two points in time to which medieval universalism owed its temporal unity: the advent of Christ retained significance for the periodization of world history. And it has done so ever since. Though there are now (as there were then) many alternatives to reckoning time from the birth of Christ, and though attempts are sometimes made to loosen the connection between our form of dating and its roots in a particular religion by substituting the abbreviations C.E. (common era) or B.C.E. (before the common era) for A.D. (*anno Domini,* in the year of the Lord) and B.C. (before Christ), the number of years accompanied by those abbreviations still points to the birth of Christ with a clarity that can be embarrassing in gatherings whose judgment on the significance of Christ is not unanimous.

But humanists did succeed (because they tried) in destroying belief in the temporal unity of the period since the birth of Christ. They were certain that the Holy Roman Empire had undergone a change that was not really for the better and in any case was so deep that the unity of the period from antiquity to the present had to be considered a mirage. Some of them even thought the Roman empire was altogether dead and gone.[20] They abandoned the doctrine of the four world monarchies, and they invented the concept of the Dark or Middle Ages in order to capture the long period of decline by which they believed their own time to be divided from the glories of antiquity.[21] In all of these regards they were assisted by reformers, Protestant as well as Catholic, who performed a parallel operation on the body of the universal church by replacing the search for endurance and continuity with that for the recovery of origins. Once they succeeded in destroying the unity of the period, it did not take long before expectations of the end of the world gave way to an unbounded future extending without limits to all eternity.[22] Thus humanists and reformers joined forces to dislodge the ruling heads of medieval universalism from their preeminence over the final stage of history and relegated them to a barbaric interval between a resplendent classical antiquity and a renascent modern age. That was a blow from which the authority of pope and emperor was never to recover.

The division of history into ancient, medieval, and modern (and the division of the historical profession into corresponding branches) is not simply better than the theory of the four world monarchies. Nor is it merely different. It rather is abiding testimony to the victory that the party of the historical revolt won over its opponents in a great civil war that shook early modern Europe to its foundations. By exploding the temporal unity of the period from ancient times to the present, the humanists changed truths that had enjoyed apparently unshakable permanence into mere antiquities. They transformed things that seemed self-evidently true into things of the past that were henceforth impossible to know without a special effort. They demoted the universal power of pope and emperor from present experience to an aspect of history that had to be judged by means of evidence. Exploiting the potential inherent in altering temporal perspectives was their greatest accomplishment. And the unthinking facility with which historians have until recently applied the tripartite division of history into ancient, medieval, and modern, not merely to the history of Europe or to their own profession, but to the history of the entire world, merely confirms the one-sided nature of the victory.

History thus arrived on the scene with an energy quite different from that which it commands today. This energy was not confined to history in the narrow sense. The affirmation of the self that was integral to the rise of history extended across the entire realm of thought and action. It took shape in new forms of science (heliocentric astronomy, inertial motion, experiments), new forms of law (positive, natural, and moral), new forms of religion (salvation by faith alone, priesthood of all believers, treatment of works and ceremonies as indifferent), and the development of three-dimensional perspective in painting.[23] As the adoption of the three-dimensional perspective turned medieval painting from an attempt to reflect eternity into an antiquated style, so the adoption of the temporal perspective in studying texts transformed medieval scholarship from an attempt to access sources of eternal authority into a poor sort of history. As three-dimensional perspective transformed visual images from symbols of transcendence into representations of physical objects in natural space, so history transformed writings from means of communicating eternal truths into records of the particular thoughts and actions of some particular person at some particular time and place. New forms of painting established definite links between visual images and particular things, so that the images could be said to represent the things. New forms of reading established definite links between writings and persons, so that the writings could be said to serve as evidence for the intentions of their authors. As three-dimensional perspective subjected visual reality to domination by the particular point in space from where it was inspected by the observer (shifting the locus of visual authority from objects perceived to the observer perceiving them), so temporal perspective subjected temporal reality to domination by the particular point in time from which it was inspected by the historian (shifting the locus of authority from things enduring over time to the examiner of the past). Both stood for new forms of freedom and responsibility. Both imposed standards of objectivity on different (visual and temporal) aspects of reality.

At that time the dialectical relationship between the two sides of history was filled with greater tension than it ever was thereafter. Greater, too, therefore, was the creative energy with which historians asserted new forms of consciousness against the claims of universal authorities. Objective knowledge of the past was at a minimum, a plan of action not yet undertaken, a distant dream, the contents of an unwritten book. A new perspective had been adopted. But nothing had been seen clearly yet. Compared with the knowledge we command today, contemporary knowledge of what had happened during antiquity and the Middle Ages was raw and scarce. Objectivity may be the last quality to be attributed to early modern historians. Few things can be more striking than the freedom with which they sent a motley gang of facts into battles over the meaning of the past that the most thoroughly annotated histories today would scarcely dare to witness from afar.

Assertions of individual autonomy were similarly scarce. On some occasions they may have been made with a clarity too startling to have lapsed into oblivion. One thinks of Luther defying the emperor in Worms, Sir Thomas More beheaded at the command of Henry VIII, and Giordano Bruno burned alive in Rome. But if such acts of self-assertion proved unforgettable, it was only because they flew so flagrantly in the face of the ordinary course of things. They were a promise and a dream of things to come, no more. Meanwhile the world continued to follow well-trodden paths of custom and tradition. Inertia rules society as much as it rules physics. Nothing is easier than to identify the many ways in which early modern people thought and behaved just like their predecessors. It would take centuries before the notions of individual autonomy and personal responsibility that underlay the humanist reconceptualization of time were turned into the common property of millions of citizens in modern nation states, most of them taught to read and write at public expense, none of them willing to have their freedom limited by anyone's mere custom, and all of them regularly called upon to do their civic duties and exercise their civic rights.

Nonetheless, history gained its hold over the European mind as the result of a revolution. Historical perspective permitted humanists to offer an interpretation of authorities like the Bible and Roman law that was not merely new or better but of a different kind: interpretation with reference to time that viewed a text as the result of human agency, distinguished one time from another, and made that difference the principle of its approach. They changed the order of the world. Equipped with objectivity, they relegated medieval universalism so firmly to the past that one can barely speak of it today without provoking suspicions of heresy, treason, or irrelevance. They put the faith in evidence so firmly into place that things unrecorded and unrecordable seem to have lost all chance of gaining recognition. They won what has to count as one of the more one-sided victories in the long line of humanity's attempts to remake the world in its own image.

An Elementary Confusion

Yet this was never how they saw themselves. From their own point of view, they started no rebellion. They were on the defense. They were restoring ancient truths. If they took the initiative, they did it only because their enemies' ignorance, corruption, and tyrannical abuse of power left them no other choice. They were compelled to act by knowledge, faith, and truth. They brought about rebirths and reformations, renaissances of antiquity and returns to the true spirit of the original church. They served Christ and the classics. Self-assertion was not on their list of things to do.

An elementary confusion thus led to a victory whose winners remained oblivious, unconscious even, of the true novelty of their own enterprise. The progress that they really made was confused in their own minds with mere improvements to an existing pattern for which they needed no justification. It seemed simply true. It seemed to justify itself. It had been known before. It merely needed to be stated once again in all its pristine purity. As Columbus confused the new lands he found across the ocean with the old lands that he had set out to search for, so the historians confused the new world they opened up to human examination with the old world they studied. The novelty of the historical perspective was submerged beneath a generic claim on truth—as if there were no difference between reading texts and treating them as evidence, between remembering the past and dividing it from the present.

They had, of course, good intellectual reasons not to regard themselves as revolutionaries. The scrutiny of ancient texts as such was scarcely new. Humanists and reformers expanded the number and kinds of documents to which attention had to be paid, improved on older interpretations, and cast their ideas in different literary genres. But new texts had been discovered and translated throughout the Middle Ages, and some of them were far more dangerous to papal and imperial authority than, say, the letters of Cicero or

Tacitus's *Germania,* which humanists added to the list of books worth reading later on. In that respect the work of humanists was thoroughly continuous with that of their forebears. Pope and emperor themselves drew their legitimacy from the Bible, the writings of the fathers, and Roman law, all of them ancient texts. And medieval scholars had developed the study of ancient texts in glosses, commentaries, questions, sums, and other genres to heights of technical and stylistic perfection that only modern prejudice can fail to reward with the unstinting admiration they deserve.

The philosophy of Aristotle, to mention only the most obvious example, was pagan to the core. It posed a manifest threat to Catholic belief in God's creation of the world out of nothing and the personal immortality of the soul. It is not without reason that Aristotle's writings on metaphysics and natural philosophy were officially prohibited early in the thirteenth century. They could hardly have been integrated into the teaching of medieval schools without an effort that well-nigh consumed the intellectual ability of Saint Thomas Aquinas and his Dominican companions. Even after Aquinas the bond between ancient, pagan, Greek philosophy and modern, Christian, European theology was never more than tenuous. And yet Aristotle's metaphysics was so successfully incorporated into medieval thought that he came to be known as "the philosopher" (*philosophus*), with an authority analogous to that of Saint Paul, known as "the apostle" (*apostolus*), without any mention of his name. Compared to that amazing act of interpretive assimilation, the work of humanists could justifiably be seen as just another step on the long road from ignorance to knowledge.

A charitable view may therefore attribute this elementary confusion to mere lack of intellectual acuity and the old human habit of falling victim to the seductive clarity of writing. There may have simply been no way to recognize that progress came from a new frame of mind and new conceptions of the good.[24] More likely, however, confusion over the nature of the historical revolt must be attributed to a fear of the authorities so powerful that it could not be openly acknowledged. The protagonists of the historical revolt were only too well aware that the authorities would accuse them of overturning the established order. But if they could convince themselves that, far from breaking with the past, they were reviving it, that they were doing nothing but telling the truth, except to tell it better, then they were safe. And so they did. Maintaining that their interpretation of the texts was merely a better understanding of the same ancient sources on which the authorities themselves relied (only more of them, and in more authentic form), they were oblivious to the charge of heresy. The continuity with ancient truths in which they saw themselves confirmed them in the good conscience that they were right.

Only a few managed to raise their deepest fears to consciousness. Such was, I think, the case with Machiavelli, Luther, and Hobbes. All three cut through the confusions of their age to a point where the willfulness and even violence beneath the truthful exterior of the historical revolt became all too apparent. All three were willing to take responsibility for that violence by seeking to redefine the good in terms self-consciously transcending the limits of all writing. *Virtù*, faith, and absolute sovereignty are different in many ways. But none of these are written, and all of them agree in their lack of respect for law. All three had a characteristically ambiguous relationship to humanism. And in the end all three fell victim to the taboo that they had challenged. In squarely owning up to the violence inherent in the historical revolt, facing the fear of death, and forcefully demanding a degree of responsibility exceeding the capacity of contemporaries who could not imagine truth as anything but given, they merely managed to turn opinion against themselves and strengthened the taboo. Theirs are precisely the ideas that were most speedily removed from sight by authorities and revolutionaries unanimous in their conviction that order needed to be drawn from writing.

That is perhaps the reason why Machiavelli, Luther, and Hobbes have withstood the test of time more successfully than their contemporaries. Their views remain more thoroughly alive. The business they started was never finished. The threat they posed in early modern times has never been defused. It lurks barely concealed beneath the surface of modern consciousness, from where it exercises an abiding fascination. They still provoke intense hostility. With friends like these, who needed enemies? But notwithstanding their intellectual longevity and their importance as both challengers and victims of the boundaries laid down in the historical revolt, in the short term of early modern European and even modern history, all three must be considered failures. The most successful were saner and arguably more boring men like Calvin, Melanchthon, Lipsius, and even John Locke, who followed the radicals up to a point but closed the door on their most daring experiments. They defused the explosives that Machiavelli, Luther, and Hobbes had placed under all principles of order, transformed them into classics, and made their teaching safe to study in public and in school.

That gave them a decisive edge. Unconsciousness of their own place in time released the revolutionaries from self-doubt. It served them like a magic shield, made them invulnerable to attack, and allowed them to walk like innocents across the intellectual battlefields of early modern Europe, if not untouched by the fray, at least completely confident of being in the right and therefore victorious in the end. Their enemies found it impossible to grasp the source from which the historical revolt drew strength. They tried. Tried very hard. They knew that they were being threatened with sedition, that knowledge of history corroded the foundations of their authority. They did not in the least believe that the good conscience of their adversaries was justified, and they were more than willing to brand them as heretics. Indeed, if heresy can be defined as the willful rejection of statements whose truth has been sanctioned by public authority, then the historical revolt was nothing if not heretical in nature.[25] But they were never able to convict the revolutionaries of anything more incriminating than respect for the same texts on which they founded themselves. They failed to identify the heresy. Their charges never found their object and therefore failed to stick. They were as blinded by the light of history as the protagonists of the revolt.[26]

Fear of authority thus contaminated history with a subliminal degree of dishonesty that has never been altogether shed. A revolutionary transformation slipped unnoticed into the modern age under the cover of ancient or objective knowledge for which no one needed to take responsibility—indeed, could not have taken responsibility without endangering the revolution. As sovereignty was declared to be absolute and subject neither to history nor positive law nor, above all, to any papal or imperial powers, but only to a natural law defined by a new science, so history was declared to be absolute, independent of time, and subject solely to the objective faculties of the historian. As Jean Bodin once put it with chilling candor, "it is a kind of legal absurdity to say that it is in the power of the prince to act dishonestly."[27] In the same way, history made it a kind of scholarly absurdity to say it might be in the power of evidence to misrepresent the past.

The revolution remained anonymous. It was as if it had happened by itself, as if it was nothing but truth and nature coming into their own. We still have no name for it other than the exquisitely misleading names of *Renaissance* and *Reformation* that it was given in early modern times, or the meaningless name of *early modern history* given it since by historians. We still have no better name for the enemy whose rule it destroyed than *medieval universalism*—a cipher that conceals what was at stake. We still restrict the designation *revolution* to later events in England, America, France, and elsewhere, whose main achievement was not to overturn the existing order of society but merely to bring the existing order of society into conformity with principles that had long since proven their worth. The historical revolt was never called by its proper name.

The Shadow of the Emperor

But time has little patience with the devices by which we hope to extricate ourselves from change. Time is a layered manifold, composed of an infinity of things related to each other in a structure of endless subtlety in which each thing is both past and present in degrees and proportions of infinite variability. Unlike the evidence, the past straddles the boundary between subject and object, transcending and embracing both. It has a subjective side, not frozen anywhere in time like ice, but fluid like water; not fixed like a recording, but live like a performance. It slips through the meshes of whatever nets of evidence historians may be trailing. The plodding distinction between a medieval past and a modern present was always a violent imposition on the reality of time. It was an imposition that worked, because it in fact allowed the humanists to shape a new form of human life. But like all things in time, it worked only for a while.

The second phase of history's rise to eminence therefore turned out to be quite different from the first. When the Holy Roman Emperor finally stepped down from his throne and the papacy agreed to a concordat with Napoleon that turned French clerics into salaried employees of a secular state, the energy that history had brought to bear on the creation of sovereignty was finally freed from the authority of the past. The boundary the humanists had drawn between their own age and the Dark Ages ceased to be an object of contention dividing those who actively supported medieval forms of government from those opposing them in the name of modern forms of subjectivity. Henceforth the advance of sovereignty proceeded on auto-pilot, as it were, unchecked by mental reservations or significant opposition. The rulers of medieval space and time were gone. History became objective in a novel sense.

Now it began to make good sense to ask whether the Middle Ages ended in 1517 (when Luther posted his theses), in 1492 (when Columbus "discovered" America), or in 1494 (when the Italian wars began), as if the boundary a revolution had once placed into time was simply an event that happened. History no longer needed to stand for a special form of thought and action; rather, it seemed to be able to extend its understanding dispassionately to all forms of consciousness. The empire, the history of Roman law, and Gothic cathedrals acquired their historians. Historical societies were founded, sources were published in new editions, historical novels were written, scholarly journals proliferated at unprecedented speed, and historians transformed themselves from public intellectuals attempting to reshape the order of the commonwealth into professionals conducting the business of history according to the standards of professional organizations.

The fate of history in the nineteenth century thus stands in an instructive contrast to its beginnings in early modern times. Like early modern humanists, nineteenth-century historians witnessed an explosive accumulation of new evidence. Like early modern humanists, they insisted on the significance of taking a historical point of view. But if the main endeavor of early modern humanists had been to set themselves apart from the preceding age in the name of recovering a distant antiquity, the main endeavor of nineteenth century historians was to reverse that very break in the name of a historical understanding transcending all boundaries of space and time. The transformation of the Middle Ages from a tale of human ignorance into an object of intense and admiring historical examination was a surprise. For the first time, the Middle Ages moved to center stage. That reversal shows exactly what was at stake in the demand for the new level of objectivity in the examination of the past of which Ranke's famous "wie es eigentlich gewesen" still serves as the abiding motto.

As a result the meaning of the historical revolt was first attenuated and then lost. History was no longer recognized as the tool that a particular party had deployed in order to advance its cause. History was thought to be no tool at all but an impartial form of understanding, capable of encompassing all forms of humanity without distortion. History seemed no longer humanist but human. The difference was overlooked. The business of history was changed from the creation and defense of a new order of the good to its perpetuation in an unending process of self-critical revisions, of which the turn to the Middle Ages was merely the first in a long line that has not ended yet.

From that point forward, historical self-consciousness was forced to pay a growing price for the lack of self-knowledge that first led it to victory. Historical revolutionaries enjoyed good conscience so long as they were able to confront real enemies. Now that those enemies were gone, their good conscience lost its foundation. The charge of heresy was effectively brushed aside so long as it was brought by popes and emperors. But it gained most uncomfortable strength when it was brought by critics left and right with unimpeachable credentials in the service of progress who saw only too clearly that history lacked the innocence it claimed. History lost the ability to speak in any other mode than irony or cynicism.[28] And by a strange inversion, history began to embody the very authority it had so valiantly sought to overturn.

Just when the emperor seemed to have been displaced into the past forever, transformed into an impotent and insubstantial figure, a shadow of his former self, forced to retreat into a legendary mountain, that mountain turned out to be history itself. Inside that mountain the emperor survived, and from that mountain he returned, not as his former self, but as a new state of mind, the shadow cast by modernity, the insubstantial alter ego of individual autonomy, branding each of its turns with silent charges of heresy and never leaving its dark side. Under this shadow, the subjects of modernity went on to conquer empires of unprecedented magnitude, perhaps in fits of absentmindedness but not without the guilty conscience that was the price for claiming moral and scientific objectivity, and ultimately at the cost of unspeakable human sacrifice to history and nature. The shadow of the emperor brought civil war into the modern world. It turned conscience into the enemy of sovereignty and history into the enemy of nature. It inspired Napoleon to teach the world how to transform liberty, equality, and fraternity into reasons for imperial expansion. It menaced facts of politics and nature with the curse of irrational and inhumane brutality. It looms over Machiavelli, Hobbes, and Nietzsche; over politicians struggling to protect the common good from unconditional suspicions of partiality; over scientists indicted for the unintended consequences of their knowledge; and not least over historians waging a ceaseless exorcism to protect the present from the living dead.

This was the time when the monstrosities peculiar to the modern age—from Dr. Frankenstein, Count Dracula, and the man without a shadow to Dr. Moreau, Dr. Jekyll, and Mr. Hyde—gained their first hold over the European imagination and put a check on the enlightened optimism that that imagination had thought to be its final destiny. Surprised by those monsters, incapable of grasping the cause of an unease that sprang from the same unconscious source that had for so long guaranteed success, the modern state and the modern discipline of history began to display the symptoms of an affliction whose full extent would not become revealed until some time thereafter and has not yet been understood. Romanticism, imperialism, and the violence by which the twentieth century was consumed are the price that Europe paid, and has made others pay, for overturning medieval universalism on the cheap.

There is therefore a kind of displaced or stateless past, somewhere beyond the borders of the empire of history, just as there are displaced and stateless people who suffer, in addition to the aches and pains of ordinary human life, the peculiar horror of an existence unacknowledged by the authorities, for no better reason than that they happen to have come without official papers. The mere existence of that past threatens historical self-consciousness with dissolution. It does not respect the boundary between subject and object, between the record and the thing recorded. It serves as a perpetual reminder of the original act of violence by which history cut time into past and present in order to subject a share of reality to its control. Invisible to eyes trained on the evidence, it haunts the present like a ghost called forth by a historical sorcerer's apprentice and grows in strength with every effort to subject it to the dominance of history. Like a monster created by history out of the living body of time, the stateless past roams the present in search of acceptance and recognition. Like the living dead, it does not know itself (because its knowledge has been taken from it by historians), and it rises from the grave to which historians thought it could safely be consigned and takes revenge by turning on subjectivity itself in order to annihilate the boundary to which it owes its shadowy existence.

Disclaimers and Qualifications

At this point I would like to insert a few disclaimers. First, I do not mean to argue that history was invented in early modern Europe. History has a venerable pedigree that reaches back at least to Greek antiquity and, by an only slightly more liberal definition, to wherever and whenever people have tried to record the past in any way, which is to say, much further back in time than ancient Greece, to records altogether different from alphabetic writing and to places all over the globe. Neither do I mean that history first acquired its revolutionary side in early modern Europe. Even a cursory listing of works considered to be classics in a tradition with which the accident of having been born in a particular place and time have made me familiar suggests a deeper connection between history and revolution than could conceivably be limited to modern times.

Herodotus and the Persian Wars; Thucydides and the Peloponnesian War; Polybius and Rome's conquest of the Mediterranean; Livy and the destruction of the Roman republic; Tacitus and the foundation of the Roman empire; Saint Augustine and the conversion of the Roman empire to Christianity; Otto of Freising and the assertion of papal supremacy; the city chronicles of medieval Italy and the demise of the Staufen emperors: examples such as these may well lead unprejudiced observers to conclude that the study of history is bound to violent upheavals by more than sheer coincidence. Seen in this light, the efflorescence of history in the modern West is only one instance in support of the hypothesis that there exists some subterranean connection between great contributions to history, imperial expansion, revolt, and civil war. But I note that only in passing. What I mean to argue is that the early modern invention of history was a specific event in a specific context with a specific character and consequences that have yet to be fully realized.

Second, I do not mean to say that history has not changed since early modern times. There is debate about this question among historians today. Some argue that modern historical consciousness originates in the sixteenth century. Others maintain that it did not develop until later, and they insist that historicism is not to be confused with early modern historical scholarship.[29] Both sides have good points to make. It would be utterly surprising if history and consciousness had not changed over a period as long as that extending from the sixteenth to the nineteenth century. Moreover, at least one change is crucial to my own argument: the change by which history's purpose was turned from an assault on medieval universalism into an ideology that even until today continues to guarantee to history the status of an objective good so indisputable as to rise above all questions other than how best to bring it within reach.

It is that change, I think, that separates men like Hermann Conring (1606–81), who will receive attention later in this book, from, say, Giambattista Vico (1668–1744). Conring, though a latecomer to the historical revolt, was still an active participant in it—active enough, at any rate, to be aware that history was needed in order to defeat claims to universal government. Hence he was at the same time enthusiastic about the powers of history and skeptical about the trust to be attributed to its results. Vico, in contrast, is widely recognized as the first and one of the greatest representatives of the historicist spirit later embodied by Ranke and Burckhardt.[30] Vico lived not much later than Conring. Yet his confidence in history was of a different order. He represents the moment when the pursuit of historical knowledge for its own sake began to seem a reasonable goal.[31]

Change, in other words, there surely was, none greater than the transformation of history into the objective and comprehensive study of the past, carried out, apparently, for no other purpose than to understand the past on its own terms: the whole past and nothing but the past. However, one thing at least has not changed since the sixteenth century: historical consciousness depends for its meaning on some tension with a real past that really challenges the present. This was particularly true in the beginning. The new form of knowledge could never have gained ascendancy without the tension in which it stood with a past whose universal rulers were none too willing to have themselves subjected to historical analysis. But it continued to be true in the nineteenth century. If anything, the "scientific" history proclaimed in the nineteenth century was even less restrained than its predecessors in deploying evidence "objectively" in order to advance specific political goals. Historians on the right invented ancient ethnic histories, particularly of Germanic peoples, in order to promote movements of national liberation and unification that, notwithstanding their pretense of antiquity, overturned the traditional society of orders with a destructive and profoundly revolutionary energy that continues to sweep the globe today.[32] Historians on the left reciprocated with no less mythical histories of ancient modes of production that served to legitimate equally revolutionary attacks on the state in an attempt to emancipate suffering individuals from the anonymous operation of social forces that condemned humanity to a perpetual struggle between opposing classes.[33]

The understanding historicism sought was therefore neutral only in a superficial sense. If it was never clearly identified with any particular moral or political position, that was only because it enjoyed the luxury of being able to rely on the efforts of predecessors who had already won recognition for the discipline. Just like its early modern predecessor, it was never aware of its own place in time. No doubt there is a fundamental generosity inherent in historicism. It is the generosity with which Ranke and Burckhardt aimed to extend their understanding to the entire world. But like Herodotus's generosity, it rests on a victory gained in a real fight with real enemies. If that is not acknowledged, it turns into an occasion for disingenuousness and condescension.

Third, I do not mean to argue that there is any necessary conjunction between historical knowledge and violence, much less that whatever violence history does in fact entail is necessarily great or intentional. Most of the time, the harm that history does is limited to placing inconsequential blinkers on well-educated minds. Most of the time, it is more than outweighed by ignorance, hunger, war, and diseases caused by factors entirely unrelated, or even thoroughly opposed, to the professional study of the past. Some of the time, history still serves its original emancipatory purpose well. A glance at the liveliest efforts in the historical profession today will show that the best historians are always straining impatiently at the reins of superannuated fashions. Violence stems from passion. But even if history without passion should turn out to be a bad utopian dream, historians should nonetheless be able to take conscious responsibility for whatever exercise of force their work may entail in the service of whatever good keeps them devoted to the practice of their craft.

I do mean to argue this: to study history is to take a stand, to stake a claim, and to oppose real enemies. That makes it a dangerous form of knowledge, both to its enemies and to its supporters. The danger to its enemies was proved in the historical revolt. The danger to its supporters has been proved since then. In the short run, the historical revolt was followed by peace among the winners. Peace ushered in an age of unprecedented cultural and political productivity. This was the time of the Enlightenment, when the distinctions between past and present, private and public, nature and culture seemed so unquestionably built into the structure of the universe that no self-doubt impeded their elaboration in works of thought and action that remain exemplary today. In the long run, a price had to be paid for the violence history did in fact conceal. The magnitude of that price did not become apparent until the twentieth century. It cannot be reduced by mere improvements to the historical design, nor can it be paid off by nature or natural law. It requires nothing less than a declaration of independence from historical consciousness.

The Problem

The chief obstacle to independence from historical consciousness consists of the unspoken unanimity with which we consent to history. We have become so thoroughly accustomed to thinking of ourselves in terms of time that we no longer know how to cast doubt on taking a historical position. History is our second nature. Even its most articulate opponents do not know exactly how to extract themselves from it.[34] Religion may lose its faith; philosophy may lose its meaning; art may lose sight of beauty; and reason may lose its mind. No matter. When every other choice is gone, we can still turn to history and study how it all came to such a pass. History remains our last refuge. Nothing seems capable of freeing us from the illusion that history is always at our beck and call, a natural, neutral, harmless, and universally applicable form of thought.

We are not even conscious that we are taking a historical position. We act like the photographer who never looks at anything except through the lens of his camera. We seem to have lost the ability to recognize that history is merely one way of looking at the world, a good way (because our freedom depends on it), but one that neither shows everything to us nor shows anything without refraction. We take on faith the principles that "those who cannot remember the past are condemned to repeat it," that "to understand the meaning of a text, you must place it in its context first," and that "you cannot tell where you are going unless you know where you are coming from." It never occurs to us that no one can possibly know where they came from, much less where they are going, unless they know already where they are. Whoever is familiar with the experience of getting lost in a strange place knows that a map is useless unless you know where on the map you are.[35] Yet when it comes to history, we think that all we need is better maps.

Of course the unanimity of our salute to the historical revolt is neither conscious nor complete. There has been much to fight about. There have been parties of the left and right, of progress and reaction, of toleration and dissent. There have been materialists, idealists, anarchists, philologists, structuralists, poststructuralists, new historians, political historians, intellectual historians, social historians, historians of everyday life, gay historians, feminist historians, historians of minorities, historians of labor, historians of crime, and so on. The object, the methods, and the foundations of history have never been uncontested in the least. The list of historical varieties battling each other for places in the sun keeps growing by the day.

Early modern humanists themselves afford the first, and for that reason perhaps the most instructive, example of such disputes internal to history. There were among them republicans and monarchists, Ciceronians and Tacitists, champions of reason of state and champions of popular resistance to tyranny, Catholics and Protestants, skeptics, deeply pious clerics, and "atheists." Humanist ranks included laymen, monks, commoners, noblemen, noblewomen, and ruling figures in the hierarchies of church and state. In fact, humanists were so deeply divided in so many different ways that it is utterly impossible to find a single point of doctrine on which all humanists agreed.[36]

Therefore, no attempt to explain the humanist movement in terms of any special brand of theology, philosophy, or politics has succeeded so far, and none can be expected to succeed. To that extent the thesis of Hans Baron that humanism ought to be understood as the expression of a Florentine liberation movement taking shape in 1400 has to be judged a failure.[37] Far better to insist, with Paul Oskar Kristeller, on a strictly formal definition of humanism as a movement of education united by its championship of certain disciplines of knowledge (grammar, poetry, rhetoric, history, and moral philosophy) that were so far from representing a particular position as to be capable of serving diametrically opposed positions with equal facility.[38] Far better also to accept as real the continuities by which humanists were tied to Aristotelian philosophy, scholastic theology, canon law, and other medieval antecedents.

But the divisions internal to the humanist camp must all the same not be allowed to obscure their shared allegiance to a new form of thought and action. To think of this allegiance as "merely" formal is to fail to understand the significance of form.[39] Formal it may well have been. But its pervasive power derived precisely from its formality. It was a purely formal question whether to treat a given text as a timeless authority or as a piece of textual evidence to be subjected to historical analysis. Historical analysis as such did not predetermine the result of interpretation. But it did predetermine the form the interpretation had to take: whatever disputes over the meaning to be attributed to this or that particular piece of text might have divided (and did indeed divide) humanists, all of them were governed by principles of history. Conclusions may have been up for grabs. Methods of reasoning were not.

The formality of the humanist allegiance to a particular set of disciplines was neither a *mere* formality nor a weakness to be concealed or deplored. It was rather a source of tremendous intellectual strength. It permitted the liveliest of conflicts over substance without endangering the successful implementation of a new framework of thought and action. Indeed, conflicts over substance most likely helped to speed up success. They focused attention on specific matters, demanded the exercise of new faculties of interpretation, and all the more effectively distracted attention from the silent operation of a new form of thought. Because each eye saw different things, no eye could see that all were turned in a new direction. To that extent, Baron's attempt to grasp what held all humanists together, though it may have missed its mark, rests on a sound intuition about the reality and depth of the gulf dividing medieval universalism from the historical revolt.[40]

Much the same needs to be said about the battles that have divided historians since then. Like early modern humanists, historians have never stopped fighting over innumerable issues concerning the evaluation and interpretation of the evidence. Not coincidentally, their most intractable disputes have turned on history's association with violence. From Voltaire, via Marx, to the most recent postmodernist critique, the history of politics and ideas, kings and battles, diplomacy, the state, and Western civilization has justly been singled out as something dimly felt to favor domination. All these kinds of history have been recognized as somehow misrepresentative of the past, elitist, exclusive in some way that violates history's professed goals of broader understanding. Attempts have been made time and again to break the association between history and violence and to transcend the limits to which "conventional" history confines our sympathies.[41]

Those attempts have demanded much attention. The turn to the Middle Ages with which the professional study of history began in the nineteenth century was merely the first of many. Since Karl Lamprecht's famously confrontational and disastrously failed attack on conventional history, they may well have consumed the greater part of historians' energy.[42] The entire field of social and economic history has from the start been animated by a desire for a history more representative of the past than the study of politics and ideas. An entire school of historians, named after their chief journal the school of the *Annales,* has since the first quarter of the twentieth century attempted to break down the prison in which intellectual and political history previously kept the past by writing "total" history, or history of "long duration," history of underlying structures, mental and geographic, affecting all the people. In the United States the turn to the Middle Ages came later than in Europe, but it signaled the arrival of professional history with the same clarity.[43] The history of women and gender, labor history, the history of persecuted and oppressed minorities (religious, sexual, ethnic), the history of popular culture, the history of everyday life, microhistory, world history and global history, the history of political culture, critical cultural studies—all of these are motivated by similarly deeply justified frustrations with the exclusions practiced by "conventional" history. The means and methods differ, and the protagonists can fight each other bitterly. But their devotion to the task of rendering history adequate to the past is equally unflagging. Even bodily functions that used to seem suited only for physical examination are now receiving outstanding historical analysis.

No doubt our knowledge of the past has grown by leaps and bounds as a result. If historians at first restricted their attention to a narrow circle, that circle has grown with breathtaking speed until the complete subjection of the past to historical scrutiny seems to have been transformed from an ideal into an almost palpable reality. No aspect of human life can any longer claim immunity from the desire for true knowledge of the past. But there is also no doubt that none of that new knowledge has managed to define the source of the unease from which it sprang. The battles between left and right, conservatives and critics, historians of structures and historians of events, political and social historians, medievalists and modernists, post-modernists and prophets of the end of history, and so on have all remained internal to a paradigmatically modern logic that has never been dislodged since it first gained the upper hand. History, in all its variations, continues to draw strength from the conviction that there is nothing wrong with the standards of objectivity, only with their implementation. Conclusions are still up for grabs. Indeed, more up for grabs than ever. But historical consciousness itself rules silently supreme.

More than four decades ago, Reinhart Koselleck explained how the distinction between an inner, private realm of morals and an external, public realm of politics, having brought peace to the seventeenth century, threw modern politics into a crisis ever after.[44] It created the crisis by giving private individuals authority to subject the moral deficits of politics and politicians to the critique of conscience. It concealed the crisis by disguising what was in effect a political endeavor as the exercise of purely moral faculties. And no resolution was possible because the exercise of purely moral faculties was exempt by definition from political control. The pattern that resulted was paradoxical: every attempt to heal our relationship to politics by means of moral reform could only make the crisis worse.

If the argument of this book has any merit, the pattern that Koselleck identified in politics applies to history as well. History's distinction between now and then is consubstantial with the distinction between moral and political. As the distinction between moral and political led to a crisis in our relationship to politics, so the distinction between now (the present, alive, and here) and then (the past, dead, and gone) led to a crisis in our relationship to time. It produced the crisis by giving historians authority to subject the past to critical examination. It concealed the crisis by disguising what was in effect an act of self-determination as mere study of the past. And it put a solution out of reach because the study of the past was by definition exempt from political control. The pattern that resulted was paradoxical: every attempt to heal our relationship to time by means of history could only make the crisis worse.

In both cases the crisis consisted of an assault on the source of its own energy, a kind of cultural auto-immune disease. In both cases the result was a kind of irresponsibility, moral in one, historical in the other. The irresponsibility was excused by claims to objectivity: the objectivity of moral law and that of historical research. And in both cases the irresponsibility, once it had been excused, threatened to spiral out of control toward some final judgment passed by an utterly unrestrained subjectivity upon an utterly defenseless objectivity.

The result has been a deeply frustrating predicament. Now most historians will agree that history has failed, and keeps continually failing, to achieve the kind of objectivity to which history officially aspires.[45] But the faith in evidence continues to rule so effectively that the mere attempt to look for alternatives seems illegitimate. If the disputes dividing humanists in early modern times helped to fuel the elaboration of new forms of thought and action, the same disputes dividing historians today only confirm the authority of very old ideas. What could history be, if not the study of evidence? Fiction appears to be the only answer. But fiction, arguments to the contrary notwithstanding, is not the same as history, much less the same as knowledge of the past.

Hence, historians are confronted with an uncomfortable choice between two equally unattractive paths that look as though they led in opposite directions but end up in the same morass. Let us call them history with a stiff upper lip and history that wants to call the whole thing off. Stiff-upper-lip history (serious, filled with a sense of duty) insists that only one thing can explain why history has failed to reach its goals: we have not yet tried hard enough. Stiff-upper-lip history demands that we try harder. And people do. How hard they try is often nothing short of amazing. Future ages will doubtless marvel that mere mortals were able to erect such massive monuments to learning. By contrast, let's-call-the-whole-thing-off history (skeptical, filled with a sense of absurdity) pronounces the impossibility of ever knowing anything and goes to equally amazing lengths in disentangling the relationships between facts, evidence, and theory.

Both seem misguided. The search for greater objectivity is bound to deepen history's failure to tell the truth about the world of time; and pronouncing the impossibility of knowing anything at all is bound to reinforce old standards of objectivity, if only by conceding that knowledge does not qualify as real if it is not objective. At the extremes the consequences are a self-indulgent relativism taking secret advantage of standards of objectivity only apparently scorned in public, and opportunistic revivals of tradition whose authenticity is belied by the facility with which they sacrifice history to popular demand. I hope it can go without saying that neither that self-indulgence nor this opportunism may be attributed to the character of particular historians. They stem from the character of a discipline whose intellectual debts are coming due.

One might consider turning to philosophy for help. Some of the most famous accomplishments of modern philosophy have, after all, turned on attempts to come to terms with that great transformation in early modern thought that Whitehead called the historical revolt. Hegel made history the very ground of his *Phenomenology of Mind*. Nietzsche attacked the very structures of subjectivity to which the historical revolt gave rise. Heidegger offered alternatives that constitute an unanswered challenge to the historical imagination. And developments have not stood still since then. One merely needs to mention the names of Gadamer, Collingwood, Ricoeur, Foucault, Kuhn, White, Rorty, and Koselleck to recognize the lengths to which reflection on the nature and condition of historical consciousness has recently been carried.[46] There can be little doubt that historical consciousness constitutes one of the central preoccupations of modern philosophy.

And yet the fundamental problem remains entirely unsolved. Nietzsche's and Heidegger's ideas were fatally wounded by their association with the extremes of violence to which they were taken in the Third Reich. No doubt the association is unfair. But there is no doubt either that it is all too real, not arbitrary in the least but among the penalties exacted for the ascendancy of historical consciousness. More recent works may not suffer from the same association, or not to the same degree. But they succeed in steering clear of the violence on which Nietzsche and Heidegger foundered only by leaving the captivity of modern thought to history unchallenged. Gadamer's radical hermeneutics remains committed to a "fusion of horizons" that, far from letting history go, extends it to universal applicability. Foucault appears to have been guided by surer instincts. But he left history surprisingly unscathed. Nowhere is this more clearly evident than in his reliance on the conventional periodization of European history into ancient, medieval, and modern periods, his unfamiliarity with medieval matters, and a faith in the self-centered independence of modernity that seems remarkably naive compared to his philosophical sophistication.[47]

Charles Taylor's *Sources of the Self* offers a good illustration of how difficult it is not to succumb to the allure of history.[48] Here is a philosophical investigation of the first order, explicitly intended to uncover the ontological limitations that stunt our modern selves. So far so good. But though it is carried out with admirable verve on paths carefully chosen to clear the obstacles that stopped Nietzsche and Heidegger in their tracks, it falls flat the moment it encounters history. Taylor's half-hearted "Digression on Historical Explanation" shows that the difficulty has occurred to him.[49] But that can hardly serve as a substitute for demonstrating history's complicity in the naturalist reductions that he wants to undo. The shoulder-shrugging attitude with which a philosopher of such standing draws on history as though it could be trusted to take no sides in ontological disputes suggests that history prevents us far more effectively than science from raising our condition to consciousness. Philosophy, it seems, cannot be counted on to bail out history.[50]

Given this state of affairs, it may be no surprise that the sizable body of philosophy specifically devoted to analyzing historical logic—books whose titles seem to promise answers to the questions that have been raised on the preceding pages—turn out to have a different intellectual agenda.[51] Such philosophical analyses are informative about questions internal to the operation of history. They raise the intellectual activities in which historians are commonly engaged to a level of precise philosophical definition. That makes for instructive reading. But it clarifies only what history does in public, not how it works in private. If you would like to know what it is possible to learn about the past by studying the evidence, these books are for you. But they will not explain history's rise to prominence, much less its hold over our minds.

History seems to have gotten itself into the place of the barber who shaves all the men in town who do not shave themselves: because he cannot shave himself (the barber shaves no man who shaves himself) he has to shave himself (the barber shaves all the men who do not shave themselves). He is trapped in a quandary from which he cannot possibly escape . . . unless he is a woman, leaves town, or changes his profession. History is trapped in the same way. What is it? Woman, barber, man in town? What should it shave? The history on other faces? The theory on its own? What should it do? Leave town? Stop shaving? Only a decent sense of humor can keep questions like these from weighing history down. Neither historical research nor historical theory seems qualified to help us out. As Thomas Kuhn once put it, "in history, more than in any other discipline I know, the finished product of research disguises the nature of the work that produced it."[52]

The way to extricate oneself from history's spell may therefore not lie in books at all. Perhaps the only way is through experience. No one who has been subject to historical examination can fail to be struck by the discrepancy between an objective reconstruction of events and personal experience. The sharpest pain such reconstructions cause does not derive from failings of the examiner (though it is all too easily attributed to such). It rather derives from the examination. More precisely, it derives from the authority with which the examiner officially reports on the examinee. To be subject to that authority is to be violated, to feel the urge to disagree, make points of which the examiner could not have been aware, and generally to rebel against the claim that any examiner can ever speak for the examinee. Not (to say it once again) because the examiner failed his responsibility, but because he executed it; because there can be no objective account unless the evidence has first been hunted, as it were, then seized, and finally forced to do a work it never did before. No mere book can hope to teach that experience.

The Solution

When I began to write this book, I was already well aware that history only scrapes the surface of the past. To put it in terms that will be considered more closely later on, I knew that studying the past results in blurry images (chapter 2), that interpreting evidence in the context of its place and time leads to an infinite regress (chapter 3), and that interpreting evidence outside the context of its place and time is to confuse logical analysis with historical understanding (chapter 4). I knew that these problems cast such fundamental doubt on history that there was little point in doing once again what had been done before.

That stopped me right at the start from business as usual. My plan was never to write a history of the historical revolt, not even one limited to early modern Germany or to the history of historical writing. I never considered the possibility of composing the intellectual biography of some particular figure, tracing the influence of some idea, describing some cultural environment, or writing social and economic history. History as I knew it would not do. I wanted to write some other kind of history, free from the defects I saw in everything I read. I did not have an inkling what kind of history that might be. But I was certain that history needed to be improved. You could say I wanted to write bigger and better history.

It seemed a noble goal. In fact it was grandiose. It did no justice to the predicament I have described above at all. It was to underestimate the problem by a whole order of magnitude. The results were correspondingly appalling. They were just like the bumps that Wittgenstein says reason gets on its head when it runs into the limits of language.[53] They were so ugly that in the end they forced me to reckon with a nagging sense of having overlooked something important. What I had overlooked was this: an adequate understanding of the past may be within our reach. But it cannot be grasped by reason or demonstrated from the evidence. History is a limited form of knowledge. Within those limits it can do good work. Outside of those limits it cannot exist. History needs no improvement. It is as good as it has ever been. It needs to be no better.

That turned my understanding of the problem inside out. The problem is not that history has not yet gone far enough. The opposite is true: history has constantly gone too far—too far in its ambitions and too far in its claims. History is burdened with tasks it cannot possibly fulfill. It cannot tell "wie es eigentlich gewesen," and it should never have been asked to do so. That is what saps its meaning. Expecting history to reach the reality of the past is to allow oneself to be seduced by a mirage arising not from the past but from a historical imagination run amok.

My understanding of the task changed accordingly. If history is to do well what it can do, its limits need to be affirmed. Merely describing them is not enough. They are so deeply buried beneath the scholarship daily produced by professionals who cannot afford to have their concentration interrupted by doubts about the foundations of their enterprise that they are difficult to see and easy to forget. They must be shown in the concrete, and their effects need to be driven home until they cannot be ignored.

That is what I shall try to do in this book. I shall accept our condition as it is and make no attempts at novelty. There will be no new theory and no new form of history offered here. Nothing bigger, nothing better. I shall simply focus on a specific subject and practice some history on it. The subject is Hermann Conring (1606–81) and a little book entitled *Discursus novus de imperatore Romano-Germanico* or *New Discourse on the Roman-German*

Emperor that was published under Conring's name in 1642. The subject is a particle of the past chosen for the sake of illustration, no different in principle from any number of other subjects I could have chosen for the same purpose. Its advantage, if any, is that it may make it easier than other subjects would to challenge history where it hurts: at the most conservative core of its most traditional practice. The methods I shall use are perfectly commonplace as well. The only difference is the purpose of this study: not to add to our knowledge of the past but to point out its limits.

I first heard of Conring in a course on diplomatics (not the art of diplomacy but the critical study of official historical documents, particularly medieval charters) that I took as a beginning student at the Rheinische Friedrich-Wilhelms-Universität in Bonn. The lecturer, Paul Egon Hübinger, maintained that Conring had not received the attention he deserved. That caught my interest. Many years later my interest grew when I found out that Conring was trained as a physician. That was intriguing. My interest was confirmed by the advice of Arnaldo Momigliano and Michael Stolleis. But I have to confess that only hindsight permits me to articulate the reasons for a choice first guided by nothing much better than frustration, anger, and a hunch: frustration with the limits of history, anger at the sublime invisibility of chains whose effects I felt only too clearly but was incompetent to put into words, and a hunch that it would prove revealing to concentrate on a neglected but obviously important thinker whose work made a mockery of the labels commonly used to sort out early modern intellectual history.

That hunch proved better than I had any right to hope. Conring lived in a period when the adoption of a temporal perspective was still contested and the conjunction of history with violence had not yet been submerged beneath mountains of empirical detail and theoretical debates over the nature and extent of historical knowledge. He lived on the cusp between the historical revolt and its institutionalization in the Enlightenment. In his day the principles of historical analysis had already been so well developed that they were hard to miss, as opposed, for example, to their embryonic condition in the writings Marsiglio of Padua aimed against the papacy at the very beginning of the early modern period. At the same time they were still very far from having secured the dominance they have today. That helped. Studying historical thought in its nineteenth-century maturity would have crowded my view. Looking for it in earlier periods would have made me fall prey to the equivocation with which histories of historiography commonly smooth over (or vanish into) the conceptual abyss dividing medieval from modern attitudes toward time.

The fact that Conring lived in Germany consolidated the advantage obtained from his place in time. Germany never managed to join the temporal perspective on private and public sovereignty as firmly as France or England did. So Germany affords a clearer view of the relationship between history and politics than can be had elsewhere. In Germany medieval universalism, in the form of the Holy Roman Empire, managed to survive well into modern times with a vitality that has only recently been recognized and still remains surprising to historians with a conventional focus on the rise of the modern state.[54] But Germany was also the part of Europe in which the practice of "scientific" history was perfected soon after Emperor Franz II was forced by Napoleon to put an end to the imperial tradition that Charlemagne had started almost exactly a thousand years before. From Freiherr vom Stein, the foundation of the Monumenta Germaniae Historica, and Ranke via Droysen and Burckhardt (not German in the nationalist sense, but very much so in the antinationalist one) to Dilthey, Weber, Troeltsch, and Meinecke, German historical thought set the pace for the rest of Europe until the catastrophes of the twentieth century transported its intellectual energy to France, England, and the United States.[55]

That was unique. The long survival of an imperial tradition holding its own successfully against attempts to displace it into a stateless past, the exemplary intensity of Germany's turn to "scientific" history, the monstrous descent into madness that followed when Hitler managed by some black art to endow the shadow of the emperor with a real living body, the raw nerves beneath the thin skin of German culture—all these make writings from Germany more promising for anyone wishing to find the seams between history, sovereignty, and violence than are the seamless works (though seamless only by comparison) of writers such as Machiavelli, Hobbes, and Locke, written in regions conventionally praised for their more secular, rational, and progressive character.

The inconspicuousness of Conring on the landscape of professional history was a less important but not negligible source of his attraction. Apart from my own writings and brief articles in some encyclopedias and dictionaries, there is only a single English publication that focuses on him directly.[56] Even works explicitly devoted to the study of early modern political thought barely mention Conring's name—and encyclopedias like the *Encyclopedia Britannica* do not even do that.[57] The literature in German is, of course, more sizable.[58] But broadly speaking, Conring cannot be said to be familiar to anyone except a few specialists.

That made it easier to master what was already known. It furnished a welcome opportunity to march straight into the territory staked out above without first having to clear entire forests of books that were, according to my hypothesis, only too likely to put out of sight what I was looking for. But the scarcity of writings about Hermann Conring was more than a practical advantage. The lack of a body of historical literature commensurate with his significance was a clue to the forgetfulness from which I sought to wake myself. The recalcitrance with which his polyhistorism refuses to bend to the usual categories of historical analysis is an implicit challenge to the assumptions from which those categories draw their strength. That Conring's work escapes from those assumptions made it worth asking how, then, it ought to be understood.

I need not retrace the steps by which I found the means to put an inchoate frustration into words. But I would like to describe the steps by which I hope to take the reader to the same destination. Chapter 2 introduces Hermann Conring as a subject for historical attention. It opens with a brief look at the difficulties with which conventional distinctions between law and politics, state and empire, and medieval and modern history confront historians seeking to understand the origins of modern political thought. The chapter goes on to offer a reasonably detailed review of Conring's life and works in an attempt, ostensibly, to make a little headway in reaching a more adequate understanding of the origins of modern political thought.

Chapter 3 concentrates on the *New Discourse on the Roman-German Emperor.* I shall examine the circumstances of its publication, compare it with several other closely related writings, and follow its later history. I chose the *New Discourse* for three main reasons. First, because it shows as pointedly as one could wish what the historical revolt was all about. Second, because it was written early in Conring's career, at a time when he still spoke with a welcome lack of restraint. It was, in fact, the first work on questions of politics published under his name. And third, because it was (the reader may be surprised to learn) not written by himself, at least not according to the conventional understanding of authorship. Although the ideas expressed in it are definitely his, the text was an unauthorized reprint of a dissertation defended by one of his students in 1641. The *New Discourse* and the dissertation on which it was based thus are ideally suited to examine not merely Conring's thought, but also the whole set of ties by which we believe the evidence to be connected to its creators.

Chapter 4 deals with the substance of Conring's argument. That argument consists of an assault on one of the cardinal ingredients in medieval universalism: the notion that the Roman emperor ruled the world. Right at the beginning of the *New Discourse,* Conring attacked a famous formulation of that view by Bartolus of Sassoferrato (1313/14–1357), an authoritative commentator on Roman law who lived almost as long before Conring's time as Conring lived before our own. Chapter 4 pays a good deal of attention to the doctrine that Conring rejected with such undisguised antipathy. That will make it easier to clarify exactly what was at stake in Conring's turn to history.

Chapters 2, 3, and 4 are related to each other by a logical progression that leads from the surface to the bottom of the questions that this chapter has raised in the abstract. Chapter 2 largely depends on the existing historical literature and makes only brief forays into the world of primary evidence. Its function is to claim a particular plot of historical terrain for the historical investigation that follows in the succeeding chapters. It begins exactly where professional historians normally begin: with a deficiency in our present state of knowledge. Only much later will it become apparent that the deficiency is not as easy to correct as it may seem.

Chapter 3 goes deeper into the past: it seeks to draw new knowledge about the past from a piece of evidence that has not previously been examined. It relies on methods (the analysis of texts in the context of their time and place) and concepts (intention, authorship, and authenticity) that are as old as the historical revolt itself. But far from making good on the promise of better understanding, chapter 3 leads to the conclusion that the historical reality at issue (what Conring really thought) lies beyond the reach of historical research. Authorship and authenticity turn out to be concepts that deceive, and context offers no guidance firm enough to grasp the meaning of the text. Chapter 3 ends with a Pyrrhic victory: it makes a certain contribution to our current state of knowledge, but at the cost of eroding the foundations on which our current state of knowledge rests.

Chapter 4 takes the progression to its conclusion. It seeks to grasp the substance of Conring's argument by contrasting it with that which he rejected. The substance of his argument, however, turns out to be very strange—indeed, to be no argument at all, but an incommensurability impossible to understand in terms of historical development and carefully concealed by Conring with one of those intellectual sleights of hand that led the historical revolt to victory. Chapter 4 lands in a logical dead end out of which history does not seem qualified to lead. Chapter 5 draws conclusions.

What I am offering the reader here, in other words, is neither history nor theory. Not theory, because this book turns on the historical examination of a particular aspect of the past. Not history either, because it does not aim at knowledge of the past but at that recognition of our own ignorance that Montaigne once called the surest test of judgment.[59] It offers a systematic study neither of Conring's writings as a whole nor of any one of them, nor does it make up for the lack of a biography. Still less does it pretend to deal with Bartolus and the history of Roman law. If I insist on conducting a special historical investigation by analyzing primary evidence that will compel the reader to struggle with an unfamiliar subject and some technical detail, I do it only because I do not think that theory can lead out of the perplexity that stares us in the face. No other way leads forward than to practice the principles of the craft in full awareness of their poverty. That this investigation is focused on Hermann Conring and his *New Discourse* results from a mixture of accident and opportunity. That Conring lies far from contemporary fashion is no impediment. All subjects in the realm of knowledge enjoy an equal right to being known. Knowledge does not discriminate.

I realize that in this project I ask my readers to peer into the historical distance while looking over their shoulder to catch a glimpse of their own subjectivity—a feat of mental acrobatics that may seem unreasonably difficult. But I know of no other way to gain perspective on history than by a double entendre of whose exasperating quality I am only too well aware. It has exasperated me no less than it may exasperate the reader. I cannot say that I have any special interest in Conring's life and works. Not that I bear him any grudges, either. I have nothing against the man, have even grown fond of him over time, to the extent at least that he permitted the degree of familiarity without which fondness is impossible. But there are many other people among the living and the dead whose company in life and letters I find no less enjoyable—a point with which I think Conring would have agreed. Nor can I claim that I have any special interest in the works of philosophy to which I have so glancingly referred above. Few things could be less philosophical than any special interest in philosophy.

I want to take you on a guided tour to the limits of history. I hope that explains why I decided firmly against a title or subtitle mentioning Conring and Bartolus. This book is not about either one of them. This book sets out to show in one instance what separates us in all instances from an adequate understanding of the past. It seeks to clarify the significance of history by means of an example taken from the times when early modern European people changed their mind about the past and, consequently, about politics and nature. It aims to show that mind itself, including mind informed by a historical perspective, changes over time. What changes is not merely what we think, or how we think, or what we mean by thinking, but that faculty itself by means of which we think that we think. If the book has any overriding purpose, it is only to lift the spell with which history keeps us in thrall.

2

The Subject: Hermann Conring

This is the first of three chapters in the guided tour I promised. It is devoted to what historians like to call a gap in our knowledge. The gap lies in early modern European historical and political thought, and it contains the life and works of Hermann Conring. I shall begin by describing the location of the gap and the reasons it seems worth filling. Then I shall fill it with information gathered from primary and secondary sources. I shall take care to arrange that information in a fashion appropriate to the subject and instructive to the reader. Other gaps would require different arrangements. But the principle would be the same.

The State of the Art

In recent decades historians have paid much attention to early modern European political thought. This is especially true of the English-speaking world, where Donald Kelley, Francis Oakley, J. G. A. Pocock, Quentin Skinner, and Brian Tierney (to mention in alphabetical order the names of a few especially distinguished authors) have placed the study of early modern political thought on a new foundation.[1] But similar observations can be made about writers in the German language, such as Otto Brunner, Horst Dreitzel, Jürgen Habermas, Reinhart Koselleck, Gerhard Oestreich, and Michael Stolleis,[2] as well as Italians such as Giorgio Chittolini, Paolo Prodi, and Diego Quaglioni.[3] Only French and Spanish scholars seem to have remained somewhat on the sidelines.[4]

The causes behind this expenditure of scholarly energy are not obvious. But its effect has been great progress in understanding early modern political thought. Whereas until not so long ago one could refer interested readers only to such classics as John Allen's *History of Political Thought in the*

Sixteenth Century (1928) or Pierre Mesnard's *L'essor de la philosophie politique au XVIe siècle* (1936), both of them outstanding but seriously dated, there is now a whole body of scholarship that is growing by the day and illuminating the landscape of early modern political thought in ever finer detail.[5]

Nonetheless, some obstacles still lie ahead. Chief among them is a conceptual difficulty. The central phenomenon in the history of early modern political thought is the development of a separate sphere of politics, as distinct from religion, law, morals, and history, along with the distinction of religion, law, morals, and history from each other in a larger process leading from medieval "wholeness" to modern specialization.[6] That development is manifestly impossible to understand if the result to which it led in the end is presupposed at the beginning. Quentin Skinner has famously warned against the "mythology of doctrines" and the temptation to read the history of political thought backward.[7] But the fame of his warnings seems to exceed our ability to heed them. Instead of showing how politics came to be defined as a separate sphere of human thought and action in a world where no such sphere previously existed, we still presuppose the existence of "politics," pursue its origins as far back in time as our means permit, then further, and all the while refrain from sidelong glances at things that do not fit the presupposition—never mind that such things may be crucial for understanding how modern politics came into being.

Three of the most important things thus relegated to the periphery are law (excluded by the boundary between politics and law), the Middle Ages (excluded by the boundary between modern and medieval), and the Holy Roman Empire (excluded by the boundary between state and empire). These are not the only exclusions that could be mentioned,[8] but they are representative of many others and are especially important. Each deserves more comment.

It is something of a commonplace that historians of political thought pay too little attention to the history of law. Historians of law, it is only fair to add, reciprocate with similar disregard for the history of political thought. There are, of course, good reasons for that division of labor. Anyone who has ever worked with medieval or early modern legal writings knows that they are poorly published, rarely translated, and difficult to use. They are written in genres entirely different from those of political thought as it is usually understood, and they cannot be mined without much technical expertise. Many of them consist of dispersed commentaries on particular passages of law whose connection to political ideas is opaque unless examined closely. Even when they are offered in the form of discursive treatises with more obviously theoretical relevance, they are suffused with references to underlying legal texts and glosses as impossible to overlook as they are laborious to trace. Works by philosophers like Marsiglio of Padua (c. 1280–1343) at the beginning of the period or Thomas Hobbes (1588–1679) and John Locke (1632–1704) at its end are more self-contained, deal with something that looks more like "political thought," and make for much more inviting reading than the glosses of Accursius (c. 1182–1260) or the commentaries of Bartolus of Sassoferrato (1313/14–1357) on Justinian's *Corpus Iuris,* not to mention a collection of medieval and early modern legal expertise by many different authors like the *Tractatus universi iuris*.[9] Little wonder that authors like Marsiglio of Padua, Thomas Hobbes, and John Locke figure more prominently in the history of political thought than Accursius or Bartolus.

But the history of early modern political thought is incomplete if it does not include the jurists. Medieval and early modern jurists traveled across much of the intellectual territory that was later taken over by political theorists. Many of the most prominent contributors to early modern political thought were professionally trained in law. Francesco Guicciardini (1483–1540), Jean Bodin (1529/30–1596), and Hugo Grotius (1583–1645) are three particularly well-known cases. Such men defined the concepts that are fundamental to modern political thought. State and sovereignty are only the most obvious. Property and contract belong in the same class.

That has been recognized for quite some time.[10] But even though German and Italian historians of political thought pay more attention to law than American and English ones, practice is lagging far behind theory.[11] With the notable exception of medieval canon law, where the divide between law and political thought has been bridged by Walter Ullmann, Brian Tierney, Francis Oakley, and their students, and occasional bright spots, such as the work of Gaines Post, the histories of law and political thought continue to exist in splendid isolation from each other.[12] That is fine, so long as the distinction between law and politics can be presupposed. But it is fatal where that distinction is itself at issue.

The case is only slightly better with the boundary between medieval and modern political thought. The difficulties that impede our understanding of the Middle Ages are similar to those just mentioned for understanding law. Until recently, one might almost have said that medieval political thought was beyond the scope of historians of early modern political thought. That is no longer true. The days when the Renaissance and the Reformation were thought to mark an absolute divide between medieval and modern history are gone.[13] The importance of medieval canon law for modern politics is now more widely recognized. Modernists are entering into encouraging conversations with medievalists and vice versa. There are new translations of medieval writers on questions of politics, and names like John of Salisbury (c. 1115/20–1180), John Quidort of Paris (c. 1240–1306), and William of Ockham (c. 1280/85–1349) are no longer as foreign to students of modern political thought as they once were.[14] Thanks to the efforts of James Burns and Quentin Skinner, we even have histories of political thought that treat medieval and early modern political thought almost in one breath.[15]

But only *almost* in one breath. The chronological boundary that defined the books of John Allen and Pierre Mesnard has been weakened. But even in its weakened state, it still dominates our thinking. We have not yet found a way of crossing it without falling into one of two vices: belittling the differences that separate medieval jurists like Bartolus from modern theorists of sovereignty like Jean Bodin, or pressing them into the Procrustean bed of a convenient but superficial dichotomy. In the former case, medieval thinkers are elevated to the status of having invented everything that matters, while their modern successors are demoted to the status of mere elaborators or imitators of the medieval heritage.[16] In the latter case, modern thinkers are given credit for taking the crucial step to modernity, while their medieval forebears are reproved for their failure to take that step themselves.[17] A kind of chronological Orientalism compels us to oscillate between dismissing medieval people as barbarians and revering them as the creators of our civilization.[18] A history that manages to pay them due respect without ignoring how they differ from ourselves has not yet been written.

Finally, concerning the boundary between state and empire, the origin of politics is regularly sought in the city-states of Italy or the territorial monarchies of France and England, but not in the Germanies, much less the Holy Roman Empire.[19] Whereas early modern Germans are recognized for having produced significant works on religion, law, and history, they are rarely considered to have made contributions of any real significance to political thought until the Enlightenment.[20] Histories of early modern political thought abound in references to Machiavelli, Bodin, Hobbes, and Locke. Germans are scarcely mentioned.

This is to forget that modern politics is unimaginable without the redefinition of the relation between politics and religion that Martin Luther (1483–1546) demanded and obtained. It was the Reformation that made the separation of religion, law, and history from politics inevitable.[21] It may be true that the results went further or deeper in Germany than elsewhere. Certainly the boundary dividing state from society, as well as that dividing public from private affairs, was drawn differently in Germany than in France or England. Certainly the Holy Roman Empire never developed into a state like France or England. Hence politics and political thought in Germany do not look like politics and political thought in other countries. Hence it may have been more difficult for Germans to arrive at a satisfactory understanding, not to mention a satisfactory practice, of politics than it was for their neighbors.[22] But none of that justifies the superficial treatment given to German developments in early modern political thought. If it is accepted that the Reformation was important for the development of European political thought in general, it is hard to understand why the thinking of Germans in the century following the Reformation should not have been important for the development of European political thought as well—never mind that it proceeded along unfamiliar paths and does not seem to qualify as "political." German developments were part of a European process. That process is impossible to understand unless the understanding includes Germany.[23]

Whoever wishes to improve our understanding of early modern political thought should therefore read more than Machiavelli, Hobbes, and Locke. Their writings deserve the detailed investigations to which they have been subjected. They are classics. They laid down the boundaries between medieval and modern, law and politics, state and society. Their logic has governed modern thinking ever since it was first put into place. But here that logic is to be confronted. That is why I shall focus on an author and a writing just about as far from classic as they come: Hermann Conring and his *New Discourse on the Roman-German Emperor*.

Conring's Youth

Hermann Conring was born on 9 November 1606, in Norden, a small but, by the standards of the time, not insignificant harbor town in East Frisia, a large territory on the North Sea coast of Germany.[24] East Frisia extended from the Netherlands in the west to Hamburg in the east. It was perhaps the largest German territory whose ruling house, the counts of Cirksena, had not yet managed to rise to princely status by the time of Conring's birth.[25] Many years later, in 1654, Conring himself helped to persuade Emperor Ferdinand III to elevate Count Enno Ludwig to the rank of prince. But even then the change in status was limited to the title of Enno Ludwig and his heirs. East Frisia itself remained a county and did not gain the separate voice in the imperial diet that was normally granted to principalities.[26]

Norden adopted Luther's interpretation of the Gospel in 1527, relatively early in the Reformation, and held fast to Lutheran beliefs thereafter. Like other Lutheran communities in East Frisia and the population of the countryside, it was loyal to the counts, staunch Lutherans themselves. Emden, however, by far the most important city in East Frisia because of its size, wealth, and far-flung connections as a major center of northern European trade and industry, was a stronghold of Calvinism.[27] For a while it served as a refuge for Calvinists in exile and a center of Calvinist agitation second in importance only to Geneva itself. Emden was a world apart from Lutheran East Frisia. Conflicts between a powerful Calvinist city, Lutheran counts, and their Lutheran supporters in smaller towns and the countryside dominated the politics of the region. They must have acquainted Conring early on with the consequences of Protestant disunity, and perhaps they fostered both his lasting attachment to Lutheran princes and his fondness for the religious climate prevailing in the Netherlands.

Conring's mother, Galatea Copin, was descended from an old East Frisian family. She was the daughter of a Lutheran minister who preached in Pilsum and later in Delft. Though we know next to nothing about her life, not even the dates of her birth and death, we do know that she was much younger than her husband. We also know that she was well educated and that she taught her son the rudiments of Latin.

Conring's paternal grandfather, Johannes Conring (dates unknown) was an immigrant to East Frisia. He was born in the vicinity of Billerbeck in Westphalia, not far from Münster, where Conring's family name can be documented since the fourteenth century, but emigrated from Westphalia to the Netherlands, where he preached as a Lutheran in Drenthe. The time of his departure is uncertain. One imagines that he left Westphalia in the midst of the turmoil surrounding the sensational establishment and bloody collapse of the Anabaptist kingdom in Münster.[28] But if he thought the Netherlands would offer him lasting refuge, he was mistaken. He had to leave around 1550, again, it seems, for reasons of religious conflict. We do not know what led him to settle in Norden. It certainly helped that East Frisia was well connected to the Netherlands and that Norden was firmly Lutheran. In Norden, at last, Johannes Conring was welcome. He married a local woman by the name of Maria Meiners, had two sons, and rose to respectability as a member of Norden's town council.

Conring's father, also named Hermann Conring (c. 1553–1644), was a Lutheran minister. Having studied theology in Rostock and Wittenberg, he began to preach in Hinte near Emden in 1588. In 1600 conflicts between Calvinists and Lutherans forced him to renounce his position. Hinte turned Calvinist. Twelve years later, in 1612, he became pastor of Norden. But he had moved there earlier, and it seems likely that he began to preach there no later than 1603. Having been born about 1553, he was more than fifty years old when his son Hermann was born. He died in 1644 at over ninety years of age after more than forty years of service in Norden.

A grandfather who preached the Lutheran faith and whom religious strife drove repeatedly from home until he struck roots in the welcoming soil of a small Lutheran community in the north German provinces, another grandfather who preached the Lutheran faith and whose family was long entrenched in the north German provinces, a father trained in theology at two leading Lutheran universities, and a young and well-educated mother, all of them committed Lutherans; a small town where the father served as minister and the grandfather as councilor; a ruling house of Lutheran counts distinguished by little besides their territory's size; and a large Calvinist city in the vicinity: there you have an image of the small world of rival faiths and learning into which Conring was born.

He had nine siblings, eight sisters and one older brother named Johannes (1593–1642). Except for one younger sister, he was the youngest child. His brother preceded him to the University of Helmstedt in 1611 to study theology and later became a minister in Utrecht. None of his sisters lived to become adults. Two died soon after they were born. The other six died of the plague in 1611, an epidemic that his older brother seems to have escaped only because he had just left for Helmstedt. Hermann himself fell violently ill but survived.

One can only imagine what Conring's near-mortal illness and the death of six sisters soon after his only brother had gone off to study may have meant. Not yet quite five years old, but old enough to experience loss and pain, he found himself a solitary child with the memory of a close brush with death. Historians have on occasion liked to speculate about the effect of these events on Conring's body, mind, and character. Some believe they turned him into a sickly, sensitive, anxious, unhappy, outstandingly intelligent but not quite normal boy who grew up to become a man of morally questionable character.[29] Others see a man who may have kept a scar or two to remind him of the plague but was otherwise tough, resilient, and full of energy till old age began to take its toll.[30] But it seems futile to speculate whether or not his later choice of medicine as a profession, his physical appearance, his famously small stature, or his illnesses later in life may or may not be attributed to his childhood encounter with the plague. In the absence of any evidence, the illness can with equal plausibility be imagined to have left him weakened and to have strengthened him in the long run. It is certain only that Conring knew from early on that everything in life can change and life itself can come to an end.

Conring was not yet six years old when he entered the German school of Norden in 1612, but still that was, for the times, comparatively late. Perhaps he was delayed by the need to recover from the plague. One year later he entered the Latin school and stayed there for seven years. We know little about his teachers except two names: Johann Oldewelt, principal from 1613 to 1618, who is reported to have published a *Facula ludi Nordensis* and a Latin grammar, and Hibbe Magnus, principal from 1619 to 1624. The names suggest that these were local men. Conring's quick rise to scholarly eminence suggests that they taught him well. But he seems to have been more inspired by their predecessor, Hermann Mesander, a pastor and former principal of the Latin school who figures prominently in Conring's earliest recorded writings.[31]

These writings consist of two Latin essays. They were written in 1620, toward the very end of Conring's life in Norden. Neither was finished, and they were never published. The manuscripts of both were lost at some point in the twentieth century. But they survived long enough for Conring's biographer Ernst von Moeller to inspect them before the outbreak of World War I and to describe them in detail.[32] The first was an imitation of Lipsius's *Satyra Menippea* (not to be confused with the more famous *Satire Ménippée,* in which French *politiques* expressed their support for Henry IV of France). It purported to describe a dream in which the dreamer, Conring, visits Rome, encounters the greatest ancient and modern poets, and accompanies Mesander, who happens to be there as well, to a meeting of the literary senate in the temple of Apollo, where Virgil and Plautus preside over a debate on the art of poetry. The second essay consisted of an imaginary dialogue between Conring and Mesander comparing ancient with modern times and weighing the question of which of the two deserved to be preferred.

Neither of these "boyish undertakings" (*conatus pueriles*) was, or claimed to be, original. But both exhibited Conring's dexterity in Latin and his considerable familiarity with ancient classical literature as it was taught in the standard Latin curriculum of the time. More particularly, they exhibited his acquaintance with the leading Latin writers of his day at both of the universities where he was soon going to study: Johannes Caselius (1533–1613) at Helmstedt, and Justus Lipsius (1547–1606), Joseph Scaliger (1540–1609), and Daniel Heinsius (1580–1655) at Leiden.[33] They also establish his preoccupation with one of the most basic questions of his time: who was better? The ancients or the moderns? And how was anyone to judge? These essays may be counted as the earliest manifestation of Conring's intellectual ambition and the earliest expression of his fascination with the great reorganization of Europe's temporal perspective.

Conring dedicated his imitation of Lipsius's *Satyra Menippea* to his brother Johannes, who was still studying in Helmstedt at the time. Johannes showed it to his teachers; perhaps it had been written for that purpose. And the teachers were impressed. One of them, Cornelius Martini (1568–1621), soon wrote to Conring's father inviting him to send Hermann to the University of Helmstedt. He promised to take him under his wing and, as was not unusual at the time, put him up in his own house. The invitation was accepted. On 25 October 1620, at not quite fourteen years of age, Hermann Conring was registered as a student in the faculty of philosophy at the University of Helmstedt.

Student in Helmstedt

At the time Helmstedt boasted one of the leading Protestant universities in Europe.[34] Like the more famous University of Leiden, it was a modern Protestant university that had been founded in the 1570s. It served the lower Saxon territories ruled by the various lines of the princely house of Welf (chief among them Brunswick-Wolfenbüttel, Hanover, and Lüneburg) as a source of well-trained graduates for the various clerical, bureaucratic, and courtly positions at the disposal of the several princes. In this regard it resembled other Protestant universities, including those of Leipzig, Wittenberg, and Jena, which served the upper Saxon territories held by the various lines of the house of Wettin in similar fashion. But Helmstedt embodied a more open-minded spirit than most other German Protestant universities of the time. Throughout the seventeenth century, it remained true to a combination of Aristotelian philosophy and humanist erudition that had been pioneered by Philipp Melanchthon (1497–1560) and brought to Helmstedt by Melanchthon's student Johannes Caselius (1533–1613).[35] On that score it differed sharply from the fundamentalist Lutheran orthodoxy prevailing elsewhere.

Until the 1620s the University of Helmstedt just about rivaled Leiden in distinction. Close to seventeen thousand students went to study there in the first half-century of its existence, a more-than-respectable number and a clear indication of its reputation as one of the most advanced universities in northern Europe. Then the Thirty Years War caused it to fall behind. The university recovered after the 1630s, and Conring's fame played no small part in that, as did its reorganization under Duke August of Brunswick-Wolfenbüttel.[36] But it never gained the eminence that it might have enjoyed without the unhappy effects of the war. In the 1740s it began to decline into obscurity, eclipsed by the new university in Göttingen that drew on the opulent resources of Hanover and became the archetypal German Enlightenment university. King Jerome of Westphalia closed the University of Helmstedt in 1810.

Conring studied in Helmstedt from 1620 to 1625. As was usual for a beginning student, he took most of his courses from the faculty of philosophy. In most universities of the time, philosophy ranked below the faculties of theology, medicine, and law. In Helmstedt, however, that was not so. Thanks largely to the influence of Johannes Caselius and the support of the dukes, the faculty of philosophy was considered equal to the other faculties—a small but telling indication of the enlightened intellectual climate that characterized Helmstedt, and a harbinger of the victory that philosophy would gain over theology in the eighteenth century.[37]

We know very little about the courses Conring took at Helmstedt, but we do know the members of the faculty to whom he was close. In his application to be appointed Helmstedt's professor of natural philosophy in 1632, he mentioned four of them: Cornelius Martini, Rudolf Diephold, Christoph Heidmann, and Nicolaus Gran.

Of these Cornelius Martini (1568–1621) was the oldest and the most important for Conring's intellectual development. He was born in the Netherlands but had studied at Helmstedt with Johannes Caselius and was appointed to a chair of philosophy in 1592. Along with Caselius himself, he was one of the leading intellectuals of the university in its early history, best known for teaching Aristotle's logic. His origins may have strengthened the links between Helmstedt and the Netherlands from which Conring himself was soon going to benefit. In spite of his early death, in 1621, only one year after Conring arrived in Helmstedt, we may assume that he prepared the ground for Conring's mastery of the Aristotelian corpus.

The other three were lesser lights. Rudolf Diephold (1572–1626) was chiefly responsible for Greek, which he had taught since 1605, but also taught history and geography. Conring moved into his house after Martini died. Christoph Heidmann (1582–1627) taught rhetoric, ethics, and politics. Nicolaus Gran (1569–1631) came from Sweden and was the only one in this group not to have studied with Caselius. He taught natural philosophy or "physics" beginning in 1613 in a chair that Conring was going to occupy from 1632 to 1637.

Martini, Diephold, Heidmann, and Gran taught Conring the well-articulated forms of late humanism and a supple mastery of Aristotelian philosophy. Humanism and Aristotelianism became two equally important dimensions of Conring's thought. They differed from each other in age and intellectual substance. Humanism was a comparatively recent movement and privileged the study of culture. Aristotelianism was of far older vintage, was rooted deeply in the medieval centuries, and privileged the study of logic and nature. But far from being incompatible, they complemented and reinforced each other with a productive tension that fired Conring's imagination. Aristotelianism furnished a reassuringly comprehensive system, and humanism a critical spirit of innovation that kept the reassurance from growing stale. Both were indispensable to Conring's intellectual accomplishment, the former supplying breadth and the latter critical discrimination. It was for equipping him with this kind of education that Conring thanked his professors when he acknowledged them in his application to succeed Nicolaus Gran as Helmstedt's professor of natural philosophy in 1632.[38]

Conring had somewhat different relations with two other members of the Helmstedt faculty: Georg Calixt and Konrad Hornejus. Although he did not list them alongside his teachers in his application of 1632, they had been his mentors since the 1620s and watched over his academic progress. He failed to acknowledge his debt openly to them in 1632 almost certainly because they were involved in helping to secure the chair for him. Besides, he had already thanked them on an earlier occasion by dedicating one of his first published writings to them, a disputation titled *On the Origin of Forms*—a classic Aristotelian problem of particular significance to Calixt's theology—that was printed in Leiden in 1630.[39]

Georg Calixt (1586–1656) was, together with Conring, the most important thinker at Helmstedt in the seventeenth century.[40] Having studied at Helmstedt with Johannes Caselius and Cornelius Martini, he was appointed professor of theology in 1614. He soon occupied a unique position among German Protestant theologians, because he sought to distance himself from the conservatism associated with Lutheran orthodoxy at the Universities of Leipzig and Wittenberg. His goal was the reunion of all different branches of Christianity, and he was willing to engage with Catholics. The basis on which he advocated confessional reunion was Scripture as interpreted according to the "consensus of antiquity." He was convinced that the first five centuries of the Christian era had developed a shared understanding of the Bible that all later ages could rely on as a secure foundation. Orthodox Lutherans, by contrast, insisted on a biblical fundamentalism that considered interpreting the Bible (whether according to the "consensus of antiquity" or by any other means) unnecessary if not dangerous. For them, the Bible was inspired word for word, and it required not interpretation but close attention to the text. The text interpreted itself. Catholics were happy to engage in interpretation of the Bible but far from willing to limit it to the "consensus of antiquity." They insisted that divine inspiration could be drawn from an unwritten tradition extending without interruption from the first days of Christianity to the present and, under the guidance of the papacy, beyond. Calixt's reliance on the consensus of the ancient fathers amounts to a rejection of both of these positions and an attempt to find a middle ground by an exercise in history and theological hermeneutics.[41] There is no doubt that in taking this position Calixt furnished Conring with a model.

Like Calixt, Konrad Hornejus (1590–1649) was the son of a minister and a student of Caselius and Martini. He was appointed to an extraordinary chair of logic in 1619 and thus became Martini's colleague in the faculty of philosophy. In 1622, following Martini's death, he became his successor, and in 1628 he was appointed professor of theology. That put him in a position to help Calixt to deepen the imprint of Aristotelian philosophy on the Helmstedt faculty of theology. But his stature in Conring's mind never matched that of Calixt.

A few more remarks may be in order to characterize this group of six professors who played a special part in Conring's education. They were of course united by a common attachment to the University of Helmstedt. All of them except Nicolaus Gran had studied with Johannes Caselius, who in turn had studied with Melanchthon in Wittenberg. All of them embodied a vital link to Melanchthon's form of Christian education. And all of them were sworn to the revival of Aristotelian philosophy that so unexpectedly echoed the scholasticism of medieval universities in the Protestant halls of modern learning and yet foreshadowed the intellectual freedom of the Enlightenment.

But there are interesting differences, too. The "philosophers" Martini, Diephold, and Gran were born around 1570 (Heidmann not until 1582) and passed away during the early phases of the Thirty Years War, before Conring returned from Leiden in 1631. They were a generation older, and their relations with Conring remained on a more formal level. The theologians Calixt and Hornejus were much younger and lived to the middle of the century. Their association with Conring was longer and deeper.

Conring was particularly close to Calixt. He defended Calixt's theology on more than one occasion. He shared his abhorrence for papal supremacy. Both called it the "Hildebrandine heresy," after the monk who dared, as Pope Gregory VII, to depose Emperor Henry IV in 1076. Both were convinced that papal supremacy was a crucial impediment to peace. Like Calixt, Conring valued the "consensus of antiquity" over Tridentine tradition and orthodox Lutheran insistence on Scripture. Like Calixt, he engaged in theological controversies with the Jesuit Vitus Erbermann, the Capuchin Valerianus Magni, and the Protestant Matthias Wasmuth, a student of the redoubtable Abraham Calov, who was Calixt's most vocal Protestant opponent. Above all he applied Calixt's habits of mind to areas of thought with which Calixt himself was not directly occupied.

Calixt's insistence, for example, that theology was a rational form of knowledge that had to be systematically distinguished from the faith is perfectly analogous to the spirit in which Conring distinguished between areas of thought that were commonly treated together.[42] This was especially so with politics: Conring never tired of explaining that politics constituted a separate realm of thought and action, whose independence from law, theology, and morals had to be protected from the unfounded claims of jurists and theologians. He liked to refer to Machiavelli as the most important writer to have made that point.[43] But it may well have been Calixt's insistence on the difference between faith and theology that furnished Conring with the crucial intellectual model for integrating Machiavelli's vision of politics into a view of the world that gave more room to theology and law than Machiavelli would have been prepared to countenance.

Something similar may be said about Calixt's refusal to accept the orthodox Lutheran position on the Bible. That refusal may have fed Conring's conviction that no text can be understood apart from the historical context in which it was written. If Calixt practiced historical theology by relying on the consensus of antiquity as a guide to the proper interpretation of Scripture, Conring practiced historical jurisprudence by relying on the context in which Roman law was written as a guide to the proper interpretation of law. He applied those principles to the history of law with stunning success in one of his most celebrated writings, the *Historical Commentary on the Origin of German Law* of 1643.[44] That this work was at least in part written in order to rebut a Catholic attack on Calixt's ideas about the history of Roman law is as good an indication as any of the intellectual proximity of Conring and Calixt. Conring pursued his studies of history and law independently, and there is good evidence that Calixt did not always see eye to eye with him.[45] But without his guidance Conring would scarcely have carried historical criticism as far as he eventually did.

The Thirty Years War began in 1618. In 1623 the troops of the Count of Mansfeld devastated East Frisia. Conring was forced to interrupt his studies and go home in order to assist his parents. In 1624, when the crisis had passed, he returned to Helmstedt and resumed his studies. Early in 1625 his studies were cut short again. This time the war had come to Helmstedt itself and brought the plague along with it. Conring went home again. Most other students left the university at the same time, and so did most of the professors. Calixt and Gran alone remained. The university was forced to suspend its operation and did not reopen until the fall of 1628.[46]

In 1625 the war thus put an end to Conring's student days in Helmstedt and to the happiest period in the history of the university. Fortunately he had well-connected teachers. Since 1607 at the latest, Calixt had enjoyed friendly relations with Mathias van Overbeck, the son of a wealthy merchant in Leiden and an admirer of Johannes Caselius, much devoted to the cause of scholarship. He had the means to act on his devotion and had already once invited Calixt to come to Leiden. Calixt preferred to stay in Germany, but he called qualified protégés to Overbeck's attention.

Student in Leiden

Thus it happened that in 1626 Hermann Conring went on Calixt's recommendation to Leiden to begin a course of studies supported by the generosity of Mathias van Overbeck and live in his house. He did not go alone. Two other students from Helmstedt enjoyed Overbeck's support at the same time. One was Christoph Schrader (1601–80), five years Conring's senior, who had preceded him to Leiden the year before. Schrader had studied with the same teachers in Helmstedt as Conring had since 1621, and he was going to become Conring's colleague. From 1635 until his death in 1680, he taught rhetoric at the University of Helmstedt. The other was Andreas Kinderling (1595–1664), a student of Martini's who tutored Overbeck's children and from 1638 until his death in 1664 taught first logic, then physics, at the University of Helmstedt.

Leiden changed Conring's life. If Florence was the capital of humanism in the heyday of the Italian Renaissance, Leiden was the capital of humanism in the late northern Renaissance. The university, founded just two years earlier than Helmstedt, enjoyed a well-deserved reputation as the most vibrant center of late humanism in Protestant Europe.[47] It housed scholars of a European reputation like Lipsius, Scaliger, and Grotius who maintained a level of learning hardly matched elsewhere. And more than learning was involved. Here, in the United Provinces and in the midst of the long-drawn-out battle between a Protestant republic defending its freedom and a Catholic monarchy threatening that freedom, the humanist reorganization of early modern Europe reached a peak of productive and influential activity. Students flocked to Leiden from all over Europe, and when they left again to enter careers in high political, administrative, clerical, or academic office, they took with them a distinctive ethos and a distinctive model of action imprinted on them by a combination of neo-Stoic moral and political philosophy on the one hand and, on the other, deep skepticism about the possibilities of human happiness. That equipment undergirded a sense of service and duty to governments capable of keeping the peace by force of arms, money, and, where necessary, fraud. Dissimulation and honesty, force and duty, learning and drill all went into the mix. Leiden played a central role not only in educating the most gifted youth of Protestant Europe, but also in imbuing a northern European Protestant elite of political and military leaders with a cohesive moral and intellectual code that would govern their thought and action for a century.

When Conring moved from Helmstedt to Leiden, he entered a new world. He exchanged the small towns and war-torn lands of lower Saxony for wide open horizons. The United Provinces enjoyed the self-confidence of having successfully defended their freedom from Spain, the most powerful monarchy in all of Europe, and were just about to turn the prowess of their traders into the foundation for a universal empire of a different sort. Conring gained firsthand familiarity with moderate Calvinists, Arminians, and Remonstrants. He encountered a degree of religious freedom that seemed impossible to equal in Germany, not even in the relatively open climate prevailing at the University of Helmstedt, at a time when Calvinists, Lutherans, and counter-reformatory Catholics were fighting with growing bitterness for control of their destinies. True, even in the United Provinces, religion and conscience were subjected to public persecution. Grotius and Oldenbarnevelt had been tried in 1618, Arminianism had been banned in 1619, and the careers of two of Conring's teachers, Gerhard Johannes Vossius (1577–1649) and Caspar Barlaeus (1584–1648), had suffered as a result.[48] But persecution was relatively mild and brief. Arminians returned to official respectability in 1630 and founded the Athenaeum in Amsterdam, where they were able to teach their views in freedom and where Vossius and Barlaeus accepted professorships in 1631.[49]

The years that Conring spent on this cosmopolitan training ground must have left a decisive mark on his development. But the glory of Leiden in its heyday contrasts sharply with the scarcity of our knowledge about his studies there. We know nothing about the friendships he formed, the circles in which he traveled, or what he read. He must have had close contacts with his fellow students from Helmstedt, Christoph Schrader and Andreas Kinderling. He collected excerpts on philosophy and history.[50] We know that Vossius, Barlaeus, and Heinsius were his most important teachers. We know that he continued the studies he had begun in Helmstedt, acquired a professional knowledge of medicine, and began to collect information about the states of all the world—an enterprise that would culminate much later in a famous course he taught on the same subject. We know that he published his first writings and began to edit the works of other writers.[51] But we know neither exactly what he studied nor what his teachers meant to him.[52]

One can make educated guesses. Heinsius's edition of Aristotle's *Politics* surely shaped Conring's approach to a work that he himself was going to edit on two separate occasions later on, because it was the basic textbook the University of Helmstedt required him to use in his lectures on politics.[53] Vossius may have had a similar impact on Conring's reading of history, and, since he was an Arminian who had barely managed to hold onto his position before moving to Amsterdam, he may have deepened Conring's appreciation of theology. Something similar may be said about Barlaeus, who was not only more outspokenly Arminian but also familiar with medicine; he may therefore have been closer to Conring at a time when Conring had apparently just settled on making his career in the medical profession.

But the only reliable information about Conring's intellectual life in Leiden (other than whatever unpublished documents may be languishing in archives) consists of the three disputations that he published there. The first, *On Body Heat,* published in 1627, dealt with a question he would revisit twenty years later in one of his major works of medicine.[54] The third, *On the Origin of Forms,* published in 1630, dealt with a classical problem of Aristotelian philosophy: the question whether or not form can exist apart from matter.[55] It was this disputation that Conring dedicated to Calixt and Hornejus. The second is the most interesting for our purposes. Entitled *Theses variae de morali prudentia* or *Various Theses on Moral Prudence,* it was published in 1629 and defended under the presidency of the philosopher Franco Burgersdicius.

The *Various Theses on Moral Prudence* was devoted to elaborating a form of morality founded entirely on natural reason, as opposed to moral theology and jurisprudence. It drew a sharp distinction between natural law and positive law. It drew a parallel distinction between moral philosophy and jurisprudence, as two separate disciplines of knowledge devoted, respectively, to natural law and positive law: moral philosophy was given theoretical responsibility for natural law, whereas jurisprudence was restricted to the study of positive law. This may be taken as an early expression of Conring's desire to take natural law out of the hands of jurists and theologians. His theses were briefly stated, but the point they made proved to be fundamental to his thought, perhaps his most important departure from Aristotelian ideas. Much later, in 1662, his chief work on political theory, *De civili prudentia* or *On Civil Prudence,* would found politics on natural reason just as, on a much smaller scale, the *Various Theses on Moral Prudence* tried to do for principles of morality in 1629.

Moeller plausibly maintained that this approach revealed the influence of Hugo Grotius, whose magnum opus *De iure belli ac pacis libri tres* or *Three*

Books on the Law of War and Peace had only recently been published in Paris, in 1625.[56] Grotius (1583–1645) deserves more than passing comment, both because of his intrinsic significance and because of his impact on Conring's ideas. He is often described as the founder of modern international law (in language not coincidentally analogous to that in which Conring is described as the founder of German legal history) and as one of the most creative minds in the tradition of legal and political thought in early modern times.[57] His influence on Conring has never been examined, and our understanding of his own writings leaves much to be desired.[58] But there is no doubt that Conring knew about him from an early age and respected him enormously. Grotius had himself been educated at the University of Leiden. His works were circulating there among his followers, and Conring must have paid attention. Later he wrote detailed annotations to Grotius's *De veritate religionis christianae,* easily the most frequently published and widely read of all of Grotius's writings.[59] He corresponded with him on a few occasions.[60] He drew repeatedly on Grotius for intellectual support in the *New Discourse on the Roman-German Emperor,* which we shall consider more closely in the following chapter.[61] And when he died in 1681, his library included more books by Grotius than by Aristotle, Galen, Cicero, and many others whom Conring surely reckoned among the greatest thinkers and writers of all time. Only three authors were represented by more books than Grotius: Conring's friend and teacher Georg Calixt, Erasmus, and Martin Luther.[62] It was more than flattery when Goebel, in his edition of Conring's *Opera,* made a point of comparing Conring's achievement to that of Grotius and came to the conclusion that both were equally original and widely respected scholars of European stature who opened new avenues of learning.[63] There were good reasons for seeing them joined by a spirit that broke new intellectual ground and distinguished them from their contemporaries.

We do thus have some grasp of the relationship between Conring's studies in Leiden and his later work. Clearly he was already thinking about questions in politics and medicine that would preoccupy him for decades to come. He had already made some elementary decisions about what kinds of answers he was willing to accept. But overall our picture of his studies in Leiden remains disappointingly vague.

At the Crossroads

The year 1631 marked a turning point. Conring's teachers Vossius and Barlaeus left Leiden to take up positions at the newly founded Athenaeum in Amsterdam, and his financial support from Overbeck was running out at the same time. What to do? He received an offer from Paris to serve as a physician to the German students living there. We know nothing about the circumstances, only that he declined. Perhaps it was because he knew no French, or because the career of an émigré physician did not appeal to him. Perhaps the offer did not appear reliable.[64] Where to go? He had grown accustomed to freedom, intellectual excitement, and a reasonable degree of peace in the Netherlands. He did not relish the prospect of returning to a Germany divided by religious intransigence and torn by some of the worst fighting of the Thirty Years War. But in June of 1631 he received a letter from Calixt that called for a quick decision.

Calixt had found another way of furthering his pupil's fortunes. He wrote that Arnold Engelbrecht, the chancellor of Brunswick-Wolfenbüttel, was prepared, presumably on Calixt's recommendation, to employ Conring as tutor to his son. The promised salary was high. More important, Conring was given to understand that if he accepted Engelbrecht's invitation, he could expect to succeed to the professorship of natural philosophy at the University of Helmstedt that had just been vacated by the death of his teacher Nicolaus Gran. That promised the security of long-term employment and an academic career at his alma mater.

Calixt's letter arrived on 26 June 1631. On 27 June Conring wrote to Barlaeus in Amsterdam and asked him for advice. The letter he wrote that day has often been singled out as one of the most interesting documents for Conring's biography, because it offers unusually detailed insight into his state of mind at a decisive moment.[65] He described the terms of the offer and explained his dilemma. On the one hand, he was attracted by the chance of a professorship in Helmstedt. On the other hand, he was appalled that, once there, he would be forced to deny his fondness for the Arminians. He did not say so, but he must have been aware that professors at the University of Helmstedt were obliged to swear a solemn oath to their employer, the duke of Brunswick-Wolfenbüttel, on the Augsburg Confession and the *Corpus doctrinae Julium,* an official collection of documents codifying the religious confession that was mandatory in the duchy of Brunswick-Wolfenbüttel. Both the university, officially known as the *Academia Julia,* and the *Corpus doctrinae Julium* were named after Duke Julius, the orthodox Lutheran founder of the university. His less orthodox successors had loosened the link between the official faith and the university's intellectual life, but the formal obligations remained fully in effect.[66]

No wonder Conring was attracted by the freedom he had found in the Netherlands. As events would prove soon enough, he had good reason to be afraid that back in Helmstedt he might have to conceal his beliefs not only from his enemies, but even from friends and mentors like Hornejus and Calixt. His conscience, he wrote to Barlaeus, warned against compromise. He would prefer to stay in the Netherlands, even if that entailed living in straitened circumstances. He reminded Barlaeus that he had offered his services to the Remonstrants in the past, and he repeated his offer now. Barlaeus himself had suffered for his Arminian convictions and had only recently managed to gain a secure position as professor. He knew what it meant to confront the pressure for religious conformity. He could be expected to understand, and he would give good advice. He might even be able to offer something better than good advice. Perhaps, Conring suggested, there was a chance for him to teach in some subsidiary fashion in Amsterdam, at least for the time being. Perhaps there was even the prospect of an academic career in the Netherlands.

The letter conveys both Conring's anxieties about returning to Germany and the extent of his trust in Barlaeus. Whether it should be taken at face value is a different matter. It was calculated to gain Barlaeus's sympathy. It may have exaggerated Conring's anxiety and misrepresented the depth of his religious scruples. It is unlikely, after all, that Calixt would just then have made advances on Conring's behalf with the chancellor of Brunswick-Wolfenbüttel if Conring himself had not invited them, if only by informing Calixt that his fellowship in Leiden was running out. But if he had calculated that an offer of employment from Brunswick would provoke a counteroffer from Barlaeus, he was disappointed. Whether or not Barlaeus believed Conring's protestations—and the tone of his response suggests a healthy skepticism—we do not know. But he did make it clear that he was in no position to offer anything of substance. The Remonstrants had only recently been readmitted to respectability. They could be glad to have escaped from persecution. Dispensing patronage to students from Germany was not within their power. He advised Conring in kind but certain terms to accept the offer from Helmstedt. He would be better off with a secure position in Helmstedt than free to think but penniless without a job in the Netherlands. Of course, Barlaeus added, Conring could and should not go if going would violate his conscience. But he may well have suspected that Conring's conscience was less troubled than he said, and possibly less troubled than he knew.

That left Conring in no doubt. His life as a student in the Netherlands was over. His career as a university professor in Germany was about to begin. He wrote to Helmstedt to accept Engelbrecht's offer and thank Calixt for his help. He left Leiden in November 1631 and soon after assumed his position as tutor to the son of the chancellor of Brunswick-Wolfenbüttel. As promised, he did not have to tutor him for very long. On 18 August 1632 he was appointed professor of natural philosophy and placed under the required oath.[67] That was expected. Less expectedly, Conring was given responsibility for teaching rhetoric as well. The idea probably came from Chancellor Engelbrecht. The chair of rhetoric had been vacant since 1627, and Engelbrecht would have saved money by asking one professor to do the work of two.[68] Combining the work of two professors in the hands of one so as to save on salaries was common practice, and Conring could have turned in a creditable performance. But the device did not have the effect intended. Conring seems to have resented his appointment to the chair of rhetoric and paid no attention whatsoever to the responsibilities that it entailed.[69] The chair remained as good as vacant until it was filled in 1635 by Christoph Schrader, Conring's fellow student from his Leiden days.

Another event occurred in 1632 that had at least as much significance for Conring's future as his return to Germany and his appointment to a professorship. He befriended Jacob Lampadius, professor of public law at the University of Helmstedt. Lampadius (1593–1649) was one of the more important seventeenth-century German writers on public law.[70] Indeed, he ranks as one of the more important personalities in Germany's public life. Having studied at Helmstedt, Marburg, and Giessen, he was promoted to doctor of both canon and Roman law at the University of Heidelberg in 1619 for a dissertation on the public law of the Holy Roman Empire and began to teach in Helmstedt in 1621.[71] Soon after Conring made his acquaintance, he entered on a career as councilor at the court of Brunswick-Wolfenbüttel and later as vice chancellor at the court of Hanover. After 1643 he was going to represent the duchy of Brunswick-Lüneburg at Osnabrück and Münster, distinguishing himself as one of the leaders of the Protestant cause in the negotiations that culminated in the Peace of Westphalia.

In 1632, however, when peace was still in the distant future, the war had once again made teaching in Helmstedt impossible. Like many of his colleagues, Lampadius was passing time in the security of Brunswick, waiting for courses in Helmstedt to resume. He moved into the house of Chancellor Engelbrecht, where Conring had just arrived to tutor Engelbrecht's son. Conring and Lampadius appear to have taken an immediate liking to each other. They entered into conversations about the condition of Germany, about war and diplomacy, about the history of the empire, its law, and the need for peace. These conversations changed Conring's interests and the trajectory of his career more profoundly than any event since he decided to study medicine.

Lampadius was the man who opened Conring's eyes to the connection between politics and history. At the time, the history of Germany was poorly known, clouded in myths largely taken from legend and historically ill-informed readings of Roman law that were propagated by narrow-minded and self-serving jurists—or so, at least, it would seem to Conring. He himself had so far learned about the past only what he imagined to be necessary for someone who intended to become a physician and natural scientist, which is to say, not much at all. "For while I was still in the Netherlands," he wrote many years later, "I had already learned something about the condition of our own and other states. But only a little bit. Just as much, to be precise, as seemed necessary to manage successfully the social life of someone who practiced medicine and was most interested in natural philosophy."[72] Now that changed. To destroy those myths about the German past, to reveal the ignorance on which they rested, and to replace them with knowledge drawn from a systematic study of surviving records became an objective that would fuel Conring's intellectual endeavors with unabating energy for the remainder of his life.

Here was a piece of knowledge really worth having. A piece of knowledge that mattered no less than the medicine on which Conring had so far concentrated. Bodily health remained a worthwhile goal. But peace for the body politic was more exciting. And peace was impossible to secure for Germany so long as the contending parties divided over visions of the future that followed from conflicting visions of the past. Ignorance of the history of Germany and its law was more than an academic failing. It was a cause of war. And history was more than a remedy for ignorance of the past. It was medicine for the state, a matter of supreme political importance. History could clear the public mind, helping to distinguish symptoms from causes of the disease afflicting the body politic. It could immunize the commonwealth against the ailments that had brought Germany near to destruction. It could do so by depriving jurists of the grounds on which they subordinated politics to law in order to take politics into their own misguided hands. History was able to liberate politics from law. In the hands of discriminating men of state, who knew that the common good ranked higher than the law and who were not deceived about the true state of affairs by faulty notions of the past, history would clear the road for Germany to reach a lasting peace.

Conring immediately set to work. Still in Lampadius's company, he immersed himself in two of the most important works he was going to deploy as a teacher of future men of state: Christoph Lehmann's massive chronicle of Speyer and Lampadius's own dissertation on the Holy Roman Empire.[73] From the former, which ranges far more widely than its title suggests, he learned about the "form" of the empire during its entire history in far greater depth than the sketchy knowledge he had acquired during his studies in the Netherlands.[74] From the latter he learned about the jurisdiction (*iurisdictio*) or constitution (*constitutio*) of the Roman-German empire—or, as he eventually preferred to call it, the Roman-German state (*respublica Romano-Germanica*).[75] The preface he wrote for a new edition of Lampadius's work in 1671 still conveys the excitement with which, a generation earlier, he had first seized on a subject that changed his life and satisfied his main ambitions: thirst for knowledge, teaching the young, and service to the common good.[76]

Getting Established

To begin with, however, Conring had to focus on his duties as a professor of natural philosophy. On 19 September 1632 he gave his inaugural address. He spoke in praise of Aristotle, a subject that allowed him to signal both his willingness to follow the traditions that were mandatory at the University of Helmstedt and his refusal to place blind obedience to authority above his dedication to the truth. Taking advantage of a familiar commonplace, he reminded his listeners that Aristotle himself had not hesitated to place his dedication to the truth above the authority of his teacher Plato. Aristotle was not well followed by unquestioning submission to authority, including Aristotle's own. Conring knew that his first public appearance would set the tone for his future, and he did not wish to offend. But neither did he wish to give up the freedom he had enjoyed in the Netherlands. He was testing limits.

The limits were immediately pointed out to him. It seems his speculations on the relationship between faith and reason upset both Calixt and Hornejus, because they threatened to rock the confessional boat at an inopportune time. They asked him to destroy the pages of his inaugural address that had already been printed. He refused, but with the mediation of Christoph Schrader he offered to tone down the passages that gave offense. And so it was agreed. What these passages may have been we shall probably never know. We have the lecture only in the expurgated version that found its way into the edition of his *Opera* by Johann Wilhelm Goebel.[77] But we have confirmation that Conring's fears about Germany had not been unfounded. On his first foray into public debate, he was reined in, not by enemies, but by his most important friends. That was an important lesson about the value of silence and dissimulation.[78] Germany was not the Netherlands.

Soon after giving his inaugural address, Conring returned to the safety of Brunswick once more. The war was still too close to Helmstedt to permit the resumption of normal academic life. He did not actually begin to lecture on natural philosophy until the fall of 1633. But lecturing to students took only part of his attention anyway. His first priority was to achieve a measure of financial stability. His income as a professor of natural philosophy was not enough to raise a family. Worse, it was unreliable. His appointment was subject to termination on six months notice at any time, and the dukes of Brunswick-Wolfenbüttel, themselves in financial straits, were not at all forthcoming in paying their professors either punctually or in full.

That helps to explain why Conring concentrated on completing the studies of medicine that he began in Leiden. Medicine was a profession that could be relied upon to yield an income both steady and sufficient. In his appointment of 1632 he was described as a candidate of medicine, meaning that he had not yet brought his studies to completion. Two years later, in 1634, he did complete them under the supervision of his teacher Johann Wolf with the public defense of a dissertation on scurvy—a common illness during the war and one that Conring studied further on several occasions.[79] That earned him the title of licentiate and the right to teach medicine. Two years after that, on 21 April 1636, he was formally promoted to the degrees of Doctor of Medicine and Doctor of Philosophy, and in the following year he was appointed to one of the two professorships that made up the faculty of medicine.[80]

On the same day on which Conring received his doctoral degrees, he married Anna Maria Stucke. That may strike readers today as strange. But it was not so strange according to the standards of the time. The licentiate that Conring earned in 1634 was perfectly sufficient to certify him as a professionally trained physician. His promotion to the doctorate two years later was less an act of intellectual significance than a solemn ceremony to seal his membership in the guild of academic teachers. It entailed considerable expenses and mattered for his reputation—not his qualification. As he explained in a letter to a friend, he needed his medical practice in order to earn a living, and he needed the doctorate because his patients would otherwise not take him seriously as a physician.[81] Without the promotion he might not have been able to support a family; without a family he would have needed to pay less attention to his reputation. That his promotion coincided with his wedding suggests that both acts were more important for his place in society than for his intellectual life.

Anna Maria Stucke (1616–94) was the daughter of Johann Stucke (1587–1653), and Johann Stucke, like Lampadius, was a professor of law at the University of Helmstedt on his way to high public office.[82] Only days before the wedding, perhaps not by coincidence, Duke August had appointed Stucke as his privy councilor and vice chancellor of Brunswick-Wolfenbüttel. In 1638 he succeeded Arnold Engelbrecht, Conring's old benefactor, as chancellor in Hanover. In 1649 he entered Swedish service and worked until his death in 1653 for Queen Christina of Sweden as chancellor for the territories of Bremen and Verden, which Sweden had only recently acquired in the Peace of Westphalia.

Stucke was a wealthy and well-connected man. He was going to bestow much of his wealth on Conring and put his political connections to good use for him as well. When he moved to Hanover in 1638, he turned the magnificent and brand-new house that he had just built for himself in Helmstedt over to his son-in-law, who thus became the owner of one of the most glamorous pieces of real estate in town.[83] Another piece of real estate that Conring would acquire from his father-in-law, by inheritance after Stucke's death in 1653, consisted of a large estate in the vicinity of Helmstedt. The marriage to Stucke's daughter helped Conring become a landlord of substance and one of the richest men in Helmstedt.

About Anna Maria Stucke herself, however, we know next to nothing. There is an anecdote that on the day of their wedding and his promotion, Conring gave her the choice between marrying the Doctor of Medicine and marrying the Doctor of Philosophy. She is said to have chosen the Doctor of Medicine. She bore eleven children: three sons and eight daughters, of whom two sons and two daughters died young.[84]

By the late 1630s, Conring had thus achieved a degree of academic and financial security that allowed him to breathe more easily. From that time on, his life was going to follow a more settled course. There were a few travels, there were illnesses, and there was a private life about which we are singularly ill informed. But on the whole, apart from the disputes provoked by his scholarship, the rest of his life unfolded with the calm characteristic of someone making his mark by teaching and writing. Henceforth the main events to be reported in Conring's life consist of books he published, courses he taught, and the directions in which he pursued his scholarship.

For one or two years after his appointment to the faculty of medicine in 1637, Conring continued to take care of business left over from his five years of teaching in the faculty of philosophy. He officially resigned from his position as professor of natural philosophy as soon as he joined the faculty of medicine. But he went on to lecture and supervise dissertations on natural philosophy and published an introduction to natural philosophy in 1638.[85] He had originally meant to survey the whole field of natural philosophy according to a systematic plan that he laid out in some detail. But the plan was never carried to completion. Preoccupied with getting his career in order, with gaining a degree in medicine, with establishing a practice, and with his first, informal courses on politics, Conring lacked the time to finish this survey of elementary knowledge. Perhaps he lacked the inclination too. The *Introduction to Natural Philosophy* of 1638 serves as a fitting monument to the five years he spent as an apprentice teacher in the faculty of philosophy and the pleasure he must have felt about leaving this stage of his career behind. In 1639 he ceased lecturing and supervising dissertations in natural philosophy altogether. Thereafter his interests were completely focused on medicine and politics.

Medicine came first.[86] Until 1643 Conring was preoccupied with an extensive program of investigations into the production and circulation of the blood, prompted by his curiosity and William Harvey's revolutionary theory about the circulation of the blood, which had first seen the light in Frankfurt in 1628, while Conring was still studying in Leiden.[87] For several years he conducted experiments and vivisections designed to test the validity of Harvey's views. The results were first published sequentially in ten separate academic exercises, each of which was defended by one of his students in a public academic exercise.[88] Once the series was complete, all ten were published under Conring's name in 1643 as a single volume on the circulation of the blood, *De sanguinis generatione et motu naturali* or *The Generation and Circulation of the Blood by Nature*. This may be counted as his most original contribution to the Scientific Revolution as commonly understood. More than any of his other writings, it was based directly on experiments. It dealt with a central question in the science of his day and lent significant support to Harvey on the Continent. By hindsight Conring may seem merely to have consented to what Harvey had made obvious. But Harvey's theory and Conring's endorsement were far from obvious until better optical instruments, almost two decades later, permitted the first observation of capillaries.

The Generation and Circulation of the Blood represented the culmination of a major research effort that had taken several years of concentrated work. It was followed in relatively quick succession by several other books on a variety of medical subjects that, though equally substantial, may have been easier to write and did not involve Conring in similarly extensive experiments. First, in 1645, came a work that may be said to lie on the borderline between medicine and history—the only one of Conring's many contributions to medicine that Goebel saw fit to include in his edition of the *Opera*. Entitled *Dissertation on the Bodily Constitution of Ancient and Contemporary Germans*, it was a curious, quasi-anthropological, quasi-racist piece of writing in which Conring exercised his knowledge of medicine to speculate on reasons for the differences he noticed between ancient Germans as Tacitus described them in his *Germania* (tall, blond, and blue-eyed) and the Germans with whom he was familiar (tall, blond, and blue-eyed only on occasion).[89] He thought the Germans of his day did not measure up to those of antiquity. He did not think that climate was to blame, thus parting company with a favorite theme of Hippocrates. Intermarriage between differently constituted peoples seemed to him more important. But most of his attention focused on diet and nutrition: too much bread, alcohol, and tobacco, too little meat, milk, butter, and cheese—those were the factors that he judged most important in explaining the apparent deterioration in the physique of his compatriots.

Two years later, in 1647, Conring published a major treatise on another question of great interest to the science of the times. It was the same question to which he had devoted his first published dissertation twenty years earlier. Entitled *De calido innato sive igne animali* or *On Innate Warmth and Animal Fire*, it aimed to identify the source from which the human body drew its ability to heat itself. One year later, in 1648, he published yet another major work, a highly critical examination of the chemical philosophy of Paracelsus and the mythic medicine believed to have been taught in ancient Egypt by Hermes Trismegistus.[90] This may be termed a systematic and forceful attack on the single most important alternative to the kind of academic medicine with which Conring identified himself. Unlike his earlier writings, it was designed not to establish the truth of new scientific doctrines, but rather to defend new scientific doctrines from what he judged to be charlatanry and unfounded speculation. It has received barely any scrutiny, most likely because his negative judgment of Paracelsian medicine was for a long time shared by historians of science. But it is the only one among his works on medicine to which he returned later on. He expanded it, revised it, and added an important preface that contains one of the clearest descriptions of the principles of judgment and investigation on which he thought science ought to be founded.[91] He published this expanded version in 1669 and dedicated it to Jean Baptiste Colbert, to whom he had by then developed good connections.[92]

Apart from this, Conring's last major publication in the field of medicine was a survey of medical knowledge as a whole, published in 1654 under the title *Introduction to the Complete Art of Medicine and Each of Its Parts*. It may be said to form the capstone of his medical studies, just as the incomplete *Introduction to Natural Philosophy* of 1638 did for his studies of natural philosophy.[93] Its literary form was similar. It consisted of a compilation of dissertations written by Conring's students, except that in this case the compilation was treated as a dissertation in its own right, the whole of which was defended by his student Sebastian Scheffer in a public examination on 29 April 1654—a detail worth special mention given the questions of authorship surrounding those seventeenth-century dissertations of which Conring's *New Discourse on the Roman-German Emperor* will turn out to furnish an instructive case.[94] In terms of content, the *Introduction to the Complete Art of Medicine* was a systematically organized review of the entire library of medical writings that had been produced from antiquity to Conring's time. It was organized according to the main fields of medicine that students had to master and paid special attention to guiding them directly to the best literature on every important question. It was reprinted twice and seems to have remained useful as a textbook into the early eighteenth century.[95]

Two major studies on two major questions of contemporary medical science; an anthropological excursus into the physique of ancient Germans; a comprehensive critique of a brand of medicine that Conring believed to be unscientific; and a comprehensive review of the best medical knowledge available in print: these were the most substantial contributions Conring made to the medical literature of his day during the decade of his most intense activity as a physician. Add to this list a few minor works that he wrote during the same years, the works by other authors that he edited, and the roughly thirty dissertations he supervised from his appointment in 1637 to 1650, and the whole amounts to a deep stream of scientific productivity running through the first half of Conring's life as an established member of the academy.[96]

Rethinking Politics and Law

All the more impressive is the energy with which Conring applied himself at the same time to the study of politics. Lampadius had helped him to conceptualize the task: a systematic rethinking of politics on the basis of a new understanding of German history and law. As early as the mid-1630s he began to enter on that task by teaching two different courses, roughly in alternating years, though always with interruptions and exceptions: one on Aristotle's politics and one on the history of the Holy Roman Empire. These courses were taught privately, not in fulfillment of his official responsibilities as professor of natural philosophy. They were intended to complement each other, as knowledge of the general principles ruling all bodies politic complements knowledge of the particular body politic in which Conring happened to be living. They comprise the dual goal he would henceforth pursue: a systematic understanding of the nature, method, and object of political science in the abstract; and a detailed, empirical, historical grasp of particular bodies politic in the concrete. In this setting students, including his former pupil the son of Chancellor Engelbrecht, wrote dissertations that constitute our earliest evidence for his political ideas.[97]

So as to rest his teaching on a good textual foundation, Conring edited the necessary books. He published Lampadius's dissertation on the empire under the new and characteristically different title *On the Roman-German State* in 1634, just as soon as his courses began. This was going to serve him as a textbook until the end of his career. He had it republished twice soon after, in 1640 and 1642, and three decades after that, in 1671, he edited it with a substantial commentary of his own, in which, on the basis of years of sustained reflection and with all due respect, he indicated where in his judgment Lampadius's work was incomplete or misleading.[98] In 1637 he published Aristotle's *Politics* in the translation of Giphanius. In 1656 he published it again, but this time in the translation of Petrus Victorius and with the Greek text of Heinsius.[99] In the same context I should mention that in 1635 he published a new edition of the founding document for humanist investigations into the origins of Germany, Tacitus's *Germania,* which had not been discovered until the fifteenth century.[100] This he would republish twice, in 1652 and 1678. He introduced it with a programmatic preface explaining his approach to history in general and German history in particular. The views he stated there were fundamental. He reaffirmed them without change in 1678, three years before he died.[101]

At the same time he was beginning to develop a new view of political science. Initially he planned to present it in the form of an introduction to Aristotle's *Politics*. But it proved more complicated than he expected. The treatise *On Civil Prudence* that he eventually wrote instead would not appear in print until 1662, almost a generation later. By that time it had grown far beyond a mere introduction to Aristotle's *Politics*. It was a major theoretical accomplishment. "No other book," he exclaimed with evident exasperation, "was so disgustingly difficult for me to write."[102] Small wonder that in the 1630s he limited himself to writing an introduction that was more closely focused on the *Politics*. It appeared together with the edition he published in 1637.[103]

Having repeatedly lectured on politics in terms of Aristotle and Germany in terms of Lampadius; having supervised a good number of dissertations on questions of politics; having all the while taught, first natural philosophy, then medicine; and having published books in both of those fields, Conring was ready by the early 1640s to put his political ideas into print. He lacked only time and occasion. Time, at least some of it, came in 1643 when he completed his study on the circulation of the blood. The occasion came almost simultaneously, when his old friend and colleague in the faculty of theology, Georg Calixt, was attacked for having raised doubts about the standing of Roman law in Germany. Conring immediately rose to the challenge. The result was two equally pathbreaking studies on Germany, its law, and its relationship to the Roman empire that appeared in quick succession in 1643 and 1644.

The first was Conring's celebrated *De origine iuris Germanici commentarius historicus* or *Historical Commentary on the Origin of German Law*.[104] Among all of Conring's writings, this has been the favorite of historians and has received the lion's share of their attention. Almost every historian who has dealt with Conring in any way at all has had something to say about this work.[105] It was this book that earned him the appellations "founder of German legal history" from Stobbe and "protagonist of German law" from Moeller.[106] It exploded the notion that Roman law was formally binding on Germany, a myth commonly called the Lotharian legend because it rested on the efforts of sixteenth-century humanists, Melanchthon above others, to propagate the idea that Emperor Lothar II of Supplinburg (also known as Lothar III, because he was the third king of that name, though only the second emperor) had officially adopted the Roman *Corpus Iuris* in 1137 as the sole law of Germany, abolished all other kinds of law, and prohibited any changes in the law for the future.[107] Conring not only demonstrated that that story was difficult to believe in its own right and unsupported by any evidence (which had been pointed out before, not least by Calixt), but also (and far more importantly) explained that Roman law had advanced into Germany much later and had done so simply because late medieval German jurists had studied law in Italy, where Roman law was taught as a matter of course. This was the first convincing explanation of how Roman law acquired its standing in Germany's courts. It has never been superseded. Almost at a single stroke, it revealed the perception of Roman law as a source of timeless truths to be the product of historical circumstance, and it transformed Roman law itself into just one body of human laws among many others, all of which were equally subject to history and change.

This did not mean, of course, that Roman law was instantly going to be written out of Germany. It had entered far too deeply into the minds of German jurists, the practices of German courts, and the institutions of German government, from the imperial chamber court down to cities and territorial administrations, to be susceptible to swift dislocation. In some ways the basis for Roman law's hold over Germany that Conring himself uncovered in the Italian training of German students was more enduring than any statutory act by Emperor Lothar II could ever have been. At the same time, Conring's pragmatic identification of the training of German students in Italy as the real source from which Roman law had drawn its power opened the road to legal history. It required a reinterpretation of Roman law along the lines of the so-called *usus modernus Pandectarum*—the modern practice of treating Roman law as a source not of binding law, but of exemplary models of legal analysis and system-building.[108] Not least, it invited new legislation and led Conring to call explicitly for the kind of legal codification that would not get seriously under way until the Prussian reforms of the eighteenth century and was not completed until the publication of the German civil code in 1900.

The second major work was entitled *De Germanorum imperio Romano* or *The Roman Empire of the Germans* and published early in 1644. Though it is less frequently remarked upon, it has with good reason been called Conring's chef d'oeuvre on the constitution of Germany.[109] Its subject was not the history of German or Roman law but the relationship between Germany and the Roman empire. That subject will demand more of our attention below. But it will help to say something about it now.

The basic point was simple. Conring insisted on a sharp conceptual distinction between two separate states, Germany and the Roman empire. The former was ruled by the king of Germany, the latter by the emperor of Rome. It just so happened, Conring argued, that for several centuries the same persons had been both king of Germany and emperor of Rome. Hence the two states had come to be thought of as one. But the union of their supreme offices in the hands of a single person was no reason to lose the constitutional distinction from sight. From Conring's point of view, Germany and the Roman empire were now, as they had always been, two separate entities, each equally sovereign, each with its own government, its own law, its own history, its own institutions, and its own territorial boundaries.

That theory was clear and radical, even revolutionary. It flew in the face of a tradition extending back at least to the Staufen emperors of the twelfth century and the Ottonians of the tenth, if not to Charlemagne himself. According to that tradition, Germany was merely part of an empire that had existed without interruption since antiquity, had not only witnessed the advent of Christ in the age of Augustus but had also submitted itself to Christianity in the times of Constantine, had been transferred by the pope from the Romans to the Franks, and was going to endure until the end of the world.[110] According to Conring that tradition was a pure figment of the imagination. Not that there was no Roman empire at all. There was. But it was hardly holy; it had shrunk to a tiny territory clustered around the city of Rome; and its ability to endure until the end of time was subject to considerable doubt. If the pope had anything to do with it, it was not because he was the pope, but because he was a leading Roman citizen who had transferred the Roman empire to the Franks as such.

In reality, of course, the kingdom of Germany and the Roman empire had for centuries been so closely intertwined that German kings, far from being called "kings of Germany" had normally been called "kings of the Romans," not to mention the intricate connections by which "Roman" offices were intertwined with "German" ones in ways that Conring now wanted to undo. That made it impossible to disentangle the kingdom of Germany from the Roman empire simply by means of positing a conceptual distinction. Specific geographic, legal, and institutional boundaries had to be drawn in all the many places where Germany and the Roman empire had actually been combined. About a decade later, Conring was going to complete much of this task in a work explicitly devoted to fixing the boundaries of what he then called the German empire—a work with less theoretical appeal than *The Roman Empire of the Germans* but enormous practical significance and a proportionate degree of popularity, neither of which have yet been studied by historians.[111] The upshot of that endeavor, put as simply as possible (without mentioning details concerning territories like Burgundy, the kingdom of Bohemia, the duchies of Schleswig and Lorraine, or the cantons of Switzerland), was that "Germany" included everything that had previously been considered part of the Holy Roman Empire minus northern Italy and the papal states. The Roman empire was defined as the municipal government of Rome and its environs—a government in the hands of the pope and, in Conring's mind, of dubious constitutional validity.

No less important was the question why Germany and the Roman empire had entered into a relationship so close that their respective independence had become difficult to see. Conring gave a straightforward answer. Germans had conquered Rome, or what was left of Rome after the dust kicked up by their invasions had settled over early medieval Europe. Germans had never, strictly speaking, annexed the Roman empire to German territories. But German and Roman lands had been bound together by the Roman surrender to German rulers. It was this union that was signified by the combination of royal rulership over Germany with imperial rulership over Rome in the hands of one single person. The union obviously mattered. But it did nothing, or at least should not have done anything, to obscure the basic point of constitutional law: Germany and Rome were separate states.

In Conring's mind the Roman empire thus had no universality at all. Germany and Rome were two separate, sovereign states, with different histories and different boundaries but equal standing in the community of sovereign nations, free to enter into treaties with each other, free also to make war, to conquer and be conquered by each other because they both belonged to the same species in the realm of political animals—the species *state*.[112] To that extent nationalistic interpretations of Conring's thought in the nineteenth and twentieth centuries were right. Conring worked hard to establish both Germany's former greatness and its contemporary independence as a free and sovereign nation among the nations of the world. Nationalistic interpretations were wrong only to attribute to nationalist sentiments what was founded on an entirely unsentimental devotion to principles of political sovereignty and international law that were still being hammered out on the anvil of religious war.

The Roman Empire of the Germans thus was a perfect complement to the *Historical Commentary on the Origin of German Law*. The latter proved that Roman law had crept into German practice for purely pragmatic reasons; the former proved that those pragmatic reasons had obscured the true constitutional relationship. The latter drew its force from Conring's revealing attention to the actual, empirically observable means by which Roman law had gained ascendancy in Germany; the former drew its force from a simple, but powerful, conceptual dichotomy between two sovereign states. They reinforced each other. Both were original and radical at once. Both reinterpreted the history of Germany along lines that soon proved to be so utterly convincing as to become commonplace.[113]

Public Intellectual

The success of *The Roman Empire of the Germans* and the *Historical Commentary on the Origin of German Law* helped to spread Conring's fame until it reached the ears of a monarch who not only was directly interested in the constitutional affairs of Germany but also happened to be one of the greatest patrons of scholarship in the seventeenth century: Queen Christina of Sweden, since 1648 one of the sovereigns guaranteeing the Peace of Westphalia and thus deeply involved in German politics. No doubt it helped that Johannes Stucke, Conring's father-in-law, had good connections to the Swedish state. As early as 1644 he introduced Conring to representatives of the Swedish Crown.[114] And his accession to the chancellorship of the new Swedish territories of Bremen and Verden in 1649 can only have helped to strengthen those ties still further.

In 1650 Queen Christina invited Conring to Stockholm.[115] He went. She conferred on him the title of royal counselor and court physician. If he had wanted to, he could have stayed. This was not his first opportunity to leave Helmstedt. In 1638 he had been offered a professorship of medicine at the University of Wittenberg, where he would have succeeded Daniel Sennert. He decided to stay in Helmstedt in return for an increase in his salary. Stockholm, however, was another matter, as was the court of a queen who made a point of attracting scholars from all over Europe, including Descartes, who had only recently accepted a similar invitation to Stockholm and had died shortly before Conring arrived.[116] One wonders how Conring's views would have been affected if he had met Descartes in Sweden. But there is little doubt that Queen Christina's invitation lifted Conring to a place on the stage of European scholarship more prominent than any that Wittenberg could have offered him.

Nonetheless, after three months in Stockholm, Conring decided to go back. He returned to Germany and used his enhanced prestige to improve his life in Helmstedt. The time was right. Just one year earlier, in 1649 he had been appointed privy counselor and court physician to Juliane, regent of East Frisia. He had already written to Duke August of Brunswick-Wolfenbüttel to point out how much distinction his presence conferred on the University of Helmstedt.[117] Not much had happened as a result. Promotions in the East Frisian courtly hierarchy may not have impressed the duke. But Stockholm did. Confronted with the possibility that Conring might actually leave, Duke August, on the advice of Johannes Schwartzkopf, his chancellor, established a new professorship for politics in the faculty of philosophy. He used the simple expedient of dividing in two the existing chair for ethics and politics that Conring's teacher Heidmann had once occupied: one for ethics, and one for politics. He offered the chair for politics to Conring and promised that he could hold it in addition to his chair in medicine. That not only amounted to a formal recognition of his standing as a writer on politics. It also gave him the right to teach publicly the courses he had taught privately since the mid-1630s. Perhaps more to the point, it carried a substantial second salary and the prospect of further emoluments—a well-deserved reversal of the unwanted measure by which Chancellor Engelbrecht had saddled Conring in 1632 with the responsibility for two chairs in return for the salary of only one.

Conring hesitated. In early 1651 he was still thinking seriously about moving to Sweden.[118] He wanted to know whether resuming a position in the faculty of philosophy, from which he had resigned in 1637, would require him to shoulder the administrative offices of dean and proctor that were routinely taken up by every member of the faculty. He was concerned about the added work involved in filling a second chair and asked for clarification of how he would be expected to divide his time between the dual tasks of teaching medicine and politics. The response could hardly have been more generous. The chancellor agreed to exempt Conring from the administrative duties normally incumbent on members of the faculty of philosophy and placed the matter of how to meet his responsibilities as a teacher of politics and medicine entirely at his discretion. Conring was still obliged to teach politics according to Aristotle. But even that appears to have been something of a formality. In 1661, at least, Conring felt free to rely on Cellarius's compendium, explicitly because he was dissatisfied with Aristotle.[119]

The middle of the century thus marked another turning point in Conring's life, though one far less dramatic than 1631. If 1631 saw his return to Germany, 1650 confirmed that he would stay. It was, as far as we can tell, his best opportunity to leave. By this time the anxieties that had once moved him to seek employment in the Netherlands were gone. Peace was returning to Germany, and Conring had little reason to look for fundamental change. He could be proud of his accomplishments. He was, if not yet downright wealthy, at least financially secure. Only two years later, in 1652, he purchased a sizable estate not far from Helmstedt.[120] He had risen to intellectual prominence and had managed to convert his prestige into the freedom to devote himself to the matters closest to his heart. Henceforth, at ten o'clock on Monday, Tuesday, Thursday, and Friday during the academic year, he would teach politics, no longer *privatim,* as he had done since the mid-1630s, but *ordinarie,* alternating annually between the *Politics* of Aristotle and the "nature and constitution of the Roman-German commonwealth or empire."[121] To be more precise, he was going to teach only when more urgent business or personal affairs did not keep him away. He had the freedom to absent himself from teaching often and for considerable lengths of time. He stayed at home when he was ill and taught at home when it was cold in winter. He suspended classes in order to visit a church on one of his estates. In 1671 he took off the whole month of October in order to attend his daughter's wedding. It was a rare occasion when in 1661 the visitors appointed to examine the university pointedly stated that the cold walk from Conring's house to the lecture hall in winter was no good reason for him to teach at home.[122]

Conring continued to teach and practice medicine until the end of his life. In this regard 1650 amounted to no turning point at all. But from now on, medicine took second place to politics.[123] With the exception of his revisit to Paracelsus in 1669, he produced no substantial new work on medicine. And even though he continued to supervise medical dissertations, their frequency fell by more than half.[124] Politics, by contrast, consumed ever more of his attention, both as a teacher of popular courses and as a well-known expert with a reputation far beyond the boundaries of Brunswick-Wolfenbüttel for an uncanny ability to sort out conflicting legal claims, a subtle understanding of competing interests, and a willingness to offer his scientific expertise as a consultant to any client who could pay. Increasingly he sought and found opportunities to extend his activities beyond teaching and writing in Helmstedt to advising minor and major rulers inside and outside the Holy Roman Empire on their affairs.

As a result, the rhythm of Conring's publications began to fluctuate between the competing demands of theory and practice. First came a sudden burst of theory. In the winter of 1649–50 he lectured on "civil prudence," at long last resuming work on that systematic treatise on the principles of political science that he had first contemplated in the 1630s. In 1650 and 1651 he supervised a series of dissertations devoted to the same subject.[125] In 1651 he presided over a famously important dissertation on "reason of state" that reached a new level of dispassionate clarity and conceptual sophistication in the German debate on that celebrated concept.[126] These were his largest steps toward a systematic treatment of political theory so far. They signal not only his old theoretical resolve and his new freedom as a professor of politics but also the return of peace to Germany and the reflection that peace made possible. He continued to teach courses on politics and presided over political dissertations for the next quarter-century. But it took him more than ten years to complete his general treatise on political theory, which he finished in 1662.[127] Too often he spoke out on affairs of more immediate concern.

Perhaps the most important, and certainly the earliest, question of the day on which Conring took an outspoken stand arose directly from the Peace of Westphalia. Hostility between the confessions did not exactly cease in 1648. Peace was still vulnerable to attacks on religious grounds. Conring responded by seeking to promote understanding between the confessions while at the same time defending the peace against confessional assaults. His first venture onto this treacherous terrain came early in 1648, during the final negotiations before the Peace of Westphalia was signed. Hiding his true identity even from friends behind a pseudonym—Irenaeus Eubulus, which might be translated as Pacific Goodwill—and throwing potential enemies off the track by posing as a moderate Catholic, he advocated peace between Protestants and Catholics as a laudable cause for both parties.[128] Once peace had been declared, he stepped forth in his own name. In 1657 he expanded the arguments of Irenaeus Eubulus and published them with a wealth of supporting documents.[129] He put further effort into reprinting works by Georg Witzel and Georg Cassander, sixteenth-century Catholic authors who had tried to pave the road toward confessional reconciliation with arguments on which Calixt had also drawn.[130] Religious peace ranked high on Conring's agenda.

But not religious peace at any price. He saw no room for compromise with claims for the supremacy or infallibility of the pope. When it came to the papacy, he was as intransigent as any Catholic could be—or John Locke in the *Letter concerning Toleration* that (never mind its title) withheld toleration from Catholics.[131] Pope Innocent X rejected the Peace of Westphalia because it extended equal treatment to Protestants and Catholics. In 1651 and again in 1654, Conring took up the challenge.[132] He denied the right of Innocent X to declare the Peace of Westphalia null and void, and he came forth in 1653 with an impassioned defense of its validity—one of the few pieces of writings that he published both in Latin and in German.[133] When his attacks were countered by Catholic responses, he doggedly stood his ground for several rounds with his opponents.[134] And once, in 1651, he entered into debate with the Jesuit Johannes Mulmann on the question of purgatory.[135]

If these writings were intended to protect the empire from attacks on religious grounds, the treatise *The Borders of the German Empire in Two Books* that I already mentioned was written during the same years in order to stabilize the empire's territorial condition.[136] This was not, as might be thought at first, a work of geography. It was an investigation into legal and diplomatic history whose purpose was to settle which territories did, and which did not, belong to that German empire that Conring had so sharply distinguished from Rome, and whose constitution had now officially been placed on a new foundation. It reviewed, territory by territory, state by state, the borders dividing the empire from its neighbors; their development over time, from early medieval beginnings until the conclusion of the Peace of Westphalia; and the justice of whatever claims and counterclaims could still be made for including or not including a given territory in the empire.

This was no small task at a time when territorial boundaries were still uncertain, when foreign powers participated routinely in the affairs of the empire, and when Louis XIV was just beginning to embark on his well-known policy of relentless nibbling at the empire's substance under the pretext of reuniting unjustly alienated parts of France with the motherland. It was only fitting that Conring dedicated *The Borders of the German Empire* to the Great Elector Friedrich Wilhelm of Brandenburg, and perhaps also that a pirated edition was published by Martin in Lyon—a city that had once lain within the empire's borders.[137] But *The Borders of the German Empire* was of interest from many different points of view. It proved to be more popular than Conring's endeavors in the field of pure political theory. It had already been reprinted twice when Goebel reprinted it again in Conring's *Opera* in 1730, and it attracted the attention of Emperor Leopold I himself. He asked Conring to carry the story beyond the time of the Peace of Westphalia.[138] But with his attention divided between the demands of theory and practice, and confronted with an amount of empirical information that no one had ever sought to gather in similarly systematic fashion, Conring was pressed for time. He did not manage to respond to the emperor's requests until the last year of his life, and even then responded only incompletely in the form of the *Third Book on the Borders of the German Empire* shortly before he died.[139]

It was probably about the same time, in the early 1650s, and for similar reasons that Conring began to collect notes for the *The State of Europe, with Special Reference to the German Empire*, a history of Europe and the Holy Roman Empire in the years following the Peace of Westphalia that Goebel published posthumously in 1730 from a manuscript for which we do not know the exact date of writing.[140] This work nicely complemented *The Borders of the German Empire*. The latter dealt with the period preceding the Peace of Westphalia, and the former dealt with the period following it. Like *The Borders of the German Empire*, *The State of Europe* sought to establish a foundation on which to base political decisions about the good of the commonwealth. But it was differently conceived. It was not limited to the empire but included all of Europe. More important, it did not merely focus on tracing the boundaries of the empire but was intent on grasping its entire "state" or "condition." It was a mixture of contemporary history and the sort of statistics that Conring was one of the first to conceptualize and that would flourish at the University of Göttingen in the eighteenth century.[141]

Conring's support for the Peace of Westphalia was deep, sustained, and public. It was also founded on new principles of historical analysis and political theory. That surely helps to explain his growing popularity with students. In 1658 about one hundred students signed up for his course on Germany. In 1668 he told the university examiners that he had never less than thirty students in his course on politics, and sometimes many more.[142] Those numbers were more than respectable at a time when the entire University of Helmstedt counted only about three hundred students.[143] Conring's desire to imbue a younger generation of future civil servants and men of state with a sound understanding of politics was bearing fruit. We have no way to measure the influence his teaching had on the conduct of German politics. But we have reason to believe that it was real.

The best-known case in point concerns Johann Christian von Boineburg (1622–72), a man so prominent in the affairs of the empire and so important for Conring's own career that he deserves some special mention.[144] Boineburg descended from an old Hessian noble family. He first met Conring during the 1640s as a student in Helmstedt. They took a liking to each other. In December 1643, Conring entrusted Boineburg with the defense of *The Roman Empire of the Germans* in a public academic disputation—an unmistakable sign of his respect for Boineburg's intellectual gifts. Their friendship continued without any apparent interruption after Boineburg's departure from Helmstedt in the mid-1640s. It is documented in a voluminous correspondence that began (judging by surviving records) in 1650 and lasted until Boineburg's death in 1672.[145] These letters traverse the whole intellectual space measured out by Conring's inimitable combination of history with politics, science with religion, and scholarship with close attention to contemporary affairs. It is a mine of information about the intellectual and political life of the Holy Roman Empire in the third quarter of the seventeenth century.

Boineburg spent the first few years after his graduation from Helmstedt in the service of his Hessian rulers, requiring him, coincidentally, to go on a two-year journey to Sweden that may well have smoothed the way for Conring's own journey there. In 1652 he met and befriended Johann Philipp von Schönborn, archbishop elector of Mainz. That changed his life. Schönborn was an exceptionally energetic man.[146] He had ideas about the proper relationship between the princes, France, and the empire, and he meant to take advantage of the rights given him by the empire's constitution. His rights were considerable: the archbishop of Mainz was one of the seven princes who elected the emperor; he had the prerogative of crowning the emperor in Frankfurt; he was arch-chancellor of the Holy Roman Empire; and as arch-chancellor he presided over the meetings of the imperial diet.[147] Even though the standing of Mainz had suffered during the Thirty Years War, its potential was by no means negligible.

Boineburg was just the man to put the archbishop's plans into effect: intelligent, ambitious, even arrogant, well traveled, well trained, and in spite of his youth already equipped with some experience in imperial politics. Schönborn invited him to Mainz. Boineburg was eager to come. The difficulty was that a Lutheran could hardly serve the archbishop of Mainz in any official capacity. That caused some soul-searching on Boineburg's part and interesting epistolary exchanges between himself and his old teacher.[148] Conring did his best to stop Boineburg from bowing to what he considered papist pressure. But in the end Boineburg converted nonetheless. There is no reason to believe that his conversion was not a matter of conviction as much as expediency. From Calixt and even Conring himself he had learned to insist not on confessional distinctions, but on a "consensus of antiquity" that made it possible to see both Catholic and Lutheran confessions as expressions of one underlying Christianity.

Having converted to Catholicism, Boineburg became high marshal of the archbishop's court and president of his council. For about ten years he shaped the foreign policy of Mainz, and thus of the imperial estates. This is not the place to enter into more detail about his character and policies. Suffice it to say that in the end the ties he wove to France and the self-confidence with which he moved, sometimes quite independently of the archbishop, upon the diplomatic stage earned him the enmity of the imperial court in Vienna, ruined his chances to become imperial vice chancellor, and, assisted by some plotting by local enemies, led to his fall from grace in 1664. After a few months of imprisonment, he was reconciled with the archbishop and had the satisfaction of seeing his enemies suffer the archbishop's wrath in turn. But he was never able to return to politics. He spent the remaining years of his life in close scholarly collaboration with Leibniz, his protégé, devising plans to strengthen German unity, reconcile the confessions, found a scientific society for all of Germany, and redirect Louis XIV's acquisitive attention from Germany to Egypt.[149]

Whether or not Conring had any hand in shaping Boineburg's politics or, through Boineburg, Leibniz's career, are questions that await investigation. But it may be worth noting that Leibniz went on to serve the same dukes of Brunswick-Wolfenbüttel who employed Conring and became director of the great library in Wolfenbüttel that had been founded by the same Duke August of Brunswick-Wolfenbüttel (1579–1666) with whom Conring stood in a particularly close intellectual relationship.[150] We know that Boineburg's conversion did no lasting damage to his friendship with Conring. And we can hardly go wrong in thinking that Boineburg's preoccupation with the political unity of the German state and his admiration for the France of Louis XIV reflect judgments about the nature of politics and the significance of sovereignty that he had learned in Conring's courses. At least in this sense, Boineburg's case shows the extent to which Conring's desire to reform German politics by means of education bore fruit outside the university.

Adviser to Princes

Boineburg matters not only as an example of the influence that Conring exercised on the next generation of Germany's political elite. He matters also because the power that he gained allowed him to open doors through which his former teacher would have found it difficult to walk alone. In the mid-1650s, he asked Conring to defend the rights of the archbishop of Mainz in the coronation of the emperor against the claims of his chief rival, the archbishop of Cologne. In 1655 Conring published a vindication of the rights of Mainz, first anonymously, then under his own name.[151] This provoked a flurry of exchanges to which Conring was only one of several contributors.¹⁵² But in the end his vigorous defense of the rights of Mainz prevailed, both at the time and in the judgment of historians.¹⁵³ That earned Conring the ill favor of the archbishop of Cologne. But it also gained him goodwill in Mainz and strengthened his reputation as an authority on the constitution of the empire.

Boineburg was involved again when Conring accepted a commission to defend the rights of the Count Palatine against the Bavarian elector.¹⁵⁴ More important, Boineburg helped Conring to establish a connection to the court of France that was going to prove highly lucrative—and a source of some embarrassment to nineteenth-century historians who found it difficult to reconcile Conring's willingness to offer expertise for money with what they believed to be his duties to the German nation.¹⁵⁵ The commentary on Machiavelli's *Prince* that Conring completed in 1661 was one of the first occasions when the French connection took effect. It carried a dedication to the French foreign minister Hugues de Lionne, the successor of Mazarin, clearly designed to win his favor, and was sent to him with Boineburg's assistance. It earned Conring a letter expressing the minister's appreciation for his scholarship and, when Conring persisted in driving home the point that he desired more than appreciation, a gold chain and watch.¹⁵⁶ From that time forward, Conring's contacts with the court of Louis XIV continued more or less without interruption until the mid-1670s, melding fluidly with Colbert's practice of dispensing French pensions to scholars all over Europe to marshal their learning in support of France.¹⁵⁷

Soon Conring went beyond flattering dedications. In 1662, with the mediation of Boineburg, but without great public fanfare, he conveyed a favorable opinion on the treaty between Charles IV of Lorraine and Louis XIV. In 1667 he wrote to defend France's rights to the Spanish Netherlands. In 1668 he maintained that the king of France had a right to be considered a candidate in elections of the emperor.¹⁵⁸ In 1669 he dedicated the second edition of his work on hermetic medicine to Colbert.¹⁵⁹ In about 1670 he composed a memorandum outlining a strategy for the king of France to defeat his Dutch and English enemies, not by military confrontation, which Conring expected to have disastrous results for France, but by building a commercial empire in the Mediterranean in order to increase French national wealth.¹⁶⁰ At about the same time, he composed an unpublished advisory on the Triple Alliance.¹⁶¹ And in 1671 he suggested once again that Louis XIV might consider aspiring to the imperial crown.

Boineburg thus gave Conring a series of opportunities to prove his expertise as a public commentator on questions of politics, law, and the German constitution. He gave him access to the court of Mainz and, through Mainz, to that of France. These were perhaps the most important political connections that Conring managed to build on his career as a professor. They were certainly among the most lucrative and demonstrate abundantly the importance of personal patronage. But they were not the only ones. Conring acted as legal and political adviser to his lords, the dukes of Brunswick-Wolfenbüttel.[162] He maintained his ties to Sweden, the other great guarantor of the Peace of Westphalia next to France. Sweden had been the first great court to ask for his services. Though he had passed on Queen Christina's invitation to take up residence in Stockholm, he continued to enjoy the favor of the Swedish Crown and continued to work on its behalf. In 1652 he published a defense of Sweden's authority over the city of Bremen, denying the independence that Bremen claimed as a free imperial city.[163] In 1655 and 1656 he wrote in support of Sweden's rights in Poland.[164] He edited writings by authors like Mithobius and Starovolski that helped the court of Sweden to make its case abroad.[165] There is little reason to believe that Conring would have been equally active on behalf of Sweden if his father-in-law had not opened doors to him in Stockholm like those that Boineburg was opening in Mainz and in Versailles.

Over time Conring may have become less dependent on personal patronage. His own reputation increasingly sufficed to earn him invitations to intervene in one or another fashion on behalf of one or another of the many parties vying for a share of the parts of political life that the settlement of Westphalia had not defined. Three, all of them dating from the year 1666, are especially worth mentioning. They came from Denmark, Lindau, and Cologne. King Frederick III of Denmark asked Conring for his advice on how to solidify the absolute monarchy that had been imposed on Denmark in 1660 and confirmed by a *Lex regia* in 1665 but still encountered serious opposition. Conring responded with a memorandum supporting absolute monarchy in principle but counseling moderation in executing absolutist policies.[166] He also wrote two memoranda supporting Danish fishing rights in the North Sea.[167]

In the same year, 1666, the city of Lindau asked him for help in its attempt to gain control over a nearby convent. His proof that the charter on which the convent based its independence from Lindau's jurisdiction was a forgery did not appear until 1672. But it was worth the wait. It ranks among Conring's best works of historical criticism and is still regularly cited as one of the most important early demonstrations of the principles that Jean Mabillon and others transformed into the systematic historical criticism of ancient charters now known as diplomatics.[168]

Finally, the city of Cologne asked Conring in 1666 to defend its rights against the archbishop of Cologne. Conring was hesitant, explaining that he had opposed the archbishop before and was not eager to repeat the exercise. But three years later, in 1669, he consented, presumably because Cologne persisted and offered to pay him well. He visited the city, searched the archives, and produced a massive analysis in support of the city's claims that has never been published. It and *The State of Europe* are perhaps the most important writings by Conring never to have received detailed attention.[169]

Conring was not selfless in furnishing his expertise to so many different clients. Like consultants nowadays—scientific, political, or economic—he offered his advice expecting tangible rewards. Nor was he shy about making demands when he did not believe his service had been properly rewarded. The rewards came in the form of titles, offices, and payments.[170] Princes usually rewarded Conring with titles and offices. East Frisia's regent Juliane made him her privy counselor and court physician in 1649. Queen Christina of Sweden made him royal counselor and court physician in 1650. King Charles X of Sweden made him privy counselor and court physician in 1658.[171] The duke of Brunswick-Wolfenbüttel named him his privy counselor in 1660. And the king of Denmark named him his privy counselor in 1669 and rewarded him with an annual payment of one thousand talers—a lucrative appointment that, because of the enmity between Denmark and Sweden, compelled Conring at long last to loosen the ties to Sweden that had first been established in the 1640s.[172] The cities did not give him titles, but they paid. Cologne is said to have paid four hundred talers. France also paid. Indeed, France paid particularly handsomely, in keeping with the reputation maintained by the Sun King. From 1664 until 1673 Conring received nine hundred pounds each year and no less than fifteen hundred pounds in 1671.[173]

Such tangible rewards for scholarly expertise used to strike some historians as evidence for Conring's venality, duplicity, and other blemishes on his character.[174] Moeller was perhaps the first to dismiss such accusations as unworthy of serious attention.[175] And Erik Wolf, it seems, was one of the last who found it necessary to formulate a nuanced judgment.[176] Since then the issue has mostly been raised in order to be brushed aside, and justifiably. There is no reason to doubt that Conring was motivated by self-interest or that he knew exactly how to use the evidence to his clients' best advantage. Nor is there any doubt that in so doing he sometimes came close to contradicting himself, or even did contradict himself. But none of that proves that he violated, consciously or unconsciously, the principles to which he was explicitly committed. More plausibly, his conduct can be seen as evidence of the difficulties faced by even the most clear-headed contemporaries in an age when the entire moral, religious, and political order of Europe was shaken to its foundations. If anything, Conring deserves to be respected for the detachment with which—in spite of all upheavals—he managed to advise political opponents with equally professional expertise.[177]

Harvest

In the late 1650s, Conring returned to political theory. In 1656 he published a new edition of Aristotle's *Politics* in Heinsius's version of the Greek text, accompanied by the Latin translation of Victorius and a detailed introduction that analyzed the logic and notoriously knotty arrangement of the books into which the *Politics* is divided. In 1658 and 1659 he followed up with courses on Machiavelli's *Prince* that led to a new edition of the *Prince,* in the Latin translation of Sylvester Telio, but also to the composition of an extended commentary on Machiavelli's thought and the extent to which it deserved to be approved. It was this commentary that Conring dedicated to the French foreign minister in 1661.[178] In 1662 he finally completed the treatise on the principles of politics, *On Civil Prudence,* that he had first contemplated in the 1630s, the first chapters of which he had worked out in the early 1650s.[179] *On Civil Prudence* was meant only as an introduction to political science. Nonetheless, it turned out to be so large a volume that Conring was concerned about its reception. To expedite the dissemination of ideas that it had cost him so much time and trouble to put into writing, he condensed the work to its bare essentials and published an abbreviated version in 1663 as *Propolitica or Short Introduction to Political Philosophy.*[180] This furnishes the most immediate access to the ideas that Conring himself judged to be central to his thought. Unfortunately, for reasons difficult to understand, Goebel did not include it in his edition of Conring's *Opera.*

Thereafter Conring resumed his studies of the Holy Roman Empire and other states of the world. In 1662 he lectured on Germany, relying once again on Lampadius's old book, and on the states of Europe overall, relying mostly on information that he himself had gathered over time. In 1666 and 1669 he supervised three dissertations on aspects of the imperial constitution.[181] These rounded out the series of dissertations that he directed in the 1630s and early 1640s. They were the first that he devoted to the constitutional structure of Germany since Blume defended his dissertation on the German episcopate in 1647, well before Conring had even been appointed to a chair in politics.[182] In 1671 he published a revised edition of Lampadius's work on the empire and, for the first time, included his own commentary, at least as far as he had been able to carry it.[183] And in 1674 he collected the most important dissertations on the Holy Roman Empire that had been written under his guidance, revised some of them substantially, and published all of them in a single compendium under his name.[184]

The lectures that Conring gave during those years on the states of Europe and the knowledge he thought necessary to assess any specific body politic were popular and widely known. He contemplated turning them into a book, as he had done with other lectures in the past. But he was rudely anticipated by the publication of Philipp Oldenburger's unauthorized transcript in 1675.[185] He responded with a declaration warning his readers not to confuse Oldenburger's pirated rendition with his own ideas.[186] But he never managed to replace it with his own. It was left to Johann Wilhelm Goebel to publish what he found in manuscripts that Conring left behind.[187] Conring seems to have realized only too well how thin the knowledge was that he compiled from variegated sources and may not have thought it worth publication. Nonetheless, his work is still widely considered to have staked out the field of statistics that was later cultivated at the University of Göttingen.[188]

In the late 1670s, Conring's health began to wane. From 1677 to 1679 he taught only on rare occasions. He published no substantial new work. In 1680 he taught his course on Germany one last time. In the same year he retired, but he continued to draw his full salary as a special favor from the dukes of Brunswick-Wolfenbüttel to thank him for the outstanding services he had rendered for almost half a century. In 1681 he managed to complete additions to his work on the boundaries of the German empire.[189] In July of the same year he presided over his last dissertation.[190]

Conring died on 12 December 1681. On 28 December he was laid to rest in the church across the street from the estate in Gross Twülpstedt, not far to the north of Helmstedt, that he had bought in 1652. He left behind three estates, the house in Helmstedt, and a library of well over 4,500 titles bound in more than three thousand volumes that qualifies as one of the larger private collections of the time.[191] He was survived by his wife, his son, and three daughters.[192] His body lies in a coffin in a small vaulted crypt flanking the north wall of the church and reserved to members of his family. The coffin stands in plain sight and is inscribed "Hermanni Conringii reliquiae."

A Blurry Image

This completes the first of three steps that I proposed to take toward a better understanding of the limits of history. Let us briefly review where it has taken us. I started by identifying a certain problem in contemporary historical scholarship. I claimed that our understanding of the origin of modern political thought suffers from a conceptual shortcoming: it presupposes the very categories of analysis whose origin it is intended to explain. In order to substantiate that claim, I pointed to three areas of historical life commonly slighted by historians of modern political thought: the history of law, the history of the Middle Ages, and the history of the Holy Roman Empire. These exclusions, I maintained, are complementary: one is conceptual, one chronological, and one geographical. In combination they narrow our field of vision to an area nicely preconfigured to guarantee before the inquiry has even started the outcome whose origin is ostensibly in question. The outcome is guaranteed to be political (because law has been excluded), modern (because things medieval have been set aside), and centered on the nation-state (because the Holy Roman Empire has been declared a quaint anachronism). How were those blinkers made? What makes them so alluring? How can we get rid of them?

In search of answers to those questions, I turned attention away from classics in the history of early modern political thought and to Hermann Conring instead. Conring was not classic. But he was deeply implicated in all three of the areas commonly excluded from the study of modern political thought: he focused on the history of law; he did so for medieval as well as modern times; and he paid especially close attention to the Holy Roman Empire. That combination of characteristics was perfect for our purpose. Hence I went on to describe Hermann Conring's life, his education, and the writings that he produced during his long career as a professor at the University of Helmstedt.

What I have done so far may thus be taken as an illustration of business as usual among historians: I took off from the diagnosis of a certain problem in (what is often called) our current state of knowledge; I offered therapy by means of new evidence, or evidence at least that has (historians like to say) not yet received the attention it deserves; and I entered upon a course of treatment that was intended to produce (the language goes) a more adequate understanding of the past. Problem, diagnosis, new evidence, and a more adequate understanding of the past: these are the terms by which historians usually justify what they do.

Some readers may object that this is not business as usual at all. At best it is an illustration of business as usual some time ago. It focuses on a hoary subject (the origin of the modern state), lumbers down a well-beaten track (the life and works of X), and marches blindly past the insights historians have gained in the more recent past. There are other things that we would like to know. What was life in early modern Helmstedt really like? What role did women play? Who went hungry, who went cold, who suffered from the plague? How did the people organize their day? How did they socialize? What did they dream? What did they fear? What did they think of sex? How did they treat their children? What was the meaning of old age? Did they know how to read? Why did they burn witches at the stake? What made them happy and what made them mad? Not to dignify such questions with attention may hardly seem to qualify as business as usual at all.

But such objections, were they made, would miss the point. All forms of history, including those embodied in the most recent scholarship, rest on the same elementary assumptions about the difference between primary evidence and secondary literature, between the present and the past. Those assumptions place limits on our understanding. It makes no difference whether we take a conventional approach or not. For in the elementary sense at issue here, the most old-fashioned kind of history exemplifies the historian's business as well as the most recent publications do. Indeed, there is a sense in which a conventional approach is more suitable to our purpose. If we want to uncover limits inherent in the study of history as such, we must be careful not to confuse them with limits inherent merely in our choice of some particular subject or approach. Far better for our purposes to focus on a subject like Conring, just because we already know only too well how many aspects of the past it eliminates from consideration. That makes it easier to recognize what history excludes from understanding, not because it is conventional, but because it is history.

Instead of turning our sights to subjects of more contemporary interest, we shall therefore intensify our inspection of the subject that has been introduced. So far we have only a blurry image. We have relied on secondary literature and largely limited ourselves to summarizing what was already known (if only to a small group of German-speaking scholars). Now we have to confront the evidence directly and do original research.

3

The Context: *Discursus Novus*

The preceding chapter was designed to fill a gap in our knowledge. It did so by accumulating information and putting it into a systematic order. Most history proceeds like this. There is much merit in such work, particularly if the information is fragmentary and dispersed. But if we want to understand the role that Hermann Conring played in history exactly, we need to change our method from accumulation to analysis. In this chapter we shall therefore concentrate on one of Conring's writings and subject it to one of the most powerful tools at the disposal of historians: putting it into the context of its time and place.

An Unhappy Author

Sometime in 1642 a slender quarto volume, no more than forty pages long, with the title *Discursus novus de imperatore Romano-Germanico* or *New Discourse on the Roman-German Emperor,* was published under the name of Hermann Conring. Judged by the standards of the time, the title page was bare. It carried the name of the (supposed) author, the title, and the date of publication. That was all. No indication of the place where it was published. No mention of the printer. And none of the florid details with which seventeenth-century printers were happy to adorn the title pages of their books in an effort to attract potential buyers.

The *New Discourse* was a small book, but it dealt with a big subject. Right from the start, it turned to one of the fundamental questions for the self-understanding of early modern Europeans in general and Germans in particular: did the Roman empire still exist, or had it long since vanished from the face of the earth? The answer was both simple and provocative: either the Roman empire had disappeared completely, or it had shrunk to an empty title and a tiny piece of land consisting of the city of Rome and its environs—a title and a piece of land that were now in the hands of the pope. In neither case was there any reason for German kings to continue to pretend that they were Roman emperors, much less for them to march into Italy, at great expense and no small danger to their persons, in order to have themselves crowned by the bishop of Rome.[1]

Those were bold things to say at a time when many people—and by no means only inconsequential people—still believed, or at least pretended to believe, that the Roman empire was the last of four world monarchies and was not going to vanish from the face of the earth until the world itself came to an end.[2] For centuries the Roman empire had been so closely linked to the kingdom of Germany that the two had become virtually indistinguishable from each other in the minds of many contemporaries. Depending on your historical perspective, the ties between them were at least as old as the imperial coronation of Otto the Great in 962, and possibly as old as Rome itself. Jacob Lampadius, for example, began his account of "jurisdiction" in the Holy Roman Empire with the foundation of Rome in 753 B.C.[3] And Lampadius was by no means exceptional. He is worth special mention only because he was a Protestant friend of Conring who did more than anyone else to turn Conring's attention to the history of the empire. As for enemies, while Conring was contemplating the demise of the empire, Ferdinand II, a king from the house of Habsburg who had been thoroughly imbued with the vigor of counter-reformatory Catholicism, was conducting a European war in order to bring his Protestant enemies to heel and restore those universal rights to which he believed himself entitled as ruler of precisely the Roman empire.[4]

Toward the middle of 1643, the *New Discourse* fell into the hands of its supposed author.[5] He did not like what he saw. He considered the publication of the *New Discourse* evidence for the depths to which contemporary morals had sunk. He would never have dreamed that anyone should have dared to publish so shoddy a piece of writing under his good name, especially not while he was still among the living. He was saddened by the cowardice that had prevented the printer from identifying himself or the place of publication on the title page. He was dismayed by the rapacious shrewdness with which that same printer had invented an "insolent" title for this "primitive supposititious child." He was appalled by the damage done to his reputation. And he saw no other remedy to save his reputation than to do something he would much rather have avoided, namely, to write a better book on the same subject. That book was entitled *De Germanorum imperio Romano* or *The Roman Empire of the Germans*. It was published in the first days of 1644, and it was in his preface to that book that Conring offered his unflattering assessment of the *New Discourse*.[6]

Those were strong words. Small wonder that a century later Johann Wilhelm Goebel did not include the *New Discourse* in his edition of Conring's *Opera* but placed it on a list of "writings the author did not acknowledge as his own and his heirs do not acknowledge either."[7] Small wonder that historians since then have more or less ignored the *New Discourse*.[8] But that is a pity. For the *New Discourse* was identical with a work entitled *Exercitatio de imperatore Romano Germanico* or *Exercise on the Roman German Emperor*, over whose publication Conring himself had presided in 1641. He had no qualms about calling that work "my *Exercise*,"[9] he republished it in 1674,[10] and Goebel had no hesitation whatsoever to include it in Conring's *Opera*.[11] More important, the teachings of the *New Discourse* are, with a few telling exceptions, indistinguishable from those of *The Roman Empire of the Germans*, the very work ostensibly written in order to supersede the shoddy scholarship of the *New Discourse*. Far from shoddy, the *New Discourse* was, in fact, the first publication in which Conring's fundamental ideas about the relationship between Germany and the Roman empire were circulated to a larger audience. It was also the most pointed. Which is almost certainly why it was reprinted in yet another pirated edition in 1655, long after *The Roman Empire of the Germans* had appeared in print.[12]

What are we to make of this curious state of affairs? What is the relationship between the *New Discourse,* which Conring rejected, the *Exercise on the Roman German Emperor,* which he published and republished, and *The Roman Empire of the Germans,* which is acknowledged to have been one of his most important writings? Does any of them furnish authentic access to his thought? Of which was he the author? What did he really think? In order to throw some light on these and more general questions about authorship and authenticity, I shall now trace the history of the *New Discourse* and the works to which it is most closely related.[13]

The Original

The history of the *New Discourse* began, so far as we can tell, not long before 8 May 1641.[14] That was the day on which a student by the name of Bogislaus Otho von Hoym submitted the *Exercitatio de imperatore Romano Germanico* or *Exercise on the Roman German Emperor* to a public examination at the University of Helmstedt over which Conring was presiding.[15]

At the time such examinations had two different functions.[16] One was to certify that the student deserved to be awarded an academic degree, not unlike dissertation defenses today. The other did not entitle the student to any degree but gave him an opportunity to demonstrate in public that he had understood his professor's lectures. Both types of examination were conducted in public and based on a printed text that was derived from the lectures of the professor who presided over the examination. Sometimes the student wrote the text, sometimes the professor, sometimes both, but there were few cases in which the professor's lectures did not ultimately furnish the basis both of the examination and of the accompanying text. In all cases the student was expected to defend the text by responding orally to questions and criticisms raised by the audience in disputation.

These texts were referred to as *theses, exercitationes, disputationes,* or *dissertationes*—all of them varieties of the same literary species with subtle differences that are impossible to define with any precision except in concrete instances. Theses that were printed for an examination of the more elevated type (the one that led to the award of a doctoral degree) were usually identified as "inaugural" dissertations. Both inaugural and noninaugural dissertations could vary enormously in length and presentation. Some were printed on a single page containing a few tersely stated theses designed for little more than getting the oral argument under way. Others were longer than one hundred pages containing detailed arguments and copious evidence in support of each thesis, along with ornate prefatory matter like dedications, congratulations, and letters to the reader.

Often these *theses, exercitationes, disputationes,* or *dissertationes* concluded with a set of so-called corollaries (*corollaria*).[17] Corollaries consisted of tersely stated propositions that stood in a definite logical relationship to the preceding text: they had not been addressed before, but they did follow directly, by way of logical inference or deduction, from points that had already been considered. Corollaries thus stood and fell together with the main body of the text. The student was probably expected to prove their validity in the course of the disputation by demonstrating how they followed from the substance of the dissertation. In this fashion he could display his mastery of the subject matter while maintaining a definite distinction between his professor's authority and his own.

Seventeenth-century dissertations were thus altogether different from dissertations written by graduate students in universities today. Today, a dissertation is meant to prove that a student has mastered the principles of an academic discipline to such an extent that she or he is capable of turning out a work of craftsmanship on her or his own strength. That is the central condition on which a Ph.D. degree is granted. The dissertation must be an original piece of writing, expressing the student's own ideas, resting on independent research, and presenting insights that may well have been gained with the help of teachers but must not have been taken *from* them. If the dissertation cannot be considered an original piece of writing and research, the student has failed the test. Hence plagiarism—the unacknowledged copying of the work of others so as to pass it off as one's own—is among the worst possible offenses a student can commit today. Dissertations nowadays rest squarely on concepts of authorship, originality, and responsibility that require clear lines of separation between the student and the teachers.

Matters were altogether different with dissertations in seventeenth-century Germany. Of course they served a similar purpose in a similar setting: to certify a student's mastery of the principles of an academic discipline in a university examination. Indeed, the student was expected to prove his originality as well. But the burden of that proof rested on his ability to speak up orally in public defense of a written text containing theses developed by his professor. It did not rest on the written text. Whether the text was written by the student, the professor, or both was a subsidiary question. It was assumed that the dissertation would in any case reflect the professor's teaching and that the student's qualifications were to be judged by the live performance.

This will confuse contemporary readers who, like contemporary students, expect written dissertations to be original works of writing and research composed in their entirety by the student. It will be difficult for them to know what to make of dissertations that merely repeat the professor's lessons. They will be tempted to dismiss such dissertations as so many pieces of plagiarism or, at best, inferior copies of the original ideas and lectures from which they were derived. Since the present investigation is focused directly on the text of a seventeenth-century dissertation in order to determine exactly what Hermann Conring thought about the theses it contained, it will be useful to dispel such confusions from the start and cast as much light as possible on the degree to which professors did, or did not, take a hand in writing the dissertations defended by their students. Fortunately for our purposes, Conring's oeuvre is rich enough to furnish examples across the entire range of possibilities.

At one extreme there are dissertations that were written by the student. Such was the case with the dissertation on principles of moral philosophy that Conring himself defended in 1629 under the supervision of his professor Franco Burgersdicius. He signed the dedication "A. & R.," meaning "author and respondent."[18] Here the student did not orally defend (as a "respondent") theses copied from the lectures of his professor (the *praeses* or "president" at the defense); he had actually written them himself. The care with which Conring noted his dual role as author and respondent demonstrates that those were usually not the same. It also shows that Conring was keenly aware of the distinction and determined to document his authorship for a dissertation that would otherwise have been attributed to Burgersdicius.

At the opposite extreme we have *dissertationes* and *exercitationes* that were, as far as we can tell, written entirely by the professor. Obvious examples of this sort are the "dissertations" that Conring published on the bodily constitution of ancient and contemporary Germans in 1645, on a law of the Theodosian Code in 1655, and on the German empire in 1671 and the famous *Historical-Political Exercise on the Study of Particular States* that was published posthumously in Goebel's edition of Conring's *Opera*.[19] These were so completely Conring's own works that they seem never to have been defended by any student responding in any public disputation to questions from any audience whatever. In these cases *dissertation* simply figures in the title of a work written entirely by an author who also happened to be a professor at the University of Helmstedt and happened to have students who regularly responded under his presidency in defense of dissertations that he had not written in their entirety. That terms such as *dissertatio, disputatio,* or *exercitatio* could be used interchangeably for works written by professors and works defended by students in academic examinations shows nicely how closely they were related to each other in the seventeenth-century academic mind.

From the dissertation written entirely by the professor but never defended by a student, it was but one short step to the dissertation written entirely by the professor that *was* defended by a student. Here the line dividing the written work from the oral defense is particularly clear: the professor did the writing, and the student was responsible for the defense. Such cases seem to have been just as rare as their opposite, in which the student was both sole author and respondent. Two separate factors had to come together: ability on the part of the student and trust in that ability on the part of the professor. The public expression of such trust by a professor presiding over a disputation in which the fate of words unequivocally his own was left in the hands of his student, and the chance for the student to justify that trust by a public display of his abilities in defense of his professor's work constituted a special responsibility and a special honor. It therefore comes as no surprise that the best example consists of *The Roman Empire of the Germans,* one of Conring's most important works and one defended in a public academic disputation by Johann Christian von Boineburg, almost certainly Conring's most distinguished student.[20]

Most examples of dissertations associated with Conring's name fall between the extremes. They were written under his guidance and defended by students under his supervision but were not actually written by him. In such cases it is never completely clear how much of the text simply repeats what Conring himself would have said and how much may be attributed to the student's formulations.

Two main types can be distinguished. One consists of individual dissertations devoted to subjects of particular interest to the professor. Most of the dissertations written under Conring's guidance on questions of politics and history fall into that category. One of the best examples is the famous *Dissertation on Reason of State* that Conring published in 1651.[21] This was defended by a student named Heinrich Voss and is justly considered to give us insight into Conring's thinking on a particularly important subject of debate at the time. But even so it cannot simply be considered Conring's work.[22]

The other type is best exemplified by Conring's introductions to natural philosophy and medicine and by his books on the circulation of the blood and body heat.[23] These works comprise the majority of Conring's publications in medicine and natural philosophy. But all of them consist of compilations of dissertations, each of which had been written to cover a certain aspect of the field and all of which in combination cover the field as a whole. Hence one suspects that the overall design of these books, the arrangement of parts that were first separately published as dissertations, and the substance of the text itself reflect Conring's own teaching closely.

That is certainly the case with the introductions to medicine and natural philosophy. Their purpose was not to break new ground but to familiarize students with a well-established field of study. They left little room for originality on the part of any of the students defending the underlying dissertations, if only because neither the student nor the professor was expected to demonstrate any more originality than necessary to master an authoritative tradition of scientific knowledge and convey it coherently to the audience. And yet they began as dissertations. Indeed, the introduction to medicine not only consists of a series of chapters "for the most part compiled from Hermann Conring's public dissertations," but it was itself also treated as a dissertation and was defended as such in a public disputation on 29 April 1654 by Conring's student Sebastian Scheffer.[24] Here, it seems, the mere act of compiling previously published dissertations sufficed to produce yet another one. But that does not make Sebastian Scheffer the author of this work any more than the students who had previously defended parts of this work in "Hermann Conring's public dissertations." That textbooks could not only consist of bundled academic dissertations but could also themselves be treated as dissertations illustrates the contrast between our expectations of originality and the function of such dissertations at the time particularly nicely.

The works that Conring wrote on the circulation of the blood and on body heat, in contrast, clearly show Professor Conring at his most original, seeking to break new ground, with students following in his tracks. That ten separate dissertations on the circulation of the blood were first defended by ten of Conring's students and then combined into a single volume and published under Conring's name in 1643 is surely not a sad instance of professorial plagiarism in which Conring took ruthless advantage of the results that an exceptionally original and cooperative crew of ten students had produced by their own research. This was his book, and the ten students were his agents. At most they helped him to write up the results of a scientific project that he designed and carried forward for several years, and they were given an opportunity to prove their understanding of his work by defending it in a public examination.

Such examples explain why seventeenth-century dissertations are usually included among the works of the professor under whose presidency they were defended. All other circumstances being equal, the professor was normally responsible for the content of the dissertation, and the student merely for its oral defense. And yet it is important to keep in mind that a student may always have contributed something to a dissertation. Conring, as we shall see below, took pride in encouraging his students to think and write for themselves.[25] Hence the only way to disentangle the professor's authorship from that of his students in dissertations that cannot be clearly attributed to one or the other is to do it case by case.

Such is the task before us. For Bogislaus Otho von Hoym's *Exercise on the Roman German Emperor* falls clearly in the large range of dissertations somewhere between the two extremes: the title page announced the date of the examination, named Hermann Conring as the presiding examiner, and spelled out that the text was "mostly" (*praecipue*) based on Conring's lectures.[26] The text, divided into fifty-six numbered theses and printed on forty-four unnumbered pages, served as the foundation for a public academic exercise of the lesser variety, not an inaugural dissertation. And it concluded with seven corollaries.[27] One may therefore wonder who exactly wrote the *Exercise on the Roman German Emperor* and how accurately it represented the views of Hermann Conring. But there is no doubt at all that it is an authentic record of the text that Bogislaus Otho von Hoym defended and that Hermann Conring approved for publication in May of 1641.[28] In order to distinguish this original text from the other versions in which it appeared later on, I shall refer to it as the *Exercise* of 1641, or von Hoym's *Exercise*.

Three years later, in the preface to *The Roman Empire of the Germans,*

Conring would maintain that von Hoym clearly identified himself as the author (*auctor*) of the *Exercise* of 1641, that he had taken "only some matters" (*nonnulla tantum*) from Conring's "lectures" (*discursibus*) and had taken the rest from "elsewhere" (*aliunde*).²⁹ But that is thoroughly misleading. Von Hoym did say that his dissertation was "mostly" (*praecipue*) based on Conring's lectures. And if it was "mostly" based on Conring's lectures, one must assume that it came "partly" from elsewhere. But von Hoym left it entirely open how much he actually took from elsewhere, and he said nothing at all about what "elsewhere" might have meant. Given the similarities between the *Exercise* of 1641 and *The Roman Empire of the Germans* of 1644, described below, it seems likely that whatever he did take from other sources cannot have amounted to a lot—if it amounted to anything whatsoever. Perhaps the "mostly" in the title of his *Exercise* served him as a fig leaf with which to disguise the scarcity of his own contributions (a sentence here, a reference there?). Perhaps there were no such contributions at all. Or perhaps the "mostly" was a hedge against the charge that he had failed to report Conring's views with the necessary accuracy. What matters, regardless of the extent of von Hoym's own contributions, is this: von Hoym described himself as a "Pomeranian knight," but certainly not as the "author" of the *Exercise*— a point Conring must surely have noticed since he himself had once been careful to describe himself as "author and respondent" of a dissertation he wrote while studying in Leiden.

If von Hoym's *Exercise* had been a run-of-the-mill thesis, his examination might very well have been the last that anyone would hear of it. Throughout the seventeenth century, at universities in Germany and elsewhere, year in year out, such theses were duly published and defended with dulling regularity by students who rarely looked back to what was seldom more than a simple demonstration that they had understood their teacher's Latin lectures and a ticket of admission to a career in public or academic service. Tens of thousands of such dissertations have been preserved in European libraries. It is doubtful that many of them have been read since the day they were defended. Only recently have historians begun to pay closer attention to the massive amount of information they contain about early modern intellectual life and the conditions by which it was shaped.³⁰

But von Hoym's *Exercise* was not run-of-the-mill. It dealt with one of the most important constitutional questions of the day and contained some rather radical conclusions presented in unguarded language. It was the first time that Conring's ideas about the emperor and the relationship between Germany and the Roman empire were put into print.³¹ It would not take him much longer to establish his reputation as a leading interpreter of the history and law of the German empire. Only two years later, in 1643, he published the *Historical Commentary on the Origin of German Law,* a milestone in the long debate on the relationship between Roman law and the German constitution. Hence the *Exercise* received more than the usual amount of attention, recurred in more different printed versions, and had a much longer life than dissertations usually had.[32]

The Pirated Edition

The first of those other versions was, of course, the *New Discourse on the Roman-German Emperor* itself, that "primitive supposititious child" whose birth Conring found so upsetting. It was published in 1642, about one year after von Hoym's *Exercise,* in an unknown place, probably the Netherlands.[33]

I said that the *New Discourse* was identical with von Hoym's *Exercise.* But that is not literally true. There are differences. Most are purely external.[34] Misprints in von Hoym's *Exercise* were sometimes corrected in the *New Discourse.*[35] There is even a reference to Grotius's *Laws of War and Peace* that was misprinted in von Hoym's *Exercise* but corrected in the *New Discourse.*[36] Clearly, whoever printed the *New Discourse* was either knowledgeable enough to recognize a garbled reference to an important statement by Grotius at first sight or careful enough to check. But there are also perfectly obvious misprints in the *Exercise* that were not corrected in the *New Discourse.*[37] Evidently the effort to correct misprints was only intermittent.

The most important differences between von Hoym's *Exercise* and the *New Discourse,* however, are of an entirely different nature. They occur at the beginning of the text and at the end. At the beginning, on the title page, the *New Discourse* bears only the name of Hermann Conring, the title *Discursus novus de imperatore Romano-Germanico,* and an indication that it was published in 1642.[38] At the end it omits the seven corollaries that were printed on the final two pages of von Hoym's *Exercise.* The *New Discourse* thus suppressed all references to the academic setting in which the text had originated and concealed the identity of the respondent who had presented it to public examination under Conring's guidance. It even dropped the word *thesis* from the numbering of the first chapter on the first page of the text, the only place where it occurred in the *Exercise.* All of this led readers to believe that they were being offered chapters in a book, as opposed to the consecutively numbered theses of an academic exercise.

These may not seem like major differences either. Their effect, however, was to transform the nature of the work. We should not let ourselves be deceived by the fact that the *Exercise* of 1641 was printed like a book. Printing was simply the most efficient means available for distributing a written text, regardless of whether it was to be discussed by the students and faculty of a single university or read by the learned in all of Europe. Dissertations printed by the Helmstedt printers were meant to circulate within the classrooms of the university. They were accessories to an event whose essence consisted of the student's live performance.[39] They were not, or were only coincidentally, intended to reach a larger audience. Had more modern technologies been available, the *Exercise* of 1641 would probably have been photocopied or placed on a publicly accessible computer, not put into print.

The *Exercise* of 1641, in other words, was not a "book." It merely looked like one. It was a paper intended to serve as the written basis for the oral examination of a student. That is what it was, and that is how it presented itself to its readers. The *New Discourse,* on the other hand, presented itself as a book—a work written and published by Conring himself for dissemination to the European reading public. That was a very different thing.

In order to grasp the difference more precisely, it may be useful to invoke the distinction between locutionary content and illocutionary acts that Quentin Skinner has so successfully introduced to the history of political thought.[40] Locutionary content consists of things that people say (or, by extension, write). Illocutionary acts consist of things that people do in saying whatever they happen to be saying (or writing). The distinction is necessary because the very same words can be used to convey entirely different meanings. A "good morning" spoken to a child just woken by a parent not long after sunrise, for example, has an entirely different meaning from a "good morning" spoken by a professor waking a student in his class during a lecture at some point in the early afternoon. The locution is the same, but parent and professor are doing different things with it.

Illocutionary acts determine the meaning of words and sentences on a more fundamental level than does locutionary content. Locutionary content is like the ripples on the surface of a pond. Illocutionary acts are like the spring from which the pond is fed. But in spite of their importance, illocutionary acts are difficult to study, precisely because they differ from whatever words are spoken. Words spoken are easily studied. Words written still more easily. Words are code. Unspoken acts are not. Different illocutionary acts are usually expressed in different spoken words that differ from each other precisely so that they can convey different illocutionary acts. In such cases the difference between unspoken acts and spoken words remains invisible, as it were. The different unspoken acts are so deeply embedded in the different words by which they are expressed as to be indistinguishable from them. That makes it easy to assume that different words all by themselves convey the different meanings—as if meaning were identical with code.

Sometimes, however, illocutionary acts emerge from beneath the surface by which they are ordinarily concealed. They do so most obviously when identical words are used to convey different meanings. When the locutions are identical and yet their meanings obviously different, it becomes clear that the locutionary surface must not be confused with the illocutionary substance, that the code is not the same as the meaning. That is why it is worth the effort of comparing the words of different authors on the same question, or different writings by a single author, or different works by different authors over time. Such comparisons make it possible to track down instances in which identical (or nearly identical) words were spoken in different circumstances. Not at all, as one might think, because identical locutions establish identical meanings, but because identical locutions furnish a precious opportunity to grasp the illocutionary act that they embody, and thereby to determine what the author really meant.

The rare occasions on which identical words can be found to have been used on different occasions are therefore moments of excitement for anyone interested in meaning. Those are the moments when it seems possible to perceive speech acts directly, as it were, divested of the verbal clothes in which they are usually dressed. Those are the moments when it seems possible to communicate directly with the speaker, to break through the code and grasp the meaning without mediation. Those are the moments when we believe we really understand.

Comparing the *Exercise on the Roman German Emperor* with the *New Discourse* leads to precisely such a moment. Von Hoym's *Exercise* had the same locutionary content as the *New Discourse:* both were using the same words. But they were performing different illocutionary acts. That is exciting for us, because it promises us the pleasure of looking through the surface of Conring's words and discovering what he really meant. It was exciting for Conring, too, although for very different reasons. He, too, was looking through the surface of his words and discovered what someone really meant, except that it was an anonymous printer who had turned his words to a purpose that he had not intended.

We may leave it undecided whether or not the printer was motivated by the greed that Conring attributed to him. Perhaps he was motivated by a commendable desire to bring Conring's ideas to the attention of the audience they deserved. But whatever his motivation, he did perform an illocutionary act of which Conring was not the author. Leaving aside for now the question whether Conring did or did not subscribe to the locutionary content shared by the *Exercise on the Roman German Emperor* and the *New Discourse* (whether or not he approved the words and sentences), as well as the further question whether he did or did not subscribe to the illocutionary acts performed by the *Exercise on the Roman German Emperor* (whether or not he approved what von Hoym was doing in putting those words and sentences into print and defending them in public), there is no doubt at all that he angrily disapproved the illocutionary acts performed by the *New Discourse*. In the *New Discourse* Conring found his words turned against himself. His excitement therefore did not manifest itself in the pleasure of understanding that we may feel upon comparing the *New Discourse* with the *Exercise on the Roman German Emperor,* but in the anger of an author who discovered that someone whom he did not even know had given his words a meaning he did not want them to have.

There is nothing more frustrating for a speaker or a writer than the possibility that the audience may fail to follow across the great divide between words and meaning—may fail to grasp the illocutionary act below the locutionary surface, may fail to "get it"; nothing more disconcerting than that the audience may walk away believing to have understood when it has done nothing of the kind; and nothing more enraging than having one's own words turned against oneself by someone taking malicious advantage of the difference between words and meaning. That is what Conring must have felt on reading the *New Discourse*. The printers of the *New Discourse* had turned his words against him by making them "his" words. His anger was the anger of speechlessness.

The cause of Conring's anger was thus not merely that von Hoym's *Exercise* had been reprinted without his permission. It was that reprinting the *Exercise* under the title of a *New Discourse on the Roman-German Emperor* violated his own freedom of speech. It bound his name in public to radical ideas about the empire under "a title that was not only insolent, but even dangerous at a time when war was still raging," as he was going to put it more than thirty years later.[41] It exposed him to a certain risk that, though it may not have been as large as he imagined or pretended, was not negligible and to which he had in any case not given his consent. By suppressing all mention of Bogislaus Otho von Hoym and the academic setting in which the *New Discourse* had originated, it usurped a degree of authenticity and authority that Conring did not wish to claim—at least not yet and not in public. Authenticity, because the ideas were presented as Conring's "own." And authority, because they were presented as the author's considered judgment, his "discourse," published for dissemination to the educated European public. In all these ways, the publication of the *New Discourse* left Conring straining for speech, straining for a means of proving that those words, though his, did not mean what others had made them mean.

Conring's anger, however, must not be allowed to obscure the central fact about the relationship between von Hoym's *Exercise* and the *New Discourse:* the text of the two versions is word for word the same.[42] On the locutionary level, the words of the *New Discourse* were Conring's own or, at the very least, the words of a student to which he had given his formal approval in a public examination. The "legitimate child" and the "supposititious child" may have worn different clothes. They may even have done different things. But on the evidence of their bodies, they were identical twins. Conring was angry not because they differed but because one of them had gotten out of his control.

We can only speculate about the circumstances that led to the publication of the *New Discourse*. Perhaps Bogislaus Otho von Hoym had a hand in it. More likely it was someone else, someone who was familiar with Conring's work or had come across the *Exercise* of 1641 by accident, but in any event it was someone who was convinced that its contents were too interesting to languish in the obscurity of a Helmstedt dissertation.[43] We do know that Conring had nothing to do with the publication of the *New Discourse* and never managed to find out who did, or at least he did not say so in any recorded piece of information.[44] We also know he disapproved it vehemently. The *New Discourse* was a pirated edition to which he had not given his approval, masquerading under his good name as if he were its author, as if this were the best he had been able to say on a subject of such great significance.

It was not the best. Conring soon set about correcting whatever damage he feared the publication of the *New Discourse* had done to his reputation.[45] Publicly, he declared his unhappiness about having to take time away from his medical research and teaching in order to devote attention to a subject that now threatened to attract unwanted scrutiny and was not unlikely to embroil him in more of the contentious debates that characterized much of his career. "Although I would much rather have devoted myself to other things, I found myself compelled against my will—I know not how—to undertake a project equally far removed from my mind and my way of life. For I was neither free to skirt, nor did I want to undertake, an effort whole worlds apart, as they say, from that study of medicine to which I am drawn both by choice and by my academic responsibilities."[46]

Public expressions of unhappiness, however, must be taken with a grain of salt. Ever since meeting with Jacob Lampadius, Conring had been at least as deeply interested in the history and constitution of the empire as in medicine. And since about 1634 he had regularly acted on that interest by teaching a private lecture course on the subject.[47] The publication of the *New Discourse* gave Conring an occasion, perhaps a little sooner than he had wished, to publish a systematic and detailed account of his ideas about a subject that had been close to his heart all along. That led to the next step in the history of the *New Discourse*.

The Rebuttal

Early in 1644, only about half a year after the *New Discourse* had fallen into his hands, Hermann Conring published *De Germanorum imperio Romano liber unus* or *One Book on the Roman Empire of the Germans*.[48] He introduced it with a letter of dedication to his lord, Duke August of Brunswick-Lüneburg, and a letter "To the Reader."[49] In the letter to the duke, he explained why he had taken time away from his official duties in the faculty of medicine to write a book on politics. He defined his subject as Germany's identification with the Roman empire and its laws—"that name and those laws by which our Germany's fame has for centuries been raised above all other states of Europe (although their true significance is difficult to understand and commonly misconstrued)."[50] He declared that widespread confusion about the relationship between Germany and the Roman empire had damaged Germany's liberty and dignity.[51] He spoke of the miserable condition of Germany, of his desire to come to the assistance of his people, and of his hope that Germany would be restored to its former glory.[52] But he mentioned the circumstances that had compelled him to write only in passing.[53]

He was more specific in the letter "To the Reader." He repeated that he would much rather have devoted himself to medicine than to a subject that had once given him great pleasure but now pained him deeply: "I will not conceal from you, dear reader, that I was forced against my will and better judgment to write the book that I am publishing herewith. For since I am engaged in medicine, I have no time to spare for such diversions. Moreover, Germany is in such misery today that one can hardly think about its former rights and constitution—a subject, I confess, that once gave me the greatest pleasure—without the deepest grief. And since such grief afflicts almost all good German citizens anyway, the mind recoils from contemplations that can only double the pain."[54] But then he went into a detailed description of the circumstances that had led him to overcome his revulsion. It was there that he described von Hoym's *Exercise* in the terms considered above, protesting that von Hoym had openly declared himself to be the author of the

Exercise and taken "only some matters" from Conring's lectures. It was there that he attacked the unknown printers for publishing the *New Discourse* under his name, complaining about its "insolent" title and the omission of the corollaries. And it was there that he declared his intention to restore his reputation and set the record straight.

The official date of publication, 1644, is slightly misleading. The printed letter of dedication to Duke August was dated 23 December 1643. Soon after, on 8 January 1644, he signed and sealed a handwritten letter to the duke, explaining why he had dedicated *The Roman Empire of the Germans* to him, apologizing once again for having taken time away from his duties as professor of medicine, and enclosing it with a dedicatory copy of *The Roman Empire of the Germans* as a personal gift to Duke August. That copy and the accompanying letter are still preserved in the Herzog August Bibliothek in Wolfenbüttel.[55] In spite of the official date of publication, *The Roman Empire of the Germans* may thus have been printed before the year 1643 was out—a small point, but worth keeping in mind.[56]

The body of *The Roman Empire of the Germans* consisted of thirteen lengthy chapters that went over much of the same ground as the *Exercise on the Roman German Emperor* and the *New Discourse*.[57] But the book was an altogether more impressive piece of work. Conring himself called it with a certain degree of understatement a mere "booklet" and "a book, though small in size, by no means negligible in its argument."[58] Even so, this booklet was more than three times as long as the *New Discourse*. It included more detailed information and many more references to primary and secondary sources. In the *New Discourse*, for example, Conring had simply claimed that the Romans had ruled only part of the world. In *The Roman Empire of the Germans*, he specified exactly how large a part: one sixth of the world known at the time—a hazardous but nonetheless informative estimate.[59] In the *New Discourse* he had never mentioned Dante's *Monarchy*, one of the most obvious targets for an attack on universal monarchy. Now he did mention it.[60] Questions that had merely been touched upon in the *New Discourse* were now taken up at leisure. What exactly was the meaning of the charter recording Emperor Otto the Great's donation to the papacy? Was it a forgery or was it genuine? How could you tell?[61] What was the significance, in regard to these questions, of a famously relevant passage in canon law on the validity of the Ottonian donation?[62] There was an entirely new account of the papacy's rebellion against Emperor Leo the Isaurian in the eighth century.[63] There was a critical examination of the practice by which the kings of Germany had for centuries been called "King of the Romans," accompanied by a long quotation from the conclusion of Abbot Trithemius's

*Compendium.*⁶⁴ There was a little excursus on the question whether the imperial power of Charlemagne had been transmitted to his descendants by rights of heredity.⁶⁵ And so on.

The Roman Empire of the Germans closed with an appendix to which there was no parallel in the *New Discourse*. It contained two excerpts from the writings of two celebrated sixteenth-century authors on politics that Conring clearly judged to be excellent examples of up-to-date political science supporting his analysis. Both were copied from Goldast's *Monarchy*, a well-known anthology of writings on the relationship between empire and papacy.⁶⁶ The first was a brief but striking statement about papal power attributed to Pierre Pithou (1539–96), one of the leading champions of the independence of the French church and a critic of the papacy.⁶⁷ The second was a much longer passage from the *History of Italy* by Guicciardini (1483–1540), showing how the papacy had transformed the spiritual power of the church into a source of purely secular advantage. Conring, following his source, called it "Guicciardini's discourse on the origin of secular power in the Roman church" and made sure to draw attention to it on the title page of *The Roman Empire of the Germans*.⁶⁸

But *The Roman Empire of the Germans* was not merely longer, more detailed, and better documented. It was also more clearly structured and argued. Each of the thirteen chapters had a heading succinctly stating content and thesis, so that the table of contents alone amounts to a neat summary of Conring's argument.⁶⁹ There was more explicit reasoning. There was more attention to underlying principles of law and philosophy, sometimes taking the form of little excursions from a purely historical line of analysis. Where, for example, the *New Discourse* had simply insisted that the Bible could not always be taken literally, *The Roman Empire of the Germans* offered reasons why the Bible sometimes spoke in metaphors.⁷⁰ And where the *New Discourse* had simply asserted that the Romans had irrevocably subjected themselves to German control in the days of Otto the Great, *The Roman Empire of the Germans* analyzed the differences between temporary, perpetual, personal, and institutional acts of submission.⁷¹

Above all else, there were more clearly drawn distinctions. Where the *New Discourse* had raised a general question whether the Roman empire continued to exist, *The Roman Empire of the Germans* distinguished between three different possibilities: (1) the Roman empire continued to exist as a mere title, although the actual empire had vanished; (2) the Roman empire continued to exist as a universal empire that would last until the end of the world; and (3) the Roman empire continued to exist as a German-Italian empire pretty much like any other state with no rights to the rest of the world.⁷² Where the *New Discourse* had attacked the papacy's usurpation of imperial rights in general terms, the final chapter of *The Roman Empire of the Germans* identified precisely six principles comprising the "Hildebrandine heresy."⁷³

Sometimes *The Roman Empire of the Germans* went further than merely to clarify the *New Discourse*. Take, for example, the different kinds of law. The *New Discourse* had distinguished between three kinds of law: divine law (positive law made by God and revealed in the Bible); natural law (rational law derived from "known principles of nature"); and human law (positive law made by human beings).⁷⁴ That was conventional. *The Roman Empire of the Germans,* by contrast, offered a double distinction between two overlapping sets of law. First, it distinguished between eternal and positive law (according to the different standing of law in time). Second, it distinguished between divine and human law (according to the source from which eternal and positive law derived).⁷⁵ Thus, on the one hand, one more kind of law was added: four, not three, kinds now had to be considered. Two were divine, namely, the eternal law by which God governed the world and the positive law that God had revealed in the Bible. And two were human, namely, the eternal law to which human beings had access through their natural reason and the positive law by which they legislated for their bodies politic. On the other hand, the juxtaposition of three different kinds of law was now transformed into a sharp dichotomy between divine and human law. This was more than an improvement on the presentation of the relationship between the different kinds of law. It was a different view of that relationship itself.

On closer inspection, however, the differences between *The Roman Empire of the Germans* and the *New Discourse* turn out to be superficial. The resemblances, by contrast, are substantial and profound. Never mind the length, arrangement, and appearance of *The Roman Empire of the Germans*. Never mind the greater conceptual sophistication, the more abundant documentation, the different account of the principles of law. The case it makes is fundamentally the same. It begins with the same questions. It uses the same means to answer them. It proceeds in the same fashion from the fall of Rome via Charlemagne and Otto the Great to (more or less) present times. It gives the same (novel) significance to the coronation of Charlemagne on Christmas Day 800, and it dwells at the same length and with the same grave emphasis on the reign of Otto the Great. It adopts the same periodization, offers the same evidence (though more of it), and arrives at the same conclusions on the same grounds.⁷⁶

Most important, it agrees completely with the *New Discourse* on the essential points: Germany was an independent, sovereign state, and the king of Germany ruled Germany by rights that were completely independent from his rights as Roman emperor (and the king of Italy ruled Italy by equally independent rights). The Roman emperor as such had no right to rule Germany or Italy at all, because the Roman empire had never ruled the world in fact, nor had it had any right to rule the world by law. The Roman empire itself had long since shriveled to the city and environs of Rome, and the city and environs of Rome were actually under the control of the papacy. On those points there was no difference whatsoever. At bottom, the substance of *The Roman Empire of the Germans* is the same as that of the *Exercise on the Roman German Emperor* and the *New Discourse*.

The same applies to the form of *The Roman Empire of the Germans*. There, too, the difference is more striking at first sight. The *New Discourse* was a mere dissertation produced by one of Conring's students, defended and approved under his supervision but angrily rejected when published under his name. *The Roman Empire of the Germans,* however, was a real book, published by Conring under his own name, avowedly in order to correct misleading impressions created by the *New Discourse*. The former is of doubtful authenticity. The latter is not. And what is more, the authenticity of the latter was proffered explicitly in order to unmask the former's lack of it.

These formal differences, however, turn out to be no less deceptive than the substantive ones. As it happens, *The Roman Empire of the Germans* was also first presented to the public as an academic dissertation by one of Conring's students. The dissertation was entitled *De imperio Romano Germanorum Disputatio* or *Disputation on the Roman Empire of the Germans,* the student was Johann Christian von Boineburg, Conring's most distinguished protégé, and the defense took place on two separate occasions in December 1643, a few days before *The Roman Empire of the Germans* officially appeared in print.[77] All that remains of this event are two printed pages bearing the announcement of Boineburg's first disputation for 6 December 1643 and three corollaries to be considered on that date.[78] The announcement of the second disputation, if one was ever printed—it may have been made orally on the occasion of the first—has not been preserved. We do not know when it took place, nor is there any separately printed version of the text that Boineburg defended. But that does not mean that the text of Boineburg's disputation has been lost.[79] It rather means that Boineburg must have defended the text of Conring's *Roman Empire of the Germans*. As pointed out above, *The Roman Empire of the Germans* was printed near the end of 1643.[80] Even if the printing was not yet completed on the day of Boineburg's first disputation, he may have made use of galleys. Whatever the physical form of the text that Boineburg used, there is no doubt that it was identical with that published as Conring's book under Conring's name. Conring said so himself in his prefatory letter to the reader: "I wrote this booklet out of necessity. But I also took advantage of the opportunity to present it in two parts in the academic arena, as an appropriate service to students whom only Hercules could instill with an adequate understanding of our state from a young age."[81]

The publication of *The Roman Empire of the Germans* thus furnishes an interesting point of comparison to the *Exercise on the Roman German Emperor*. Unlike the *Exercise on the Roman German Emperor*, it was acknowledged by Conring to have been written by him and published under his own name. It did not consist of notes taken from his lectures, and the student who defended it, though more distinguished than von Hoym, does not appear to have had any hand in its composition. Like the *Exercise on the Roman German Emperor*, however, it was first presented to the public in an academic disputation at the University of Helmstedt.

This was no mere formality. Conring made sure that everyone would know. For inattentive readers he inserted a separate little statement between his prefatory letters and the table of contents to inform them that "JOHANN CHRISTIAN VON BOINEBURG defended this work in the usual academic fashion on two separate occasions"—with Boineburg's name printed in capital letters.[82] On at least one occasion, he referred to *The Roman Empire of the Germans* directly as a "disputation."[83] Moreover, though the text defended by von Boineburg did not consist of notes taken from Conring's lectures, it surely incorporated notes that Conring himself had prepared for lectures on the Holy Roman Empire that both von Hoym and Boineburg had attended. Lacking transcripts of those lectures, we shall never know how closely the text of *The Roman Empire of the Germans* resembles the words Conring delivered in class. But given the speed with which it was written, it can hardly be considered anything other than Conring's own systematic presentation of ideas on which he had been lecturing for close to ten years. The *Exercise on the Roman German Emperor* (like the *New Discourse*) and *The Roman Empire of the Germans* thus differed only in the detail and precision with which they reported Conring's ideas. But they were fundamentally alike in that all of them reported the same ideas—and in that none of them may be confused with the shape in which Conring first presented those ideas in his lectures, much less those ideas themselves.

What Conring really thought about the relationship between Germany and the Roman empire and just how the *Exercise on the Roman German Emperor* is related to *The Roman Empire of the Germans* will therefore not become apparent (insofar as it can become apparent at all) until we have examined and compared their contents in more detail. But even now it should be clear that the difference between them is impossible to grasp by declaring Conring to be the author of *The Roman Empire of the Germans* but not of the *Exercise on the Roman German Emperor*—or, for that matter, of the *New Discourse*.

There is one point, however, on which *The Roman Empire of the Germans* of 1644 does seem to differ substantially from the *Exercise* of 1641. That point concerns the question whether the Roman empire had ceased to exist. The *Exercise* (and thus the *New Discourse*) concluded that the Roman empire was gone and that German kings were wasting their time going to Rome to exercise imperial rights. *The Roman Empire of the Germans,* by contrast, concluded that the Roman empire was not gone at all and that German kings ought to do everything in their power to rescue it from papal usurpation. Since this is the central issue, it demands close scrutiny.

It will be useful to begin by quoting the conclusion of the *New Discourse* (and the *Exercise*) in detail. It came in chapter 52:

> I am not now going to analyze whether four hundred years of possession is enough for the popes to have acquired [by prescription] a genuine right over what they first took by force and crime, especially since in all of that time, few emperors seem to have disputed the case. But this, at least, seems certain: if after so many years of prescription, our kings and emperors have lost all those true and ancient rights of the emperors, there is no longer any reason why some of them should vainly boast I-know-not-what lordship over the world or the city of Rome; much less, why emperors elect should at great expense and overwhelming danger march into Italy in order to obtain the imperial crown from the Roman bishop. The conclusion is not difficult to perceive: since the eastern Roman empire has long since been destroyed by the Turks and hardly anything of the western empire is left to our emperors except the imperial title, it is perhaps not wrong to affirm that either the Roman empire has perished completely or, if you put aside the question of whether or not the papacy had the right to usurp the imperial title and confer it on others, that the imperial power is now actually in the hands of the Roman pope.[84]

That was straightforward. It established a clear alternative: either the Roman empire had ceased to exist completely, or it had been reduced to a mere shadow of its former self that had fallen into the hands of the papacy. To be sure, the alternative was hedged with due caution as something that was "perhaps not wrong to affirm" and merely "seemed certain." That left some room for compromise. Equally significant, the question of prescription remained unanswered. But no reader could be left uncertain about the thrust of this conclusion: for all practical purposes, the Roman empire was dead and gone.

Before we compare this conclusion to that of *The Roman Empire of the Germans,* the issue of prescription needs special consideration. Prescription was a principle of Roman law by which the uncontested possession of a certain thing over a certain period of time earned the possessor a genuine right of property, no matter how it had originally been acquired.[85] Prescription thus made it possible to secure present property relations by law, even if they were known to have originated in acts of violence or if their origin was shrouded in the mists of time. Only one thing was necessary for prescription to take effect: a certain length of time—ten, twenty, thirty, or a hundred years, depending on the kind of property—during which no one had challenged the rights of the possessor.

Prescription was a crucial ingredient in Conring's argument. It helped him to explain how the violent force with which early medieval Germans had conquered the Roman empire could, over time, have been turned into a genuine right. But it suffered from a decisive weakness: it stemmed from Roman law—and Conring could hardly draw on Roman law to justify German conquests of Roman lands without admitting that Roman law applied to Germans. His entire case was meant to prove the opposite: that Roman law was simply the particular law of one ancient state, not a source of universal or international law. Applying the Roman law of prescription to relations between Germans and Romans during the early Middle Ages threatened to lead him into a blatant self-contradiction from which there was no escape except by admitting precisely what he was seeking to deny: that the Roman emperor did have the right to rule, if not the world, at least relations between states.

It was Grotius who furnished Conring with a way out of this predicament. In his *Laws of War and Peace,* Grotius, like Conring, had to address the place of Roman law in the contemporary world. He had come to similar conclusions, on similar grounds, and by a similar route, including even a similar discussion of the rights of Charlemagne.[86] He had also had to face the question of prescription: was it rooted in positive Roman law, or could it be established on independent grounds? He turned to that question in book 2, chapter 4, "On Assumed Abandonment of Ownership and Occupation Consequent Thereon; and Wherein This Differs from Ownership by Usucapion and by Prescription."[87] He started from the assertion that boundary disputes between sovereign states could never be brought to anything other than a violent resolution unless the passage of time was taken into consideration. Not to take the passage of time into consideration when sorting out relations between sovereign states was illegitimate in principle, not merely because of Roman law. As Grotius put it, "we ought to think that good should be expected of men; and for that reason it ought not to be supposed that they have such a disposition that, out of consideration for a mere perishable thing, they would wish a fellow man to live in a continual state of sin. Without such abandonment of ownership, such a result often cannot be avoided."[88]

The passage of time alone, however, was not enough to create a right. Grotius was clear in his mind that in and of itself time does nothing at all: "Time, in fact, in its own nature has no effective force; nothing is done by time, though everything is done in time."[89] But something else did have effective force, namely, the will of the parties to a dispute—and the passage of time did help to ascertain what that will was. If after a certain length of time, whose extent would need to be specified according to the circumstances, someone whose rights had been violated had neither declared his intention to recover those rights nor taken any of the legal actions available to him in order to accomplish (or at the very least to register) such an intention, he could be presumed to have given up his rights. Although the passage of time had no direct effect, it did serve as a means to determine something that had a direct effect, namely, the intention of the injured party, even if no intention was formally expressed. And the injured party's intention to surrender its right constituted proper grounds for turning what had begun as violent occupation into a legal right. Prescription could thus be shown to rest neither on Roman law nor on the mere passage of time, but on the nature of disputes between independent agents and the will of the conflicting parties. Prescription was a matter of natural reason. It applied to relations between sovereign states no less than to relations between the inhabitants of any particular state.

This was the argument on which Conring relied.[90] Prescription, now safely detached from Roman law and reestablished on grounds of natural reason, permitted him to argue that the violence with which early medieval German tribes had conquered the Roman empire had, over time, been transmuted into legitimate rule. Prescription was the foundation for the legitimacy of Germany's claim to rule the Roman empire. But it was more than that. Prescription united in a single issue some of the most fundamental elements in the historical revolt: sovereignty, the relationship between independent states, the intention of individual agents, their responsibility, property, and the passage of time as a source of meaning. Rights that could with equal justice be conceived as timeless and universal thus were subjected to the logic of individual agency, sovereign wills, and the passage of time. The same logic conferred upon prescription a timelessly rational validity that had previously been ascribed to Roman law. Roman law lost its timeless validity and was demoted to the standing of mere positive law. In all these ways prescription was crucial to Conring's case. No wonder he insisted more than once that it was founded on natural law. This is no matter of purely technical significance. It signals the pivotal role played by a new view of time in the creation of modern ideas of law.

The author of the *New Discourse* applied this new logic enthusiastically to the German conquest of the Roman empire. But he did not apply it to the force with which the papacy had seized the Roman empire from German kings. He raised, but did not answer, the question whether prescription made the papacy's control of the Roman empire just as legitimate as it had made the German conquest of the Roman empire. In principle the door was thus left open to reasserting German claims over the Roman empire. But the author of the *New Discourse* clearly considered that door to be of little practical significance. The tone of his conclusion left no doubt as to the fundamental point: the kings of Germany had lost control over what little of the Roman empire was left. There was no point in trying to override that fact by clamoring for the enforcement of superannuated rights.

Overall, the conclusion of the *New Discourse* thus amounted to a ringing declaration that the Roman empire was gone. The time had come to recognize Germany as an empire instead. Or so one could at least infer from the terminology of the *Exercise on the Roman German Emperor* and the *New Discourse*. Both formulated the central issue in terms of a German empire, rather than the Roman empire, much less the Holy Roman Empire, or even the "Holy Roman Empire of the German Nation." The phrase *German empire, Imperium Germanicum,* appears in the first sentence of the *New Discourse*.[91] It appears also in the title and the body of another dissertation that Conring supervised in 1641.[92] As far as the *Exercise on the Roman German Emperor* and the *New Discourse* were concerned, the Roman empire was gone and had been replaced by a German empire.

In hindsight, this may seem obvious. Charles V in 1530 was the last emperor who had been properly crowned by the pope—and he was crowned in Bologna, not in Rome. The last emperor crowned by the pope in Rome was Charles's great-grandfather Frederick III in 1452. And since the demise of the Hohenstaufen dynasty in the middle of the thirteenth century, only three other German kings had been crowned emperor by popes or papal legates (Henry VII in 1312, Charles IV in 1355, and Sigismund in 1433). The vehemence with which the *New Discourse* protests against a practice that had not been followed at all for more than a century and only intermittently for three centuries before that may therefore seem slightly misplaced. But if we dispense with the benefit of hindsight, it is perhaps better seen as evidence for the powerful spell cast by the imperial heritage far beyond its mere physical survival.

That is certainly how it looks from the perspective of *The Roman Empire of the Germans*. If the *New Discourse* was willing to let the Roman empire go the way of all temporal things, *The Roman Empire of the Germans* was thoroughly unwilling. Its title distinguished carefully between Germans and the Roman empire, not only implying that there was no such thing as a German empire, but also suggesting ever so gently that the Roman empire was very much alive and well—or at least alive and well enough to be ruled by Germans. If in the years before the publication of the *New Discourse* Conring had sometimes been willing to speak of a German empire, in the years following he was punctilious about distinguishing between, on the one hand, Germany or the kingdom of Germany and, on the other, the Roman empire. He never referred to a German empire (*imperium Germanicum*), as the *New Discourse* had done, or a Roman-German republic, or a Roman-German empire, as he had done on the title pages of his edition of Jacob Lampadius's book on the empire.[93] That was the practice he followed in the title of *The Roman Empire of the Germans* and maintained consistently throughout the text. As he explained in his prefatory letter to Duke August, he regarded the confusion between Germany and the Roman empire as more than a matter of semantics. It was a real and dangerous source of doubts about the sovereignty of Germany. He hoped that clear terminology would remove those doubts and help to liberate Germany from the papacy's interference.[94]

As time passed, however, his terminology changed again. In 1647 he published two dissertations that spoke merely of Germany or "the German commonwealth."[95] In the 1650s "the German Empire" reappeared in the title of *The Borders of the German Empire*.[96] And from 1666 onward, he seems to have preferred combinations like "Roman-German empire" (*imperium Romano-Germanicum*), "Roman-German Commonwealth" (*respublica Romano-Germanica*), or "Commonwealth of the German empire" (*respublica imperii Germanici*).[97] The shifting terminology reflects the difficulty Conring faced in giving clear expression to a complex and evolving state of affairs. It suggests that the *New Discourse*'s distressingly public reference to a German empire led him, if only for a while, to distinguish more sharply between Germany and the Roman empire than he may have wanted (or may have done in his lectures) and delayed the time when he became comfortable with combining the Roman and the German element in a single term again. But whatever may be learned from the terminology in the titles of Conring's books, and whatever the degree of Conring's willingness to call Germany an empire at one time or another, *The Roman Empire of the Germans* left no doubt at all about two points: there was a Roman empire, and that empire was not to be confused with Germany.

The final chapter of *The Roman Empire of the Germans* stated that view in unmistakable language. The heading of the chapter announced that "the empire over the city of Rome and the rights attached thereto still belong to Germany, even though the pope has torn them to pieces in every which way."[98] The body of the chapter insisted that the Roman empire continued to exist and continued to belong to the kings of Germany. No concessions to prescription here. And at the conclusion of the chapter, coinciding with the conclusion of the entire book, he issued a powerful endorsement of imperial rights over Rome and a fiery indictment of the papacy, borrowed from no less an authority on Roman law than Cino of Pistoia (1270–1336/7):

> Since, therefore, the popes had no right whatsoever to cast the power of the emperor off of themselves and out of the city of Rome, it is evident that the rights enjoyed by the emperors until the age of Hildebrand, however much the pontiffs may have been battering them, subsist in their entirety today. I shall therefore finish this disputation by quoting words attributed to the noble juriconsult Cino of Pistoia: "The pastors of the church have become rapacious wolves, insatiably lusting after temporal things and filled with the ambition to rule. They have striven and continue to strive to usurp the empire and imperial rights by various illicit means. That is why under their governance the entire world has been placed into evil and the power of tyrants. I believe that the time for God's vengeance upon them is close. If only it were closer!"[99]

This is the only real difference between *The Roman Empire of the Germans,* on the one hand, and the *Exercise on the Roman German Emperor* and the *New Discourse,* on the other. But it is obviously crucial. Where the *Exercise* and the *New Discourse* seemed willing to countenance the disappearance of the empire or to surrender its remainders on grounds of prescription to the papacy, *The Roman Empire of the Germans* upheld the position that the empire belonged to the king of Germany and railed in sharp language against the "Hildebrandine heresy." Where the *New Discourse* directed its wrath against Bartolus because of his support of the empire's universal rights, *The Roman Empire of the Germans* reserved its anger for the papacy, while praising Cino of Pistoia, teacher of Bartolus, friend of Dante, and a great Ghibelline defender of universal monarchy, if only for a time. As far as the existence of the empire was concerned, *The Roman Empire of the Germans* looked more conservative and more inimical to the papacy.

What Conring Really Thought

What, then, did Conring really think? Did he think that the Roman empire was for all practical purposes gone, or did he think that it constituted a fundamental ingredient in the power of German kings? Did he think what was written in the *Exercise on the Roman German Emperor* and the *New Discourse*? Or did he think what was written in the last chapter of *The Roman Empire of the Germans*?

We could take the difference at face value. This would mean that Conring really thought what he wrote in the conclusion of *The Roman Empire of the Germans:* that the Roman empire continued to exist and continued to be ruled by the kings of Germany. Perhaps the conclusion of the *Exercise* reflects what he believed in 1641 but not what he believed in 1643. Perhaps we are dealing with a change of mind. The publication of the *New Discourse* may have prompted him to write *The Roman Empire of the Germans* in order to clarify his change of mind. In that case *The Roman Empire of the Germans* ought to be seen as a correction of the *New Discourse*.

Perhaps, however, the conclusion of the *Exercise* never did reflect what Conring really thought. It might only reflect a case Conring allowed Bogislaus Otho von Hoym to make in print with which he personally disagreed. Perhaps the publication of the *New Discourse* prompted him to write *The Roman Empire of the Germans* in order to set the record straight. In that case *The Roman Empire of the Germans* ought to be seen as the rebuttal of the *New Discourse,* which is the way it introduced itself to its readers.

Then again, we need not take the difference between the *Exercise* and *The Roman Empire of the Germans* at face value at all. We can easily imagine that Conring accepted the conclusion of the *Exercise* in 1641 and continued to accept it in 1643 and 1644, despite its conflict with the conclusion of *The Roman Empire of the Germans*. He might, for example, have considered it as the result to which the logic of his argument was leading if it was pursued to its extremes but not as a position he was prepared to defend in public. He might have been willing to entertain the extinction of the Roman empire as a subject for examination in an academic exercise based on a text printed for circulation within the university but not willing to adopt the same point of view in the face of the authorities. Perhaps the publication of the *New Discourse* forced his hand by tying his name in public to a doctrine with which he did in fact agree, but for which he was not prepared to take responsibility. Perhaps he found himself compelled to adopt a conclusion in public with which he disagreed in private. In that case the difference between the *Exercise* and *The Roman Empire of the Germans* would not reflect what Conring really thought, but merely what he felt at liberty to say. Perhaps he did not "really" believe either conclusion. Perhaps the question what he "really" believed is not the right question to ask.

The first of these possibilities (that *The Roman Empire of the Germans* ought to be seen as a correction of the *Exercise*) can be dismissed almost out of hand. It is a commonplace in the literature on Conring's intellectual life that traces of intellectual development are difficult to find. He formulated his basic ideas early and remained faithful to them throughout his career.[100] There is no reason to believe that it was any different with a point as fundamental as the question of whether the Roman empire continued to exist and who was in charge of it. He had been deeply preoccupied with the constitution of the empire since 1632, when he met Jacob Lampadius. He had published Lampadius's dissertation on the empire in 1634 and reprinted it in 1640 and 1642. He had taught a private course of lectures on the subject since the mid-1630s. If he had changed his mind between 1641 and 1643, someone was bound to notice. He himself might be expected to have acknowledged such an important change of mind in order both to disavow the *New Discourse* and to ridicule the printer who published it for having missed his mark. But the preface to *The Roman Empire of the Germans* is perfectly clear about the reasons why Conring distanced himself from the *New Discourse*. Those reasons had nothing to do with his having changed his mind, but everything to do with wishing not to be held accountable for the contents of a piece of writing published against his will.

What about the second possibility (that the conclusion of the *Exercise* states a case Conring allowed Bogislaus Otto von Hoym to make in his examination, but with which he did not himself agree)? That looks like an attractive explanation at first sight. Conring was proud of the freedom he gave his students. He thought it best to interfere as little as possible with the formulations they chose on their own. He wanted them to learn how to take responsibility for their work and for the risks that inevitably entailed. As far as he was concerned, his contribution was limited to offering them correct instruction, removing obvious mistakes, and adding whatever essential observations had escaped their understanding. Or so at least we may infer from his own description, late in life, of the manner in which he treated his students' dissertations: "So as to develop the talent and industry of the more gifted youths, I took care to make them experience the danger of their own pen, so to speak. I limited myself to giving them accurate instruction by lecturing on everything they needed to know, amending whatever they had stated improperly and adding whatever seemed to have escaped their youthful understanding—all the while insisting on leading them by the hand, as it were, to a more refined understanding of the subject matter."[101]

Those principles were among his distinguishing characteristics as a teacher. They have lost none of their attraction in the intervening centuries. They expressed a pedagogical desire for his students to progress as rapidly as possible to intellectual maturity. They made him a remarkably enlightened teacher at an early time, a man who believed that learning comes from doing, that students need to be given sufficient leeway to try out their talents, if necessary by missing a step here and there, so as to recognize their proper strength, and to learn from error by confronting "the danger of their own pen."

It seems entirely reasonable to presume that Conring allowed Bogislaus Otho von Hoym to write his dissertation on those same principles. One could therefore infer that the conclusion of the *Exercise* represents just one of those missteps that Conring permitted his students but not a conclusion with which he himself would have agreed. One could then maintain that Conring presented his own conclusion in *The Roman Empire of the Germans* precisely because he disagreed with the conclusion of the *Exercise*.

A moment's reflection, however, dissolves the plausibility of that line of thinking. The issue here is not of giving leeway to a student, nor is it one of missing a step. The issue concerns the single most important point made in the *Exercise*, the point of culmination and convergence for all the evidence and reasoning it deploys. It may well have been that very point that led an anonymous printer to reprint the *Exercise* and entitle it a *New Discourse on the Roman-German Emperor*. Can we believe that Conring would have allowed one of his students to maintain a novel conclusion on a matter of such significance if it flatly contradicted his considered judgment? Hardly. Conring did give his students leeway in writing their dissertations, but he did not allow them to defend a thesis that he considered to be downright wrong. By his own account, if he found such statements, he corrected them.[102] If he had disagreed with the conclusion of the *Exercise*, he would not have let it stand.

Besides, if he had disagreed with the conclusion of the *Exercise*, young Bogislaus Otho von Hoym would scarcely have put it into writing. Would he have risked incurring his teacher's displeasure by declaring that German kings were wasting time in chasing after ancient imperial glories if he had had any reason to suspect that Conring thought otherwise? Pufendorf, perhaps, or Leibniz, or even Boineburg might have incurred such risks. Not von Hoym. More likely he stated clearly, if naively, what Conring had said in his lectures with more circumspection. More likely he defended a conclusion suggested to him by his teacher's lectures without realizing just what it was that he was putting into print. More likely Conring permitted him to do so because, at bottom, he agreed. All teachers are familiar with the shock of recognizing their own ideas in formulations by their students that are cruder than they would have liked but not, unfortunately, simply false.

That leaves the third possibility: the difference between the conclusions of the *Exercise* and *The Roman Empire of the Germans* must not be taken at face value. Both tell us what Conring "really" thought, except that they were formulated under different circumstances. Different formulations in different circumstances create the illusion of a substantive disagreement. But in fact Conring was "really" thinking the same.

If that is true, it must be possible to identify an underlying agreement between the *New Discourse* and *The Roman Empire of the Germans*. Such an agreement does in fact exist. It turns on one of those clear distinctions in which *The Roman Empire of the Germans* excelled in comparison to the *New Discourse,* namely, the distinction between different meanings of the term *Roman empire*. At the very beginning of *The Roman Empire of the Germans,* Conring pointed out that his contemporaries used the term *Roman empire* to refer to three very different things: some thought it was a mere title with no corresponding reality at all, because the old Roman empire had long since vanished; some thought it was a universal empire that, though presently in straitened circumstances, could reassert its universal rights and would surely last until the end of the world; some, finally, thought that its remainders had been absorbed into a German-Italian state with no rights to the rest of the world at all.[103] But it took Conring until chapter 11 to state, in an inconspicuous place, without fanfare, almost in passing, the most important conclusion that he himself was prepared to draw on the basis of that distinction: the Roman empire in the sense of a universal monarchy was gone. The Roman empire survived only in the form of control over the city of Rome.[104] It was more than a mere title. The Roman empire still possessed a political reality. But only on the assumption that government over a single city qualified as an empire. "If you take 'Roman empire' to refer to some vast state whose rights belong to the city of Rome, as was the case in antiquity, then the Roman empire has long since altogether vanished. But if the government of a single city deserves the majesty of that title, then the Roman empire continues to exist even today."[105] There is no contradiction here to anything that Conring maintained in the *New Discourse*.

The same distinction between the Roman empire defined as a "vast commonwealth" and as the municipal government of Rome gave Conring an opportunity to dispose of objections to the demise of the Roman empire that were founded on the Apocalypse. He seized the opportunity just as soon as he had established the distinction.[106] There was no doubt, Conring stated, that the words written in the Apocalypse about Babylon deserved to be applied to Rome.[107] According to the Apocalypse, however, Babylon was going to endure till the end of the world. Hence there had to be some sense in which the Roman empire would continue to exist as a "vast commonwealth." And so there was. But it was a countersense. It was the perverted sense in which the papacy ruled over an empire of its own perverse design. The Catholic Church was Babylon. The Catholic Church was that enduring vast Roman empire that could be expected to last until the end of the world. But it was an empire only of sorts, because it was different from any "natural" commonwealth. It was no normal state like Germany or, for that matter, the ancient Roman empire itself. It was, just as the Apocalypse had written about Babylon, a *horribilis et sacra tyrannis:*

> Everybody knows that for many centuries the Roman pope has exercised a gigantic kind of monarchy over the church of Christ that reaches almost all over the world, on the pretense that Saint Peter himself conferred it on the city of Rome. He has prostituted the sanctity of Christian teaching with indulgences, benefices, and dispensations. He has even subjected kings and princes to himself, not by force of arms, but by a strange kind of religion. And by such means he aims to make his realm eternal. Hence even today there still exists some vast kind of Roman empire. But its nature is quite different from that of other states. This Roman monarchy will endure as long as the city of Rome itself. But that is not the kind of empire that belongs to Germany, nor is it our purpose here to expose this horrible accursed tyranny.[108]

The concluding phrase is virtually untranslatable. It plays effectively on the horrors of tyranny and the double meaning of the word *sacer,* which can mean both "sacred" and its opposite, "cursed." But it leaves no doubt about the execrable nature of the tyranny itself.

It also leaves no doubt about Conring's views on the Roman empire. They may be summed up in three separate propositions. The Roman empire in the sense of a "vast commonwealth"—a maximum empire—was long gone. The Roman empire predicted by the Apocalypse to endure until the end of the world did still exist. But it was not an empire, strictly speaking, and it had nothing to do with Germany. It was an anti-empire, a monstrous aberration, a perversion of spiritual power by which the papacy had transformed its preeminent role in the Christian church into a tyranny—an evil empire. The only sense in which the Roman empire could still be said to exist for real was that which referred to the municipal government of Rome, and then only on condition that government over a single city qualified as empire—a minimum empire.

That demonstrates how sharply the conclusion of *The Roman Empire of the Germans* was actually limited. Unlike the *New Discourse,* it did proclaim that the kings of Germany ought not to rest until they had reclaimed their rightful power over the Roman empire from the papacy . . . which meant the municipal government of Rome. One wonders how favorable to their cause imperial loyalists could have considered a conclusion that gave with one hand what it took with the other. This helps to explain how the conclusion of the *New Discourse* differed from the conclusion of *The Roman Empire of the Germans.* The *New Discourse* spoke loosely about the demise of the Roman empire without specifying the sense in which it had, and the sense in which it had not, vanished. The *New Discourse* also left open the possibility that prescription had put the papacy into legitimate control of the small bit of land that now paraded under the name of Roman empire. And the *New Discourse* did not consider that bit of land worth much attention. Apart from that, both texts are in complete agreement.

The disagreement between the *New Discourse* and *The Roman Empire of the Germans* thus turned solely on a different evaluation of the proper attitude to be taken toward that minimum empire that could still be said to exist. The *New Discourse* considered the shriveling of the Roman empire sufficiently advanced to pronounce it altogether gone, not as a matter of indisputable fact, because the remainders were still there, but as a reasonable attitude to take toward those remainders that it was "perhaps not wrong to affirm." The *New Discourse* also left it undecided whether the papacy's actual possession of Rome was legitimate. Perhaps prescription had transformed the papacy's control over the municipal government of Rome into legitimate rule. Perhaps it had not. *The Roman Empire of the Germans,* by contrast, dug in its heels. It insisted that the Roman empire, shriveled or not, did still exist. It insisted also that the papacy's control over Rome was decidedly illegitimate. And it concluded with such emphasis, such passion, such rhetorical vehemence that it well-nigh obliterated any memory of that other conclusion that Conring had drawn in the same work, only earlier, with less passion and more detachment: that the maximum Roman empire was long gone.

Both attitudes were reasonable. Both had advantages and both had disadvantages. The *New Discourse* was simpler and more forward-looking. Given the lack of proportion between Roman imperial claims to world domination and the actual extent of the empire to which those claims had been confined, it was reasonable to declare the empire defunct. Perhaps that did amount to a proleptic anticipation of the empire's demise. But hindsight proves that the anticipation was justified. Five or six generations were enough to turn it into fact. And given that the Roman empire was, if not gone, at least a goner, there was little point in unraveling the question whether the magic of prescription had transformed the papacy's possession of that goner from the usurpation that it was when it began in the eleventh century into legitimate rule half a millennium later. Why fuss about prescriptive rights to nothing much? Better to close the *New Discourse* without proposing an indelicately definite rejection of the papacy's rights to whatever little bits of empire were left.

It was just as reasonable, however, not to anticipate the future but to insist that the Roman empire, shriveled or not, did still exist. The empire might have been going, but it was not gone just yet—and in the presence of the dying, it is impolite to speak of death. It was similarly reasonable to insist that the magic of prescription had never allowed the papacy to transform its usurpation of control over Rome into legitimate rule. That did of course require Conring to explain why prescription should have been able to work its magic in favor of early medieval German kings but not of high medieval Hildebrandine popes. But such an explanation was not hard to find. He thought there was a difference. The original proprietors of the Roman empire had eventually ceased to contest the conquests of the Germans. In so doing, they had surrendered their rights and allowed prescription to take effect.[109] The German emperors, however, had never surrendered their rights and had never ceased to contest the legitimacy of papal rule.[110] The prescriptive clock did measure the growth of rights over time with equal fairness to early medieval Germans and the papacy. But in the case of the papacy it had never begun to tick.

In sum, the single apparently substantial difference between the original *Exercise* and *New Discourse,* on the one hand, and *The Roman Empire of the Germans,* on the other, does not deserve to be taken at face value. The case made by all three works is fundamentally the same. Whatever differences can be discerned turn out to be superficial, misleading, a matter of appearance and emphasis. The central teaching is identical.

We have a lovely bit of evidence to prove that, in spite of his protestations to the contrary, Conring actually thought so, too. Fortunately for our purposes, he said so in a place where it could be recorded, many years later, when the publication of the *New Discourse* lay far enough in the past that he no longer felt a pressing need to convince his audience that it was nothing but a "primitive, supposititious child." That place was lectures on the Holy

Roman Empire that were not published until Goebel included them in his edition of the *Opera*. In those lectures Conring stated flatly that the *Exercise* of 1641 could be considered a "compendium" of *The Roman Empire of the Germans* and even encouraged his students to rely on the *Exercise* if they had any trouble locating a copy of *The Roman Empire of the Germans*—without, of course, adding that the *New Discourse* contained precisely the same text.[111] We could not ask for better confirmation that the *Exercise on the Roman German Emperor*, the *New Discourse*, and *The Roman Empire of the Germans* reflected the same ideas: the very author who had once rejected the *Exercise on the Roman German Emperor* and the *New Discourse* in such uncompromising terms believed their resemblance to *The Roman Empire of the Germans* to be so close that the former could serve as substitutes for the latter.

What, then, did Conring really think? One could say this: he thought that in one (fundamental) sense the Roman empire was gone, while in another (restricted) sense it still continued to exist. He thought that the remainder of the Roman empire was not worth much attention. Confusion over the true relationship between Germany and the Roman empire had been the cause of much misery. In his opinion, the Roman empire occupied more space in the imagination of his contemporaries than it deserved. He sought to free them of their illusions by clarifying what the Roman empire had been once upon a time, what it was now, what it was not, and what it had never been. He hoped to persuade them that a bit of land in central Italy and memories of ancient glories were no good reason to throw Germany into war—much less a good foundation for realizing dreams of universal monarchy. He would much rather have had his fellow citizens forget about Rome and turn to the business at hand. That business was to make peace and rebuild Germany from the ravages of war. But he was not going to let his thoughts be turned into a weapon to be used against Germany. If anyone contested Germany's sovereign rights, he would insist on them with the same passion as his most determined enemies—even if the enemy turned out to be the pope and if the rights in question concerned that little bit of land in central Italy. Given sufficient provocation, he maintained Germany's rights over the last remaining vestiges of the Roman empire as vigorously as the most ardent defenders of universal monarchy.

Perhaps Conring himself put it best when, in his dedication to Duke August of Brunswick-Lüneburg, he explained why he had written *The Roman Empire of the Germans*:

> I believe I ought to come to the assistance of our people, so that they will not be deceived by the double meaning of that name "Roman empire" by which Germany is now constantly being called, and fall into worse doubts about the

sovereignty of their country. I also believe I ought to repel the insolence of those Roman popes who strive to wrest from the people of Germany not only possession of the city of Rome itself but also the right of possessing it. True enough, the misery of Germany today is such that we can barely defend ourselves at home. Germany is turning almost completely into a desert. Under these circumstances there is hardly much room for planning the recovery of losses in other places. Yet even so, it is worthwhile to reach for Germany's old rights, if only in the mind, lest gradually our present ills obliterate their memory completely. For who can tell? Perhaps a merciful divinity will end our present suffering before too long, and Germany will rise again to its former glory.[112]

What Conring Actually Said

The differences between the *New Discourse* and *The Roman Empire of the Germans* have thus turned out to consist of additions, clarifications, and differently placed emphases. But analysis must not stop here. If *The Roman Empire of the Germans* agreed with the *New Discourse*, why did Conring not say so himself? Why did he make our task more complicated than it had to be?

According to Conring's own account, in his preface to *The Roman Empire of the Germans,* there were four reasons that he rejected the *New Discourse:* it named him as the author; it carried an insolent title; it concealed the name and location of the printer; and it omitted the corollaries by which it could have been recognized as an academic exercise. Those grounds can be summed up in a single sentence: the *New Discourse* was flying under false colors. Conspicuously missing from the list is any statement to the effect that the *New Discourse* came to the wrong conclusion. Instead he labeled it "a primitive and supposititious child" (*crudus ac supposititius foetus*). That offers a memorable and, shall we say, pregnant image of the attitude Conring took toward the *New Discourse* and the grounds on which he rejected it. The attitude was that of an unwilling father; the grounds were those of illegitimacy.

He could hardly have done otherwise. He was in a bind. He knew that the contents of the *New Discourse* were identical with those of the *Exercise.* But though the *Exercise* was just as crude as the *New Discourse,* it was anything but supposititious. It was the product of a student whose publication he himself had formally approved. There was no doubt about the legitimacy of that child. His rejection of the *New Discourse* thus turns exclusively on questions of authority, responsibility, and property. It turns on meaning only in the narrow sense of the illocutionary act by which the printers of the *New Discourse* had invested it with a meaning that Conring had not intended. Conring was well within his rights to deny his responsibility for that. He had perhaps less right to deny responsibility for the words that von Hoym had printed in his *Exercise*. But he had no right at all to deny responsibility for the case that the *New Discourse* and the *Exercise on the Roman German Emperor* made. That case was what he thought himself.

That is the underlying reason why Goebel, Conring's editor, was right to state in such precisely chosen terms not that Conring disagreed with the conclusions of the *New Discourse* but that the "author" (*auctor*) did not acknowledge the *New Discourse* as his "own" (*suum*) piece of writing and that his heirs did not do so either.[113] Why mention heirs? Heirs cannot inherit meaning. But heirs do inherit property. And property was all that Conring had defended in rejecting the *New Discourse*. The reason he had likened it to a child was more than just metaphorical. The similarity was real. What he pronounced over the *New Discourse* was not an act of disagreement but one of disinheritance, a denial not of truth but of responsibility.

The differences between the *New Discourse* and *The Roman Empire of the Germans* were meant to confirm that denial of responsibility. Given that the *New Discourse* contained Conring's own views, he could not very well reclaim his rights by presenting different ideas. He had to present the same ideas and yet to sever his responsibility for the meaning they gained in the *New Discourse*. He accomplished that objective by wielding the same tool with which the printers of the *New Discourse* had purloined his authorship in the first place: by exploiting the distinction between locutionary content and illocutionary act. The printers of the *New Discourse* had used his locutions to perform an illocutionary act of which he was not the author. What better remedy than to reverse the procedure? So he produced a new and more substantial work, gave it an introduction that seemed to reject the *New Discourse* without qualification, added new material, explicated matters so far left implicit, and concluded that the Roman empire not only continued to exist but also deserved to be recovered by German kings. That conclusion was circumscribed by an extremely narrow definition of the term *Roman empire* and by new clarity about the inapplicability of prescription to the papacy's usurpation, precluding real contradictions between *The Roman Empire of the Germans* and the *New Discourse*. But Conring did not say so where his readers needed to be told. Whoever reads the conclusion of *The Roman Empire of the Germans* must be impressed by the passion with which Conring demanded that Germany's imperial rights over Rome be taken back from the papacy. Whoever compares it to the *New Discourse* has to be struck by the blithe disregard for Germany's imperial tradition with which those rights were there dismissed as unworthy of attention. The effect was to invest *The Roman Empire of the Germans* with an illocutionary act that seemed to take back what the *New Discourse* had asserted.

That strategy was well designed for Conring to reclaim his rights. But it did more than that. It placed authorship where it did not belong and refused it where it was appropriate. It drew a distinction between Conring's "own" thoughts and those of "another" that was no more legitimate than the identity between the two to which the printers of the *New Discourse* had pretended. It may have enabled him to dispel the suspicion that the *New Discourse* might actually contain his thoughts. It led his readers to imagine a distance between the *New Discourse* and *The Roman Empire of the Germans* that was unreal. He magnified that distance by silence on points that might have narrowed it and emphasis on points that served to make it greater. In short, though the *New Discourse* and *The Roman Empire of the Germans* make the same case, they are not alike at all. The former is a simpler and more honest piece of writing. The latter is more sophisticated, but also decidedly duplicitous.

Honesty and Dissimulation

What shall we make of this duplicity? The obvious first answer is that Conring was running scared. His studies had convinced him that the Roman empire was a thing of the past. He had been willing to state that conviction in a private course of lectures, even to make it the subject of one of his students' dissertations. But when the dissertation was published under his own name, his courage failed. Now it was no longer a question of debating the Holy Roman Empire with the children of lower Saxon noblemen. Now he would have to defend his views not in class, but in court, not before students, but face to face with the emperor whose rights he had denied. What to do? He could not deny von Hoym's dissertation. But he could carp on its imperfections, complain about the damage to his reputation, draw fine distinctions, veil his beliefs, publish a new book, and mislead his readers in order to escape responsibility for his own ideas.

This view is not implausible. A similar tendency to adjust his statements with, let us say, notable pliancy, a similar preference for nuance over clarity, and a failure to stand up for his convictions when called on to explain himself can be observed on other occasions. The oath he swore on the *Corpus Julium* in 1632, in spite of the misgivings he had expressed to Barlaeus in 1631, immediately comes to mind. His willingness to modify the printed text of his inaugural lecture of 1632 to suit the wishes of Calixt and Hornejus is equally to the point. The positions he took, and sometimes changed, on sensitive political issues in the 1650s and 1660s (the relationship between the empire and the duchy of Lorraine, the rights of the Palatinate versus those of Bavaria, the rights of Sweden and France) were suited to his patrons' wishes.[114] The evidence for lack of character may never be compelling, but it is far too voluminous to be dismissed as insignificant.

This was no secret to contemporaries. Among those who knew, we may count whoever paid for Conring's written expertise. Not, of course, that paying beneficiaries can be expected to have made their gratitude for his pliancy known. To publicize the agility with which Conring could lean in this or that direction without toppling from his scholarly foundations would have been self-defeating. Hence it is difficult to document whether or not his patrons thought his scholarship to be as sound as their interest led them to maintain. Conversely, his enemies would have been likely to proclaim that Conring's scholarship went to the highest bidder, because their interest led them to discredit his opinion. Until there is a well-documented biography, it will therefore be difficult to form a fair impression of what contemporaries thought of Conring's character.

One judgment is worth quoting because it comes from Samuel von Pufendorf. Remembering their conversations, Pufendorf said that "in most respects Conring agreed with me about the state of Germany and freely shared writings of his with me that part company with popular opinion. But even though he expressed himself frankly on any number of issues, he clearly kept a great deal to himself in order to avoid offending the powerful or provoking the anger of Catholics."[115] Pufendorf was an unusual case. He was a keen observer and had a mind of great originality that took beginnings made by men like Conring to entirely new lengths. Born in 1632, the same year as Locke and Spinoza, he belonged to a new generation. He did not have Conring's memories of war and was more accustomed to the peace for which Conring's generation still had to fight. He may have been more willing to engage in the public display of privately held conviction, and he may have overestimated Conring's reticence. But his observation rings completely true, which is surely why Goebel included it in his collection of testimonies to Conring's life and works.[116] It lends some credence to the image of a man who lacked the courage to publicize his judgment in the teeth of opposition. From there it is but one short step to the man whose judgment was for sale.

But plausible is not the same as true. Conring is best known for writings that overturned conventional wisdom in widely separated fields of knowledge. These were not the works of a prevaricator who adjusted his ideas in whichever direction the winds of fortune happened to be blowing. They sprang from a powerful mind that knew how to build a case on principles and how to make it withstand critique. They testify to a combination of clarity, knowledge, and judgment that put great adversaries on the defensive. Repeatedly he challenged opponents as powerful as the archbishop of

Cologne and the emperor on the stage of public debate. Repeatedly he confronted Catholic opposition. And repeatedly he engaged in protracted polemics to defend his point of view against public attack. Prudent he may have been. But timid he was not.

Besides, more was at stake than Conring's personal well-being. At stake was the question how to bring one of the most destructive wars in European history to a conclusion and lay foundations for a lasting peace. That required more than a proper understanding of Germany's condition. It required the will and the ability to give that understanding public effect. Radical statements about the disappearance of the Roman empire, however true, were little help in that endeavor. They were more likely to poison still further an atmosphere already poisoned than to promote the peace. It was more prudent to take the conservative position that the kings of Germany retained their rights to the Roman empire and mollify Protestants by sharpening attacks on the papacy.

The price that Bogislaus Philipp of Chemnitz paid for publishing his famous *Dissertation on Reason of State in Our Roman-German Empire* under the pseudonym of Hippolithus a Lapide, only two years before the *New Discourse* appeared in print, may well have served as a salutary lesson.[117] Chemnitz minced no words. But though historians enjoy the candor of his assault on the Holy Roman Empire and the house of Habsburg, contemporaries regarded it as wanton recklessness. It earned him the hatred of his enemies, cost him the respect of his friends, and forced him into permanent exile from Germany. Chemnitz came to regret the bluntness with which he had indulged himself. And word of his regret was transmitted to posterity by none other than our Hermann Conring.[118]

In short, there were good reasons for Conring to distance himself from the ideas expressed in the *New Discourse,* especially if they were really his ideas. Those reasons had nothing to do with truth. But neither did they consist of lies or purely personal advantage. They arose from considerations of public interest and the part that Conring hoped to play in making peace. His reputation was more than just a boost to his vanity. It was a tool that gave effect to his ideas. It increased their reach and influence. It was not lightly to be put at risk with friend and foe for the brief satisfaction of having spoken his mind without reservation. There was a principle at stake. The principle consisted of "Plato's conviction that the laws of the commonwealth ought not to be subjected to public scrutiny unless they can be examined without danger to the public peace of civil society [publica civilis societatis tranquillitas]."[119] That is how Conring put it when he described his attitude toward dissertations.

We seem to be confronted with two mutually incompatible assessments. One sees Conring as an opportunist, the other as a man of principle. He was cynical or misanthropic in one view, generous or philanthropic in the other. They draw on the same evidence. They even overlap to some degree. Misanthropes can, after all, admit that considerations of principle and the public good may have played a certain part in shaping Conring's conduct. And philanthropes can freely grant that Conring's private interest may have been on his mind as well when he declared his love for the common good. But the issue turns on the relative importance of interest and principle. On that score the cynical and generous interpretations are implacably opposed. For one it is his selfishness that tips the scales, and for the other his sincerity. How shall we judge?

Historians have on the whole preferred the misanthropic view. That is perhaps their calling. Their confidence was greatest in the late nineteenth and early twentieth centuries. Assured by faith in national sovereignty, they took Conring's willingness to modify his stance as evidence for flaws of character. But as national sovereignty itself became a matter of some doubt, their confidence gave way to hesitation. Gone are the days when Conring could be upbraided for lack of loyalty to the nation without raising questions about the historian's own integrity. Historians are nowadays more likely to explain that loyalty to the nation ought not to be expected from a late humanist professor at one of the territorial universities of the Holy Roman Empire. But the rejection of nationalist criteria of judgment can hardly substitute for an answer to the underlying question. That Conring sometimes bent the truth and profited from doing so seems true beyond a reasonable doubt. But was he justified? That question is entirely alive.

It may be thought that historians can leave moral judgment to one side and concentrate on fact. Not so. Did Conring lie or did he tell the truth? Did he defend himself from danger, or did he work for the common good? Those *are* questions of fact. Our description of the relationship between the *New Discourse* and *The Roman Empire of the Germans,* our interpretation of Conring's thought, our understanding of *The Roman Empire of the Germans*—in short, our assessment of Conring's place in history and thus our assessment of that history itself are all impossible without an answer to the question of just what it was that he was doing when he rebutted the *New Discourse:* bending the truth for personal advantage or serving the common good? To skirt the question is not to practice abstention from unfounded moral speculation. It rather is to abdicate historical responsibility and give free rein to hidden judgments made in passing without attention to the grounds on which they might or might not be justified. Arnaldo Momigliano put it concisely:

"What history-writing without moral judgments would be is difficult for me to envisage, because I have not yet seen it."[120]

No hope is therefore to be placed on acknowledging the merits of the cynical and generous interpretations and leaving it at that. They are exclusive of each other. There is no middle of the road. To declare that Conring was motivated by self-interest and also by the public good without defining where the two part company is not a palatable interpretation. It is an indigestible concoction that will, sooner or later, upset even omnivorous interpretive metabolisms. Self-interest and the common good need to be served on separate platters if they are to be served at all.

Self-Doubt and Self-Denial

Let us step back and take a larger view. What were the basic factors that Conring needed to consider in order to make up his mind? First and foremost there was the empire itself. The Holy Roman Empire may have seemed dead and gone to the author of the *Exercise on the Roman German Emperor.* It certainly seemed gone to generations of nineteenth- and twentieth-century historians. But it did not seem gone to the author of *The Roman Empire of the Germans,* and his judgment has in recent decades been corroborated by a shift in scholarship. The flippant dismissal of the Holy Roman Empire as neither holy, nor Roman, nor an empire, so popular ever since Voltaire gave it currency, has yielded to new respect for a body politic that managed to secure a good measure of protection to smaller imperial estates, helped to keep a decent peace in Europe from the Peace of Westphalia to the Napoleonic Wars, and allowed the Enlightenment to flourish in the Germanies. Contrary to lingering fragments of once common wisdom, the Holy Roman Empire enjoyed real political vitality.[121]

That posed a problem for Conring's politics. He was convinced that the empire was one of the major causes of the war that had well-nigh destroyed Germany. And he desired peace. As a Protestant he abhorred Catholic attempts to restore papal supremacy. As the subject of a German territorial prince, he sought to defend his ruler's rights against imperial encroachments. As a historian he contested the identification of Habsburg rulers with Roman emperors whom Roman law had once endowed with the right to rule the world. And as a student of politics, he rejected universal monarchy. From his perspective the empire was a pernicious anachronism, destructive to the common good. And yet there were the Habsburgs imposing that anachronism with undeniable effect. No matter how certain he was of being right, there was the empire's ability to muster forces out of proportion to its supposed unreality. No matter how conclusive Conring's analysis, it did not capture the true condition of his age. There was a real disjunction between the truth of his analysis and daily experience.

That made the question of the Holy Roman Empire both complicated and exciting. The excitement is palpable in his writings. It is equally palpable in the profusion of books on the public law of Germany that began to pour from German presses at the beginning of the seventeenth century.[122] Conring may have been exceptional in the clarity with which he anticipated the empire's demise. But he was not at all alone in his preoccupation with its condition. No one could tell exactly how to make sense of contemporary experience. Everyone was familiar with the old verities about the four world monarchies and the end of the world. You learned those things in school. But no one knew whether they were true. The question was up for grabs. The answers were conflicting. Some liked the old verities. Some hated them. Some were convinced they had discovered a way out of the uncertainty. But in the middle of a war and in the absence of consensus about the empire's rights and nature, people could not tell precisely where their interest lay. Whatever answer was proposed had consequences, and it was impossible to predict whom those effects would harm or benefit. Cognitive dissonance ruled the day. Politics was in the grip of deep confusion.

A similar confusion prevailed in matters of religion. With hindsight, the distinction between Protestants and Catholics is as clear as the empire's demise. But hindsight obscures the difficulties faced at the time. Of course, some points of difference were fairly obvious. Catholics accepted submission to the papacy, the decrees of the council of Trent, the claims of Habsburg rulers, and so on. Protestants did not. But the real question was, Who counted as Catholic and who as Protestant? What did it mean to be one or the other? How could you tell about your neighbors, how could your neighbors tell about you? Was it possible to choose? Were you somehow assigned to one camp or the other by forces out of your control?

Duke Maximilian of Bavaria was just as Catholic as the emperor. But he can hardly be said to have supported the emperor without considering his own interest. Cardinals Richelieu and Mazarin were Catholic, and yet they presided over French attacks on Catholic imperial soil. The prince electors of Saxony preceded all other Protestant estates in dignity and power. Their Universities of Wittenberg and Leipzig stood as true bulwarks of orthodox Lutheranism. And yet time and again they sided with a Catholic emperor against their Lutheran peers—not to mention the Calvinist Palatinate. Sweden was a state of impeccably Lutheran credentials. And yet it battled Protestant German princes without remorse. Conversions from one confession to another, often more than one in a person's life, were common. They form one of the guiding themes in Grimmelshausen's *Simplicius Simplicissimus,* perhaps the greatest piece of German literature between the high Middle Ages and the Enlightenment.[123] Should they be taken as evidence for lack of faith? They rather demonstrate how difficult faith was to keep. Language itself, Thucydides might have exclaimed, had changed its meaning.

The depth of this confusion about the most fundamental questions of religious and political identity is the most important factor to keep in mind for grasping Conring's meaning. Another consists of his attachment to the university. The university afforded shelter from the confusion destroying the "public peace of civil society." The university was a society of its own—not a civil society, much less a political one, but nonetheless a corporate body, chartered by a prince, recognized in law, with its own rules of conduct, its own government, its own jurisdiction, and its own people. The university united a body of men (no women for some time to come) in the knowledge that they enjoyed the right, indeed, had the obligation to examine questions like that of the Holy Roman Empire to the best of their ability. Of course that right was limited. Professors depended for their income on their prince; they were bound by the oath they had to swear on the confession of their state; they were subject to statutes governing their conduct, their courses, and the very books they were allowed to assign. They were expected to adhere to methods of lecture and disputation, of reading and analysis, of philology and interpretation—all in Latin—that set university men apart from ordinary people, that constituted the dominant model of rationality, and that determined what counted as evidence, what as fact, and what could be considered proof. The concept of academic freedom, *libertas philosophandi,* was not unknown. But its extent was sharply circumscribed.

Yet it was real. It offered shelter, if not from the confusion reigning overall, at least from its debilitating consequences. The university was a place where questions could be explored in a peace and quiet that, though never more than relative, contrasted with the war beyond. There young and old were safe to examine questions about the future of the commonwealth. University printers published a flood of answers, some more successful, some less, but all of them with the potential to steer public debate in new directions, and many of the answers were in the shape of dissertations just like the *Exercise on the Roman German Emperor.* The university gave you a place where you could think and say what needed to be said.

We have an interesting complaint from Catholic delegates to the imperial diet of Regensburg in 1641 about the freedom with which university dissertations examined questions of great public sensitivity—interesting in part because 1641 happens to be the year in which Conring published the *Exercise on the Roman German Emperor*.[124] But the very unhappiness voiced by the delegates at Regensburg confirms the freedom that the university secured to students and faculty to deal with important issues and the attention with which political estates registered what was written there and sold in stores.

For all of these reasons, Conring cherished the university. To him, the university represented as much of the peace and freedom he had once found in the Netherlands as he was ever going to enjoy in Germany. He needed it.[125] The university, of course, was not the only place where he could have worked for the common good, and writing on matters of politics, history, and law was not the only road he could have chosen. There were other possibilities. He himself had once chosen one of them. For it seems fair to say that medicine served Conring as an effective way of escaping from the confusion over the common good under which Germans labored in the seventeenth century. Medicine did not make peace. But neither did it make war. The personal, bodily, private health that it did bring about made for a cleaner conscience than was possible in the realm of public and religious affairs. So much the more momentous was Conring's decision in 1631 to return to Germany and live the life of a professor. That choice was existential. From that time forward, his ability to meet his responsibility depended on the university. The university gave him the freedom to think constructively about the common good and protection from the hostility his thoughts were certain to provoke. But both that freedom and that protection depended on the boundary by which the university was separated from the world outside, a boundary physical, legal, and intellectual all at once.

That boundary was broken by the printers of the *New Discourse*. In taking one of Conring's students' dissertations and publishing it under his name, they did not merely call unwanted attention to his ideas. They threatened his ability to continue along the path on which he had determined to conduct his life. They risked the freedom on which he depended for his life and the reputation that was his stock in trade. They threatened his existence. In that sense the deception he practiced in *The Roman Empire of the Germans* was meant to save his life.

One other fundamental point to be considered consists of Conring's loyalty to Luther's faith—the faith for which his ancestors had suffered exile and because of which Germany was in the midst of war. Perhaps the most instructive way to plumb the meaning of Conring's action is to contrast it with what Luther did in 1517. Like Conring in 1642, Luther in 1517 was a professor in his midthirties at a northern German university of relatively recent vintage. Like Conring, he had struggled in relative obscurity with questions fundamental but abstract. Like Conring, he chose an academic disputation on a set of printed theses—ninety-five theses on indulgences—to come forth with his ideas. And like Conring, he soon discovered that his theses escaped from his control.

The differences, of course, are also telling. Luther was a monk and theologian, Conring a layman and professor of medicine. Luther disputed on indulgences in his own name; Conring presided over a disputation on the empire by one of his students. Luther's theses sparked events of world-historical importance; by comparison the *Exercise on the Roman German Emperor* drew barely a flicker of attention. But for the sake of understanding Conring's reaction to the publication of the *New Discourse,* no difference matters more than this: when Luther discovered that his theses had escaped from his control, he did not retreat. The outcry provoked by his ideas spurred him to sharpen his ideas still further. His opponents gave him many an opportunity to soften his views, recant his most provocative positions, accept a compromise. Conring might well have seen such opportunities as golden bridges on the road to peace. Not Luther. Luther did not believe himself to be at liberty where it concerned the truth. As he once put it in the famous letter to Pope Leo X that accompanied his tract *The Freedom of a Christian,* "There is no dispute about morals between me and anyone else, only about the word of truth."[126] He was perfectly willing to compromise, but only on matters that permitted compromise. The truth was no such matter. Conscience compelled him to stand by the truth. Conscience gave him the courage to say his final "no" at that memorable meeting in Worms in 1521. Face to face with the emperor, confronted with the overwhelming authority of the Holy Roman Empire's assembled rulers, threatened with exclusion from the company of the living and the dead, Luther refused to change his stand and publicly stood by ideas that were only too likely to earn him death.

That conduct, far more than his theology (we may doubt that it was understood by more than a few contemporaries), fueled a surge of popular enthusiasm for his cause and person that neither pope nor emperor knew how to contain. A public display of personal conviction in the face of death can have explosive power. It unveils and thereby destroys the symbolic order that mediates the normal operation of vested interests. It draws its power from the clarity with which it proves in a single act, even a single word, that force can be resisted. It promises liberation from the conventions channeling our conduct into narrow compartments safely divided from each other, restricting our mental, moral, and even our physical shapes to limits that we were taught not to cross by parents, teachers, and the pain that follows from transgressing them. Breaking such boundaries holds the promise of a life lived freely on grounds of conviction, instead of one burdened by compromise. That promise of freedom and self-determination, that revelation of his self to the world, that ruthless honesty gave Luther credibility. Theology mattered to those who wanted reasons. Without theology Luther himself could surely not have acted as he did. In that sense theology is crucial to understanding the history of the Reformation. But Luther's action spoke more loudly than his words. It announced a change in the most basic rules of order. Conscience had stood up to the emperor, and the emperor had failed to silence it. Henceforth conscience was never again to disappear from the stage of politics. Conscience was there for good. The question was merely how large a part of the stage it would subject to its control.

That question was going to unsettle Europe for close to two centuries. Luther himself may have believed that all true Christians would rally round the truth his conscience had compelled him to put forth. He may have expected peace. More likely he expected a gathering of friends and enemies of Christ into two camps and a cataclysmic battle between the forces of good and evil that would end only with the end of the world itself.[127] What he did not expect was what actually happened: not the battle between good and evil and the end of the world, but an endless frittering away of the world amid a numbing proliferation of conflicts between an unimaginable number of combatants, none of whom were confident of their alliance with anybody else and few of whom were confident of themselves. Conscience had entered politics. But far from uniting the good to the fight the evil, it merely divided every party against itself. In the end no image seemed more appropriate than a state of nature that was a state of war.

How to make peace in wars that conscience had unleashed? That was the question Luther's insistence on the truth bequeathed to posterity. When Conring began to teach at the University of Helmstedt, the question was unanswered. Peace had not yet been made in Europe, and nowhere less so than in Germany. In Germany the understanding that was signed in Augsburg in 1555 had seemed to offer a solution. All parties had forsworn the use of violence in questions of religion. That was a great accomplishment. But it was not enough to bring about peace. Beneath the surface the conflict between conscience and power, truth and tradition, morality and custom remained entirely unresolved. Conflict had merely been delayed at the cost of returning with much greater fury half a century later.

Eventually peace was going to be built on the distinction between public and private affairs. Conscience had fought with pope and emperor for control of the world. Both had claimed universal rights. When both realized that victory was out of reach, they agreed to divide the spoils. And in so doing they transformed themselves into the shape in which we have known them ever since: a conscience that makes no claims on politics and a politics that makes no claims on conscience.[128] Conscience was recognized, but only as a private voice that had no right to public force, except indirectly, through peaceful debate. Augsburg's abstention from settling questions of religion by force was thus kept intact. But it was also made legitimate by a new distinction between politics and religion that had lain beyond the imagination of the sixteenth century. Sovereigns reciprocated by surrendering the rights claimed by their universal predecessors to govern the consciences of their subjects. Religious faith was abandoned as a foundation of the commonwealth. Its place was taken by a faith in the distinction between public and private matters that helped to restore obedience to law. Sovereigns regained the right to keep the peace by exercising force, but only in a sphere defined as free from the imperatives with which conscience confronted them. By means of the distinction between private and public affairs, church and state, morality and positive law, Europe thus managed to build the institutions that brought back peace and then enabled it to extend its reach across the globe—much as by means of the distinction between spiritual office and temporal fief, pope and emperor had managed at an earlier time in European history to divide the world between themselves and put an end to the Investiture Controversy, that high medieval analog to the early modern wars of religion.[129]

In Conring's day, however, none of that was clear. There was as yet no way to distinguish the voice of conscience from the voice that called for public peace. No one could have foreseen that conscience would be persuaded to retreat into a separate, private chamber. The only thing that was certain was that conscience meant war. The age was fundamentally confused by forces that Luther's clarity had set in motion. And it was this confusion that Conring had to master when the *Exercise on the Roman German Emperor* escaped from his control. We may be sure that he was well aware of what conscience asked of him. The heir of two generations of Lutheran ministers, he knew as much about the word, the faith, and the truth as anyone. In this regard he stood in direct continuity to Luther. Beneath the restraint of his academic prose, one senses the yearning for an opportunity to prove himself as Luther had proved himself in Worms. But one can also feel his deep conviction that such an opportunity would never come. Perhaps the world has only a limited supply of energy for what Luther did. Luther used up a century's worth of the clarity that was required to set the example. Perhaps on some level Conring resented the limits that Luther's exercise of freedom had set to his own. For unlike Luther, Conring had more than a century's worth of experience to prove that conscience in politics means war. He knew first-hand. He had repeatedly been forced to change his life because of religious war. He tried to avoid the hardest choices by staying in the Netherlands. When that proved impossible, he decided to devote his life to establishing some reasonable order among the claims that tore his world apart. He hoped to promote the peace by showing where conscience ended and where politics began, where tradition still held fast and where sovereignty was free to rule. If conscience had bound Luther to a clear path of action, conscience bound Conring to self-doubt and self-denial.

We have an instructive statement from early in Conring's career. It comes from his inaugural address, consists of words spoken directly to his audience, and reveals a combination of fear, respect, courage, honesty, despair, and dissimulation that is as revealing in its brevity as it is typical of the age: "Although there is no way for me not to offend you at all, I decided that I would offend you least if I said only what each of you has hitherto been used to approve and applaud, in private and in public, without sectarian prejudice."[130] The Latin could be translated differently. Conring had *peccare* (to sin) in the place of "offend." He had *sine amore, sine odio* (without love, without hate) in the place of "without sectarian prejudice." But "sin," "love," and "hate" no longer have the meanings that made them suitable to Conring's purpose. They have become so personal and private that they can nowadays hardly be used without concealing the impersonal, objective, and public nature of Conring's point. The very difficulty of translating Conring's language into our own testifies to the degree to which a boundary has come down between private and public matters excluding things like "sin," "love," and "hate" from the public arena in which Conring confronted them.

The larger point is Conring's certainty that he could not say anything at all without giving offense. That was the lesson drawn from a century of religious dispute. Gone was the faith that conscience could be relied upon for peace. Whether he chose to speak for tradition (and thus restrained the truth) or for the truth (and thus against tradition), he would offend. He knew he would offend. And he spoke anyway. But he did not know why he should. A hundred years of war had sapped the conviction that allowed Luther to offend. What was there left to say? Only what Conring knew his audience to have maintained in both spheres, private as well as public. The distinction between private and public was central to his dilemma. But only insofar as it permitted him to say what was beyond dispute in either sphere.

Those few words speak volumes about the distance, not merely temporal, but moral, religious, and political all in one, that separates Conring from Luther. Conring chose not to say what was merely politic. To that degree he saved the command of conscience to tell the truth. But neither did he choose to say simply what was true. He limited himself to that smallest common denominator that satisfied private and public needs at once, and he excluded everything else from expression—and this in full awareness that even the smallest common denominator would give offense.

It is tempting to call the result baroque. Conring deliberately chose confusion. Neither the truth would do, nor mere convention. They had to be subjected to some strange mental alchemy producing speech from which the inner truth was gone in order to preserve the peace, and from which convention was gone as well in order to preserve honesty. That alchemy defined *The Roman Empire of the Germans*. It reveals a predicament directly the reverse of Luther's. Luther had risked his life for the sake of conscience. Conring risked conscience for the sake of life. Luther was compelled by conscience to enter confrontation. Conring compelled his conscience to avoid confrontation. Luther played fast and loose with peace. Conring played fast and loose with honesty—or rather, played with it slowly and with deliberation. Where Luther moved with every step more rapidly into confrontation, never hesitating for more than a moment to open yet another door on views that had hitherto been forbidden, Conring closed door after door, retreated again and again, deliberately, cautiously, dissimulating at every opportunity, always covering his tracks, always prepared to feint. Where Luther revealed himself in table talk that challenged decorum as a point of principle, Conring veiled himself in decorum of such opacity as to obscure his inner life from us and, not at all unlikely, from himself.

This of course does not settle the question of justification. Much less does it determine whatever motives may have impelled Conring to act or not to act. Both of the obvious interpretations advanced above still retain more or less equal weight. Misanthropes still may suspect Conring of selfishness. And philanthropes may still defend his motives from assault. But the point is that Conring was able to be neither selfish nor public-spirited without equivocation. Not because of any failing peculiar to his person, much less because of any outstanding virtue, but because the age afflicted everyone with the same failing. Only fools and favorites of the gods were exempt. The boundaries between self and other, mine and thine, individual and community, were gone. There was no self other than a long succession of different masks to be tried out upon the stage of life as needed for the occasion. There was no common good other than one contested in its very possibility by religious war. Language itself had lost its capacity to communicate understanding. Only after the return of peace would it again seem possible to give meaningful answers to the question "selfish or not?"

And that was going to take time. The Peace of Westphalia was signed in 1648. But peace first needed to be examined, tested, and proved lasting before conscience, chastened by war and civilized to keep to private matters, could be allowed to reemerge into the bright light of a new "public sphere" in which debates could be carried out without instantly stirring fears that order would collapse.[131] Sovereigns first needed to prove to themselves and to their critics that they were able to endure. Pufendorf, a generation younger than Conring, was further along the road to self-confidence. But it took generations for the fruits of peace to mature. Peace was difficult to envision and impossible to realize when Conring wrote *The Roman Empire of the Germans*.

An Elementary Uncertainty

Confusion about the empire, confusion about religious truth, attachment to the university, conditions changed since Luther's time by war—these are only a few of many factors that went into Conring's thought. But we need not consider more. For at this point the whole interpretive scaffolding that we set up before has fallen down. There remains only one conclusion that we can state with real conviction: what Conring really thought about the Holy Roman Empire is utterly impossible to say, not because anything is wrong with our method or because he hid what he thought too successfully for us to reach our goal, but because the goal itself is a chimera. Conring's thought was real enough. But it was also fundamentally uncertain, shifting, indefinable, not because he had failed to make up his mind, but on the contrary because he had tried to make up his mind to the best of his superlative ability, and in full knowledge of the demand for clarity that had been raised by Luther. Conring was a man who thought. That much is true. He thought hard and deep. But he lacked the good fortune that allows some of the people some of the time to fix the question in their minds and formulate fixed answers. His mind did not stand still. The man and his ideas refuse to be defined. What Conring really thought includes an irreducible element of doubt. That doubt is basic to humanity, and it ought to be basic to intellectual history as well. Perhaps the very notion of "real thought" is an oxymoron.[132]

Conring himself was thoroughly aware of this. He knew better than his interpreters how deeply uncertain, shifting, pliant his views were. What else, if not that knowledge, gave him the energy to set out to find firm land somewhere amid the swirling ocean of a daily changing world? "Opinion," he once wrote, "is a disease both sacred and accursed. And yet it rules this world like nothing else."[133] Such views are not untypical. What was untypical was only the clarity with which Conring grasped the uncertainty of his condition, the courage with which he confronted the demons of untruth, and the stoicism with which he resigned himself to an unending struggle. His method was different from Descartes's; his inspiration was the same.

That helps to explain the sadness pervading Conring's life. The limitations he imposed on himself for the sake of reestablishing a clear relationship between the self and the common good came at a considerable human price. His motto speaks of a dejection woven into the fabric of the age: "Quantum est in rebus inane!"—How meaningless the world![134] His portrait hints at his temperament. It speaks of self-discipline in the face of emptiness. It speaks of sacrifices made without knowing their worth. It shows the face of a man who could never be sure of his own motives because they were never quite his own, a man experienced in the art of presenting a mask to the world that hid not guilt, but doubt. If Luther was at one time able to bear the weight of the world's oppression on the strength of a solitary conscience because his conscience left him no other choice, Conring bore the same weight sadly and willingly, knowing full well that every choice he made could have been altered or avoided. Resisting his own moral impulse for the sake of peace cost him the certainty of moral conviction. It made him pay for the common good in the coin of his own moral integrity.

That explains why men like Luther are much more popular objects of historians' attention (favorable or unfavorable) than men like Hermann Conring. Breaking the shackles of convention is more appealing or more frightening, but in any case more exciting, than putting on new steely ones, even if they are put on voluntarily and for the sake of peace. It is also much easier to understand. Entire libraries have been written about Luther, the Reformation, and the Enlightenment. Historians prefer to apply their skills to periods when the element of duplicity that came to be ingrained in the modern world had not yet shown itself (because the distinction between public and private had not yet been drawn) or was already so fully internalized as to have become invisible again (because the distinction between public and private had become a given). The passage in between has baffled them and made them avert their eyes as if, somehow, the modern world originated in a great leap from the Reformation to the Enlightenment, from faith to reason, without touching, or being touched by, events in between. That aversion is an inverted form of tribute to the threat that Conring had to face and that his person still poses to modern self-confidence.

Conring matters, not as an individual but as a type, not as a thinker to whose influence later developments may be traced but as a clue, a symbol, a man whose thoughts and actions throw light on the process by which Germany and Europe were led from the Reformation to the Enlightenment. He helps us to understand how much that process differs from progress. Progress there surely was, and there was more to come. But it came only because people like Conring consciously suppressed themselves in acts of self-immolation. Their suppression of themselves has long since been forgotten. It cannot be unearthed without unease. And yet it needs to be examined because it laid the foundation for the modern world.

But it seems ill-advised to search for more clarity about Conring's intention. Such searches may deflect unwanted attention from doubts about the legitimacy of the orders on which they are carried out. But they will not succeed in grasping the meaning of Conring's duplicity. We would do better to admire the extent to which Conring managed to tell the truth, avoiding both flat-out self-contradiction and flat-out lies. He reconciled the views he held as an academic protected by the university with those he held as a citizen of the German state that he hoped to steer to peace. He held both in the balance. The balance was precarious. But it was not dishonest, except in the sense in which all children of Adam are. It was the price without which the separation of private from public matters, of conscience from politics, could not have been completed. It furnished the foundation on which freedom of conscience could be granted by every sovereign state without having to fear religious war. If freedom of conscience is fundamental to modern politics, this has come about only because men like Conring found ways of teaching conscience how to absent itself from politics.

Contrary to appearances, *The Roman Empire of the Germans* thus was not clearer than the *Exercise on the Roman German Emperor* or the *New Discourse*. It looked clearer because of its improved logical instrumentarium. In reality it was more confused. It was more confused because it was written in greater awareness of political reality. Greater clarity was possible inside the university. The university, its methods, its texts, and its corporate identity endowed professors with the authority they needed to be clear. Later on—much later on—the same kind of authority was going to be claimed by every citizen. And sovereign states would furnish such authority to citizens by means of a public education that extended the mastery of texts from a small Latinate elite to every adult speaker of the vernacular—but only because they could trust their citizens to be predisposed, by customs of long standing, to practice the sacrifice that Conring learned how to practice on himself without the help of custom.

The Aftermath

If Conring thought that once *The Roman Empire of the Germans* had appeared in print, he would no longer have to worry about the *New Discourse,* he was disappointed. In 1655 an anonymous "society" of printers in Embrun republished the *New Discourse* under his name in yet another pirated edition as part of a volume entitled *De imperii Germanici republica acroamata sex historico-politica* or *Six Historico-Political Lessons on the Commonwealth of the German Empire.*[135] The *Six Historico-Political Lessons* was a compilation of every dissertation written under Conring's supervision about the constitution of the German empire since 1641. The dissertations dealt with all of the imperial estates as a whole, with each of them individually (the prince electors, the bishops, the secular princes, and the cities), and with the courts of justice.[136] The *Six Historico-Political Lessons* thus constituted something like a compendium on the constitution of the Holy Roman Empire.

The *New Discourse* occupied a special place in that compendium. It was not counted as one of the six lessons but singled out on the title page and placed as a separate treatise at the end of the collection.[137] It was also endowed with new and improved titles: *Tractatus de imperatore Romano Germanico* or *Treatise on the Roman German Emperor* on the title page and *De imperatore Romano Germanico discursus historico-politicus* or *Historico-Political Discourse on the Roman German Emperor* in the body of the text. That helps to confirm the importance the printers attributed to this particular dissertation. More important, the printers evidently knew that in response to the publication of the *New Discourse,* Conring had written a much larger work in which his ideas had been more systematically stated: *The Roman Empire of the Germans* of 1644. They did not reprint *The Roman Empire of the Germans* as a whole, presumably because its length would have upset the balance of their volume. Perhaps they preferred the more candid argumentation of the *New Discourse.* But they did borrow four (long) chapters from *The Roman Empire of the Germans* and substituted them for eighteen (much shorter) chapters of the *New Discourse* that occupied roughly the same place in the development of the argument. The beginning and the end were lifted from the *New Discourse.* But a substantial section in the middle was copied from *The Roman Empire of the Germans.*[138] The *Historico-Political Discourse on the Roman German Emperor* of 1655 thus is an entirely unreliable hybrid corresponding to no single work ever written by Conring or one of his students.

We do not know why the printers chose to publish the *New Discourse* in yet another unauthorized version, but the reasons are easy to imagine. Compared to the *New Discourse, The Roman Empire of the Germans* of 1644 lacked punch. To be sure, it advertised itself as a better statement of Conring's views. That was a good reason for students of the German constitution to give it their preference. But for most readers, it may have been difficult to see how it improved on the *New Discourse*. The *New Discourse* had the same basic structure—so much so that the printers of Embrun saw no difficulty in fitting some of the chapters of *The Roman Empire of the Germans* into the text without disturbing the flow of the argument—used the same basic methods to prove its points, and finished more quickly without allowing itself to be encumbered by scholarly qualifications and detailed annotations. More to the point, it came to a more candid and provocative conclusion.

Those, one suspects, were the considerations that made it seem worthwhile to publish a collection of Conring's dissertations at a time when the *New Discourse* must have gone out of print. It also agrees with what we know from Conring himself. According to information he had in 1674, the hybrid *Historico-Political Discourse* of 1655 had spread to France, Italy, Spain, and England.[139] Given that French, Italian, Spanish, and English readers may be presumed to have been less interested in the details of Conring's thinking than in the clear-cut theses put forth by the *New Discourse,* it would naturally have received the most attention where it had been published to begin with, namely, abroad. If Conring succeeded in limiting the distribution of the *New Discourse* at all, it was limited only in Germany.

In the end Conring himself was forced to recognize that the *New Discourse* had taken on a life of its own and that the same was true of the other dissertations on the constitution of the Roman empire that had been defended by his students. Even while continuing to insist that it was wrong to regard these dissertations as his own works, strictly speaking, he acknowledged that the public relied on them for effective introductions to the constitutional structure of the Holy Roman Empire. There were good reasons that they had come to be regarded as if they were written by him and had acquired a reputation for containing information not to be found elsewhere. Under those circumstances it was neither right nor possible for him to continue to refuse to take a hand in their circulation, if only in order to prevent further misrepresentations.

> Because these exercises are not entirely my work, I have let them go their own merry way so far, content to see them scatter singly here and there, not caring one way or another, busy enough with writings that were properly my own. Now, however, several reasons have forced me to change my mind. For I have noticed that many eminent scholars in all sorts of places (not only in Germany but elsewhere, too) attribute all of these dissertations without any distinction to myself

alone, even in print. . . . The generous judgment and the praise of outstanding men, moreover, have convinced the general public that these exercises contain much useful information that no one else has put together and that cannot be found in any other place. Which is the reason why they are in as much demand as they are difficult to obtain.

These and other considerations have led me to devote myself to them once more, though I have hardly time to spare. It simply did not seem right to abandon all affection for works of which at least the greatest part was in reality my doing, so much the less since common, albeit erroneous, consent attributed them long ago to me alone. As no small injury has already been done both to the public good and to me personally by pirated editions and ill-judged changes in the text, I considered it both my duty and necessary to protect my reputation that I at least prevent any further injury—for there is no way to undo what has been done.[140]

That was the reasoning that prompted Conring to set the record straight. He collected all of the dissertations on the constitution of the Holy Roman Empire that he had supervised, arranged them in chronological order, and published them in a single volume entitled *Exercitationes academicae de republica imperii Germanici* or *Academic Exercises on the Republic of the German Empire* in 1674. Seven, including the *New Discourse,* had been available to the editors of the *Six Historico-Political Lessons* in 1655. In the 1660s Conring had supervised three more: two about the imperial diet in 1666, and one about the "officials" of the empire, which is to say the prince electors, in 1669.[141] These were now added to the group that was included in the *Six Historico-Political Lessons,* making a total of ten.

At first Conring had merely planned to reprint the dissertations as they were. But as he began rereading them, he realized that he would have to make some changes.[142] For the most part he limited himself to revising imprecise formulations, adding cautionary clauses, and correcting outright errors. He definitely did not consider it worth his effort to check the accuracy of each detail. The *Academic Exercises* is full of misprinted dates and garbled references copied directly from the originals. But although Conring's changes were limited in scope, some touched on points of substance, and one dissertation was thoroughly overhauled. It dealt with the place of the bishops in the constitution of the empire, a subject Conring considered especially important and poorly understood.[143] Finally, he wrote a preface to explain exactly how these dissertations had come into existence and how closely they represented his own views.[144]

The result was a compendium similar in conception to the unauthorized

Six Historico-Political Lessons of 1655 but different in four ways: it was authorized by Conring himself, it included all of the details about the academic origin of each dissertation, it included three new dissertations, and it improved on the text of the originals. In this way the *Exercise on the Roman German Emperor* finally received a qualified endorsement from the man who had for so long refused to describe himself as its author.

It needs to be emphasized all the more that the text of the *Exercise on the Roman German Emperor* that Conring published in 1674 was neither identical with von Hoym's *Exercise* of 1641 nor with its twin, the *New Discourse*—and of course not with the hybrid printed in the *Six Historico-Political Lessons* in 1655. Most of the differences are again minor. There are the usual changes in typography, orthography, and punctuation. Old misprints were sometimes corrected, and new ones were introduced. On some occasions Conring rephrased a sentence, straightened out some convoluted grammar, or added conceptual precision.

At one point, however, Conring went well beyond cosmetic change. That point came—no surprise—in the conclusion. He made three changes that look small but that had major implications. He changed the cautious opening phrase "this, at least, seems certain" into the still more cautious "this, at least, does not seem to be wrong." He made the clause "much less why they should go to Rome" more cautious by adding a "perhaps" after "much less." And above all, he qualified the crucial condition that furnished the basis for the entire chapter by adding an unequivocal parenthesis: "which cannot be admitted by any means." Henceforth the key sentence of chapter 52 stated: "This, at least, does not seem to be wrong: if after so many years of prescription our kings and emperors have lost all those true and ancient rights of the emperors (which cannot be admitted by any means), then there is no longer any reason...."[145]

That changed the conclusion into its opposite. The original asserted that "the Roman empire has perished completely or . . . that the imperial power is now actually in the hands of the Roman pope." The revision denied it. The revision did not fit smoothly into the logic of a text that went on to discourage German kings from claiming lordship over the city of Rome or trying to secure imperial coronation in Rome. Why not do just those things if it "cannot not be admitted by any means" that the German king had lost his rights in Rome? But it also brought the conclusion of the *Exercise on the Roman German Emperor* into line with the conclusion of *The Roman Empire of the Germans*. That shows nicely how directly Conring's unhappiness with the *Exercise on the Roman German Emperor* was focused on the conclusion. He made no other changes of any real significance. It was the conclusion of the

Exercise of 1641 that gave too much away by brushing the question of prescription aside. It was the conclusion that had needed to be stifled when the *New Discourse* was published in 1642. He tried to stifle it by publishing *The Roman Empire of the Germans* in 1644. But it was reasserted by the printers of the *Six Historico-Political Lessons* in 1655. And so he stifled it once again in 1674, this time rewriting the text of the *Exercise on the Roman German Emperor* himself.

Conring also revisited *The Roman Empire of the Germans*. Over the years he had repeatedly announced his intention to prepare a second edition.[146] He did compile substantial notes in preparation of that task.[147] But he died in 1681 before it was completed. It was left to his son, Hermann Conring Jr., to publish a revised edition in 1694 with notes that Conring had collected.[148] It was this second edition that Goebel included in his edition of Conring's *Opera*.[149]

The main differences between the first and the second edition of *The Roman Empire of the Germans* are easily described. First, Conring junior subdivided each of the thirteen long chapters of *The Roman Empire of the Germans* into short paragraphs, which made it easier to refer to the text with precision. Second, he added a two-page index of the sources on which Conring senior had relied, as well as a somewhat more detailed subject index.[150] Third, he inserted a "New Letter to the Reader" in which Conring senior explained with some contrition why he had attributed the short statement about the temporal power of the pope to Pierre Pithou.[151] Fourth, he incorporated Conring senior's additions into the body of the text. He did not identify these notes explicitly, although he did usually start them with a brief signal to the reader that he would now "see" another reference or "add" another passage.[152] But their extent cannot be reliably identified unless the edition of 1694 is compared line by line with the edition of 1644.

Most of the additions consist of minor reformulations and new or expanded references to the literature. Some extend to whole paragraphs and include new thoughts and arguments.[153] And one is so interesting for Conring's understanding of the Roman empire that it deserves special mention. It concerned his interpretation of the Apocalypse. In 1644 Conring had expressed his agreement with the view that the Apocalypse could be applied to the Roman empire.[154] Admittedly it did not apply to the Roman empire properly speaking, but only to a perverted version of the Roman empire that was ruled by the pope and that Protestants like himself considered identical with the Catholic Church. But at least in that perverted sense, the Roman empire could be expected to endure until the end of the world, just as the

Apocalypse had predicted. In 1644 Conring thus still seemed concerned to preserve the traditional faith in the truth of the Apocalypse's prophecies about the Roman empire. At some time before his death, however, he observed that "it is nonetheless plausible that the city and empire of Rome in this particular sense as well will eventually come to ruin at some point that may very well arrive long before the last days of the world."[155] That is a small but telling piece of evidence that in the second half of the seventeenth century the European imagination began to leave apocalyptic expectations further behind and to postpone the end of the world to a time that was about to become indefinite.[156]

In 1730 Johann Wilhelm Goebel had to decide which of the several versions of the *Exercise on the Roman German Emperor* to include in his edition of Conring's *Opera*.[157] Not surprisingly, he chose the revised version that Conring had published in 1674.[158] He simply copied what he found. He did not compare the earlier versions in which the *New Discourse* had been published. He did not indicate how closely the *New Discourse* of 1642 resembled the original *Exercise* of 1641, nor did he identify any of the changes that Conring had introduced in his revisions. The *Academic Exercises* of 1674, after all, presented itself as an authoritative collection of Conring's dissertations on the empire. That made it seem unnecessary to track down copies of originals that had already become rare. There is only one respect in which his edition differs: it contains a sizable number of footnotes at the bottom of the page. These were added by Goebel himself. They offer points of detail and references to relevant writings by Conring and other authors.

The history of the *New Discourse* thus ends on an ironic note. The text that Conring originally approved in 1641 and that was reprinted in the *New Discourse* in 1642 became the least likely to be read and most likely to be rejected as spurious. The version most likely to be accepted as genuine because officially sanctioned by Conring, and most likely to be read because reprinted in the *Opera*, departed from the original in at least one crucial respect: it turned the conclusion upside down. Thus the canonical edition of Conring's works helped to conceal a conclusion that he is more than likely to have contemplated seriously in 1641, and from which he dissociated himself in 1644 most likely because its unwanted publication forced his hand.

In the end Conring thus gained a qualified victory in his battle to banish the *New Discourse* from recognition. It was no longer understood that he rejected the *New Discourse* mostly because of the form in which it had been published. It was forgotten that the *Historico-Political Discourse on the Roman German Emperor* in the *Six Historico-Political Lessons* of 1655 was an unreliable hybrid. And no one realized that Goebel's reprint in the *Opera* obscured the willingness with which, at an early and unguarded moment, Conring had consigned the Roman empire to the past.

Authorship and Authenticity

A simple lesson may be drawn from this analysis: there is no way—no way at all—to fathom Conring's meaning. Not that the story I have told need be regarded as an idle waste of time. I may flatter myself to have formulated a nuanced range of interpretive possibilities and to have probed them to a considerable depth. I think I have shown convincingly that works of which Conring refused to declare himself the author seem at least on occasion to reveal his thinking with greater authenticity than works of which he was proud to declare his authorship. I have established that the *New Discourse* is worth reading for insight into Conring's mind, in spite of the anger with which he denounced its publication. Perhaps we may consider him its author-once-removed. And I have shown that *The Roman Empire of the Germans* veiled certain aspects of his thinking in subtle and deliberate obfuscations. Perhaps we may consider him its author-in-law.

These are no negligible bits of knowledge. But they are nothing like a grasp on Conring's meaning. They only represent the distance we have gone so far. Of course we can now look back and count the obstacles we scaled. But Conring's meaning is still ahead of us. Of course we could use sharper tools. Historians have amassed an armory of interpretive devices, of which this chapter has only used a modest sample. Of course we could prolong the chase. But it would never end.

If there is anything worth learning from this chapter, it is that meaning is not like a thing that can be grasped or measured; it is like the open space between two things that merely seem to touch. As the horizon is the point where the sky appears to touch the sea, so meaning is the point where thought appears to merge into expression. As no one can sail to the horizon, so no one can reach the point of meaning. As you move closer, you find more space between the thought and the expression. Meaning will only reveal itself to those who look at the horizon and stop to recognize that no horizon can be reached. That is why we have grasped Conring's meaning with anything like certainty at but one single point: the point at which he angrily rejected the *New Discourse* as inauthentic. Not by grasping what Conring really thought, but by confronting the distance dividing his thought from its expression.

Readers who are convinced that meaning is meaningless unless it can be fixed (like butterflies on pins) may find this a dispiriting conclusion. They will be tempted to limit its validity to this particular case. They will point out that the *New Discourse* is a peculiar piece of writing that was produced in trying times. No wonder it is difficult to tell what Conring really meant by focusing on words he did not really write about a subject on which he was afraid to speak his mind. Surely that is no reason to conclude that writers never really speak their minds and readers never grasp their meaning.

Indeed. That it is not. Writers do speak their minds, and readers do grasp their meaning. But not beyond the limits sketched above, and never without an irreducible remainder that does not lend itself to rational analysis. As Wittgenstein put it, "there is indeed the inexpressible. This *shows* itself; it is the mystical."[159] If that remainder is a cause of anxiety, no consolation will be had from seeking to confine it to this particular case. Of course the case is unusual. But in which sense? In that an author was found out to have endorsed a risky proposition; had his words used against his own intention; and that, as a result, we have much evidence with which to document the distance between Conring's thought and its expression. Of course his circumstances are peculiar to seventeenth-century dissertations and the contentious climate in which they were produced. But the absence of such circumstances hardly proves that otherwise thought and expression coincide. It only proves that normally the distance is easier to ignore.

What is peculiar about the case of the *New Discourse* is only that it reveals with such unsettling clarity how fragile is the bond between what we say and what we mean. We do not like to think about the ease with which our words escape from our control. And yet nothing is easier than to endow words with a meaning their author never wished them to have. Often, as in the case of the *New Discourse* (and countless news reports of so-called leaks), it is enough to publish them. The simple act of making public what was said in private can change the meaning beyond all recognition without changing a single word. If publishing is not enough, the words can always be placed into a context in which their meaning is so altered that the author has no choice but to abandon the expression he gave to his thought himself, not because he changed his mind, but on the contrary in order to preserve his meaning. There is no way around this possibility. It is a simple function of the distinction between locutionary surface and illocutionary act. Whether someone exploits that difference in order to force an author to jettison his words is a matter of pure chance. When chance becomes reality, we are confronted with different statements by authors struggling to hold on to their meaning. When it does not, we are confronted with seemingly fixed ideas. But in all cases, the certainty with which we may claim to have grasped an author's meaning is nothing more than a function of the inventiveness with which his words already have, or have not yet, been placed in other contexts. Which is why even the most authoritative interpretation of any text retains its authority only until someone comes along and adds one novel observation to the sum total previously considered.

Yes. Conring's case was unusual: he was unlucky. But the same fate can fall on anyone who ever tries at any time to put thoughts into words. If the audience has faith in the author's good intention, they will understand accordingly. If they do not, there are not words enough in any language to get the point across. The real conclusion of this chapter must therefore be that there exists no royal road to meaning. No piece of writing leads directly to anybody's thought. No piece of writing and no piece of language either. Thought and words, content and form, meaning and code are heterogeneous, and their heterogeneity is irreducible. Of course there are ways that lead from one to the other: ways of expression and ways of understanding. But none of them are safe. That makes real understanding not impossible, but fundamentally uncertain.

The upshot for authorship and authenticity can be simply stated. "Author" is a good concept for settling disputes over the extent to which people own their writings. Authorship is about responsibility and property. Whoever has the responsibility for any given piece of writing, that person is the author. And since the author accepts responsibility, he or she is entitled to corresponding rights. "Of persons artificial, some have their words and actions *owned* by those whom they represent. And then the person is the *actor*, and he that owneth his words and actions is the AUTHOR, in which case the actor acteth by authority. For that which in speaking of goods and possessions is called an *owner* (and in Latin *dominus,* in Greek *kurios*), speaking of actions is called author." That is how Thomas Hobbes joined ownership to authorship, in words that penetrated straight to the early modern heart of the matter a few years after the *New Discourse* was printed.[160] When Goebel pointed out that Conring did not acknowledge the *New Discourse* as "his own," he described the relationship between Conring and the *New Discourse* well in terms of law. But the legal relationship between an "author" and "his" writings is surely different from the creative relationship between a person and ideas. "Author" is a concept far too crude to capture both. Code can be owned. Meaning cannot.

Some of the reasons for this conclusion are specific to the case examined here: that of a dissertation, based on a professor's lectures, defended by a student, pirated, improved and expanded, pirated once again, reconsidered, and reprinted in several different editions. When so many ideas appear in so many different guises and with the indisputable participation of several different individuals for very different reasons, it may seem evident that the creative relationship between author and writing is so fluid that the author's ideas cannot be pinned to any definite expression. The same may not seem nearly so evident in the case of, say, a single piece of writing, different from all others, indisputably attributed to just one single person, and published on just one occasion in one form, although perhaps in many different copies— the case of what we normally believe to be "a book." But the difference is one only of degree, of accidents by which some writings are reproduced in different versions and some writers are compelled to retrieve their rights from pirates and usurpers, whereas others are not. Some authors enjoy good fortune. They put their ideas into writing once and then leave it at that. They do not have to reckon with the kind of opposition that forces others to abandon this or that formulation. Life may never lead them to change their mind simply because it may never force them to revisit what they wrote. Such authors may happily identify with what they wrote. They may not realize how much they owe to sheer good luck. Conring did. He knew that the links between author and writing are tenuous, hard to create and easy to destroy. About the dissertations defended by his students, he wrote that they were "both mine and not mine."[161] That captures the relationship between the author and the writing best.

As far as authenticity is concerned, none of the works considered here may claim to represent Conring's meaning fully, but all may claim to represent it to a respectable degree—even the hybrid of 1655. Authentic meaning can hardly manifest itself directly in locutions whose meaning is known, indeed intended, to diverge from the illocutionary act by which they are proposed. And yet it manifests itself to some degree. The lesson seems to be that authenticity is not to be expected from the routine deciphering of code. Authentic meaning manifests itself most clearly when the routine breaks down, as when the publication of the *New Discourse* disturbed the meaning of the *Exercise on the Roman German Emperor*—or when Luther pronounced his great no. That does appear to open a clear view on the writer's mind, precisely because it insists on the distinction between true meaning and a particular expression. Perhaps that "no, this is not what I mean" is the only form in which true meaning can really be expressed. Perhaps misunderstanding is a prerequisite for authenticity. Perhaps we must first recognize that we have failed to understand correctly in order to believe that we may understand at all.

To the Vanishing Point

This completes the second step in our journey. In this chapter we dug deep into the loose earth of the past to reach solid foundations. I asked a simple question: what did Conring really think? But that simple question proved impossible to answer. We may guess, of course. In fact, we may guess with great precision, and we could make it greater still. Whole libraries of primary and secondary sources are waiting to be read. But no matter how elaborate our analysis, how thick our description, how long our book, we shall not know what Conring really thought. For in the end it has turned out that Conring's thought refuses to be pinned to any fixed description. It slithers from our grasp because it is alive, a shifting mental substance moving along with Conring's life, his fears, his wishes, the doubts from which his understanding grew, and all the other circumstances of his time and place. It changed and changes still. It escapes all past and present forms of intellectual subjugation. It will not stay within the boundaries of any book. The instant we try to get it under our control, it retreats. The more determinedly we track it down, the more swiftly it vanishes into the distance. We know the distance we have covered, but the distance still ahead of us is infinite. And what is more, Conring himself seems to have been aware of that.

But this need hardly be the end. We need not claim that we have fathomed Conring's mind in order to be certain that we have grasped some certain knowledge of the past. Apart from the author and whatever context shaped his thought, there is the text he wrote. We can read that. It speaks to us directly. Did he mean what he wrote? Perhaps. Perhaps not. Perhaps he did not know. In any case we have his book. We can forget about his mind. The book contained an argument that marked a definite advance, dispelling medieval ignorance and myth. It changed the understanding of the past. That change is worth attention independently of whether anyone can forge an iron chain with which to fasten it forever to any author's mind. We shall therefore now put a stop to the pursuit of author, circumstances, and intentions. We shall forget the context and turn to the text instead.

4

The Text: Bartolus of Sassoferrato

In the preceding chapter, we tried to understand what Conring really thought. We learned a lot. But we did not reach our goal. Like Tantalus, we found ourselves grasping for fruits that lay perpetually just beyond our extended fingers. Upon reflection we had to realize that our efforts, though not in vain, would never lead to the desired end.

In this chapter we shall pursue a different route. Instead of burrowing more deeply into Conring's mind, we shall focus on the argument that he directed against his intellectual opponents. We shall abstract completely from the question whether it is possible to understand his argument without knowing its source. We have already tried to reach the source and met insuperable obstacles. Those obstacles are the exception entitling us to shift our focus. We shall forget about the source and look at the argument itself.

It will be useful to begin with a review of what the *New Discourse* actually said.[1] That will raise new questions in the reader's mind. What, for example, shall we make of the anachronistic manner in which Conring speaks constantly of Germany and Italy and the empire as states that waxed and waned in size and power but otherwise appear to be exempt from history, as if they were some self-subsistent substances, hypostases of history, so many pawns and officers deployed in a game of universal chess? Did those states really exist? (Most historians today would answer no.) Were they really as similar to each other in their essential nature as Conring makes it seem? (Hardly.) What were the boundaries of Germany? (Difficult to say, and impossible to answer except in detail.) What were the tenets of that Roman law from which he sought to emancipate Germany? (Depends on what you mean by "Roman law": ancient Roman law? medieval Roman law? interpreted according to the glossators? the commentators?) Is his understanding of the three crowns representing Germany, Italy, and the empire accurate? (Probably not.) And so on.

Questions like these will not detain us here. We shall remain content to paraphrase the argument as stated.[2] Whether or not it holds up to the best knowledge of medieval history today is a matter that we can safely put aside. Indeed, we had better put it aside in a book whose purpose is not to add to our knowledge of the past in particular respects (except incidentally), but to test the limits of history.

The Argument

The *New Discourse* opens with a few straightforward questions: did the king of Germany have the right to consider himself Roman emperor? Did the Roman empire still exist? If it no longer existed, what had happened to rights formerly held by Roman emperors? Had they disappeared along with the empire itself, or had they perhaps been passed on to someone else? If so, who held them now?[3]

According to the received wisdom, the answers to those questions were obvious. Of course the Roman empire continued to exist. Of course the king of Germany was Roman emperor. Everybody knew that Charlemagne had taken control of the Roman empire in A.D. 800 and that, after a tumultuous but relatively brief interlude, the imperial crown had been handed to Otto the Great in 962. Since then the empire had remained in the hands of German kings. What reason could there have been to doubt that it continued to be so? True, the papacy had been meddling in imperial affairs ever since the conflict between Pope Gregory VII and Emperor Henry IV in the eleventh century. The kings of France and England refused to submit to the emperor. No German king had actually been crowned emperor in Rome since 1452. And for the last twenty years or so, the emperor had been fighting a bitter war against German princes and foreign monarchs. Those matters cast serious doubt on the efficacy of imperial power. But they were no reason to conclude that the empire had ceased to exist or that it was no longer in the hands of German kings. Much less were they a reason to deny that the Roman emperor was lord of the world, *dominus mundi*. Bartolus of Sassoferrato (1313/14–1357), perhaps the greatest jurist of the Middle Ages, had said as much. More than that, Bartolus had raised a charge of heresy against whoever doubted that the emperor was lord of the world.[4]

This was not merely Bartolus's opinion. It was a principle rooted in both of the two books from which old Europe drew its most basic truths: the Bible and the Roman law. Roman law explicitly called the emperor *dominus mundi*, and Saint Luke explicitly acknowledged the emperor's universal power when he wrote that "there went out a decree from Caesar Augustus, that all the world should be taxed."[5] There was nothing ambiguous about those words. Since they were found in writings of unimpeachable authority, one of them containing God's own words, the other containing laws pronounced by an emperor whose power God had sanctioned, they lent unassailable support to countless medieval thinkers who regarded the emperor as the supreme ruler of the universe.[6] Emperor Sigismund had read them to the Council of Constance on Christmas Day 1414 "in his capacity of a deacon of the church, standing at the lectern with his imperial crown on his head and his drawn sword in his hand."[7] And they remained alive at least until the end of the sixteenth century.[8]

It is therefore no accident that Bartolus of Sassoferrato was the first writer whom Conring identified by name and attacked for upholding precisely that belief in the emperor's universal lordship. Nor is it an accident that Conring did not bother to state exactly where in his many writings Bartolus had upheld the emperor's universal rights. It was the tradition that Conring wanted to attack. Bartolus merely served him as a figurehead, convenient because of his fame and authority, worthy of singling out for opprobrium but hardly deserving of detailed attention. It seems unlikely that Conring consulted Bartolus's own writings. He seems to have drawn his knowledge from Hugo Grotius's *Laws of War and Peace,* a book on which he relied repeatedly for texts and arguments that were essential to his case.[9] Grotius not only quoted the passage in which Bartolus had charged opponents of the emperor's universal lordship with heresy, but he also launched an attack on Bartolus strikingly similar to the one that Conring was about to launch himself.[10]

Conring never acknowledged that his attack on Bartolus was borrowed from Grotius's *Laws of War and Peace*.[11] But he made sure his readers would know the sources Bartolus quoted in support of the emperor's right to rule the world: the Bible and Roman law. And for the benefit of readers who wanted to know whether or not those sources could be supplemented with passages from pagan writers of classical antiquity whose rise to prominence, thanks to the humanist movement, had been one of the greatest changes in the mind of Europe since the days of Bartolus, he added references to Petronius and Dionysius of Halicarnassus, two classical authors who confirmed the universality of Roman rule in polished Greek and Latin. To quote Conring himself:

> Famous men declare that the entire world once obeyed the Romans, or should at least have obeyed them. Bartolus himself, the great luminary of jurisconsults, not

to mention anybody else, was so certain of this truth that he did not hesitate to brand conflicting views as heresy. Usually this opinion is buttressed by quoting from the Gospel of Luke that "there went out a decree from Caesar Augustus, that all the world should be taxed," where the extent of the Roman empire is defined as the whole world, or from Justinian's *Corpus Iuris,* where dominion over the world is often attributed to the emperor, or finally from ancient writers like Petronius, who said that "the Roman conqueror now held the whole world," and Dionysius of Halicarnassus, book 1, chapter 3, according to whom "the city of the Romans rules all quarters of the earth—or those at least which are accessible and inhabited by human beings."[12]

Such was the common wisdom that Conring set out to challenge. He stated clearly how he would challenge it. "First of all," he said, "we need to know what actually or legally belonged to the Roman empire at the time when Rome was flourishing."[13] This short sentence, offered without explanation or apology, as though there were no reason whatsoever to dispute its truth, is perhaps the single most important sentence in the treatise. It furnishes the logical foundation of Conring's entire argument, and it implies the strategy by which he would overturn the common wisdom. The strategy consisted of three simple steps. First, he would consider how far the power of Rome had actually (*reapse*) extended in antiquity: a question of fact. Second, he would consider whether the ancient Romans had been entitled (*iure*) to rule the world: a question of right. And third, he would recount the history of Rome's imperial power in actuality and law, from antiquity to the present: a question of historical development. The first two steps were announced in his opening salvo; the third was left implied, as though it were a matter of course.

For our purposes it must be underscored that all three steps were historical in nature: the question of fact obviously so, because it concerned the actual extent of the Roman empire in antiquity; the question of right also, though less obviously, because it concerned the rights possessed by the Roman empire in antiquity; and the third most obviously of all, because it concerned development over time presented in a historical narrative. Conring's approach to the issue presupposed that history was qualified to answer questions of right.[14] Endorsing that presupposition without explanation was to prejudge the case. Later on we must therefore consider the implications of Conring's opening move, apparently so innocuous but in truth so heavily fraught with hidden assumptions about the nature of time and eternity, mind and matter, law and religion. For now we shall go on to trace the manner in which he executed his strategy.

The question of ancient fact was easily disposed of.[15] True, the Gospel of Luke did say that "there went out a decree from Caesar Augustus, that all the world should be taxed." But this was not to be taken literally, "for it is evident in itself and has long since been pointed out by the best scholars that even the Bible often tends to some exaggeration."[16] True again, the extent of the ancient Roman empire had been remarkable. But never universal. The Roman empire had never even included all of Europe, much less all of Africa or Asia, not to mention the New World, of whose very existence the Romans had been completely unaware. That was enough to complete the first step in refuting Bartolus.

Now Roman law did call the emperor *dominus mundi,* lord of the world, and it was of course conceivable that the limited extent of the Roman empire merely reflected some kind of illegal violation of the emperor's universal rights. The second step in the argument therefore was to take up the question of right. That demanded a little more attention.[17] There were, Conring asserted, three and only three sources from which the Roman empire could have drawn the right to rule the world: natural law, the Bible, and human law.[18] But Conring maintained that there was no statement in the Bible whatsoever that gave the Romans the right to rule the world.[19] Divine law could be ruled out as a foundation of universal Roman rule. Natural law came next. Natural law, like divine law, was universal in scope. But unlike divine law, it could be discovered without divine revelation, because it consisted of principles accessible to human reason without religious enlightenment. If natural law had said anything about the Roman emperor, it might have served as a foundation for his right to rule the world. Unfortunately for Bartolus, it did not. It dealt with entirely different subjects—and Conring did not even dignify the conjecture that it addressed the Roman emperor's right to rule the world with a detailed account of the subjects with which it did deal.[20] Natural law could also be ruled out as a foundation of universal Roman rule.

That left human law, and more specifically Roman law. Roman law posed the most serious problem, because it really did call the emperor *dominus mundi.* But as far as Conring was concerned, "even a child can see that the civil law of the city of Rome could not possibly have given the Romans the right to rule the world; for how could the entire world have been bound by a law that was established by a single people in their city?"[21] Moreover, the Romans themselves had never claimed such a right. Quite on the contrary, they had been careful to characterize their laws as civil laws precisely in order to distinguish them from natural law.[22] Obviously the civil law of Rome was limited in its reach. Obviously it offered no basis on which to erect any claims to universal rule.²³ Even the rights the Romans had actually held were not immutable. By the Romans' own account, Conring explained, those rights had been acquired in the same way in which rights were acquired all the time: by conquest, contract, donations, and similar means. They were not universal, and as they had been acquired, so they could be lost.

At this early point, Conring had already completed the two most important steps in his argument: he had established that the ancient Roman emperor had neither ruled the world in fact nor had the right to rule the world. It remained to show in a third step what had happened in the times following antiquity. That was going to take up most of the remaining forty-three chapters of the *New Discourse*. But it was not a fundamental issue. It never came close to threatening the points that Conring had established by the end of chapter 13.

In the following chapters, Conring went on to show how the Roman empire diminished during the early Middle Ages.²⁴ German tribes invaded and took possession of most Roman territories in the west. By the eighth century, far from defending their rights, the Romans had in effect acknowledged the conquests of the Germans as irreversible. The Romans certainly recognized the independence of Germany, because they had never ruled Germany to begin with. But they also recognized the independence of England, France, and Spain, where they had been thoroughly defeated.²⁵

The case of Italy was more complex. Italy was divided into three different regions.²⁶ The north was controlled by the Lombards, the middle by the bishop of Rome, and the south by the eastern Roman empire. But though there was some dispute over the boundaries between the parts of Italy, this was certain: neither the Lombard kingdom in the north nor the Byzantine south could be considered part of the western Roman empire. It followed, so Conring declared, that by the time of Charlemagne, the western Roman empire had shrunk to the part of central Italy that still remained under the control of the bishop and people of Rome.²⁷

What, then, was the meaning of the famous ceremony on Christmas Day A.D. 800 when Pope Leo III and the citizens of Rome acclaimed Charlemagne as Roman emperor?²⁸ Conring believed it could not possibly have been to give Charlemagne the right to rule the kingdoms of the Franks and the Lombards. Charlemagne had acquired those kingdoms on his own and long before. Nor could it have been to give him the right to rule the parts of Italy controlled by the eastern Roman emperors, much less the eastern Roman empire itself. The emperors of eastern Rome were in legitimate control of their empire, and the bishop and citizens of Rome had no right to deprive them of their power. They did, however, have the right to confer on Charlemagne power over whatever was in their own control, and that, as Conring had just shown, was a small part of central Italy. What Charlemagne acquired by becoming Roman emperor thus was the right to rule over the part of Italy that was under the control of the pope. That, and nothing more than that, was the meaning of his imperial title.

By this stage Conring had thus given a preliminary answer to the questions posed at the beginning of the *New Discourse:* the Roman empire still existed at the time of Charlemagne but had already lost its ancient grandeur. What mattered was Charlemagne's power as king of the Franks and the Lombards. His imperial office was a minor addition to that power, full of symbolic importance but lacking in real weight.

Understanding Charlemagne's relationship to the Roman empire, however, was not the same as understanding the relationship between the Roman empire and the kings of Germany. For Charlemagne had not been king of Germany. He had been king of the Franks and the Lombards. It was only later that his realm was divided into various pieces and that one of those pieces would come to be known as Germany. Conring therefore went on to consider whether the pattern established by Charlemagne changed once the Carolingian empire had come to be divided into Germany, France, and Italy.[29]

As a matter of principle, Conring began, it was conceivable that the relationship between the Roman empire and the rest of Europe changed after Charlemagne. The Roman empire could have begun to grow again. It could have reconquered some of the areas it had lost to the Germans. Hitherto independent states could also have subjected themselves to the Roman emperor voluntarily. But what was conceivable in principle had not happened in fact.

Obviously nothing of the sort had happened in France, Spain, England, Sweden, and other states in the north and east of Europe.[30] These were never conquered by any Romans, nor had they ever subjected themselves to Rome. Conring was equally sure that nothing like this had happened in Germany or Italy either. But that was more difficult to prove. For ever since the renewal of the Roman empire under Otto the Great, the kingdoms of Germany and of Lombard Italy had been joined to the Roman empire (the small part of central Italy that Charlemagne acquired when he became Roman emperor) by an everlasting alliance. Moreover, Conring pointed out, unlike their Carolingian predecessors, the later kings of Germany and Italy had rarely troubled to distinguish their rights as kings from their rights as Roman emperors. Italy and Germany had been called "Roman empire," as if there had been only one single state, and the rulers of Italy and Germany had been called Roman emperors, as if there had been only a single ruler. That made it seem that Germany and Italy had after all subjected themselves to the Roman empire.[31] Hence Conring had to take some time to clarify the actual state of affairs.[32]

The details of that investigation were complicated, but the upshot was simple. There was no evidence at all, Conring insisted, that Germany or the Lombard kingdom of Italy had ever subjected themselves to the Roman empire in any way. If they had done so, it would have been an act of major constitutional importance that could not have been performed without the consent of the estates. But there was no trace of evidence that any estates had ever given their consent to such an act.[33] Clearly Germany and Italy remained independent sovereign states, each with its own freely elected king. That was nicely symbolized by the three separate crowns for Germany, Italy, and the empire that were separately bestowed in Aix-la-Chapelle, Pavia, and Rome.[34] The citizens of Rome, by contrast, did in fact surrender the right of electing the emperor to the Germans. It followed that if anyone had been subjected to anyone at all, it was not Germans to Romans but the other way around.[35]

That cleared the way for Conring to give his considered answer to the question about the constitutional relationship between Germany, Italy, and the Roman emperor: the Roman emperor had no right to rule Germany or Italy.[36] He only had the right to rule the center of Italy around the city of Rome. The kingdom of Germany and the kingdom of Lombard Italy were sovereign states. They had their own heads of state, they did not belong to the Roman empire, and they were not subject to Roman law. Of course it had often happened that the king of Germany, the king of Italy, and the emperor were one and the same person. But speaking constitutionally, that was coincidence. The sovereignty of Germany and Italy remained secure.[37]

In the following chapters, Conring added a second conclusion that followed more or less seamlessly from the first: the pope had no right to intervene in the affairs of Germany at all.[38] The pope was a Roman citizen. As such he did have rights where empire and emperor were concerned. Together with the other citizens of Rome, he had conferred the Roman empire on Charlemagne and had played a major role in imperial coronations since. Perhaps he even had the right to remove the empire from Germany—though seeing that the Romans had surrendered to the Germans the right to elect the emperor, and that the Germans had never given it back, Conring considered that a doubtful matter. But whatever rights the pope may have had in the empire, he had no rights in Germany.

That left the question whether the empire continued to exist.[39] Conring returned to the ground he had already covered in considering the question of whether Germany and Italy had voluntarily subjected themselves to the Roman empire. But now he looked at it from the imperial perspective. He concluded that although the Roman empire had shrunk in size, emperors like Otto the Great, Otto III, and Henry III had exercised full imperial rights over the city of Rome, including the right to a decisive say in the election of the bishop of Rome. In that sense the empire had continued to exist under their rule. But matters had taken a drastic turn for the worse at the time of Henry IV, when Pope Gregory VII claimed control over the empire for the papacy. That claim was as unprecedented as it was unfounded. Later emperors had done their best to fight it. But in the end they were defeated. As a result the power of the emperor had not been exercised in Rome for more than four hundred years.[40]

The main conclusion of the *New Discourse* followed in chapter 52: either the Roman empire had ceased to exist altogether, or it had been reduced to a mere shadow of its former self, which was now in the hands of the Roman pope. There was perhaps some doubt about the legitimacy of the papacy's control over the empire, even after four hundred years of prescription. But there was no doubt at all that kings of Germany were wasting time and money on trips to Rome in order to obtain a purely ceremonial title that allowed them nothing better than to "vainly boast I-know-not-what lordship over the world or the city of Rome."

In the final chapters of the *New Discourse,* Conring answered three potential objections to his conclusion: that it conflicted with the Bible, violated Roman law, and belittled the dignity of the emperor.[41] Concerning the Bible, there was the conventional theory, founded on certain passages in the book of Daniel and the New Testament, that the history of the world was governed by four successive world monarchies, that the Roman empire was the last of these, and that it would endure until the end of the world. Conring insisted that this theory lacked all basis in historical fact. There had been far more monarchies, indeed, empires, than merely four, both in biblical times and after, so that "the whole idea that there will be only four great monarchies or world empires is more of a rumor than a fact."[42] Besides, the Old Testament had been written at a time when the Roman empire did not even yet exist. That made it rather difficult to turn the dreams of Nebuchadnezzar and Daniel into predictions that it would last forever. How could they have predicted the endurance of an empire that Daniel never even knew?[43] Matters were somewhat different with the New Testament, for by that time the Roman empire surely did exist, and the Apocalypse did link its destruction to the end of the world—but that was an issue that Conring declined to pursue, leaving the reader with some suspicion that he had no good answer to one of the more serious objections from the Bible.[44]

Concerning Roman law, there were "a great many professors of Roman law from the times of Emperor Lothar down to our own age" who tried to make the case that the king of Germany had the same rights over the world as had once been held by Emperor Justinian or even Emperor Augustus.[45] But Conring dismissed such arguments with derision. They rested on the belief that "every single piece in the body of Roman laws is founded on the law of nature and therefore true for all times." That belief was "totally false." The Romans themselves had defined their law as the law of the city of Rome and had distinguished it sharply from natural law. They obviously did not mean Roman law to be identified with natural law, nor did they believe their law gave the emperor any right to rule the world. Roman law was simply the positive law of a state that had all but ceased to exist. To apply that law to the contemporary affairs of other states, without any regard to their sovereignty and without any recognition of the changes that had intervened since antiquity, was "good for starting wars and throwing the world into turmoil." But in terms of legal reason, it was "frivolous, to say nothing worse. . . . It is simply silly to believe that everyone who succeeds someone else in name or any other way also succeeds to rights that may have been in effect a hundred or a thousand years ago. It is in fact no less absurd than the opinion of those who pretend that Charles V had a right to occupy America because he was emperor and thus lord of the world."[46] The fact of the matter was that Germany and Italy, like other states, enjoyed full sovereignty without thereby violating Roman law in the least.

The dignity of the emperor, finally, was safe.[47] Conring pointed out that there was a difference between considering the king of Germany as one sovereign among many and saying that all sovereigns were alike. True, the king of Germany, even with his imperial title, had no right to interfere in the affairs of other sovereign states. True, he was not the lord of the world. In that sense he was just like any other sovereign. But there was an order of precedence among sovereigns, and in that order the king of Germany still occupied first place, not because he held the imperial title, but because his title corresponded to a reality: since the times of Otto the Great, Germany had been the greatest state in Europe. On those grounds the emperor's dignity remained intact.[48]

Joining the Issue

Such was the argument Conring presented to his readers. Its thrust was simple. It was designed to destroy the common wisdom according to which the Roman emperor governed the world. And so it did, although of course not single-handedly. It took the efforts of many early modern thinkers with similar ideas to transform the universal lordship of the emperor from a widely shared belief into a quaint myth buried in dead letters, preserved in libraries, and studied by none but a few historians. It is now so far gone as to have lost its meaning almost beyond recovery. The question is, How come? How did it lose its meaning? What gave Conring's argument the power to accomplish such an amazing feat of mental reengineering?

Contemporary readers are likely to treat that question with impatience. The reason the universal lordship of the Roman emperor was transformed into a myth, they may well say, is obvious: Conring was right and Bartolus was wrong. Universal lordship did not need to be transformed into a myth at all; a myth is just what it had always been. Obviously the Roman emperor had never ruled the world, and obviously he never had the right to rule the world, either. Who could dispute it? Who would dispute it? No wonder Bartolus has been forgotten. Granted, he was intelligent. A certain kind of intellectual pleasure can therefore still be found in puzzling through his logic. But fundamentally he was misguided. Far better we refrain from looking too closely. We might despair over the depths of corruption into which the human mind can fall. Let us rejoice instead that we no longer need to waste our time on stating the obvious. The Roman emperor "lord of the world"? Please! That thought is nothing but one outrageous strand in the dismal web of half-truths, misunderstandings, and outright lies that were spread for centuries by ill-instructed lawyers and self-righteous clerics whose willingness to place one more layer of incomprehensible metaphysics on top of another was exceeded only by their ignorance of history.

That, of course, is caricature. Even readers who know nothing about the train of thought by which Bartolus was led to maintain the universal lordship of the emperor (assuming that he did) may hesitate before embracing it without reflection. We have been brought up on the principle that different historical periods need to be understood on their own terms. We know we must be fair to people in different times and places. Bartolus was one of those people. He may have been misguided, but surely less through any fault of his own than through the fault of his times. We must treat him with historical civility. If we have properly absorbed the lessons of modern education, we will not tell him to his face that he was an ignorant fool. We may not even admit the thought to ourselves. It would be wrong. It would be uncivilized. It would be unhistorical. But neither shall we treat him as our peer.

When Conring announces that the Roman empire never extended over the whole world and concludes that the Roman emperor's so-called universal lordship is the figment of an overly excited legal imagination, we respond "of course!" When early modern humanists like Conring entered upon the task of collecting, editing, and analyzing the records of what had actually happened in the past, we emerged from the Dark Ages. We woke up from that mad dream of misinformation that held the European mind in thrall for so many centuries. Now we are no longer in the throes of ignorance. We have an armory of critical editions, handbooks, monographs, articles, and bibliographies at our beck and call, more accurate and more detailed than Conring could have dreamed. We know what happened in the past, and if we do not know the past completely, we surely know that no Roman emperor ever was lord of the world.

The best that Bartolus can expect from us, therefore, is compassion, condescension, and antiquarian curiosity. We shall point out that his thinking was confined by the circumstances of his time and place. If he protests and asks for a hearing that does not prejudge the issue in our favor, we shall explain why thoughts like his do not deserve a hearing in any contemporary court. We shall soften the blow to his dignity with assurances of how well we understand the reasons why he thought the way he did. We shall invite him into our (perhaps unwanted) company and admit that our thinking is no less limited by circumstance than his. We shall indulge his whims, and we may even flatter him by tracing the history of his conceits. But we shall do so only on condition that he stays safely past and does not rise up from the dead.

This inability to reckon with the possibility that Bartolus might have been right and to admit that we just might be wrong, not only about the past (if our history is bad) but also about ourselves (if even good history obscures our view)—that is the greatest obstacle that must be overcome in order to achieve the purpose of this book.[49] On the following pages I shall therefore try to explain Bartolus's case in favor of universal lordship. More precisely, I shall explain as much of it as needed in order to recognize Conring's accomplishment as something other than the discovery of an obvious fact. I will pay no attention to the context in which Bartolus was working and pass over questions concerning the transmission of his writings.[50] Any attempt to deal with such issues would merely lead straight back into the methodological dead end that we encountered in the preceding chapter. Instead, I shall take my cue from the specific point in the works of Bartolus that Conring identified with the common wisdom and explore its conceptual vicinity at leisure. That will, I hope, suffice to take a step outside the logic of Conring's argument and thereby neutralize the spell of assumptions about the past and its relationship to politics that he was one of many to put into place.

The Roman People

The passage where Bartolus called charges of heresy down on whoever doubted that the emperor was lord of the world came in the middle of his commentary on one of the laws in the *Digest,* the largest of the four volumes of the *Corpus Iuris,* the body of ancient Roman law that Emperor Justinian had codified in the sixth century A.D. and that had been subjected to intensive analysis since the revival of jurisprudence in western Europe in the eleventh century.[51] The Roman law in question was number 24 in title 15 of the forty-ninth book in the *Digest.*

Digest 49.15.24 occupied merely a few lines among hundreds of pages and thousands of laws measuring the length and breadth of the ancient Roman legal imagination. The passage in Bartolus's commentary that gave such offense to Conring was similarly inconspicuous amid a body of analytic writings comprising several large folio volumes. On the surface, both the Roman law and Bartolus's commentary on it look like tiny particles of legal matter floating in a veritable ocean of jurisprudence so vast that they are difficult to locate, let alone distinguish from their surroundings. Yet both of them have fundamental conceptual significance. In order to isolate that significance, let us begin by stating simply what *Digest* 45.15.24 had to say, and then what Bartolus said about that.

Digest 49.15.24 came from the writings of the ancient Roman jurist Ulpian. Its purpose was to clarify what it meant to be an enemy of Rome (*hostis*), strictly speaking. Ulpian determined that only those people deserved to be called enemies of Rome who found themselves in a state of war with the Romans. Such a state of war could come about in two main ways: by the Romans' declaring war on their enemies or by the enemies' declaring war on the Romans. Ulpian mentioned Germans and Parthians as examples.[52]

Any number of other ways can of course be imagined in which people could have expressed enmity to the Roman state. But none of those ways would have made them enemies of Rome in the technical sense. Legally speaking, such people were mere "bandits" (*latrunculi*) or "robbers" (*praedones*).[53] According to Ulpian, you did not become an enemy of Rome merely because you had broken the law or otherwise entered into conflict with the power of the Roman state. You became an enemy of Rome only through specific public actions resulting in a formally recognized state of war. Not just anyone was able to perform such actions. For example, subjects of the Roman state were not legally able to perform them, unless perhaps the Roman state itself decided to declare war on those subjects. "Enemy of Rome," in other words, was something like a title of respect in reverse, reserved for those whom Rome considered in some sense its equal.

The distinction between genuine enemies of Rome and lowly robbers was more than splitting legal hairs. It had major consequences. If you were captured by enemies of Rome, you became their slave. As a result you lost your possessions in Rome, and your marriage was dissolved as well. If you managed to escape and returned to Roman territory, your rights could be reinstated, but that did not happen automatically. You had to perform a *postliminium,* a public ceremony formalizing your escape from slavery and reinstatement of your rights as a citizen. Moreover, even after *postliminium* had been performed, your marriage did not automatically revive, and your possessions did not return to you unless you took specific action to recover them.[54]

If you were merely captured by robbers, none of this was necessary. You were never regarded as a slave, and you did not lose your civic rights. You retained your freedom under the law, your marriage remained intact, your possessions were safeguarded, and if you managed to escape from your captors, no *postliminium* was necessary to restore you to your civic rights. The difference between falling into the hands of robbers and falling into the hands of enemies of Rome could thus amount to the difference between marriage and divorce, wealth and poverty, freedom and slavery.

That, in brief, was ancient law. The question for Bartolus was how to apply that law to contemporary circumstances. This was an important issue at a time of political fragmentation and locally dispersed violence between knights, counts, dukes, kings, and (especially in Italy) cities—not to mention the global conflict between church and state, some of the most famous instances of which occurred just before and during Bartolus's lifetime, or such important enmities as that between Emperor Henry VII and King Robert of Naples.[55] People were constantly declaring their enmity to one another and constantly falling into captivity. What were the legal consequences? Did they become slaves? Did they lose their possessions? Were their marriages invalidated? And what happened when they regained their liberty?

According to the distinction laid down by Ulpian, the answer depended on whether or not a captive had fallen into the hands of enemies of Rome. And that in turn depended on the difference between people who could become enemies of Rome and subjects of the Roman state, who could only become bandits and robbers. In order to be able to apply Ulpian's distinction to people who had fallen into captivity, Bartolus thus had to find a means of distinguishing Roman people from other people. It was in search of such a means that he came to attribute significance to the right of the Roman emperor to rule the world. Acceptance of that right, so Bartolus maintained, was the most basic means by which to distinguish the Roman people from potential enemies of Rome.

How did it come to serve that function? Bartolus began by reminding his readers of Ulpian's basic point: "You need to know that as a matter of principle there are two kinds of people: first, the Roman people, and second, foreign people."[56] But who were the Roman people? According to the gloss (the standard running commentary on Roman law, completed in the thirteenth century, with which all students of Roman law were expected to be familiar), the Roman people were defined as those who obeyed the Roman empire.[57] That definition had perhaps not been problematic in antiquity, when competitors for the Roman empire were few and its boundaries reasonably clear. But it was different at the time when Bartolus was writing. The Hohenstaufen emperors had been defeated by the papacy, the empire had shrunk to small proportions, its power was very much in doubt, and its boundaries were hardly clear at all.

If you took the gloss literally, Bartolus continued, "you could therefore say that the Roman people is tiny, because only a few people actually obey the Roman empire."[58] In theory that was a perfectly acceptable interpretation. Indeed, it was precisely this interpretation that Conring was going to adopt about three hundred years later. It is worth emphasizing that Bartolus considered that line of analysis explicitly. But it did not find his favor. He thought it was more fruitful to distinguish membership in the Roman people from obedience to the Roman emperor.

Bartolus singled out four important cases involving people who did belong to the Roman people and therefore could not normally become enemies of Rome but who nonetheless did not obey the Roman emperor, at least not in every respect. The first case concerned the city-states of Tuscany and Lombardy. Those states, he argued, did not obey the Roman emperor, but they did follow Roman law and they did accept the right of the emperor to rule over all people in the world. Thus they surely belonged to the Roman people:

> There are certain people who do not obey the Roman empire completely, but do obey it in some respects, for example, because they live according to Roman law

and because they accept that the Roman emperor is the lord of all. Such is the case with the cities of Tuscany, Lombardy, and others like them. These do belong to the Roman people, for so long as the Roman people exercises its jurisdiction over them in some article, it retains its jurisdiction as a whole.[59]

The second case was slightly different but led to the same conclusion. There were people who neither obeyed the Roman emperor nor followed Roman law, but their failing to do so was authorized by the Roman emperor himself. Ultimately the freedom of such people to withhold their obedience from the emperor depended on a privilege the emperor had granted them himself and was free to withdraw again. Hence they, too, could be regarded as members of the Roman people, even though they did not obey the emperor. Here the most important case was Venice, another Italian city-state, but one with a history quite different from those of Tuscany and Lombardy:

> There are some people who do not obey the emperor at all and do not even live according to Roman law, but who justify themselves by relying on a privilege that the emperor has granted them. These also belong to the Roman people. Such is the case with the Venetians. For they themselves say that they have received their liberty from the emperor and now hold it from him by a privilege that is, as it were, precarious, because the emperor has the right to change his will and can revoke this privilege whenever he wishes.[60]

The third case constituted yet another form of independence from the emperor. The people included here neither obeyed the Roman emperor nor derived their independence from a unilaterally granted privilege that he could withdraw at will; they derived it instead from a mutual agreement that he was not at liberty to overturn whenever he so chose. The most important instance of this kind concerned the church. The Roman church, Bartolus maintained, had stepped into the place that had been vacated when the emperor retreated to Constantinople in the east, and it had done so by mutual agreement with the emperor in the famous Donation of Constantine.[61] This meant that the church did not have to obey the emperor either. But it did not abolish administration according to Roman law, much less the clergy's inclusion in the Roman people. Quite on the contrary, the Roman church governed its territories according to the same principles that had been applied by the emperor before, and the clergy, though subject to the pope rather than the emperor, did not for that reason lose the rights and privileges of Roman citizens:

> Some people do not obey the emperor but assert that they have received their freedom from him by some contract. This is the case with the provinces held by

the Roman church, which were donated to the Roman church by Emperor Constantine (assuming that this donation is valid and cannot be revoked). I say that these also belong to the Roman people. For the church of Rome exercises the same jurisdiction over those lands that was once exercised by the Roman empire, and "Roman empire" is what they call it. Hence, those provinces do not cease to belong to the Roman people, even though their administration has been conceded to someone other than the emperor. It is similar with the clergy. All forms of jurisdiction over the clergy have been granted to the pope. Does that mean that clerics cease to be Roman citizens? Certainly not, because clerics manifestly retain the right of succession.[62]

From Bartolus's point of view, the lands of the church thus continued to belong to the Roman empire, the jurisdiction exercised by the pope stood in direct continuity with the jurisdiction previously exercised by the emperor, and the clergy continued to live by Roman law.[63]

Bartolus went on to apply exactly the same logic to the last and most important of the four cases concerning people who belonged to the Roman people without obeying the emperor. This was the case of kings and princes, above all the kings of France and England, who simply refused to regard themselves as subject to the Roman emperor at all. Theirs was perhaps the most extreme in the series of four degrees of independence from the emperor—Italian city-states, Venice, the church, and northern European monarchs—that Bartolus considered in seeking to define membership in the Roman people. But even those kings and princes, he insisted, continued to be citizens of the Roman empire and members of the Roman people. More precisely, they continued to be members of the Roman people just so long as they did not dispute the emperor's right to rule the world.

That may seem like nothing more than an empty pledge of allegiance. We shall have to see later on whether it was more than that. But empty or not, it was crucial to Bartolus. For in a sense, he was convinced, the Roman empire overlapped with the Christian church, so that whoever belonged to the church also belonged to the Roman people. That explained why it would have been heretical for kings of France and England to dispute the emperor's right to rule the world, notwithstanding their refusal to obey him. They would have done more than to refuse to obey the emperor: they would have refused to acknowledge their inclusion in the church.

> I maintain that the same is true of those other kings and princes who deny that they are subject to the king of the Romans, such as the king of France, the king of England, and others like them. For so long as they admit that he is universal lord [dominus universalis], they do not cease to be Roman citizens, for the reasons

given above, even though they may remove themselves from his universal lordship [dominium universale] by virtue of privileges, prescription, or other such reasons. By the same logic, virtually all people who obey Sacred Mother Church belong to the Roman people. And if someone were to say that the lord emperor is not lord and monarch over the entire world [dominus et monarcha totius orbis], he would be a heretic, for he speaks against the determination of the church and the text of the Holy Gospel, where it says that "there went out a decree from Caesar Augustus that all the world should be surveyed," as you can read in Luke, chapter 2. Christ himself thus recognized the emperor as lord.[64]

Such was Bartolus's answer to the objection that "you could say that the Roman people is tiny, because only a few people actually obey the Roman empire." His answer turned on the distinction between obeying the emperor and being a Roman citizen. He granted that few people actually obeyed the emperor. But he did not grant that those were the only people who were to be reckoned among the citizens of Rome. He evidently saw a fundamental difference between membership in a community and obedience to the ruler of that community. The former by no means implied the latter.[65] There were many citizens in the Roman empire who belonged to the Roman people but did not obey the emperor at all. So long as they admitted that the emperor was universal lord, they qualified as Roman citizens. Otherwise they were heretics. The difference between being a good Christian and belonging to the Roman people was negligible. Accepting the emperor's right to rule the world thus came to serve Bartolus as the most fundamental and most inclusive of all criteria for determining who did belong to the Roman people and who did not.

We shall have to look more carefully at the implications of this argument for the nature of imperial power. But let us first complete this brief review of the manner in which Bartolus distinguished potential enemies of Rome from mere robbers. He had good reason to be satisfied. Of course his argument had limitations. It focused mostly on Italy, dealt rather briefly with those "other kings and princes who deny that they are subject to the king of the Romans," and said nothing at all about whatever rights the emperor could possibly have had over Roman citizens who did not obey him. It was a strictly legal argument. But it made an elegant case that, at least in terms of law, the inhabitants of Europe were members of the Roman people, and that the spiritual realm ruled by the church overlapped seamlessly with the temporal realm ruled by the emperor. That argument secured the applicability of Roman law to all Catholic Christians, regardless of whether they obeyed the emperor or not, and embodied a theory of community distinct from a theory of subjection. That was no small accomplishment.

In the remainder of his commentary on *Digest* 49.15.24, Bartolus turned to the question of who, then, might become an enemy of Rome. His answer came in two installments. First, he identified those "foreign people" (*populi extranei*) who did not belong to the Roman people because they rejected the emperor's right to rule the world. Among them he named Greeks, Mongols, Saracens, Jews, Turks, and Indians. He made sure to emphasize that these were not alike. Some of them had entered into alliances with the Romans; such was the case for the Greeks, who were allied with the Romans against the Turks. Others kept peace with the Romans and were trading with them, too; so the Mongols did. Others were formally at war with the Romans, such as the Turks and Saracens. And yet others had no relations with the Romans at all, neither relations of war nor relations of peace; that, he thought, was the case for the inhabitants of India.[66]

Foreign people differed also in the reasons for their rejection of the emperor's right to rule the world: the Greeks attributed that right to the emperor in Constantinople, the Mongols to the Great Khan, the Saracens to their own lord (whose title Bartolus did not identify), and the Jews to their lord—or so Bartolus claimed without further explanation. But the differences notwithstanding, all foreign people were united by one defining feature: none of them recognized the Roman emperor's right to rule the world.

Second, Bartolus analyzed the circumstances under which the various kinds of people he had now identified in Europe and elsewhere could become enemies of Rome. A large number of different possibilities had to be considered, ranging from pure cases of self-defense by individual people, at one extreme, to unprovoked declarations of war by self-governing communities, at the other. It would be interesting to study his views on these matters in detail, but it would lead us too far afield. Suffice it to say that he did not limit the term *enemies of Rome* exclusively to foreign peoples and that by no means all foreign peoples were automatically enemies of Rome. There were circumstances under which inhabitants of Europe could turn into enemies of Rome, and there were cases in which foreign people were friends of Rome.

A Matter of Law

The last passage quoted above is what prompted Conring to identify Bartolus by name as a champion of the emperor's right to rule the world. As we have seen, he borrowed his knowledge of Bartolus from Grotius, and he did not identify precisely where Bartolus had made the claims that Grotius attributed to him. But since we have now read Bartolus's own words, we can confirm that Conring's attack was perfectly well aimed. Bartolus did charge whoever doubted the emperor's right to rule the world with heresy. And Conring was correct in naming the verse in the Gospel of Luke that "there went out a decree from Caesar Augustus that all the world should be surveyed" as one of the pillars on which Bartolus had rested his case.

This short paragraph from Bartolus's writings thus evidently holds a key to understanding the nature of Conring's turn to history.[67] But the key is enigmatic. On the one hand, it makes one of Bartolus's most far-reaching statements about the emperor's right to rule the world. Yet, on the other hand, it insists that the kings of France and England have every right not to obey the emperor—not to mention that in previous passages he had reckoned with several other degrees of disobedience to the emperor on the part of the Italian city-states, the Venetians, and the church. What exactly the emperor's universal lordship is supposed to mean under those circumstances, and how it is to be reconciled with disobedience to him, is not obvious at all.

There surely is something very odd about a "lord and monarch over the entire world" who cannot expect obedience from "the king of France, the king of England, and others like them," or from Greeks, Mongols, Saracens, and so on. There is something equally odd about a king who admits that the emperor is lord of the world but then does not obey that lord. How could the kings of France and England possibly have admitted that the emperor "is universal lord" and then cheerfully gone on to "remove themselves from his universal lordship by virtue of a privilege, prescription, or another such reason"? What kind of universal lordship was that? What conceivable purpose could it have served to threaten anyone with heresy for denying the emperor's universal lordship if they did not have to obey the emperor in the first place? Was the very idea of a king who accepted the emperor's universal lordship without obeying him not flat-out contradictory? Why did Bartolus say that the French, the English, and the clergy merely belonged to the Roman people? Would it not have been far more logical to insist that they should have obeyed the emperor as well and that their failure to obey him was nothing but a matter of open conflict with the law?[68]

There are no answers to any of these questions in the passages just quoted.[69] Bartolus invokes the determination of the church and the example of Christ. Those are surely pertinent. But they do not allay the suspicion that the emperor's universal lordship was an empty concept—especially since

Bartolus himself does not explain what exactly he meant by the "determination of the church." If we are to understand how Conring's argument transformed the universal lordship of the emperor into a myth, we need to grasp more firmly what kind of lordship Bartolus had in mind when he called the emperor "lord and monarch over the entire world" (*dominus et monarcha totius orbis*).

The best way to begin is to insist on a basic point: Bartolus was perfectly well aware that the emperor did not rule the world in fact. His analysis of the term *enemies of Rome* alone implied as much. Elsewhere in his writings, in his commentary on the first law of Justinian's *Code*, he expressed the same awareness more clearly. According to *Code* 1.1.1, the emperor expected "all the people whom we rule with the moderation of our clemency" to follow the religion established by Saint Peter in Rome. In the Latin it began with the words *Cunctos populos* (all the people). It is therefore commonly referred to as the law *Cunctos populos*.[70]

The very words *Cunctos populos* obviously invited the question who "all the people" were. Bartolus was convinced that a proper answer had to distinguish what was right as a matter of law from what was the case as a matter of fact. The emperor no longer ruled the world as a matter of fact (and quite possibly never had). But as a matter of law, he did:

> Either the meaning of the word *rule* is understood according to law [de iure]. In that case it means that the emperor rules all the people as a matter of law and the relative pronoun *whom* is taken to be declarative, meaning simply "all the people" [without any further qualification, and regardless of whether they obey the emperor in fact]. This is what I believe the emperor meant. Or you may want to understand it according to the facts [de facto]. In that case the relative pronoun *whom* is taken to have a restrictive meaning, because there are certain people who do not in fact obey the emperor, so that "obeying the emperor" is a quality that does not apply to all in general [and the relative pronoun restricts the meaning of *rule* to people who obey the emperor in fact].[71]

Bartolus thus distinguished between two possible interpretations of the clause "whom we rule" in the phrase "all the people whom we rule." If the clause was taken *de iure*, as a matter of law, it was "declarative" (nonrestrictive). "Whom we rule with the moderation of our clemency" added to the meaning of "all the people" by pointing to a further characteristic all the people shared in addition to being ruled by the emperor. It was as if the emperor had said, "All the people whom we rule—and by the way, we happen to rule these people with the moderation of our clemency. . . ." If the clause was taken *de facto*, it was restrictive. In that sense the relative clause narrowed the meaning of "all the people" to people who were in fact ruled by the emperor, as if the emperor had said, "All the people and only the people whom we do in fact rule by the moderation of our clemency. . . ." Taken abstractly, both senses were possible. But Bartolus thought the emperor had spoken *de iure*.[72]

From the start Bartolus thus defined the emperor's universal power as a matter of law, distinguishing it sharply from whatever the matters of fact may have been. He was perfectly well aware that in fact the power of the emperor was severely limited. That was the premise of his entire attempt to define the meaning of the term *enemies of Rome*. If the emperor had ruled the world as a matter of fact, there would have been no need for his attention to foreign people, nor would there have been any need for the careful calibration with which he distinguished foreign peoples such as the Greeks, the Saracens, and the Indians from one another according to their different relationships to the Roman empire. Much less would there have been any need to distinguish between members of the Roman people who did obey the emperor and members who did not. But Bartolus was interested in law. He reckoned with the facts not because they determined what was law and what was not, but because without them the law could not be properly applied. He was thoroughly convinced that the emperor did have the right to rule all the people in the simple declarative sense as a matter of law. This was what the law maintained. As a jurist he agreed with the law, and he did so most forcefully at the very point where he stated the factual limitation of the law with the greatest clarity.[73]

The importance of that fact can hardly be overestimated. It certifies that Conring's brief portrayal of Bartolus was a caricature. Like any caricature, it seized on a characteristic and important feature—the emperor's claim to universal rule—but exaggerated that feature out of proportion. The exaggeration was perhaps justified. By the time when Conring was writing, the emperor's claim to rule the world no longer made the sort of sense it had still made to Bartolus. But deserved caricature is still caricature. It must not be confused with a fair representation of what Bartolus had taught. By Bartolus's own account, a deep gap divided the practice from the theory of the emperor's power. Just like Conring, Bartolus realized that the doctrines he found in Roman law clashed with the facts. He, too, took the clash seriously, and he struggled to solve it in a way that was intellectually tenable. To Bartolus himself the emperor's claim to rule the world already presented something of a puzzle. To be sure, Bartolus went on to solve the puzzle in favor of the law, and the manner in which he did so differed greatly from what Coning was going to say about the same question. Very much unlike

Conring, he took the emperor's right seriously as a matter of law and never dreamed of adopting a temporal perspective in which that right came to be transformed into a metaphorical expression with no contemporary weight at all. But that is hardly surprising. What is surprising, given Conring's categorical rejection of Bartolus's views, is the fundamental similarity between the two. Conring never acknowledged that.

This is our first clear piece of evidence that Conring's attack on Bartolus was something other than a refutation of Bartolus's views on grounds of fact. Yet the distinction between matters of fact and matters of law was evidently not enough for Bartolus to sustain his claims. Merely insisting on the emperor's right to rule the world as a matter of law without offering any explanation for the disparity between facts and rights would, even in his time, have struck thoughtful observers as narrow-minded legalism. More to the point, without any further explanation, Bartolus's insistence on the emperor's right to rule the world as a matter of law threw doubt upon the legitimacy of the Italian city-states and the kings of France and England. For though these did not obey the emperor, they most certainly did not simply rule de facto.

Tyrants ruled de facto. That was precisely why they were considered tyrants. But the independence of the Italian city-states from the emperor did not make them tyrannical. On the contrary, they were "emperors unto themselves" (*sibi princeps*), as Bartolus declared in a celebrated phrase, and they ruled *de iure*. The king of France ruled *de iure,* too, and could therefore be considered "an emperor in his own kingdom" (*imperator in regno suo*).[74] Those forms of rule were legitimate. And yet they did not obey the emperor. How then did they differ from tyrants? How was their right as emperors unto themselves to be reconciled with the right of the emperor to rule the world? Clearly it would not do to say the former ruled in fact and the latter ruled by law.

Bartolus never presented his understanding of the relationship between the emperor, the city-states, and the French and English monarchies in one single place. His writing followed the order of the laws in the *Corpus Iuris*. Whatever coherence it possessed depended on the underlying conceptual framework of the law and the clarity of his analysis. That is no less true of his account of the meaning of the emperor's right to rule the world than of any number of other subjects. But thankfully, he used his terms with a remarkable degree of consistency and furnished cross-references linking even widely separated passages together if they dealt with the same ideas.

I shall therefore present Bartolus's explication of the emperor's right to rule the world and the manner in which he reconciled that right with the legitimacy of territorial rulers who did not obey the emperor as a series of steps linked together, not by their location in Bartolus's writings, but by a common logic. These steps will take us first to Bartolus's understanding of empire (*imperium*), because that was the power from which the emperor derived his name, and that made him what he was. Attention to empire will almost instantly lead to jurisdiction (*iurisdictio*), because Bartolus treated empire as but one type of jurisdiction. From there I shall move on to lordship (*dominium*) in order to determine why he considered the emperor to be a lord. Once the relationship between empire, jurisdiction, and lordship is clarified, we shall find ourselves in a better position to state exactly what kind of lordship over the world Bartolus attributed to the emperor.

Imperium

One of the most important passages for grasping the nature of the emperor's power was, appropriately enough, Bartolus's commentary on the word for that power. That word, of course, was empire (*imperium*). Empire meant not only the territory over which the emperor ruled but also the power that he exercised. Hence it was crucial to determine just what that power was.

Bartolus did so in his commentary on *Digest* 2.1.3. The different types of jurisdiction that he considered there and the relationships between them are not self-evident to modern readers. But the main issues are not difficult to disentangle, and they are fundamental for understanding the peculiar right the emperor had to rule the world. It is therefore worth paying close attention to Bartolus's own words:

> Jurisdiction [iurisdictio] is divided into empire [imperium] and jurisdiction [iurisdictio], and empire is further subdivided into pure empire [imperium merum] and mixed empire [imperium mixtum]. . . .
>
> To clarify this issue, I first pose this question: what is jurisdiction, generically speaking? I answer that it is a power established by public law [potestas de iure publico introducta], as the gloss notes on *Digest* 2.1.1, where I have explained the matter in detail.
>
> Second, I ask why jurisdiction is called *iurisdictio*. The gloss answers that it is so called because it is composed of *ditio,* which means "power," and *ius* [which means "law," so that *iurisdictio* means] "power of law" [iuris potestas], as it were. That *ditio* is the same as "power" [potestas] is proved in the preface to the *Institutes,* section 1, and in *Code* 6.7.2.[75]

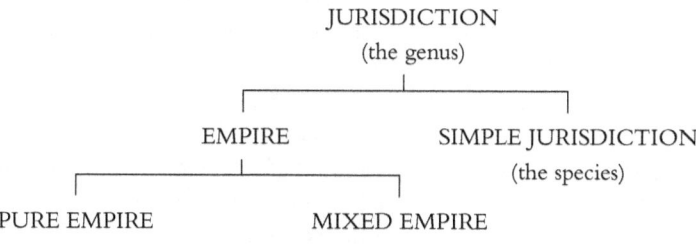

Jurisdiction and Empire

Third, I ask whether pure empire and mixed empire are included in the genus "jurisdiction." Some say that according to the law presently under consideration [*Digest* 2.1.3], they are not included, because jurisdiction and empire are there treated as separate species. But the gloss holds otherwise, and it is right to do so, as is proved above, in title 2, book 1,[76] where the gloss calls pure empire "jurisdiction," in *Novels* 15.1.1, and here [in *Digest* 2.1.3], where it says that jurisdiction is also called "power" [potestas]. For as I have just pointed out, "power" and "jurisdiction" are one and the same thing, and jurisdiction is called "jurisdiction" [iurisdictio] because it is the "power of law" [potestas iuris]. On the basis of the present text, the same is true of pure empire and mixed empire, because according to this text jurisdiction is an ingredient of empire in the same way in which a genus is an ingredient in its species, for which see *Digest* 32.1.47 and the comments there....

What then is the meaning of empire taken in an unqualified sense? I say that it is the kind of jurisdiction appropriate to the office of a noble judge. What I call "jurisdiction" takes the place of the genus in this definition, and the phrase "appropriate to the office of a noble judge" serves to distinguish this kind of jurisdiction from the jurisdiction appropriate to the office of a hired judge. The proof for this can be found in *Novels* 15.1.1.[77]

This may well seem confusing, but it is simpler than it seems at first (see the figure). The essence of the passage can be stated briefly: Bartolus defined empire by its relationship to jurisdiction, he defined jurisdiction as "power established by public law," and he divided that power into empire and jurisdiction.

Jurisdiction thus had two entirely different meanings. One referred to the genus, that is, "power established by public law"; the other referred to the species, that is, one of the two kinds of jurisdiction into which the genus was divided. The former usage included empire, the latter was specifically opposed to it.

That terminology obviously lends itself to confusion. In order to avoid confusion, Bartolus sometimes distinguished explicitly between "jurisdiction as a genus" (*iurisdictio in genere sumpta*), which included *imperium,* and jurisdiction as a species or "simple jurisdiction" (*iurisdictio simplex*), which did not. I am going to follow that practice and use *jurisdiction* or *iurisdictio* when I mean jurisdiction in the generic sense, and *simple jurisdiction* or *iurisdictio simplex* when I mean the sense specifically opposed to empire.

The terminological difficulty notwithstanding, the basic difference between empire and simple jurisdiction is clear. The difference turned on the character of the judge who exercised jurisdiction. Empire, as Bartolus said toward the end of the passage, was jurisdiction by a "noble judge," whereas simple jurisdiction was jurisdiction by a "hired" or "mercenary judge."[78] The difference between a noble judge and a hired judge was that the former could exercise his jurisdiction on his own initiative, whereas the latter could exercise it only when asked to do so by one of the parties to a lawsuit. Simple jurisdiction required some previous arrangement in which a mercenary judge was chosen to settle the dispute. Empire required no such arrangement. Empire inhered in the person of the noble judge and entitled him to settle disputes on his own initiative, independently of the wishes of the parties concerned. The right to take such initiatives was what Bartolus considered jurisdiction in the full sense of a publicly established power of law.

Another difference between the noble and the hired judge was that empire concerned public utility (*utilitas publica*), whereas simple jurisdiction concerned only private utility (*utilitas privata*)—roughly speaking, the difference between issues of legislation and criminal law, on the one hand, and issues of civil litigation on the other. But a noble judge did not exercise his jurisdiction exclusively over matters of public utility. He was entitled to deal with matters of private utility as well, and sometimes did so. That explained to Bartolus why the empire of a noble judge needed be subdivided into two subspecies: pure empire (*imperium merum*) and mixed empire (*imperium mixtum*). When a noble judge dealt solely with matters of public utility, he was exercising pure empire; when he dealt with matters of private utility, he was exercising mixed empire—mixed, that is to say, because a noble judge with empire was exercising the simple jurisdiction normally exercised by hired judges.[79]

All told, Bartolus thus distinguished three types of "powers established by public law": pure empire, mixed empire, and simple jurisdiction. He went on to subdivide each of these types into a profusion of further varieties, and he listed the legal and governmental activities appropriate to each of them as thoroughly as he was able at the appropriate points in his commentaries. We do not need to discuss the details of this classification here. It is enough to point out that Bartolus considered legislation to be the supreme function of pure empire and that even medieval readers needed systematic guidance to keep the distinctions between the different levels of jurisdiction straight.[80]

The question is how understanding empire as a kind of jurisdiction permitted Bartolus to make sense of the emperor's lordship over the world without either emptying it of genuine meaning or denying the legitimacy of territorial rulers like the Italian city-states and the northern European monarchies who were "emperors unto themselves." For that purpose it will be useful to clarify how deeply his understanding of empire and jurisdiction differed from that of ancient Roman jurists.

In antiquity, and at the most basic level, empire had simply meant "the right to give orders" (*ius imperandi*). It was therefore possible to call the binding force of a law "empire of law" (*imperium legis*), the power of the head of the family his "domestic empire" (*imperium domesticum*), and the supreme power of the Roman people the "empire of the Roman people" (*imperium populi Romani*). In a more technical sense, empire referred to "the official power of the higher magistrates (*magistratus maiores*) under the Republic, and of the emperor under the empire." This power "embraced various domains of administration, legislative initiative through proposals made before the popular assemblies (*ius agendi cum populo*), and military command."[81]

Empire thus could be used to designate a variety of things, from domestic matters to those highest public functions of the body politic that have in modern times been assigned to sovereigns. But the root from which all of these meanings grew was the ability to give and enforce orders. Hence the most characteristic form of empire was perhaps that of a general in the Roman army who had confirmed his "right to give orders" by such outstanding victories over enemies of Rome that he was rewarded with a triumphal procession through Rome and with acclamation as emperor (*imperator*). That kind of emperor truly had proved his ability to exercise empire! And it needs underscoring that such an emperor was not a legislator but a commander in chief.

Jurisdiction was defined as "the power and activity of *ius dicere*, i.e., of fixing legal principles needed in order to settle legal controversies. The term covers any judicial activity in civil matters, and in a broader sense, all activity connected with the administration of justice."[82] According to ancient Roman principles, jurisdiction was thus utterly different from empire. It was not at all defined as a right to give orders, much less as the power of a victorious general. If it had anything to do with a right to give orders at all, it was only indirectly, insofar as some sort of order might be expected to be given by a qualified magistrate after jurisdiction had settled the issues raised by a legal dispute. In principle jurisdiction was conceived as a fundamentally different kind of activity from empire.

Of course, the Roman republic was, over time, transformed into an empire, and eventually the emperor came to rule supreme over all areas of public life, including jurisdiction. Thus empire and jurisdiction came to be assimilated to each other. Since both of them eventually landed in the hands of one and the same *imperator*, it was only plausible to treat them as different manifestations of the same imperial power. One might therefore have expected Roman jurists to have formulated a theory according to which jurisdiction was a kind of empire, or perhaps Bartolus's own view according to which empire was a kind of jurisdiction. It is worth noting that they never did. To be sure, Roman jurists clearly recognized that the emperor had ultimate control over both empire and jurisdiction. Hence they tried mightily to impose clarity on the relationship between empire and jurisdiction. But they failed. "With regard to the administration of justice, *imperium* is sometimes opposed to, and distinguished from, *iurisdictio*, sometimes coherently connected with it."[83]

Moreover, since jurisdiction was now joined to empire, the jurists found themselves compelled to distinguish between two kinds of empire, depending on the kind of jurisdiction it included: "pure empire" (*imperium merum*) and "mixed empire" (*imperium mixtum*). Pure empire was reserved for "the full magisterial power. As far as jurisdiction is concerned, it is limited only to criminal matters (*ius gladii, potestas gladii*) ['the right of the sword', 'the power of the sword'] and does not include jurisdiction in civil matters. If, however, the latter was granted, too, the *imperium* was termed *imperium mixtum*."[84]

The distinction between a kind of empire that involved only matters of the sword and another kind of empire that also included jurisdiction over civil matters still reflects the underlying difference between a right to give orders (*imperium*) and a power to settle legal principles (*iurisdictio*). It was, to put it crassly, the difference between a general and a judge. And it seems that even at the height of the Roman empire, when generals had long since succeeded in concentrating all judicial power in their hands to such an extent that they had themselves become supreme judge and legislator—it seems that even then Roman jurists never quite managed to forget the fundamental difference between the right to give orders and the power to settle legal principles.

Even a cursory inspection of the ancient meanings of empire and jurisdiction (and nothing further is intended here) is thus enough to highlight how deeply Bartolus's understanding of empire differed from that of Roman antiquity, despite the similarity of his terminology. Until the very end, ancient Roman jurists thought of jurisdiction and empire as different kinds of powers that were best defined in terms of their concrete manifestations. They showed no fondness at all for the dialectical methods of logical analysis and classification, popular in medieval universities, by which Bartolus related jurisdiction and empire to each other. They remembered the fundamental difference between a power to command and the function of reconciling disputes by law. And they encountered real conceptual difficulties in relating them to each other as late as the time of Justinian, when the presence of a single emperor combining all the powers of a head of state in his person furnished a powerful impulse to define the relationship between those powers in a systematic way.[85]

Bartolus's analysis may thus have been couched in terms of ancient Roman law. And the similarity of his terminology to that of antiquity constitutes a great temptation to jump to the conclusion that he must have been struggling with the same difficulties as ancient Roman jurists did. But the temptation needs to be resisted. The terminological continuity conceals a deep conceptual break. Whereas ancient Roman jurists were uncertain about the relationship between empire and jurisdiction, Bartolus believed the relationship was cut-and-dried: jurisdiction was public power, and empire was one of its kinds.

As a result the ancient meanings of jurisdiction and empire were utterly transformed. Empire was no longer derived from any specific powers held by generals or magistrates or judges, as had been the case in ancient Rome. Instead it was defined by an overarching conceptual framework, into which Bartolus considered it his job to fit the specific powers. His treatment of jurisdiction and empire furnishes a perfect illustration of what people mean when they speak of the scholastic method and the impact of Aristotelian logic on medieval thought.[86] That method and that logic enabled Bartolus to gloss over, almost without thinking twice, a difference that ancient Roman jurists had not been able to resolve in centuries of trying.

This was a crucial step. Jurisdiction was now more fundamental than empire. It was the generic essence by which all public powers were united.

Empire, by contrast, lost its supreme position as the sole and original power to command and became something like an executive subordinate to jurisdiction. The unconditional quality by which it had been raised above jurisdiction was diluted: all public powers were now subsumed under the rule of law. The power to command obedience was merely one of them. No room was left for the power of generals or magistrates to make those unconditional commands that ancient Romans had once called *imperium.* Yet, in another sense empire was enhanced as well. It could now be regarded as the source of legislation. Instead of standing in opposition to legislation or being limited by it, legislation was now empire's highest function.[87]

At one stroke Bartolus thus blew away whatever doubts may have beset ancient Roman jurists trying to reconcile the emperor's jurisdiction with his empire. At the same time he gave a new meaning to fundamental terms of law with a long pedigree.[88] That helps explain how he was able to reconcile the emperor's lack of real power with his right to rule the world. If the ancient Roman meaning of empire had persisted without change, his task would have been more difficult. A universal commander in chief whom no one obeys, after all, really is a contradiction in terms. So is a sovereign ruler whom no one obeys—a point that Hobbes was going to make particularly clearly.[89] But Bartolus defined the emperor neither as a universal commander in chief nor as a sovereign ruler. Having transformed the question of empire into a question of jurisdiction, he defined the emperor as universal judge and legislator. Questions of obedience were consequently distinguishable from questions of empire in a way that would have been unthinkable in antiquity and became unthinkable again under sovereignty. An emperor whose most important function consists of legislation can easily be imagined to wield his empire over parts of the world where he is not obeyed or where no one has ever even heard of him. Law, after all, can still be law where it is actively resisted or ignored.

Shifting the question from empire to jurisdiction alone, however, was not enough. It might have sufficed for reconciling the emperor's universal lordship with the existence of tyrants and "foreign people," because these resisted or ignored the justice of the emperor's universal rule. The case would have been clear: the emperor's jurisdiction was valid as a matter of law, *de iure,* but not as a matter of fact, *de facto.* But this did not explain how any ruler could have recognized the emperor's universal lordship but refused to obey him and could still have been considered legitimate. If the emperor was responsible for universal jurisdiction, one should have thought that rulers who did not obey his jurisdiction were illegitimate by definition. Yet this is not what Bartolus maintained. There still remains this puzzle: how could

Bartolus have expected legitimate European rulers to bow to the emperor as the world's supreme judge and legislator without expecting them to obey his jurisdiction?

The question is made more urgent by Bartolus's insistence on calling the emperor something other than universal judge or legislator. He called him universal lord, *dominus mundi,* and he declared that it was heresy to deny not merely his jurisdiction, but his lordship, *dominium.* Now *lord* is different from *legislator,* and *lordship* is different from *jurisdiction.* Therefore, we shall have to grapple with the relationship between jurisdiction and *dominium.*

Dominium

Dominium is, like *imperium,* one of the fundamental terms of Roman law. But it is, if anything, even more fraught with confusions arising from fundamental differences in meaning that are concealed by terminological continuities. In ancient Roman law, *dominium* "denotes full legal power over a corporeal thing, the right of the owner to use it, to take proceeds therefrom, and to dispose of it freely."[90] Hence it is easy to translate as "ownership" or "property." In medieval writings, however, it must often be translated as "lordship," because the difference between private ownership and public office was not as clearly drawn as in antiquity.[91]

There was more to this than a lexical shift from one meaning (ownership) to another (lordship). One of the basic characteristics of *dominium* in classical Roman law was its indivisibility. *Dominium* was like an atom of social and material relations. Either you had *dominium* over a thing or you did not. There was nothing in between. You could not share *dominium,* at least not as a matter of principle, and you could not divide it into different components to be parceled out among different individuals. It was entirely different in medieval times. One of the most fascinating and creative exercises in medieval legal thought and practice—far from insisting on the indivisibility of *dominium*—was to find ever new ways of disentangling different elements of property or lordship from each other so that they could be parceled out to different people on different occasions and under different circumstances. This habit corresponded well to the needs of a society founded on personal obligations and framed by a hierarchy of status differentiations. But it also posed a problem: how to account for those divisions of *dominium* in terms of a Roman law that flatly ruled them out?[92]

Bartolus had his own perspective. He was of course perfectly well aware that jurisdiction and *dominium* were different. But he was also sure that they were not entirely separate. The reason was fundamental: since *dominium* did not refer merely to property but also to lordship, and since jurisdiction was one of the most important functions of any lord, they had to be related. What was that relationship?

He gave a succinct answer in his commentary on *Digest* 2.1.1. He started from a simple observation: *dominium* and jurisdiction were related to each other in that both of them represented legal powers inhering in the person or office exercising them. That person was of course a "lord." They differed from each other in that they applied to different things. *Dominium* applied to things the lord owned as his private property. This form of lordship was in the hands of anyone who owned some private property—to the extent that any medieval form of property can fairly be called private. Jurisdiction, however, applied to the territory over which the lord exercised his lordship. This form of lordship was a matter of not owning things but ruling lands. Yet it, too, inhered in the person of the lord, side-by-side with his ownership of property.

It might of course be thought that this relationship was purely accidental. That a lord combined two legal powers in his person did not prove that those powers were related to each other. But Bartolus believed they were. And as proof for their relationship, he offered none other than the emperor:

> *Dominium* is something that inheres in the person of the owner, but it applies to the thing that he owns. In the same way jurisdiction inheres in an office and in the person of the officeholder, but it applies to a territory. Jurisdiction is thus not a quality of the territory, but rather of the person. And the proof for this parallel between jurisdiction and *dominium* is this: the emperor has universal jurisdiction, as was said above, in *Digest* 1.4.1, and that is why below, in *Digest* 14.2.9, he is called lord of the world. Just as any judge may be called the prince of the city or the territory over which he presides, as is pointed out below in *Digest* 27.1.15, he may also be called the *dominus* of that entire territory as a whole, as I have repeatedly said about the emperor, especially in my commentary on the first law of the *Digest*.[93]

There was perfect symmetry between *dominium* and jurisdiction, and there was a perfectly analogical relationship between the emperor and any other lord. Every lord combined *dominium* and jurisdiction in his own person just as the emperor did, except that the emperor did so for the entire world, whereas all other lords did so only for whatever territory they happened to be ruling. The emperor alone deserved to be called "prince" in the emphatic sense that was appropriate for the ruler of the world. But in a less emphatic sense, any "judge" who exercised jurisdiction over a limited territory or a city deserved to be called a prince as well.

This struck Bartolus as a principle of exhilarating power:

> This has a consequence that is as beautiful as it is true. It is that, if the prince or someone else grants you a territory as a whole, he appears to grant you complete jurisdiction over it as well, because just as someone granting you a certain thing is said to give you *dominium* over that thing, as in *Digest* 18.1.25, so he who gives you a territory as a whole gives you the jurisdiction over it as well, because the relationship between jurisdiction and territory is the same as that between *dominium* and some particular thing.[94]

That was a stunning conclusion, truly a brilliant piece of constitutional reasoning in the medieval mode. It rested on an analogy between transfers of things owned by private owners and transfers of land ruled by public lords. If you transferred a thing to someone else, you gave that person the right to own that thing. In just the same way, Bartolus declared, if you transferred a piece of land to someone else, you gave the person the right to exercise jurisdiction over that piece of land. *Dominium* and jurisdiction were not merely similar because both inhered in a person or office. In a fundamental sense, they were identical. There was an underlying principle of lordship, of which *dominium* and jurisdiction were merely two different expressions. This underlying principle applied equally to private property and public power.

If this was a reasonable way of looking at the matter, Bartolus was well on his way to answering the question why the emperor was properly called *dominus mundi*, "lord of the world," even while faithful Christian rulers and governments refused to obey him. He was lord of the world *because* he had jurisdiction over the whole world. But was it a reasonable way? If jurisdiction and *dominium* were fundamentally identical aspects of one underlying kind of lordship, did that not entail that a person with jurisdiction owned his territory as though it were a piece of private property? *Dominium*, after all, could mean ownership. And if the ruler owned his territory, did he not own everything in his territory as well? If Bartolus was right to maintain that "the relationship between jurisdiction and territory is the same as that between *dominium* and some particular thing," where was the line dividing *dominium* from jurisdiction?

That question was almost as old as the revival of Roman jurisprudence in the eleventh century. Not coincidentally, it was one of the first to which Bartolus turned in his commentary on the *Digest*. The occasion was furnished by the first imperial constitution in the *Digest*, known by its opening word as *Omnem*. *Omnem* began by speaking about "the whole body of the law of our state."[95] Medieval jurists had long since wondered what exactly "our state" was supposed to mean. Did it mean that the state belonged to the emperor in the same way in which private property belonged to its owner? Or did it mean that the emperor had jurisdiction over the state without owning it as his property? The answer would decide what kind of lordship the emperor had.

The step that Bartolus took first was obvious and familiar. He pointed out that according to Roman law itself, the subjects of the emperor had *dominium* over their private property and that their *dominium* was indivisible. It followed, Bartolus maintained with unassailable logic, that the emperor could not possibly have the same *dominium* over the same private property:

> The gloss on the word *law* [in the constitution *Omnem*] poses the following question: since the emperor is said to have the *dominium* of universal jurisdiction, does that mean that he has *dominium* over all individual things as well?[96] That question was ventilated by Martinus and Bulgarus long ago.
>
> At first sight it might seem that, as the emperor is *dominus* of all things in the universe, he must also be *dominus* of all individual things, as is suggested by the text of *Digest* 14.2.9 and *Code* 7.37.3. . . .
>
> On the other hand, however, according to *Digest* 13.6.5, undivided *dominium* cannot belong to two people at the same time. Now I see that according to *Institutes* 2.1.11, *dominium* over individual things belongs to individual people. Hence it cannot belong to the emperor.
>
> Moreover, the right to lay a legal claim to a thing belongs to the person who has *dominium* over that thing, as is pointed out in *Digest* 6.1.23 below. But I see that according to *Digest* 6.1.1, individuals do have the right to make such claims. Hence they must have *dominium*—and if they have *dominium*, the emperor cannot have it.
>
> What shall we say? The gloss determines in favor of the opinion of Bulgarus that the emperor does not have *dominium* over individual things.[97]

That eliminated one possible answer to the question about the meaning of the emperor's role as *dominus* of the world: he did not own everything. It was true that he was called *dominus mundi* in *Digest* 14.2.9 and that according to *Code* 7.37.3, "everything is understood to belong to the prince."[98] Thus the emperor doubtless had what Bartolus called the "*dominium* of universal jurisdiction." But it was equally true that the *dominium* of universal jurisdiction was something different from *dominium* over individual things. According to Roman law itself, individual people had the right to lay a legal claim to their property in a court of law by doing what the Romans called "to vindicate a thing" (*rei vindicatio*). Since that right was reserved to those who had *dominium*, individual people clearly did have *dominium*, and since *dominium* was indivisible, the emperor equally clearly could not have the same *dominium* as well.

That point had been established as early as the twelfth century in a famous dispute between Martinus and Bulgarus, two well-known doctors of Roman law whose disagreement had exercised the jurists' imagination ever after and to whom Bartolus briefly alludes.[99] But it did not really settle the matter. It determined a right the emperor did not have: the right to private ownership over all things in the world. But it failed to determine which right, if any, the emperor did have, and it left the relationship between *dominium* and jurisdiction undecided. If the emperor was not the owner of all things in the world, what was the meaning of his "*dominium* of universal jurisdiction," and why was he called *dominus* of the world?

There were competing ways of answering that question. One of them had been taken up by the gloss. The gloss recognized that *dominium* did not exist in isolation. For even though *dominium* in the strict sense was limited to the private person who actually owned the thing, it needed to be protected by publicly established authorities. This was an especially important consideration for the church. The church had no means to defend itself and, in a legal sense, depended on the emperor for its defense against its enemies. Accordingly, it could be argued that the emperor was called *dominus* by extension.

The logic is easy to follow: ownership is not worth much unless it can be preserved intact. Hence it is plausible to include both ownership and protection of ownership in *dominium*. According to that logic, the emperor did not have strict *dominium* over all things in the world. But no one else could have strict *dominium* over them either, unless they were able to enjoy their ownership in peace and quiet. And since it was the function of the emperor to preserve such peace and quiet by protecting his subjects from violent aggression, the emperor could be called *dominus* over all things by metonymy.

In principle Bartolus endorsed that kind of reasoning:

> It needs to be said that the emperor is called *dominus mundi* by virtue of the protection and jurisdiction [that he gives to people who have *dominium* over particular things in the world], because he is obliged to defend and protect the whole world. The word "our" [in the phrase "our state" in *Omnem*], in other words, could refer to *dominium* [in the strict sense], and in that case it would not apply to the emperor. But sometimes it is used in the context of protection, and then it does apply to the emperor, as in the present case. Another proof for the same point is this: I see that people are sometimes called *dominus* because they exercise some kind of protection or administration, as in *Digest* 47.2.49 and in *Digest* 41.4.7.[100]

On this account the emperor could be called *dominus mundi*, lord of the world, not because he had *dominium* over everything in the world, but because he protected the private individuals who did. They had the *dominium*, and he was their *dominus*.

That was an attractive solution. But it had two weaknesses. One was that it reintroduced the problem of the indivisibility of *dominium*. If you argued that the emperor was *dominus* because he protected the *dominium* of private owners, did this not mean that you had divided *dominium* into different components? That would not have been allowed. The other weakness was that protecting the world was different from exercising jurisdiction over the world. Calling the emperor lord of the world because he was responsible for protecting the world did not exactly settle the question about the relationship between *dominium* and jurisdiction. If protection was the reason why the emperor was called lord of the world, what did his universal jurisdiction have to do with his lordship?

The passage just quoted is not as clear on this point as one might like. First it says that the emperor "is called lord of the world by virtue of protection and jurisdiction." That makes it seem as though protection and jurisdiction go hand in hand. But in the next sentences, jurisdiction drops out of sight, and the reasons the emperor is called *dominus* are limited to protection and administration. Does that mean that Bartolus shifted his explanation of why the emperor was called *dominus mundi* from jurisdiction to protection?

That argument has been made, but I do not believe it is valid.[101] It confuses Bartolus's discussion of one of the reasons offered by the gloss that the emperor is called *dominus mundi* with Bartolus's own account of the emperor's *dominium*. Bartolus acknowledged the point made by the gloss. But he considered the reasoning of the gloss inadequate. He made that very clear when he returned to the relationship between jurisdiction and *dominium* in his commentary on *Digest* 6.1.1. *Digest* 6.1.1 dealt with *rei vindicatio*, the procedure by which an owner, a *dominus*, sued for the recovery of private property that had been taken away from him.

> Now consider the method of pronouncing and executing judgment in a case involving [the vindication of a legal claim of *dominium* to] a certain whole [as, for example, a flock of sheep]. In a case like that, the judge may pronounce that the flock belongs to me, but the flock will nevertheless only be returned to me after any individual heads belonging to someone else have been taken away.
>
> This is why I am accustomed to say in my commentary on the constitution *Omnem* that the emperor is truly *dominus* of the whole world, even though the

glosses say that he is *dominus* only insofar as he protects everything, since different people cannot have complete *dominium* over the same thing. It is no valid counterargument that other people are *domini* over individual things, because the world is a kind of whole. Hence someone can be said to have this whole [like a *dominus*], even though the individual things do not belong to him. If someone else were to hold the world, the emperor could therefore vindicate his claim [in a court of law].[102]

Bartolus thus explicitly distinguished his own point of view from that of the gloss. The gloss thought the emperor was called *dominus mundi* only because he protected the whole world. But there had to be a better reason to call him lord of the world than that. It was, of course, true that individual things belonged to individual owners, and their *dominium* was indivisible. But the gloss had not recognized that the world was more than the sum of all the individual things in it. It was itself an individual thing, like all other individual things, and quite distinct from them. Hence there was a kind of *dominium* that applied to the world, considered not as a collection of particular things, but as a single whole, in just the same way as *dominium* applied to all individual things. *Dominium* over the world as a whole was really no different from *dominium* over particular things in the world. It was equally indivisible and equally subject to the legal procedure by which plaintiffs could establish their *dominium* over any particular thing.

In order to appreciate the significance of that solution, it will be useful to underscore how sharply the emperor's right to rule the world was circumscribed. His right was universal, but, contrary to what modern readers too easily imagine, universal was not the same as total. It was a right to the whole, but not to the parts. That difference may be difficult to grasp from a modern point of view. It may even seem absurd. But it is crucial for understanding Bartolus's case and may be crucial, too, for grasping the specific horror of tyranny in the modern world. Just as the rights of a shepherd over his flock did not include a property right over every sheep in the flock, so the emperor's right to the whole world did not include *dominium* over any particular parts of the world. His right of universal jurisdiction was just that: a right of universal, not particular, jurisdiction.

That placed definite limits on the emperor's power. For example, the emperor's right to universal jurisdiction did not allow him to issue laws concerning only certain parts of the world, much less private individuals. As Bartolus put it, "whatever pleases the prince has the power of a general law when it is done with the intention of establishing right [ius], but not if it is done with respect to specific persons, for in that case it does not abstract from particular individuals."[103] True enough, the emperor could interfere in particular matters and with particular persons in many ways, especially by granting privileges. That raised a whole host of further considerations. But none of them overturned the basic principle that imperial acts qualified as acts of universal jurisdiction only if they applied equally to all. As Bartolus asked in his commentary on *Omnem:* "Can the emperor, without cause, take away my *dominium* simply by passing a law? I say no."[104] The emperor's lordship was at one and the same time universal and firmly restricted.

In this fashion Bartolus was able to maintain his faith in the underlying identity of the emperor's universal jurisdiction with his universal *dominium*. The reason the emperor was properly called lord *of* the world had nothing to do with his *dominium* over any particular things *in* the world. He was called *dominus mundi* because he alone had *dominium* over the world considered as a single whole. It was this *dominium* that inhered in the emperor's person. And this *dominium* was so closely related to the emperor's jurisdiction that Bartolus could call it in a single phrase the "*dominium* of universal jurisdiction" (*dominium universalis iurisdictionis*), as though the two were consubstantial. The "*dominium* of universal jurisdiction" was uniquely and exclusively the emperor's right. If anyone had taken it from him, he would have been entitled to go to court and start an action of *vindicatio rei* to recover his right to rule the world. Bartolus concluded without equivocation that the emperor was "truly lord of the world" (*dominus totius mundi vere*).

The Lord of the World

This, then, was the sense in which Bartolus understood the emperor to be *dominus mundi*. He put it succinctly in his commentary on the *Code:* "Everything belongs to the Prince insofar as jurisdiction and universal *dominium* are concerned, but not as far as particular *dominium* is concerned."[105] The emperor and only the emperor had *dominium* over the world as a whole. The emperor and only the emperor had jurisdiction over the world as a whole. That was his unique prerogative.[106] His right was different in principle from the rights of all other rulers, including those who ruled legitimately over certain parts of the world. Both were legitimate, but they ruled different things. And because they ruled different things, the rulers of France and the Italian city-states could very well acknowledge the emperor's status as lord of the world without losing their independence.

Thus Bartolus solved the puzzle of how the emperor could be lord of the world even though all foreign peoples, the cities of Italy, and the kings of France and England did not obey him. As far as the latter were concerned, there was a difference between being "lord of the world" and "lord of France," "lord of England," or lord of any other territory, such as the Italian cities. The emperor was "prince" of the world. But he was not the only prince combining powers of jurisdiction and *dominium* in his person. The king of France did so as well, for France. The king of France was perfectly within his rights to claim supreme jurisdiction over France. He could even refuse to obey the emperor, in France. As individual owners were within their rights to exercise their *dominium* over individual sheep without diminishing the shepherd's right to the flock, so the kings of France and England could "remove themselves from [the emperor's] universal lordship by virtue of a privilege, prescription, or another such reason" without diminishing his right to rule the world. Conversely, the emperor had no right to interfere in the government of France. Had he done so, he would not only have interfered with particular rights of *dominium* and jurisdiction that did not belong to him; he would also have failed to act as emperor. The emperor was supposed to rule the world, not France.

That is why the king of France was properly called "emperor in his kingdom," just as any "judge" could be called "prince" in his city.[107] A superficial reading might take this phrase to mean that the king of France had the same rights as the emperor. But for Bartolus that was not the point at all. On the contrary, the point was that their rights were different. In his kingdom and only in his kingdom the king of France exercised rights like those that the emperor exercised over the world and only over the world. The reason there was no conflict was that the rights of the king of France constituted a separate set from the rights of the emperor. There was no heresy if the king of France exercised *dominium* and jurisdiction over France without obeying the emperor. There would have been heresy only if the king of France had denied the emperor's right to rule the world.

The case was obviously different with "foreign people." These people were not heretics in the strict sense of the term. A heretic was someone who had broken with the Christian faith. Most foreign people had never been Christians to begin with. Hence they could not have broken with the Christian faith. But unlike legitimate Christian rulers who did not obey the emperor, they did contest the emperor's claim to rule the world, not merely in this or that part of the world, but directly and as a whole. As Bartolus put it, "foreign people, properly speaking, are those who deny that the Roman emperor is universal lord."[108] Foreign people thus did pose a direct challenge to imperial rule, and they posed it by definition, not because they refused to obey the emperor, but because they denied that he was universal lord. That was wrong, and there was no way to change that wrong, except to move them by force or persuasion to acknowledge the emperor's universal rule. They could keep their sheep. But they had to surrender their claim to the universal flock.

In order to grasp the sense of Bartolus's definition of universal lordship, it is thus necessary to keep two separate distinctions in mind. One is the distinction between a matter of law and a matter of fact (like the distinction between the emperor's right to rule the world and the denial of that right by heretics and foreign people). The other is the distinction between one matter of law and another matter of law (like the distinction between the emperor's right to rule the world and the king of France's right to rule France).

The distinction between matters of fact and matters of law is familiar. It was this distinction that allowed Bartolus to reconcile the limited extent of the emperor's actual power with his claim to rule the whole world. It was true that the emperor's actual power was limited to a certain part of Europe. But matters of fact did not determine matters of law. Those who based their right to rule exclusively on the fact that they could do so did not rule legitimately. Such was the case with tyrants, with foreign people who qualified as enemies of Rome, and with anyone who denied the emperor's right to rule the world. They ruled by force. The distinction between fact and right thus accounted for actual cases of illegitimate rule in which the emperor's right to rule the world was directly denied. It divided the world into two camps: the camp of faithful Roman Christians, who acknowledged the emperor's universal lordship, and the camp of those who did not.

But this distinction did not account for cases in which the emperor's power was limited by someone else's legitimate rule—and it is crucial to recognize that Bartolus considered such cases possible. Those were the cases of the Italian city-states and the western European monarchies. Bartolus considered their rule to be legitimate even though they did not obey the emperor. Their rule could not be accounted for by the distinction between matters of fact and matters of law. But it could be accounted for by the distinction between different levels of jurisdiction, *dominium,* and empire, none of which were inherently or automatically tied to obedience.[109]

It is of course true that the separation of *dominium,* jurisdiction, and empire from obedience is merely a conceptual device intended to reconcile potentially conflicting rights and avoid a self-contradictory position. Even if the king of France and the emperor had adopted Bartolus's reasoning, as they surely did not, contentions would have arisen over the question whether, in a specific case, the emperor was legislating for the world, which he had every right to do, or interfering in the affairs of France, which he had no right to do. Conversely, conflicts would inevitably have arisen over the question whether in a specific instance the king of France was merely fulfilling his responsibility to France, as he ought, or resisting the emperor's right to rule the world, as he ought not. But conceptual distinctions can never be applied to specific cases without raising difficulties. Such difficulties in and of themselves do not amount to an objection to the distinctions drawn by law.

One point remains to complete this analysis, and that is to explain whence the emperor obtained his universal lordship. The explanation is simple: he derived it from the only power that could guarantee the unity of the world: from God. As Bartolus put it in his commentary on the first title of the *Digest:* "Note that even the emperor invoked the name of the Lord, and thus was Christian, as I have said above in the context of the first constitution. It follows that, had he not been Christian, he could not have been emperor, and he would not have had temporal jurisdiction."[110] He summed up like this: "The empire and the church proceeded from God as their efficient cause."[111]

Hierarchy and Sovereignty

That concludes our review of the steps by which Bartolus arrived at an understanding of the emperor's right to rule the world. The reader may already be willing to agree that there was more intellectual respectability to his ideas than could be learned from reading Conring's attack on them. But merely to collect the points that Bartolus scored one by one is not enough. Bartolus's reasoning differs not only in its particulars from the reasoning that has become familiar since the historical revolt; it differs on the whole. It rested on different assumptions and was composed of different intellectual substances. That difference must be clarified. Only then can it become apparent how Conring succeeded in turning the logic of Bartolus's reasoning inside out, corroding its intellectual core, and sweeping its decomposed ingredients from the table of European intellectual life.

Bartolus's argument turned on a point of principle. That point was that the nature of all things depends on their relationships to other things. That made them what they were. In Bartolus's universe, relationships were the constituent ingredients; things were their precipitates. No thing was inherently divided from any other thing. Of course, each thing could be considered in itself. But it could also be considered, always and by definition, as part of something else. That something else in turn could be considered in itself and as part of something else again. And the relationship between the part and the whole was merely one of many possible relationships.

The definition of anything thus was as inexhaustible as the relationships in which that thing could stand to other things. In terms of law, it followed that legal rights to anything depended on the relationships in which the thing was taken. Rights could, of course, conflict. But if they were expressed in different relationships, the conflict could be resolved. The rights did not even apply to the same things, because a thing in one relationship was not the same thing in another relationship. For real conflicts to exist, different rights had to apply not only to the same things, but to the same things in the same relationship.[112]

To take the example of the flock of sheep with which Bartolus clinched his case: you could have a right to the flock, but you could also have a right to individual sheep. You could sue to recover the flock, and the judge could adjudicate the flock to you, but that did not mean that you would get the sheep that happened to be in the flock. Some sheep belonged to other owners. They could sue for their sheep, just as you could sue for your flock. That allowed Bartolus to reconcile what appeared to be a conflict between your *dominium* and their *dominium*. There was no conflict. Both *dominia* applied to the same sheep, but they applied to them in different relationships. Yours applied to the sheep insofar as they were part of the flock; theirs applied to the sheep without reference to the flock. Those were different things and different rights. It was even conceivable—strange as it may seem to people trained to believe that things are whatever they are in themselves—that you could have *dominium* over a flock of sheep without having *dominium* over a single sheep. And why not go further still? Why not reckon with the possibility of a null flock, in which there were no sheep at all? Even then your flock need not have been destroyed and your rights to it need not have been diminished. Can I not hold the title to an account in which there is no money?

The same logic applied to things and territories. Things were like sheep, and territories were like flocks. A shepherd had the right to do with his flock as he thought fit without diminishing anyone's *dominium* to individual sheep. Just so the ruler of a territory could exercise jurisdiction over the territory without diminishing anyone's *dominium* over the things in the territory. Considered in themselves, the things were subject to a pair of two different powers: the *dominium* of their owner and the jurisdiction of the ruler of the territory. But those same things could also be considered as parts of the territory as a whole. In that sense they fell under the *dominium* of the ruler. That was why the ruler was entitled to exercise jurisdiction over things he did not actually own. Moreover, a territory could itself be considered in different relationships: as an individual thing and as part of a still larger territory. Considered as an individual thing, the territory was subject to the *dominium* of its ruler and the jurisdiction of the ruler within whose larger territory it was situated. Considered as a part of that larger territory, it fell under the *dominium* of the ruler over that larger territory. That larger territory in turn could also be considered in different relationships . . . and so on.

One could thus easily imagine things and territories as related to each other in a hierarchy, each of whose parts was like an individual thing owned by its proper *dominus,* subject to the jurisdiction of all higher-ups and equipped with jurisdiction over all lower-downs. "One *dominus* for every thing in every relationship" would have been an appropriate slogan for this conception. The number of relationships was infinite. Except, of course, that ultimately one would arrive at a territory that could no longer be considered as part of any other territory because it was itself the whole of all wholes and had no boundaries around itself except its own. That was the world, the territory of all territories, class of all classes, created by God out of nothing, entrusted by him to the emperor to rule with temporal power and to the pope for salvation. The hierarchy was universal.

In this fashion the categorical distinction between things and territories was dissolved in a universal network of hierarchical relationships. So was the parallel distinction between *dominium* and jurisdiction. Whether the ruler of a given territory or the owner of a particular thing was said to have *dominium* or jurisdiction was a function of the relationship in which they were considered. In principle, they had to have both. In principle, no ruler could have *dominium* over a territory without also having jurisdiction over the people and things included in it. That is, as we have seen, why Bartolus insisted in his commentary on *Digest* 2.1.1 that "if the prince or someone else grants you a territory as a whole, he appears to grant you complete jurisdiction over it as well."[113] One can understand the pride with which he declared this principle to be "as beautiful as it is true." In a world of lords, fiefs, and vassals, grants of jurisdiction and grants of land were the foundation of all order. To have shown that *dominium* and jurisdiction were so inextricably linked together that grants of jurisdiction were by definition included in grants of territory amounted to the formulation of a constitutional theorem of the first order.

Hierarchy explains as well why Bartolus saw an analogy between local rulers and the emperor. Marcel David believed that Bartolus may have spelled *Prince* with a capital *P* when he meant the emperor and with a lowercase *p* when he meant other lords.[114] That is an interesting suggestion. Since there was only one world, there could be only one emperor. In the emperor's case, the word *Prince* could thus have functioned like a proper name. Like a proper name, it would have deserved to be written with a capital letter.

Given the uncertainties of medieval orthography, it seems doubtful that any such usage was ever followed uniformly. But whether it was or not, Bartolus left no doubt that *prince* was something besides a name for the emperor. It had a generic meaning, too. This meaning was applicable to any kind of *dominus* with jurisdiction over any territory. A judge presiding over a city or a territory combined jurisdiction with *dominium* over his territory in the same way that the emperor combined jurisdiction with *dominium* over the world. Hence every such judge was properly called a prince. Hence it was inappropriate to segregate politics from law. At bottom politics and jurisdiction were the same.

In this fashion the distinctions that Bartolus drew between *dominium* and jurisdiction, things and territories, private property and public lordship, local noble judges and the lord of the world were suspended in an emulsion transcending all distinctions and joining all things together in a universal hierarchy in which politics, jurisdiction, and property were merely different aspects of the same order. What was the substance of that hierarchy? What was the soul by which it was animated, the living bond that joined all different things together into one universal whole? Bartolus does not say. He simply declares *dominium* and jurisdiction to be "the same," *idem,* and leaves the rest to our imagination. But there is a candidate. That candidate is *ius*. *Ius* was what was right, and *ius* entitled those who had it on their side to act with justice. *Ius* was the will of God, his providential plan for the universe, no less than the law of nature, grasped partially by human reason and cast by human ingenuity in human laws.

Of course, few questions are fraught with greater difficulty than the question of just what *ius* meant in medieval times. Did it refer to an objectively existing right order of the universe? Did it refer to the subjective rights that individual agents exercised? Or both? Was it the same as law? Was it the same as justice? What was the effect of the classification of *ius* into different types, such as *ius naturale, ius civile,* and *ius gentium*? Those questions neither need nor can be answered here. Suffice it to say that they have exercised medieval as well as modern minds and continue to form the subject of heated debates.[115]

In part the difficulty turns on the difference between modern European languages that have a single word for *ius,* combining potentially opposite (objective and subjective) meanings under one lexical umbrella (such as French *droit,* Italian *diritto,* Spanish *derecho,* and German *Recht*), and English, which does not allow anyone to ignore the difference between *law* and *right*. But the terminological problem is relatively harmless. What makes the difficulty exasperatingly resilient to rational analysis are deeply ideological conflicts between legal positivists and legal realists; jurists and moral philosophers; Germanists, Romanists, and canonists; historians favoring custom and historians favoring written law that mirror an underlying difference between medieval and modern legal thought itself.

Thomas Hobbes famously attacked jurists for confusing laws with rights: "For though they that speak of this subject use to confound *jus* and *lex* (*right* and *law*), yet they ought to be distinguished, because RIGHT consisteth in liberty to do or to forbear, whereas LAW determineth and bindeth to one of them; so that law and right differ as much as obligation and liberty, which in one and the same matter are inconsistent."[116] Ever since that point was made, the distinction between laws and rights has been constitutive of modern legal and constitutional reasoning. But there is ample reason to believe that the conjunction of laws and rights ("both law and right") was constitutive of good order in medieval legal and constitutional thought and that their disjunction ("either law or right, but not both") would have been thought pernicious. *Ius* in both of its dimensions, objective and subjective, was what Bartolus studied. *Ius* figured in his definitions of both jurisdiction and *dominium*.[117] *Ius*, one may therefore suggest, may well have furnished the substance of that hierarchy by which *dominium* and jurisdiction were linked in his imagination.[118]

Matters could hardly be more different with Conring. Bartolus focused on law; Conring focused on politics. Bartolus studied *iurisdictio;* Conring studied *prudentia civilis*. Bartolus looked to eternity; Conring looked to history. For Bartolus the universe was integrated into one hierarchy; for Conring it was divided into an infinity of separate self-subsisting parts. Bartolus maintained that politics and law were fundamentally the same, Conring that they were essentially distinct. Bartolus thought the nature of things consisted of relationships; Conring, that it consisted of an invariant essence. And so on.

At the center of those differences, there was one principle: sovereignty. Sovereignty did not allow for any hierarchy of lands and lords, much less for "princes" who need not obey their ruler but must acknowledge that he rules the world. Sovereignty made each body politic a separate entity. Sovereignty required clear boundaries in space and time where one sovereign's power met that of another. States varied in accidental qualities like size, shape, number, and constitutional arrangement. But in their essence they were identical. One thing and one thing only determined whether or not there was a state. Not law, not right, not *ius*, and certainly not jurisdiction, but sovereignty, *maiestas, summa potestas*. Wherever there was sovereignty, there was a state. The membership of such a state in the community of nations depended neither on its extent nor on the justice of its laws. The freedom of its people to make laws for themselves was enough. No lord of the world was possible or needed.

This was the principle that set Conring apart from Bartolus and aligned him with Jean Bodin, the man who made the theory of sovereignty the common stock in trade of modern political philosophy.[119] In its first sentence, the *New Discourse* drew attention to the difference between a sovereign ruler and mere magistrates: "The German empire is governed by many magistrates, but only one among them is supreme."[120] The *New Discourse* teemed with states: Germans, Lombards, Franks, Spaniards, Romans, and others all had their states. They differed in size and power, but they enjoyed the same sovereignty. Conring explicitly insisted that "by virtue of its autonomy even a small independent state, for example, the republic of Ragusa, enjoys exactly the same rights of sovereignty [maiestas] as a large one."[121] Germany was but one state among the rest, superior in rank and size, but otherwise the equal of every other commonwealth. So was the Roman empire. Hence Conring had to define the boundaries dividing the kingdom of Italy from the Roman empire and devoted one of his most important writings to the boundaries of Germany.[122] Boundaries were a question of constitutional importance as great as, for Bartolus, was the question how to relate grants of jurisdiction to grants of *dominium*. Hence Conring's preoccupation with prescription, with the time when sovereign power comes into existence and when it disappears. Without clear boundaries in space and time, there would have been no commonwealth for him to consider.

Of course there have been many different theories of sovereignty.[123] But insofar as sovereignty turns on a contrast between the styles of thought that Conring and Bartolus represent, its most important features are easy to identify. In the first place, sovereignty is indivisible.[124] There can be many officials exercising jurisdiction and executing laws enacted by the sovereign. Sovereignty may extend over territories of many different sizes. It has many different aspects, such as the right to make laws, the right to declare war and peace, the right to exercise force over its subjects, the right to command obedience to the laws, and so on. Some of these are more basic than others, and there is dispute about their number and relationship. But sovereignty itself is one. It cannot be divided into different components or parceled out to different offices. It is a singular entity.

In the second place, sovereignty demands that legislation be distinct from jurisdiction. Under the regime of sovereignty, legislation is no longer the highest type of jurisdiction in a hierarchy of jurisdictional activities that reaches from the lowliest judges to the Prince who makes laws for the entire world. Nor is it merely superior to jurisdiction. It is unique and differs from jurisdiction qualitatively. It is the key to sovereignty. If you wish to know whether a commonwealth is sovereign or not, find out whether it can make laws for itself. If you wish to know who holds the sovereignty, find out who makes the laws. The task of jurisdiction is merely to find the applicable law and apply it to the circumstances of the case. The task of legislation, however, is to devise a law where none exists so far. That requires knowledge of politics, not jurisprudence—the central point of Conring's *De civili prudentia*.

In the third place, sovereignty identifies the right to legislate with the right to enforce obedience to the sovereign will. There are other reasons for obeying law. Justice and mutual agreements are two basic alternatives. As medieval writers never tired of repeating in language tellingly impossible to reproduce in English, law was called law (*ius*) because it derived from justice (*iustitia*). But laws made by sovereigns depend neither on justice nor mutual agreements. They simply declare the sovereign will. Whether or not the sovereign will is just is an important question. But it is separate from the question whether that will must be obeyed. Laws made by sovereigns must be obeyed even if subjects think those laws are wrong.

In the fourth place, sovereigns are free to change the law at will. To use the familiar terminology of early modern times, sovereigns are absolute from law.[125] The law is but a declaration of the sovereign will. Sovereignty is therefore unconditional, as no medieval form of lordship ever was. Bodin likened it to an unconditional gift and added that gifts with conditions were not authentic gifts.[126] That is illuminating. On medieval principles a gift was part of a reciprocal exchange by definition. The lord gave the benefice or fief, and in return the man gave faith and loyalty. No gift was unconditional. Contract was the foundation of medieval politics.[127] Few things could be more telling than that Bodin conceived of sovereignty as an unconditional gift. It shows how sharply sovereignty broke with the reciprocal relations that were constitutive of hierarchy.

The novelty of this idea emerges with fierce clarity in the writings of Hobbes. But it is already fully present when Bodin declares that tyrants are sovereigns in every sense of the word, never mind their tyranny: "Yet the tyrant is nonetheless a sovereign, just as the violent possession of a robber is true and natural possession even if against the law, and those who had it previously are dispossessed."[128] Bartolus would have been horrified by that thought.[129] And horrible it may well be. But it was logical as well. If the law draws its obligatory force from sovereign will, tyrants can scarcely be distinguished from sovereign rulers by their lack of respect for law.[130]

Freedom from law, of course, is not to be confused with freedom to do anything the sovereign pleases. This is a crucial point. According to Jean Bodin himself, sovereigns are obliged to fulfill their contracts, obey natural law, and even to respect their subjects' property.[131] In this respect they do not differ from their subjects at all. But this is only so because contract, natural law, and property are now defined by their distinction from law. Between them and the law there lies a new boundary drawn by sovereignty. It roughly corresponds to the distinction between will and reason. Under the regime of sovereignty, contracts and natural law draw their obligatory force from an entirely different source from law, and rights of jurisdiction no longer form any part of property. If seventeenth-century theorists were able to maintain that legislative power derives from social contracts, that was so only because contract was now essentially distinct from law.

In short, sovereignty is incompatible with hierarchy. It denies that legislation is merely one level of jurisdiction. It denies that empire is merely one species of jurisdiction. It denies that jurisdiction and *dominium* share an underlying identity. It rebels at the thought that laws and contracts need not be opposed to one another as unilateral declarations of the sovereign will must be opposed to mutual agreements. It separates the exercise of power from the act of legislation and separates both from holding property. It denies that territories can be joined in a territorial hierarchy and that the indivisibility of *dominium* and empire can be circumvented by distinguishing between different ranks and orders for each level of the hierarchy. Above all else it denies the distinction between obedience and jurisdiction that was so crucial to Bartolus.

More than that, it makes the distinction unintelligible. Once the logic of sovereignty is accepted, membership in the community becomes impossible if it is not joined to obedience. Under sovereignty, law depends on law enforcement. Like a policeman, sovereignty is either there or not. If it is there, it is completely there. If it is not, it is not there at all. From the perspective of sovereignty, it makes no sense to say that a king must acknowledge the emperor's universal lordship but need not obey his will. Under the rule of sovereignty, a universal lord who is not universally obeyed is a contradiction in terms. He cannot be imagined to have any meaningful function. He cannot even be imagined to exist. If he may not enforce his will on all of his subjects, he is no ruler whatsoever. He is the figment of a misguided political imagination, his power a purely mystical idea.

In order to see the difference clearly, it is instructive to remember that we have not abolished the divisibility of power entirely. But we divide it in a different way. For us the divisibility of power does not derive from hierarchy, but from the difference between sovereignty and property. In Locke's famous phrase, an individual's life, liberty, and estate are property. The rights of individuals differ from sovereignty as private property differs from public power. Yet private property and public power extend to the same things: the things that people own are subject to the law. It was therefore not long before John Stuart Mill was able to call sovereignty what Locke called property: "Over himself, over his own body and mind, the individual is sovereign."[132]

The distinction between property and sovereignty thus makes for problems analogous to those Bartolus faced when he distinguished the king's *dominium* over France from the emperor's *dominium* over the world. We find it just as difficult—or just as easy—to reconcile property and individual rights with sovereignty as Bartolus did to reconcile local with universal *dominium*. That difficulty is one of the chief conundrums of modern political thought, from its articulation in early writers like Hobbes and Locke via the twists and turns through which it was put by Rousseau and John Stuart Mill, down to the excesses of totalitarian governments in the twentieth century and contemporary political theorists.

The difference between ourselves and Bartolus is therefore not that we have done away with the divisibility of power. Nor is it that we distinguish between private and public whereas he did not. He most certainly did.[133] Nor is it that he took recourse to mystical ideas—as if sovereignty were any less mystical than universal lordship. The difference is that we admit but one distinction where Bartolus admitted many. For us, the distinction between the individual and society, between the private and the public sphere, rules supreme. It is the sole foundation on which all other legitimate distinctions rest. For Bartolus it was but the general form of distinctions dividing the commonwealth into a manifold of subordinated spheres of thought and action, none of which were altogether public and none altogether private, while all of them were held together by a fine-grained structure of differentiation and relation.

The relationship that Bartolus envisioned between an owner of private property and the king of France or, for that matter, between the king of France and the emperor, is therefore merely analogous to that between modern owners of private property and their sovereign. It is not identical. It is differently conceived. In Bartolus's terms, private property was like a lord's *dominium,* just less of it. It ranged at the end of a sliding scale, where the principle of the divisibility of power finally lost effect. At that end *dominium* was indivisible. The universal lordship of the emperor was at the other end of the same sliding scale. It represented an extreme, not only of indivisibility, but also of singularity. There were many kings, lords, and judges whose various *dominia* could be divided and subdivided in infinite variety. But there was only one world. Hence there could only be one emperor. His *dominium* over the world was just as indivisible as the *dominium* of individual owners over their private property.

The *dominium* of private owners and the *dominium* of the emperor in Bartolus's thought thus resemble modern private property and modern sovereignty. But the resemblance is merely partial, because the two are linked by a hierarchy from which the extremes derive their characteristics. Bartolus's owner of private property is not a private person, strictly speaking. He is a lord who exercises jurisdiction over his holdings. It just so happens that the power he exercises over his holdings is indivisible. But even though it belongs exclusively to him, it has at least in part the character of public office. In the same way, the emperor in Bartolus's thought is not simply a sovereign exercising public functions for the common good. He is the owner of his right to rule the world. He owns that right as though it were his property. Hence Bartolus considers him entitled to sue in a court of law for his right to rule the world under the action of *rei vindicatio* that Roman law reserved for owners of private property.

Bartolus's acceptance of the independence of rulers like the king of France from the emperor is therefore not to be confused with an acknowledgment of sovereignty. Nor must his endorsement of the emperor's right to rule the world be confused with anything like an assertion of universal sovereignty. Universal lordship, yes; not universal sovereignty. Power was divisible. Indeed, the divisibility of power was a constitutional theorem of fundamental importance—and the ingenuity with which he applied that theorem to medieval circumstance in spite of the recalcitrance of Roman law may well be one of his chief claims to fame. Not to acknowledge the operation of that theorem leads to anachronistic emphases on passages in his writings that look like early endorsements of sovereignty, because they grant independence to the king of France and the Italian city-states, and a corresponding lack of attention to the limits Bartolus placed on such independence by insisting on the emperor's right to rule the world. What divides his conception of power from modern ones is not merely one or two or three ideas. It is the structure by which those ideas are held together and from which they draw their meaning.

Reason in Writing

There was a universal hierarchy. There also was a universal truth. It made good sense to use the first verse of the second chapter of the Gospel of Luke as proof for the worldwide extent of the Roman empire. One sentence was enough. More was not needed. Of course that was to take Luke's words out of their context. It may even have given them a meaning quite different from what they meant in the mind of Luke. But Luke's mind was not the point. He was not the author, anyway. He was the mouth God chose to proclaim the truth. To take his understanding of his words as the criterion of what they meant was to deny his inspiration and to assert that human beings are in command of what they say. But the command belonged to God. God was the author of the truth.

It was the same with Roman law. On no account could Roman law be treated as a mere document of legal history, much less as merely pagan. The Roman empire and its law were part of God's providential plan. Saint Paul was a Roman citizen. He wrote his longest and most famous letter to the Romans. Long before the Roman empire had been converted to Christianity, he laid down an obligation for all Christians to obey the Roman state because "there is no power but of God: the powers that be are ordained of God. Whosoever therefore resisteth the power, resisteth the ordinance of God: and they that resist shall receive to themselves damnation" (Rom. 13: 1–2 [KJV]).

If Christians were obliged to obey even pagan Roman emperors, so much more were they obliged to obey Christian Roman emperors. And that, of course, is just what the author of the *Corpus Iuris* was: a Christian Roman emperor, God's representative on earth, involved in questions of theology, writing theological treatises himself, but never once reviving the example of his pagan predecessors by going on campaign to lead a Roman army into war. In the first constitution of the *Digest,* he declared, "we rule our empire by the authority of God."[134] In the first title of the *Code*—the title beginning with that law *Cunctos populos* to which Bartolus paid such close attention—he imposed Christianity on his subjects and dealt with the nature of the Trinity and the Catholic faith.[135]

On that understanding the *Corpus Iuris* was not "Roman" law. It was a compendium of true, Christian legal reason. As medieval jurists sometimes said, the *Corpus Iuris* was "reason in writing," *ratio scripta.*[136] As the *Digest* itself said, it was "the art of the good and the equitable." And it went on to say that jurists who made it their profession to teach and practice Roman law "are deservedly called priests, because we cultivate justice and profess knowledge of the good and the equitable, separating what is equitable from what is inequitable, discriminating between the licit and the illicit, desiring to produce good conduct not merely through fear of punishment but also through the promise of rewards, teaching, if I am not mistaken, true, not feigned, philosophy."[137] The Bible was more than a book of history. For the same reason, the *Corpus Iuris* was more than the ideas of some ancient people about specific ways of dealing with contracts and property.

Of course the *Corpus Iuris* needed interpretation. Bartolus was well aware that there was room for disagreement about the meaning of Roman law, just as there was about the Bible. Both could be badly misinterpreted. No jurists and theologians would have been needed if the meaning had been obvious. But interpreters of Roman law could not expect much help from rummaging around in history. Turning to history would merely have replaced one problem with another. Indeed, it would have substituted a harder problem for an easier one. God's will was never easy to define. But surely it was more difficult to find in the distant past than in the book of laws in front of you. If there were any doubts that went beyond juristic expertise, help could be had from the "determination of the church." God himself, after all, had authorized the elected ruler of the church, the pope, successor of Saint Peter, to watch over the faith and to distinguish between right and wrong. That did not mean that the relationship between the emperor and the pope was always amicable. Much less did it mean that Bartolus was an advocate of papal supremacy. But it did mean that Christian faith and Roman law went hand in hand. "Had the emperor not been Christian, he could not have been emperor, and he would not have had temporal jurisdiction."[138]

On those grounds Bartolus was perfectly entitled to use that little phrase in *Digest* 14.2.9 where the emperor is called *dominus mundi* to justify his right to rule the world. He was aware that it was just a single phrase. He knew that it could not be made to accord with the facts without a strenuous exercise of the legal imagination. Had he been asked to give the matter any thought, he might even have agreed that what he said it meant was not what Emperor Antoninus had in his mind when he first put it into writing. But that was not the point. The point was that the *Corpus Iuris* embodied laws of God and nature. Anachronism was no vice. It was a method of finding the meaning that we believe the laws of nature have: a meaning for all time.

Conring thought very differently. Not that he dispensed with universal truth. Far from it. Like Bartolus, he was convinced that God revealed some truths to man and that man could grasp some universal truths by reason. But those truths were not to be confused with books. Books merely offered the ideas, assertions, opinions, and bits of knowledge their human authors had acquired as a result of study and experience. Before they could be trusted, they had to be subjected to critical examination. Here was a book. What did it mean? Wrong question! What did the *author* mean! That question needed to be answered. "Even the Bible often tends to some exaggeration."[139]

Conring's *New Discourse,* therefore, is quite unlike anything that Bartolus ever wrote. Whereas Bartolus roamed far and wide across the texts of Roman law in order to establish the true meaning of a term like *lord of the world*, Conring roamed far and wide across a library of books in order to determine the truth about a past for which those books were merely evidence. If Roman law defined the limits of the world for Bartolus, the world defined the limits of all books for Conring. If the context for Bartolus's work was God's providential plan, the context for Conring's work was space and time. If Bartolus believed the *Corpus Iuris* embodied truth and justice, Conring believed that it embodied conventions whose justice required judgment by the sciences of history and politics. He trusted no piece of writing. He trusted only facts. The world consisted of real things, *res*. Real things were different from books, existing on their own, apart from meaning and interpretation. That separate existence made them reliable. It made them arbiters discriminating true from false. They gave Conring the means to judge the truth of texts, of words, of *verba*, by reference to facts. Where things and words conflicted, things had the upper hand.[140]

It was a fact that Daniel could not have known about the Roman empire because he lived at a time when the Roman empire had not yet come into existence. Therefore the doctrine of four world monarchies was "more of a rumor than a fact."[141] It was a fact that the New World had not yet been discovered when the Roman empire flourished. Hence the Roman emperor could not have ruled the world. It was a fact that sovereign rulers like the king of France did not acknowledge the emperor's right to rule over their states. Hence that emperor's so-called right was nothing but an excuse for starting wars.

There was something violent in these ideas. It is the violence that we associate with Machiavelli's *Prince*, Hobbes's *Leviathan*, and Luther's hostility to the rebellious peasants. But to Conring's mind, the violence was justified by the reality. What was the point of making claims that bore no relation to the true state of affairs? Merely to ask the question was enough to dispatch Bartolus to the realm of ignorance and myth. Or so it seemed.

Missing the Point

Time to resume the argument where we left off at the beginning of this chapter. Let us remind ourselves why we left off. In the *New Discourse*, Conring took three basic steps: he established a point of fact (the Roman emperor never ruled the world); he established a point of right (the Roman emperor never had the right to rule the world); and he described the history of the Roman emperor's power from antiquity to the present (the Roman emperor's power shrank). The question was, just what did Conring accomplish with this argument? It seemed so obviously true. We took a closer look. Now we can give an answer. Conring accomplished three different things: he missed the point; he begged the question; and he changed the subject. Let us consider each of these in turn.

The argument from fact was the foundation of Conring's case. No doubt it was completely sound. But it was also utterly beside the point. Bartolus never claimed that the emperor ruled the world in the sense that Conring attributed to him. He claimed that the emperor ruled the world in a specific sense designed to account for foreign people and certain Christian rulers who did not obey his rule. To suggest otherwise was misleading and unfair. It was certainly no reason to abandon Bartolus's theory.

It cannot be stressed strongly enough that Bartolus's theory was totally immune to any factual limits on imperial power.[142] It made no difference whether the emperor was able to exercise his power over particular pieces of the world. In principle his right to rule the world was able to survive the complete extinction of his power to rule over any piece of land or over any person. Bartolus himself does not appear to have considered the possibility. But the familiar legend about the hidden emperor sleeping inside a mountain while the world is waiting for his return suggests that his theory was more than idle speculation. It spoke in legal terms about the symbolic order of society. Compared to that order, the existence of some continents the Romans did not know was simply irrelevant. If Conring had confronted Bartolus with it, Bartolus would have been well within his rights to ask, "so what?" There was only one way to prove him wrong, namely, by proving that someone other than the emperor did have the right to rule the world—which is to say, to prove the truth of what Bartolus called heresy.

Conring, of course, did nothing of the kind. The relationship between his "discovery" of facts disproving the emperor's power to rule the world and Bartolus's alleged ignorance of those facts therefore affords a nice parallel to the well-known views of Thomas Kuhn on the structure of scientific revolutions.[143] Kuhn observed that discoveries do not explain every advance in science. Discoveries often turn out to consist of complicated series of events that, far from explaining anything, need themselves to be explained. True, discoveries may lead to the development of new scientific theories accounting for new observations. But they create new difficulties, too. Some things are gained, and some are lost, and it is never altogether clear what makes new theories better than older ones. Sometimes discoveries only qualify as such in terms of the new theory whose truth they are supposed to demonstrate. Under the theory that they replace, they are exceptions or anomalies. They seem to presuppose the very change they bring about. That makes it difficult to understand just what discoveries discover.

Such is the case with Conring and Bartolus. Factual limits on the emperor's power were known to both. But there were different ways of handling them. One was to consider them as proof that the emperor did not have universal lordship. That was the route that Conring took. It was effective on the assumption that lordship was not meaningful unless it entailed real control. Another route was to regard factual limitations on the emperor's power as an anomaly that complicated the theory of universal lordship but did not prove it false. That was the route that Bartolus took. It was effective on the assumption that independently of real control, lordship had a symbolic function.

Conring's first charge against the views of Bartolus thus missed the point. It presupposed what needed to be explained: the theory of sovereignty. The facts he invoked to prove that the emperor was not lord of the world did prove that he was not *sovereign* of the world. But that was not what Bartolus had claimed. And the facts failed to prove who, if not the emperor, did rule the world. The logic of Conring's first and most basic point turns out to have been founded on a sleight of hand.

Begging the Question

Something similar applies to the second step in Conring's argument. Here there was no dispute about the facts. Both sides agreed that Roman law called the emperor *dominus mundi*. The dispute turned on the meaning of those words. Bartolus regarded them as evidence that Roman law supported universal lordship. Conring regarded them as a kind of hyperbole. Modern readers are likely to agree with Conring's point of view. The question is why? What are the grounds on which Bartolus's interpretation may be rejected as unfounded?

It does not take much reflection to see that those grounds are treacherous. First of all, from the most abstract point of view, it cannot be stressed enough that the meaning of that little phrase *dominus mundi* is not simply obvious. Could it be hyperbole? It could. Could it be the single place in Roman law where the Roman emperor's right to rule the world was stated as such? That too. Could it be that *dominus* and *mundus* each meant different things to ancient Romans, medieval Romans, and modern Romans? Of course. Are we well informed about that meaning? Not well enough. One thing and one thing only is obvious: on its face Roman law calls the emperor exactly what Bartolus said he was: lord of the world.

The dispute between Bartolus and Conring thus turns on a question of interpretation. And one does not need to know anything about contemporary schools of literary criticism or the linguistic turn in intellectual history to understand that questions of interpretation cannot be answered by reference to texts alone, especially not by reference to what is sometimes called their literal meaning.[144] The literal meaning of a text—the meaning of the letters—is either a contradiction in terms or limited to what you can learn from staring at a wall covered with undeciphered writings in a language you do not know. You see the letters. If the meaning were in the letters, what else would you need to understand? But meaning is never literal. It lies beyond the code in which it has been cast. It may be simple or complex. But it will not be found until the text has been placed in the context from which its meaning is to be derived.

The question is, Which context would that be? Opinions vary. This much seems certain: at a minimum, two conditions must be satisfied. First, you have to recognize that you are dealing with something that does actually carry some kind of meaning as opposed, for example, to ornamental drawings or random strings of ones and zeros that merely *look* like binary code. Second, you have to know the language in which the code was written. Language is the most elementary context in which a text needs to be placed if it is to yield any meaning. Those two things alone (recognizing that there is a language and understanding it) involve more assumptions about meaning and interpretation than anyone has yet been able to identify. As Wittgenstein wrote early in his life, "we tend to take the speech of a Chinese for inarticulate gurgling. Someone who understands Chinese will recognize *language* in what he hears. Similarly I often cannot discern the *humanity* in a man."[145]

It follows that debates over interpretation are badly misaligned so long as they turn on the question whether texts ought to be read in context. The answer to that question is obvious: of course they ought to be. The real question is, *Which* context? Historical, linguistic, philosophical, divine, and deconstructive? Or dancing, cookery, and sports? Disagreements about meaning can never be resolved by reference to words alone. They turn on assumptions about the language in which the words were written. Sometimes those assumptions are explicit and easy to identify. Sometimes they are implicit and deeply hidden. That can make them difficult to recognize and disagreements impossible to solve. But they are always present where meaning is at stake. Hence disagreements about the meaning of a phrase as simple as the two little words *dominus mundi* are inseparable from disagreements about the assumptions on which the very possibility of meaning rests.

That changes the nature of the case. The dispute between Bartolus and

Conring is not about the question whether the phrase *dominus mundi* did or did not mean that the emperor had the right to rule the world. The real dispute, decisive but submerged, is about the question of how meaning is to be drawn from Roman law. The meaning of the phrase *dominus mundi* is merely the tip of a logical iceberg of assumptions about the world of meaning that threatens both sides with interpretive shipwreck. It does not matter on its own account. It matters because it is so well designed to force both sides to own up to their assumptions. It functions as a kind of shibboleth distinguishing friend from foe and heretic from true believer.

What is Roman law? Is it a purely historical document? Is it past tense? Or is it present in some sense? Does it embody truths beyond the reach of time? Does it depend on the intention of the author who created it? Or does its meaning exist in separation from the minds that first put it into words? Who was its author, anyway? The ancient Roman jurists who wrote it down? The ancient Roman people who sanctioned it? The ancient Roman emperor who codified it? The God by whose grace that emperor was believed to have been appointed? The historian of law who studies it? Or all of the above?

And what is the context in which Roman law needs to be understood? Is it limited in time and space? Or does it extend to infinity? Does physics have a role to play? Does logic or statistics? Does Roman law embody a mixture of temporal and timeless truths? If so, how are the timeless truths to be distinguished from the temporal ones? Do truths about the past and truths about the present exclude each other? Or do they go hand in hand? Is there a line between the context in which the Roman law was written and that in which the historian is reading it? Where does a context end? Are there two contexts: one for the past, one for the present? Or are there many, one for each place and time? Is the variety of contexts infinite, a veritable Babel of miscommunication? Is there perhaps just one, embracing interpreter and interpretee, author and reader, nature and culture, Adam, Eve, and God?

These questions are not formulated here because there is much hope of answering them, nor because they are the only ones of their kind. Others are easy to imagine. They are formulated to clarify two truths about Conring's interpretation. One is that he had a definite position on the proper context in which to interpret Roman law. That context was historical. That is why he insisted that Roman law must never be confused with natural law. The other is that he had no good reason for assuming that his position was superior to that of Bartolus.

Bartolus was convinced that Roman law was sanctioned by God. Hence there was no better way to answer the question than to rely on Roman law itself. What he discovered was that Roman law called the emperor "lord of the world." That was a fact. Indeed, it was a fundamental fact. The question was, What did it mean? Clearly it did not mean that the emperor actually ruled the entire world. It did not even mean he was obeyed in every part of Europe. That made it difficult to understand why he was called lord of the world. You could have concluded that Roman law was wrong. But that would have been heresy.

Fortunately, the difficulty could be solved. What you needed to do was to read Roman law systematically in order to consider the various powers that were ascribed to the emperor. You had to think about the nature of those powers, define them and relate them to each other without running into contradictions. So long as you did not lose sight of the fundamental fact that Roman law called the emperor lord of the world, you could show that the emperor really did have the right to rule the world and that whatever conflicted with that right was either beside the point (the case of the kings of France and England, the cities of Italy, and so on) or in some violation of the law (the case of heretics and foreign people). The law remained intact.

Conring, in contrast, was convinced that Roman law recorded past conventions without divine authority. He did not believe that you could find its meaning as Bartolus had done. You had to seek it in the past. What he discovered was that the ancient Roman emperors had had neither the power nor the right to rule the world. That was a fact. Indeed, it was a fundamental fact. That made it difficult to understand why Roman law called the emperor lord of the world. You could have concluded that you were wrong about the limits of the emperor's power. But that would have been unscientific.

Fortunately, the difficulty could be solved. You had to distinguish carefully between different kinds of law and different periods of history. So long as you did not lose sight of the fundamental fact that Roman emperors had never ruled the world, you could show that Roman emperors did not have the right to rule the world, that the Roman empire had ceased to exist, and that whatever laws seemed to conflict with your conclusions were either beside the point (the hyperbolic language of certain Roman emperors) or in some violation of reason and nature (the case of Bartolus and his supporters).

The differences between Conring and Bartolus thus go beyond their disagreement over the meaning of a passage in Roman law. They arise from assumptions about truth and meaning that were diametrically opposed. They dealt with the same question. But they had different ideas about what the question meant. For Bartolus the fundamental fact was Roman law; for Conring, the fundamental fact was history. Their arguments are self-contained logical packages that differ from each other not merely in their conclusions, but in their entirety. They start with different assumptions and end in different places, too. They are hermetically sealed off from each other, not in all respects (there are connections, echoes, overtones, traditions connecting them), but in a fashion so elementary that the thought of one cannot be translated into the thought of the other.

To use a simple analogy: their ways of thinking are related as the circle is to the square. The circle and the square are familiar; they belong to the same stratum of reality; each can be measured, studied, and manipulated in many different ways; each can be well understood. Yet one thing is impossible, and that is to transform one into the other: no circle will be squared. The relationship between the two can only be described as an irrational proportion, a number transcending our ability to count.

The relationship between Bartolus and Conring is like this. Each is familiar in his own right. Each wrote about Roman law, the nature of the commonwealth, the relationship between law, justice, politics, religion, and so on. Each can be studied, analyzed, investigated, edited, contrasted, compared, and placed in different contexts. Each can be well understood, and they are similar in many ways. Yet one thing cannot be done: the thought of one cannot be translated into the thought of the other. Neither survives in the air from which the other draws its life. Each suffers a demonstrable and necessary loss if it is put in terms of the other. They stand for two different worlds of thought as sharply separated from each other as the world of circles is from the world of squares—and equally closely related, never mind that reason cannot completely wrap its arms round the relationship.

Hence it was not enough for Conring to offer a better interpretation of Roman law. He had to demonstrate that his interpretation was better in the interpretive key that Bartolus had chosen. That is precisely what he failed to do. For the most part, he simply ignored the issue. He specified no reasons why his (historical) interpretation deserved to be considered superior to Bartolus's (anachronistic) interpretation. He glossed over the central issue as though it did not exist. Far from answering the question why his approach to Roman law ought to have been preferred, he never even raised it. He simply asserted, as though it were self-evident, that "first of all we need to know what actually or legally belonged to the Roman empire at the time when Rome was flourishing."[146] Not one word of explanation why that is something we would really need first of all to know. The closest he came to offering a reason was to point out that "there are famous men who declare that the entire world once obeyed the Romans, or should at least have obeyed them."[147] All right. There were. We know there were. We know he disagreed with them. We grant that they were wrong about the ancient past.

But that proves nothing further than that ancient history was useful for disagreeing with famous men. What we would like to know is why ancient history was useful for understanding Roman law better than they had done. Why should those famous men have known about the past at all?

There are two brief passages in the *New Discourse* where Conring did at least draw some attention to the assumptions on which Bartolus rested his case. And they are most revealing. One of them came early in the *New Discourse*, where Conring declared that "even a child can see that the civil law of the city of Rome could not possibly have given the Romans the right to rule the world; for how could the entire world have been bound by a law that was established by a single people in their city?"[148] Here Conring identified, if only in the terms of a rhetorical question, one of the principles behind Bartolus's interpretation of Roman law: the belief that the civil law of the city of Rome did in some sense bind the entire world. The second passage came at the very end of the *New Discourse,* where Conring exclaimed that the argument of the opposition "has no force whatsoever unless you assume that there was no justifiable way for the people and emperor of Rome to lose any of their rights, or that every single piece in the body of Roman laws is founded on the law of nature and therefore true for all times. And that, of course, is totally false."[149] Here Conring identified another fundamental principle: the notion that Roman law was in some sense united with natural law.

These two passages share four telling features. First, they identify assumptions on which Conring's interpretation of Roman law might have failed. Second, they assert that those assumptions are false. Third, they offer no proof for the assertion. And fourth, they cover the lack of proof with rhetoric. Conring's interpretation refuted Bartolus's theory no more successfully than the historical study of a cookbook refutes the recipes.

One suspects that Conring was at least subliminally aware of the injustice he did to Bartolus in the process. Perhaps the rhetoric covered more than a lack of proof. Perhaps it covered a slightly guilty conscience as well. If Conring really did believe that Roman law could not be understood outside its historical context, one wonders why the same did not occur to him where Bartolus was concerned. Ought he not to have insisted that what was fair for Roman law was fair for Bartolus as well? The disparity between the historical civility with which Conring approached Roman law and the attack he launched against Bartolus reveals a guilty secret: whether or not to read a text in its historical context depends on the historian's discretion. It is not history but the historian who chooses between debating and studying the evidence. Not to have made this public was not to accept responsibility.

That leaves the third point in Conring's argument. Given the length at which he described the vicissitudes of the Roman empire from antiquity to the modern period, the reader may expect that it requires detailed attention. Not so. Logically speaking, the third point stands and falls with the preceding two. If sovereignty was the right concept to understand the power of the emperor, and if history was the right way to determine the meaning of Roman law, then of course it was necessary to determine how the empire's extent had waxed and waned over time. But neither of those conditions had been shown to be true. Conring had begged the question. The proof of his case was not that it was true. The proof was that it worked.

Changing the Subject

What Hermann Conring accomplished in the *New Discourse* was that he changed the subject and in the process changed himself. He did not merely substitute books on history for books on Roman law. He did not merely write about sovereign states, whereas Bartolus wrote about the lord of the world. He detached himself from texts and pried them open, whereas Bartolus had been content to leave them closed and make himself at home. Conring was not at home—an exile from the texts, an exile in the world. He was alone, a solitary, punctual self (Charles Taylor's term for Locke) confronted by an alien force, attempting to master it, admirable in the tenacity with which he fought for freedom from ancient authorities whom he judged to be the cause of misery and war, pitiable in his loneliness, sovereign in the knowledge that he possessed a dignity unassailable by any piece of writing because it was itself the source of writing, and hence of judgment and of truth.

Progress is not the proper name for this change. What would it have been progress toward? Conring hardly moved closer to some desirable goal. He did leave something old behind and did make something new. Progress, to the extent that it existed, took the form of waving a none-too-friendly and irreversible good-bye to Bartolus. The point is that he managed to make it happen, and never mind the reasons. The metaphor of birth is better: Conring gave birth. Not, I should like to stress, rebirth; not renaissance and certainly not reformation. Plain birth, the most elementary form of revolution that we know. Conring gave birth to a new form of thought in a new form of self. That this was painful is as natural in the realm of thought as in the realm of bodies. That it deserved in some sense to be welcomed may be natural, too. But calling it progress would seem to be self-serving.

History is ill-equipped to grasp this change. It may well have occurred in time. But it cannot be limited to time. History presupposes some underlying continuity, some self-same subject, some prime matter whose changes it can chronicle only because "it" remains in some sense the same. The subjects may vary in many ways. So may the ways of change. The libraries are full of good examples, and publishers keep adding more. But in all cases, history must be about some underlying "it." If it were otherwise, history could not fulfill its purpose.

Here it is otherwise. Here one subject has displaced another one from which it not only differs but with which it is incommensurate. There is no self-same subject here whose change could be portrayed by history. Something new has happened. A new form of life has come into the world. Grasping its novelty would be to square the circle. We could count until the end of the world and would not yet have counted long enough. We could study the evidence until the end of time and would not yet have studied long enough. In bringing history to bear on the relationship between Conring and Bartolus, we merely put ourselves on Conring's side. Like Conring, we assert that "first of all we must go back in time"—and we deceive ourselves if we believe that we can do so without breaking with Bartolus as Conring broke with him. We are a party to the proceedings. No talk of a "historical revolt" can change that fact. It can only eliminate Bartolus from consideration.

None of this means that history is a useless form of knowledge. History is useful, delightful, instructive, and even necessary. That it is insufficient to tell us what we would like to know is no more convincing an argument against its value than the lack of a rational proportion between circles and squares is an argument against mathematics. But it does mean that the invention of history amounted to a declaration of independence from the authority of ancient texts. Seeking to grasp that invention by means of history, we must fall doubly short. We do an injustice to Bartolus, because we have already taken sides. We do an injustice to Conring, too. His work was justified precisely, and only, because it did give rise to something new: a new realm of thought and action, a freedom that had not been known before. Now history is old. To practice history today may therefore honor the letter of Conring's accomplishment. But it betrays his spirit.

These are not new ideas. Yeats, Pound, and Eliot spoke of them. Nietzsche thrust them polemically into our faces. Heidegger and Wittgenstein already put them to the test. The novels of Bulgakov, Musil, Proust, and Joyce, the paintings of Picasso and Matisse all burst with them. But they have yet to shake the dominance that history exercises over the modern mind. We lack the words, as Petrarch did when the vernaculars of Europe first gained the shape in which they have been spoken since. Perhaps no other time since then has lacked the words like that. What language we now need to learn can scarcely be imagined. One thing, however, is for sure: we cannot learn it by repeating what Conring and his kind have done.

Through the Looking Glass

This completes our third step toward the limits of history. This time we more or less abandoned context. Instead we spent our energy on the alternative: comparing and contrasting two related but different kinds of arguments, proposed by different thinkers and separated from each other by a certain distance in space and time. We abstracted from the effort to determine whether our reading of the text was suitable to grasping the author's intention. We simply assumed that it was. Or rather, we assumed that it was not, but we had no other choice because of the conclusion to which we had been driven in the preceding chapter: that no human mind is ever entirely made up. Since we could not get at what Conring really thought, we hoped we might at least be able to discern the nature of his accomplishment.

That hope has now been dashed as well. Instead of grasping the nature of Conring's accomplishment, we have encountered two different conceptual systems. Each seems coherent and convincing in its own right. But between the two lies some incomprehensible divide, a nothingness transcending rational analysis. It is as though we stepped through a looking glass. The world on the other side, though strange, is not incomprehensible. It follows a logic all its own that can be mastered in a little time. You can play chess with the Red Queen. It is an interesting game. But you can never play it here. The looking glass stands in between. Were it to disappear, the worlds in front and in back would disappear as well. Two different images, two different worlds, one seemingly strange, one seemingly familiar, each somehow related to the other and yet connected by no intelligible link: that is the outcome of this chapter.

Thus, we got far enough to recognize what Conring's argument was not: it was not founded on the discovery of facts, and it did not amount to a refutation of Bartolus's argument. It missed the point and begged the question. I have used different metaphors: a circle that cannot be squared, a looking glass, a birth. The metaphors are different; the point, the same. The change consists of a novelty so simple that it exceeds the grasp of history. I called it a change of subject. But what a change of subject is still seems a little difficult to say.

And yet, in stepping through the looking glass, we have made one enlightening discovery. To study history as Conring did is to refute what Bartolus was thinking. To seek a historical understanding of the relationship between Bartolus and Conring is therefore an oxymoron: either the understanding will be historical, and then it will confirm the wall of historical consciousness that Conring built to separate himself from Bartolus. Or it will break that wall; but then it cannot be historical. A historical understanding of historical consciousness is a nonsensical endeavor. That is our chief result. Now it is time to draw conclusions.

5

The Limits of History

In the first chapter I promised to take you on a guided tour. The tour is over now. I hope you enjoyed the ride. I also hope you agree that it has ended where I said it would, at the limits of history. Only one task remains: to declare just what there was to learn on the road.

Let me review the stages. We began with a problem in contemporary scholarship on the development of modern political thought. The scholarship seemed caught in a vicious circle. It presupposed ideas like "politics" and "the state" that were only the result of the development under investigation—a kind of illegitimate anticipation of the outcome at the beginning, a prolepsis, or a projection backward onto the past of concepts that only hindsight is entitled to apply. Something was wrong with the procedure, and the result seemed biased in favor of modernity, politics, and western nation-states, against the Middle Ages, law, and the Holy Roman Empire. Our sense of equity bristled at what looked like historical discrimination playing favorites with the past, a kind of chronological Orientalism extolling Machiavelli, Hobbes, and Locke as founders of modern politics while treating Conring and Bartolus with neglect.

The way to set the record straight, it seemed, was to do better history. So we took off on an excursion to the past. We focused on a body of evidence that was well suited to our purpose but not so unwieldy as to exceed our strength: the writings of Hermann Conring. Conring was a prolific author and a penetrating analyst of the problems confronting early modern thinkers in their attempts to exit from medieval structures of authority. He played a crucial part in emancipating Germany from Roman law and helped to establish a modern understanding of German history and politics. Though he was loyal to the philosophy of Aristotle, he was also well acquainted with the ideas of Machiavelli, Bodin, and Grotius, subjecting them to critical analysis, modifying Aristotle where required, and in the process forming his own ideas. Conring seemed perfect for our purpose. For even if it turned out that he could not be ranked the equal of Machiavelli, Hobbes, or Locke, he was an expert guide to the conceptual burdens bedeviling the history of political thought.

Those were the premises from which we launched a detailed investigation. They seemed sound. Sound enough, at least, to inspire the confidence without which it is difficult to pursue any objective, scholarly or otherwise. But the results of that investigation scarcely appear to justify the hopes with which we started out. Admittedly, it was based on information from widely dispersed sources that are difficult to read. It was necessary to dig deep in certain places, and I think bright sparks of insight may have been produced here and there. Some of our progress was laborious; some was, I hope, diverting. In the process we may well have reshaped the understanding of the origin of modern politics from which we started out. But what of our objective? Have we succeeded in breaking out of that vicious circle that seemed to hold our understanding in its grip?

To that question the answer must be an unhesitating *no*. Our opening review of Conring's life and works was much too superficial to give us more than a blurry image of the historical reality we sought to understand: good enough to reveal interesting features of the past, but not good enough to grasp their sense. We tried to approach the past more closely by focusing on one of Conring's writings. But the more closely we approached, the more we were disappointed, until we had to face a disconcerting truth: instead of reaching solid ground, we found ourselves falling into a gap dividing the author's thought from its expression. We grasped at wind.

This was no accidental obstacle that we could have circumvented or removed if only we tried harder (though much room for trying harder was still left). Nor was this a peculiarity of Conring's personal condition or of the writing I chose to analyze (though their peculiarities confronted us more quickly with this result than others might have done). It was an effect of the intensity of our scrutiny. The same effect would have revealed itself if we had tried the same with any other subject (though it might have taken longer).

So we changed course and tried another way of getting at the past for real: we contrasted Conring's argument with that which it displaced. But that merely confronted us with another kind of gap: not between thought and expression, but between two different forms of thought, divided from each other not merely by differences of time and place, but by a logical dichotomy. We found no link between the two except a change of subject concealed by rhetoric—no link at all, in other words, but an unlinking; not a connection, but a dissociation; not understanding, but misunderstanding. Creative misunderstanding, to be sure, constructive even; but misunderstanding nonetheless. We found that Conring's thought, as it emerged from the contrast with Bartolus's, could not be interpreted as the result of some historical development, except by pure guessing at the connection in between.[1] Why not? Because its single most important feature, from which it drew its meaning and on which it depended for its effects, consisted of a break from the past, an act transcending the grasp of historical comprehension, a novelty under the sun (always taking Conring merely as one, and not the first, of an entire set of thinkers who favored the same novelty, and always remembering that Bartolus's meaning lies in the same gap between thought and expression where Conring's has been shown to lie). It was as incommensurable with the thought of Bartolus as the circle is with the square: both are perfectly intelligible, but they are impossible to comprehend in one intuition.

In other words, we tried three different ways out of the circle by which our vision of the past seemed to be constrained. First we tried a sort of paratactic listing of information recorded in the sources about a subject suitably chosen and defined by the historian. Second, we sought to grasp the reality behind that information by studying the meaning of one of our sources in the context of its time and place. And third, we tried to gather insight from contrasting two pertinent sources with each other. All this was perfectly good history. In fact, it may be said to have exhausted the main approaches that historians can take to the past. Perhaps that claim will not stand up to closer scrutiny. But historians who do not wish to turn history into some other kind of intellectual pursuit must take at least some variant of these three ways: the systematic presentation of information about a subject defined by the historian; the close scrutiny of evidence in the context of its time and place; and the comparative analysis of evidence according to the order of chronological development. And yet we failed. Instead of escaping from the predicament of presupposing just what we needed most to understand, we produced one blurry image and two empty spaces: a blurry image of Hermann Conring, an empty space between his thought and its expression, and another one between his thought and that of Bartolus.

This outcome can be pictured in a single image: in our attempt to get a grip upon the past, we made a mirror for ourselves and set it in the midst of time. We made it out of evidence. From the distance we see a blurry image: it looks like some object in the past. If we move closer and subject the image to analysis, we find that it is governed by something that is nothing, a central point of visual organization that dominates the reflection but lies in the virtual distance behind the reflecting glass and is neither real nor within our reach. It looks like the intention of some author but is a function of our observation. If we step through the mirror and turn round, we see an image quite similar in some ways to the first, with its own blurriness and its own vanishing point, but magically flipped from left to right. If we acquire sufficient dexterity, we can become so familiar with both sides that the strange transformation required to cross from front to back seems commonplace. But we can neither see the mirror for itself nor see both of its sides at once. They seem connected by some kind of historical development. In fact they are divided by a logical dichotomy that is a function of our reason.

The same conclusion can be stated in terms of the distinction between locutionary content and illocutionary act—and I should like to emphasize that it really is the same, no matter how different the terms may look to the reader. There is an illocutionary act that is constitutive of the activity of historians, the thing historians do with words about the past in their capacity as historians, regardless of their particular subject or method of approach. This act is to assert the truth of basic principles without which the study of the past could not proceed: that the past is gone; that it can nonetheless be turned into an object of scholarly examination by means of evidence; that the evidence was produced by some specific human agent at some specific time and place for a specific purpose; that scholarly examination can take advantage of the agent's responsibility for the evidence to reconstruct its meaning; that evidence must therefore be interpreted in the context of its own time and place; and above all, that things do have a time and a place that may be called their own. This is the act by which the mirror is created.

The distinction between locutionary content and illocutionary act is therefore more than a principle of method that historians can apply to the evidence in order to sort out its meanings. It must be applied to the historians themselves. It illuminates the meaning of their own activity. It is as fundamental to the historical enterprise as to the objects of historical examination. Each time a historian makes statements about the past, some piece of knowledge about the past is conveyed by means of a locution. The meaning of that locution depends on the illocutionary act performed by the historian. That act cannot be limited to the intention of conveying knowledge of the past. It amounts to taking a definite position in the world and excluding others on grounds that are directly related to the conditions of the historian's own time and place. It cannot be collapsed into historical neutrality.

This is not to deny how much there is to learn from history. Nor is it to assert that history is aimed at specific political results or that the past has no reality. No doubt it does. No doubt the telling of past matters can have a depth and richness of its own that all but obliterates the link between our study of the past and our role as human beings living in company with others. But I am claiming that such a link exists. The meaning of history therefore changes according to place and time as much as do the objects of historical examination. History never reaches further than our ability to suspend disbelief—and we can neither suspend our disbelief indefinitely nor extend the obligation to study evidence impartially to living an impartial life. If by *history* something more is meant than one particular limited and modern form of understanding that is itself a party to the historical proceedings it describes and is itself, therefore, sorely in need of understanding, that claim is illegitimate.

Conring probably knew all this much better than we give him credit for. He did not know the distinction between locutionary contents and illocutionary acts, of course—at least not in those terms. But he knew very clearly that knowledge of history is meaningless unless it is placed on foundations that are not historical at all. He demanded lessons from history, and he insisted that such lessons were impossible to learn without a knowledge of what he called the science of politics, precisely that *prudentia civilis* to whose elaboration he devoted the better part of his intellectual life. He stated the principle as early as 1635 in his edition of Tacitus's *Germania*: "History is only a guide to the stricter sciences. Its delights depend on the arts and sciences it serves. To grasp history's delicious fruits is therefore not given to everyone. Only those can do it who know by their own talent how to abstract general laws and universal principles from individual events, or have learned how to do so from their teachers. Once the principles are known, experiments are all it takes to arrive at absolute knowledge of reality."[2]

A little reflection on the structure of Conring's argument in the *New Discourse* will clarify the matter. The first two points he made were crucial. But they do not amount to history. They rather consist of the assertion of one fact (the Roman emperor never ruled the world) and the denial of one right (the Roman emperor never had the right to rule the world). Their meaning does not derive from the adequacy with which they portray the past. Their meaning derives from their ability to explode a certain eminently present conception of the right order of the world. They presuppose a temporal perspective, a clear awareness of the difference between what is now and what was then, and an unbending will to turn that difference to contemporary purpose by disassociating ancient law from universal truths and by subjecting law to the responsibility of individual human agents reacting on grounds of morality and nature to the particular and purely accidental circumstances of their times. They constitute a great "not so!" to the universal claims of the Roman empire and a resounding "yes!" to the sovereignty of states over politics and that of individuals over themselves. They sum up the essence of the historical revolt.

The third point of Conring's argument, by contrast, does amount to history. It consists of a narrative describing the waxing and waning of the imperial power from antiquity to the present. In terms of its logical effect, that history is entirely subordinate. Its relevance to the argument stands and falls with the adoption of a temporal perspective. In terms of rhetoric, however, the narrative is crucial. It transforms the historical revolt into what looks like nothing more than an account of what once was the case. That helps to explain the gaping holes in Conring's chronology, the uneven distribution of his attention, the sharp emphasis on Charlemagne and Otto the Great, the attack on Pope Gregory VII, the summary description of later medieval emperors, and so on. The history he told was obviously inadequate to the reality of the past. But that inadequacy could scarcely do damage to an argument that did not rest on history anyway. The past was not the point. The point was revolution. History merely served to make the point look like a reasonable story.

To characterize Conring as the founder of German legal history is therefore a misnomer. If Conring's writings have any especially illuminating value, it is not that they represent the typical activity of historians, especially not historians of law. It is rather that they help to get hold of the link by which the study of history has, since early modern times, been bound to a certain sense of self and the pursuit of a particular variety of politics. The core of Conring's project was the revolt that put historical thought in ascendance. It was the deployment of a temporal perspective in order to replace custom, divine authority, and universal hierarchy with nature, sovereignty, and individual autonomy. That was the unifying principle, the grand illocutionary act that gave meaning to all aspects of his work. In a real sense he was no historian at all. He was a physician of the body, the soul, and the commonwealth, a scientist of politics who knew precisely how to turn his dexterity with historical evidence to the service of principles that he believed to be constitutive of the common good. Nature, conscience, and sovereignty, in their novel distinction from the absent past, gave meaning and direction to the energy with which he canvassed what was written and wrote much more to set the present right. As a scientist, he trusted no mere opinions but tested them by means of experiment and observation in order to establish what he believed to be the reality of things. As a political theorist, he divided the field of the common good from religion, law, and morality and sowed it with the logic of sovereignty. As a historian, he wielded true knowledge of the past to clear the present for cultivation by properly educated citizens. And as a private individual . . . we do not really know.

We see the mask. Behind the mask, we may surmise, Conring carried on a silent conversation. Bits and pieces of that conversation surface now and then. Thus, for example, when he decided to reprint in 1652 what he had written in 1635: "I would prefer to change some of the things I wrote. But it would be improper to balance each bit of youthful labor upon the scales of a more exacting age. So long as the blemishes are not impossible to bear, they ought to be left to their own times. I see no reason why I should alter anything."[3] Those words reveal a remarkably lucid understanding of the temporal distance dividing his present self from his past self and an equally remarkable faith in the ability of his person to withstand the strains of time without loss of integrity. He must have had an even sharper sense of the distance dividing him from others, and perhaps less assurance that it could be crossed. There are good indications in the tortured opening passages of his inaugural address and in the dissimulation that Pufendorf suspected. We can guess at an internal life unfolding in loneliness and isolation. But the prolific writings he produced give us no more than glimpses. His self, by definition of modernity, is secluded from observation.

In some corner of his mind, Conring may have agreed with this assessment. The care with which he structured his argument, the vehemence with which he rejected the emperor's right to rule the world, the ruthlessness with which he refused to treat Bartolus with historical civility, the enthusiasm with which he maintained the freedom of Germany from Rome, and the mixture of courage, hesitation, and dissemblance with which he presented his case to the public—all testify to his awareness of the magnitude and danger of the task. One senses fear beneath the surface; the fear not merely of being in the wrong, but of having committed sacrilege. But one can also sense tremendous excitement. The relationship he built between himself and the world in which he lived, the kinds of judgments he felt compelled and authorized to make, the conscience that lifted him up with its strength and threw him down with its commands, the sovereigns whose rule he endorsed, the states whose common good he sought to serve, the responsibility he shouldered, and the passion with which he aimed to replace ignorance about the past with true history—all these put him light years away from Bartolus.

Here was a whole new world to be proclaimed and conquered. "First of all we need to know what actually or legally belonged to the Roman empire at the time when Rome was flourishing." In that little sentence, unaccompanied by any justification, pronounced as self-evidently true, supported by nothing whatsoever except the confidence of the historian in his own power to resurrect the past, Conring uttered modernity's declaration of independence from authority. Everything else followed from that beginning, so inconspicuous in its brevity, so obvious, apparently, so problematic in its foundations, and so momentous in its consequences. In that little sentence, truth, heresy, and progress were one and the same.

The clarity with which Conring insisted on linking history to politics is therefore not at all to be taken for granted. It sets him apart from his contemporaries and even more so from historians who study history for no other purpose than knowledge of the past. Historians who improved on Conring's version of the past in later centuries therefore did not simply improve the history he told. They also helped to complete the task that Conring had undertaken: to overturn the medieval view of order. They swathed the great debate about reality and justice on which the meaning of history had once turned in ever thicker layers of historical detail until it was removed completely out of sight. The more they succeeded, the more they hid the meaning of their success both from themselves and from others.

That process can be documented in the history of Conring's own writings. The separation of history from science, politics from law, and theology from philosophy already seemed so self-evident to Johann Wilhelm Goebel in 1730 that he could use it to justify omitting Conring's work on confessional polemics, theology, medicine, and natural philosophy from his edition of Conring's *Opera*. In so doing he may well have helped to further the purposes of Conring's works. But only by concealing the revolutionary act from which they drew their meaning: the assertion of an autonomous modern self, not limited by the past (history) but only limited by nature (science) and therefore sovereign over itself (in the realm of conscience) and constitutive of public sovereignty (as a subject and citizen of the state). A few generations later, the process was complete. When Friedrich Karl von Savigny wrote the great history of medieval Roman law that did as much to restore Roman law to a place of honor in the nineteenth century as Conring had done to expel it from that place in the seventeenth, he did not even mention Conring's name.[4] That is a good measure of the distance dividing Conring from professional historians. The revolution fell into oblivion. Its results were taken as self-evidently true, and reaction began to take its place.

Time, of course, did not stand still. We have replaced the ramshackle cottage in which Conring did his humble work with ever taller buildings of elegant design and infinite variety. From small beginnings we have gone on to great achievements. But the foundations on which our achievements rest are still the same that Conring and his fellow workers laid in early modern Europe. We have forgotten them. But we have never stepped off them. We stand with Conring on the same side of the great historical divide. We take the same historical position. We still borrow our sense of self and our vision of the future from reconstructions of the past. We share the same guilty secret, too: not history, but the historian, decides what counts as evidence and what as secondary literature, what deserves to be understood in context and what must be debated, where the past ends and where the present begins. The difference is that Conring still had to fight for history. That forced him to be direct. For us history is routine. We can be nonchalant. Only occasionally do we lift our eyes and look at what we do long enough to realize what we are doing. Maitland once lifted his eyes and said what everyone who looks can see: "Such is the unity of all history that anyone who endeavors to tell a piece of it must feel that his first sentence tears a seamless web. . . . A statute of limitations must be set; but it must be arbitrary. The web must be rent."[5] Just so. The web must be rent indeed. The web that Bartolus tried to weave.

That is why the boundary dividing the Middle Ages from modernity refuses to yield to the most well-intentioned efforts at reconciliation between the ages. The boundary is a projection of historically minded people on an unsuspecting past. Of course it is arbitrary. But it is necessary, too. Historians depend on it for their existence as historians, not as on something given, but as on something made and constantly remade. It is essential to the integrity of the modern world. Its nature is political, not historical. This is emphatically not to say that it does not exist. But the reality of a projection derives not from the object on which it is projected, but from the subject projecting it. The force of this projection is directly proportionate to the historical construction of the world that has been practiced by Europeans since early modern times. Since it is arbitrary, it can of course be moved from one chronological location to another and called by different names. It is easy to push it back into the past (from Renaissance and Reformation into the Middle Ages) and forward into the future (from early modern times to the French Revolution or the beginnings of global society). It can even be stretched out into a period.[6] But it can never be abolished, and it will not disappear until historians themselves have disappeared or changed themselves into some other kind of human being, as Bartolists once changed themselves into humanists.

The familiar habit of calling "medieval" whatever seems uncouth, bizarre, outdated, and inaccessible to reason therefore does not deserve the contempt with which it is often treated by experts in medieval history, who cannot fathom how any educated person could fall into anachronism so perverse. Far from perverse, it rests on a sound intuition that the historical reality of the Middle Ages is subsidiary to their political necessity. "Modern" is not what is recent. "Modern" is what occurs in time that can be grasped by reason. The real Middle Ages are time out of mind, history's own true past, the past that lies forever beyond the reach of history, more ancient than antiquity itself.

The frustration of historians seeking to mend the web they tore is correspondingly amusing. As if they had not torn the web themselves! As if the connection between the parts of time could be bridged if that connection had actually been severed, or needed to be bridged if it had not. As if the tear was not a necessary consequence of their attempt at historical comprehension. Hermann Conring's failure to read Bartolus in historical context is merely an early and straightforward case, almost touching in its lack of self-consciousness. Attempts to bridge the chasm between the Middle Ages and modernity today, by historians of the *longue durée* and social historians of the Reformation, to mention two prominent examples, are less straightforward. But they are no more likely to succeed.

So long as there is history, there must be a Middle Ages. So long as there are historians, there must be medievalists, a kind of party of the chronological right to the modernists who make up the chronological left, with both parties jointly engaged in maintaining the reality of one and the same projection. Hence, histories of the Middle Ages are condemned to oscillate between irreverent incomprehension and reverent idealization—or lose their meaning. So long as politics continues to rely on sovereignty and citizens exercise their right to self-determination, there needs to be some medieval period in the past from which they have progressed, no matter on which particular stretch of chronological time that progress is to be projected. All modern states define themselves by the same rupture that Conring put into effect, and all of them have histories beginning in some kind of antiquity. Chronologies may vary. But the tripartite pattern of true ancient origins, corrupt medieval intermission, and modern emergence to sovereign self-determination is built into history itself—not, to repeat, because that is what happened, but because it is a transcendental category of the historical imagination, a necessary condition for the very possibility of thinking about the past as history and living now. Wallace Stevens had it right: all history is modern history.

Parallel observations can be made about the other two exclusions mentioned at the beginning of chapter 2: empire and law.[7] As history needs a

Middle Ages from which to chart some progress toward the future, so it needs an empire against which to defend the rights of modern states and modern individuals. The empire is not simply a historical reality. Like the Middle Ages, it is a category of the historical imagination, a projection by historically minded people on an unsuspecting form of government long since replaced by something else. Histories of universal empire invariably alternate between condemning empire as an abuse of power and venerating it as a holy order. Either the empire turns out to have been just one other kind of state (which is how Conring treated it), or it turns out to have been a mystical idea (which is how it was treated by its romantic friends). The boundary between them is just as elusive, arbitrary, and necessary all at once as that between the Middle Ages and modernity. This is as it should be. History cannot expect to understand a form of politics denying significance to time and giving agency to the creator of the universe.

So it is with the distinction between "real" (modern) law and "false" (medieval) law, between real lawyers and mere historians of law. "Real" law is the positive law enacted by a sovereign state and, possibly, the moral or natural law enacted by conscience and reason. Such law can have no history. It is defined by presence and taught in schools of law. This is the only law-that-actually-is. All other law does not exactly qualify as law. It is merely some sort of law-that-is-not-really-law, because it belongs in the past and springs from no real, that is, no present, source of obligation. It can be left to historians. It consists of law that was once positive but has been abrogated since, and of custom that was never really law to begin with and has no binding force today. Perhaps it even includes the positive law that obtains in other places under the rule of other sovereign states but not right here and now. The history of those laws can be written because they are not really law but only law-that-is-no-more, law-that-never-was, and law-that-is-elsewhere. But just where the boundary between history and law ought to be drawn is fundamentally unclear.

The difficulties historians face in seeking to integrate the Middle Ages, the empire, and the law into a single vision of the history of political thought are therefore not accidental in the least. Nor are they limited to the particular empirical area of European history from about the year 1000. They are built into the study of history itself. They can be documented wherever history seeks to work its way forward by means of archives and evidence.[8] Their magnitude stands in direct proportion to the uncertainty they hide. This is not to deny, of course, that historians can succeed brilliantly at writing histories of the empire, of law, and of the Middle Ages. But it is to assert that in the very act of writing, they turn the reality they seek to grasp into a shadow of itself. Wherever the light of history shines, the empire, the law, and the Middle Ages vanish into the dark, like myth, like phantoms observable only out of the corner of the eye. Only the state, politics, and modernity remain. History may seem adequate so long as we do not look closely. But once we do (as in this book), we cannot but recognize the power of boundaries and exclusions that owe their reality to our own activity. They are not blemishes that could be blotted out if history were only better done. They are the consequence of history done best. They reassert themselves again and again no matter how confidently historians proclaim their obsolescence. Without them, history could not exist.

What we learned on the road can therefore be summed up like this: history is a form of self-assertion. That is the purpose for which it was invented. That is the purpose it still serves today. History is integral to the act by which the self gains freedom from the other, however self and other are defined. It cuts through space and time, through lived experience, and through relationships of commerce, politics, and love. It is the condition on which I claim my rights as mine in opposition to the rights of someone else. The daily production and consumption of writings about the past (or movies, television series, and pages on the World Wide Web) are only in the second place designed for the sake of knowledge about the past. In the first place they are a sacred ritual, a form of religious worship designed to keep the modern faith alive. To argue for their truth would be to fall into the trap that led some medieval Christians to believe that they could prove the truth of their religion to infidels. Thomas Aquinas was right when he insisted that such proof does not exist.

Of course historians can go on missions to the unlearned, and often they meet with great success. But no amount of history can be enough to prove the errors of their ways to historical heathens like Bartolus, who have good reasons of their own to consider history beside the point. History demands that we have faith in the propositions with which I began this book: the past is gone forever; to understand the meaning of a text, you must first put it in the context of its time and place; and you cannot tell where you are going unless you know where you are coming from. Those propositions are very good for us to have. They guarantee our freedom to go where we please so long as we do not attempt to violate the laws of nature, and to do anything we like so long as we do not restrict some other person's right to do the same. They do not oblige us to shoulder any responsibilities other than those to which we have consented of our own free will. They leave us to move on our own initiative along the trajectory of time into a future that will turn out to be another here and now. But they are not historical in nature, and they cannot be proven true.

Seen from inside, the system of belief that rests on these assumptions must seem self-evidently true to the believer. It definitely does proclaim itself as such: objective (to the extent that bias can be eliminated), scientific (to the extent that "scientific" can embrace the arts and sciences, as German *wissenschaftlich* does), and secular (to the extent that the separation of church and state is kept intact). What could be more natural than to examine surviving records in order to find out about the past? What could be less religious than to subject formerly sacred writings to historical critique? What could be more rational than to replace ignorance and myth with history? Much intellectual energy goes into fixing the degree to which history can achieve its goals. The goal itself is subject to no doubt.

Seen from outside, however, history rather appears to be the intellectual form that secularized Christianity has given to its preoccupation with the salvation of the soul. It is the same preoccupation that was in earlier times cast in the forms of theology and canon law. History is the ritual examination (especially by experts officially trained and licensed) of certain objects (mostly preserved in archives, libraries, and museums) without which the distinction between past and present could not support the weight placed on it by the established church—that modern church embodied in the nation-state whose symbols are printed on every dollar bill and whose members worship at the altar of nature. History serves to keep the modern world united. It is linked to violence in the same way that Christianity was formerly linked to the Crusades. History embodies a religious faith. That it is not recognized as such is partly due to the lack of self-awareness with which the participants in any given system of belief confuse their own belief with truth. And partly it is due to the official bargain that left clerical opponents of the modern state in charge of official religion, provided they acknowledged their defeat.

History does not permit us to step outside the realm of time in order to inspect the past from an outsider's point of view. The universe of time contains no point of Archimedes. There is no magic line dividing history from politics, no intellectual quarantine in which the health of theory could be protected from the ailments of practice. Taking a historical point of view is taking a stand—not because this or that historian's point of view is biased by political, religious, economic, or any other interests, but because it is historical. History cannot establish the origin of modern politics any more than it can validate historical thought itself. It can only clarify what we already know from other sources. Far from establishing a temporal perspective, history presupposes one. It shelters us from the experience of time; it comforts us with the illusion that subjects can be defined by their historical conditions and that change over time can be explained by historical development. "God wants it," the old crusaders would have said. The truth only begins where that illusion ends.

> One can mistrust one's own senses, but not one's own belief. If there were a verb meaning "to believe falsely," it would not have any significant first person present indicative.
>
> Wittgenstein, *Philosophical Investigations*

Notes

In citing works in the notes, short titles with dates and the following abbreviations have been used throughout. Full bibliographical data are given in the list of works cited.

Discursus novus	Hermann Conring. *Discursus novus de imperatore Romano-Germanico.* N.p., 1642.
"Gedruckte Werke"	William Ashford Kelly and Michael Stolleis. "Hermann Conring: Gedruckte Werke, 1627–1751." In *Hermann Conring, 1606–1681: Beiträge zu Leben und Werk,* ed. Michael Stolleis, 535–72. Berlin: Duncker und Humblot, 1983.
Herberger and Stolleis	Patricia Herberger and Michael Stolleis. *Hermann Conring, 1606–1681: Ein Gelehrter der Universität Helmstedt.* Wolfenbüttel: Herzog August Bibliothek, 1981.
Moeller	Ernst von Moeller. *Hermann Conring, der Vorkämpfer des deutschen Rechts, 1606–1681.* Hannover: Geibel, 1915.
Opera	Hermann Conring. *Opera.* Ed. Johann Wilhelm Goebel. 7 vols. Brunswick: Meyer, 1730. Reprint, Aalen: Scientia, 1970–73.
resp.	respondent

All translations of quotations from non-English sources are my own unless otherwise indicated. Some parts of this book require quotations from the writings of Hermann Conring and Bartolus of Sassoferrato. I have translated these quotations into English in the text and put the Latin in the notes. Adding the Latin may seem superfluous, because editions of the writings of Conring and Bartolus are relatively easily available in good academic libraries. But these editions vary in ways that are impossible to control in the absence of a critical edition, and sometimes the variants affect the meaning of the text (not to mention the accuracy of the translation). The only way to forestall confusion about the evidence on which this book draws is therefore to reproduce it in the notes.

INTRODUCTION

1. Heidegger, "Wissenschaft und Besinnung" (1954), 60.

CHAPTER ONE

1. A quick glance at the definitions of the term *history* offered by a standard dictionary of the English language will confirm that the distinction between past and present may well be the only point uniting meanings notoriously numerous and difficult to disentangle. *Webster's Third New International Dictionary of the English Language,* for example, defines history as

> **1:** a narrative of events connected with a real or imaginary object, person, or career . . . **2a:** a systematic written account comprising a chronological record of events (as affecting a city, state, nation, institution, science, or art) and usu. including a philosophical explanation of the cause and origin of such events—usu. distinguished from *annals* and *chronicle* **b:** a treatise presenting systematically related natural phenomena (as of geography, animals, or plants) . . . **c:** an account of a sick person's family and personal background, his past health, and present illness **3:** a branch of knowledge that records and explains past events as steps in the sequence of human activities: the study of the character and significance of events— usu. used with a qualifying adjective <medieval history> <European history> **4** . . . **a**(1) *obs:* a pictorial representation of an historical subject (2) *or* **history painting:** painting esp. popular in the 17th and 18th centuries in which a complex of figures conveys a story or message usu. based on history or legend **b**(1) *obs:* DRAMA 1 (2): a drama based on historical events **5a:** the events that form the subject matter of a history: a series of events clustering about some center of interest (as a nation, a department of culture, a natural epoch or evolution, a living being or a species) upon the character and significance of which these events cast light **b:** the character and significance of such a center of interest—compare LIFE HISTORY **c** *broadly:* past events <that's all history now>; *esp:* those events involving or concerned with mankind **d:** previous treatment, handling, or experience (as of a metal).

Only the kind of natural history identified in 2b may possibly not require the distinction between past and present.

2. A point well made by Tierney, *Origins of Papal Infallibility* (1972). It was sanctioned by the well-known legal tag *par in parem non habet imperium* (equals have no power over each other), which relieved sovereigns from any obligation to abide by the will of their equally sovereign predecessors. The same argument was crucial to the understanding of sovereignty first developed by Jean Bodin in his *Six livres de la république* (1576).

3. "I hereby declare, on oath, that I absolutely and entirely renounce and abjure all allegiance and fidelity to any foreign prince, potentate, state, or sovereignty, of whom or

which I have heretofore been a subject or citizen; that I will support and defend the Constitution and laws of the United States of America against all enemies, foreign and domestic; that I will bear true faith and allegiance to the same; that I will bear arms on behalf of the United States when required by the law;* that I will perform non-combatant service in the armed forces of the United States when required by the law;* that I will perform work of national importance under civilian direction when required by the law; and that I take this obligation freely without any mental reservation or purpose of evasion: so help me God." Quoted from Seckler-Hudson, *Federal Textbook on Citizenship* (1978), 13–14. This is the book I was encouraged to study in order to prepare myself for joining the citizenry of the United States of America. According to an accompanying note concerning the clauses marked with asterisks, "the Immigration and Nationality Act permits, under certain circumstances, the taking of the oath without these clauses."

4. For other views see Windelband, *Geschichte und Naturwissenschaft* (1894); Rickert, *Die Grenzen der naturwissenschaftlichen Begriffsbildung* (1902), in English *The Limits of Concept Formation in Natural Science* (1986); Rickert, *Kulturwissenschaft und Naturwissenschaft* (1926); Hempel, "Function of General Laws in History" (1942); and Hughes, *History as Art and as Science* (1964).

5. See the main definitions of the noun *subject* recorded, for example, by the *Concise Oxford Dictionary*, 5th ed.: "**1.** Person subject to political rule, any member of a State except the Sovereign, any member of a subject State . . . **2.** (log., gram.). That member of a proposition about which something is predicated, the noun or noun-equivalent with which the verb of a sentence is made to agree in number etc. . . . **3.** (philos.). Thinking & feeling entity, the mind, the ego, the conscious self, as opp. all that is external to the mind . . . **4.** Theme of discussion or description or representation, matter (to be) treated of or dealt with . . . **5.** Circumstance that gives occasion for specified feeling or action . . . **6.** Person of specified usu. undesirable bodily or mental tendencies . . ." *Webster's* definitions are more extensive, but they follow similar lines.

6. That explains the slightly embarrassed honesty with which *Webster's* definition 5a of history as "the events that form the subject matter of a history" describes these events as "clustering about some center of interest." This is decidedly vague. But it is also refreshing; defining the subject matter of history in terms of "some center of interest" is surely far closer to the actual state of affairs than defining it in terms of contexts.

7. White, *Metahistory* (1975).

8. For three equally profound but very different investigations into the nature of time along lines of thought that can here only be alluded to, see Bergson, *Essai* (1889), in English *Time and Free Will* (1910); Heidegger, *Sein und Zeit* (1927), in English *Being and Time* (1996); and Nabokov, *Ada* (1969).

9. For a study of the distinction between information and communication (especially as derived from writing), its development over the whole span of human history, and the extent to which it helps to clarify our periodization of that history, see Hobart and Schiffman, *Information Ages* (1998).

10. The distinction was classically deployed by J. L. Austin in the William James lectures of 1955, *How to Do Things with Words,* and has since then spawned a considerable body of philosophical literature. In the present context, it is most usefully approached through Tully, *Meaning and Context* (1988).

11. The term *historical revolt* is borrowed from Whitehead, *Science and the Modern World* (1967), 17; cf. Preston, "Was There an Historical Revolution?" (1977). The literature on the subject is vast, but it is itself chiefly historical in nature and therefore not

always as illuminating as one could wish; see Weiss, *Renaissance Discovery of Classical Antiquity* (1988); Cochrane, *Historians and Historiography* (1981); Franklin, *Jean Bodin and the Sixteenth-Century Revolution* (1963); Kelley, *Foundations of Modern Historical Scholarship* (1970); Huppert, *Idea of Perfect History* (1970); Ranum, *Artisans of Glory* (1980); Schiffman, *On the Threshold of Modernity* (1991); Levy, *Tudor Historical Thought* (1967); Pocock, *Ancient Constitution* (1987); Levine, *Humanism and History* (1987); Kelley and Sacks, *Historical Imagination in Early Modern Britain* (1997); Joachimsen, *Geschichtsauffassung und Geschichtsschreibung in Deutschland* (1910); Seifert, *Cognitio Historica* (1976); Hassinger, *Empirisch-rationaler Historismus* (1978); Muhlack, *Geschichtswissenschaft im Humanismus und in der Aufklärung* (1991). For a general survey, see Breisach, *Historiography* (1994). For classic statements, much cited and disputed, see Burckhardt, *Die Kultur der Renaissance in Italien* (1989), in English *Civilization of the Renaissance in Italy* (1990); Dilthey, *Weltanschauung und Analyse des Menschen* (1914); Fueter, *Geschichte der neueren Historiographie* (1911); and Meinecke, *Entstehung des Historismus* (1936), in English *Historism* (1972). For a sense of the range of conceptual approaches, compare Elias, *Über den Prozess der Zivilisation* (1939), in English *Civilizing Process* (1994); Löwith, *Meaning in History* (1949); Klempt, *Die Säkularisierung der universalhistorischen Auffassung* (1960); Toulmin and Goodfield, *Discovery of Time* (1965); Blumenberg, *Die Legitimität der Neuzeit* (1973–76), in English *Legitimacy of the Modern Age* (1983); Koselleck, *Vergangene Zukunft* (1979), in English *Futures Past* (1985); and Hoelscher, *Die Entdeckung der Zukunft* (1999).

12. This according to the definition of Kristeller, "Humanist Movement" (1979). For more about humanism, see the concise essay by Witt, "Humanist Movement" (1995); the comprehensive survey by Rabil, *Renaissance Humanism* (1988); and Witt, *In the Footsteps of the Ancients* (2000).

13. Hale, *War and Society* (1986); Parker, *Military Revolution* (1988).

14. Bonney, *Economic Systems* (1995); Stolleis, *Pecunia Nervus Rerum* (1983); Hoffmann and Norberg, *Fiscal Crises* (1994); Schnur, *Die Rolle der Juristen* (1986); Mattingly, *Renaissance Diplomacy* (1955).

15. The relationship between humanism, the Reformation, and the Scientific Revolution is a subject of such abiding interest that it is touched upon in virtually all treatments of any of these subjects. See Moeller, "German Humanists" (1972); Trinkaus and Oberman, *Pursuit of Holiness* (1974); Tracy, "Humanism and the Reformation" (1982); Spitz, "Humanism and the Protestant Reformation" (1988); Long, "Humanism and Science" (1988); Grafton, *Defenders of the Text* (1991); and Kaufmann, *Mastery of Nature* (1993).

16. Courtenay, "Nominalism and Late Medieval Religion" (1974); Oberman, "*Via Antiqua* and *Via Moderna*" (1987); Oakley, *Politics and Eternity* (1999).

17. Grafton, "Humanism and Political Theory" (1991); Martines, *Power and Imagination* (1979).

18. Oestreich, *Geist und Gestalt des frühmodernen Staates* (1969), in English *Neostoicism and the Early Modern State* (1982); Worstbrock, *Krieg und Frieden* (1986).

19. For a solid scholarly treatment of the invention of the Middle Ages, see Neddermeyer, *Mittelalter in der deutschen Historiographie* (1988).

20. For exemplary statements of this view, see Erasmus's letter to Dukes Frederick and George of Saxony, 5 June 1517; and Luther, *An den christlichen Adel deutscher Nation* (1888), 462.

21. Mommsen, "Petrarch's Conception of the 'Dark Ages'" (1959).

22. For a concise exploration of the significance of this shift, see Koselleck, "Vergangene Zukunft der frühen Neuzeit" (1979), in English "Modernity and the Planes of History" (1985).

23. See the trenchant remarks by Feyerabend, "Progress in Philosophy" (1987). Cf. the classics by Koyré, *From the Closed World to the Infinite Universe* (1968); and Kuhn, *Structure of Scientific Revolutions* (1970).

24. For language about the conception of the good, in distinction from knowledge and in opposition to "naturalist reductions," I rely on Taylor, *Sources of the Self* (1989).

25. "A heretic, by canonical definition, was one whose views were 'chosen by human perception, contrary to holy scripture, publicly avowed and obstinately defended.'" Moore, *Formation of a Persecuting Society* (1987), 68, with reference to Gratian's *Decretum* II Causa 24, quaestio 3, canons 27–31 (1879), 997–98.

26. One may well doubt that the state of affairs is much clearer today. There is a good body of literature on what has come to be known as the "voluntarist" tradition in late medieval and early modern philosophy. But its relationship to the origins of historical thinking remains deeply obscure. One of the best approaches to the issue is offered by the writings of Francis Oakley, especially "Christian Theology and the Newtonian Science" (1961), *Omnipotence, Covenant, and Order* (1984), "Absolute and Ordained Power of God in Theology" (1998), and "Absolute and Ordained Power of God and King" (1998), now reprinted in Oakley, *Politics and Eternity* (1999). For some further observations on the place of heresy in the historical revolt, see Fasolt, "Sovereignty and Heresy" (1998).

27. Bodin, *On Sovereignty* (1992), 39, from bk. 1, chap. 8, of the *Six livres de la république;* p. 156 in the French edition of the *Six livres de la république* of 1583.

28. See White, *Metahistory* (1975).

29. See Schiffman, "Renaissance Historicism Reconsidered" (1985).

30. Burke, *Vico* (1985); Berlin, *Vico and Herder* (1976).

31. Or, even more strikingly, the moment when it became possible to use history as a source of doubts about the very modernity that had brought history into existence; see Lilla, *Vico* (1993).

32. Gellner, *Nations and Nationalism* (1983); Anderson, *Imagined Communities* (1991).

33. Kolakowski, *Main Currents of Marxism* (1978).

34. I am thinking of Strauss, *Natural Right and History* (1953); Voegelin, *New Science of Politics* (1952); and Schmitt, *Politische Theologie* (1934), in English *Political Theology* (1985). None of these can be considered friends of historical consciousness. Yet for the most part, their critique only strengthens the position they attack, in spite of themselves, and never more clearly so than when the only alternative they offer consists of some kind of return to some ideal that was once realized but has been lost.

35. Taylor, *Sources of the Self* (1989), 41–42.

36. Rabil, *Renaissance Humanism* (1988), illustrates the varieties of humanism well.

37. Baron, *Crisis of the Italian Renaissance* (1966). Cf. Seigel, "'Civic Humanism' or Ciceronian Rhetoric?" (1966); Grafton, "Humanism and Political Theory" (1991); Nederman, "Humanism and Empire" (1993); Hankins, "Baron Thesis" (1995); and Witt et al., "Hans Baron's Renaissance Humanism" (1996).

38. Kristeller, *Renaissance Thought* (1961). Cf. Logan, "Substance and Form" (1977); and Nauert, "Renaissance Humanism" (1980).

39. Cf. White, *Content of the Form* (1987).

40. See the second thoughts of Nauert, "Humanism as Method" (1998).

41. This is not the place to recount the history of those attempts. For general surveys, see Barraclough, *Main Trends in History* (1991); and Iggers, *New Directions in European Historiography* (1984). For developments since the 1970s, see Stone, "Revival of Narrative" (1979); LaCapra and Kaplan, *Modern European Intellectual History* (1982); Hunt, *New Cultural History* (1989); Appleby, Hunt, and Jacob, *Telling the Truth about History* (1994); Bonnell and Hunt, *Beyond the Cultural Turn* (1999); Freedman and Spiegel, "Medievalisms Old and New" (1998); and Jenkins, *Postmodern History Reader* (1997).

42. See Chickering, *Karl Lamprecht* (1993). For the posthumous justification that Lamprecht received through the mediation of Henri Pirenne from the *Annales* historians Marc Bloch and Lucien Febvre, see Lyon, "Henri Pirenne" (1980).

43. The well-known accomplishment of Haskins, *Renaissance of the Twelfth Century* (1927). Cf. Benson and Constable, *Renaissance and Renewal in the Twelfth Century* (1982); Rosenthal and Szarmach, *Medievalism in American Culture* (1989); Van Engen, *Past and Future of Medieval Studies* (1994); and Cantor, *Inventing the Middle Ages* (1991).

44. Koselleck, *Kritik und Krise* (1959), in English *Critique and Crisis* (1988). This remains the most compelling conceptual alternative to Habermas, *Strukturwandel der Öffentlichkeit* (1962), in English *Structural Transformation of the Public Sphere* (1989).

45. For studies detailing the growth of that agreement, see Novick, *That Noble Dream* (1988); and Koselleck, Mommsen, and Rüsen, *Objektivität und Parteilichkeit* (1977).

46. Gadamer, *Wahrheit und Methode* (1972), in English *Truth and Method* (1989); Collingwood, *Idea of History* (1994); Ricoeur, *Temps et récit* (1983–85), in English *Time and Narrative* (1984–88); Foucault, *Les mots et les choses* (1966), in English *Order of Things* (1971); Kuhn, *Structure of Scientific Revolutions* (1970); White, *Metahistory* (1975); Rorty, *Philosophy and the Mirror of Nature* (1980); Koselleck, *Vergangene Zukunft* (1979), in English *Futures Past* (1985). For an introductory guide, see Skinner, *Return of Grand Theory* (1985).

47. How fruitfully Foucault's views could have been extended to medieval history is suggested by Moore, *Formation of a Persecuting Society* (1987), whose perspective on medieval history could be called Foucauldian had it not been developed quite independently.

48. Taylor, *Sources of the Self* (1989).

49. Ibid., 199–207.

50. If there is one exception, it may be Ludwig Wittgenstein, who paid less heed to history than maybe any great philosopher I know.

51. For good examples, see Walsh, *Philosophy of History* (1967); Mandelbaum, *Anatomy of Historical Knowledge* (1977); Ankersmit, *Narrative Logic* (1983); Rüsen, *Grundzüge einer Historik* (1983); Danto, *Narration and Knowledge* (1985); and Mink, *Historical Understanding* (1987). For very different observations made by practicing historians about the same issues, see the classic by Droysen, *Historik* (1977), in English *Outline of the Principles of History* (1893); Bloch, *The Historian's Craft* (1953); and Carr, *What Is History?* (1961).

52. Kuhn, *Essential Tension* (1977), x. Though the point was made almost in passing, it is precisely on the mark.

53. Wittgenstein, *Philosophical Investigations* (1953), no. 119.

54. On the reassessment of the vitality of the empire, see the essays in Boyer and Kirshner, *Politics and Society* (1986); and Aretin, *Das Alte Reich* (1993–97).

55. On the development of historical thought in Germany, see Iggers, *German Conception of History* (1983); and on its relationship to politics, see Krieger, *German Idea of Freedom* (1957).

56. Kelly, *Hermann Conring* (1993), characterized by the author on p. iii as "a revised version of the second chapter of the thesis submitted by me to the Library Association for its Fellowship in 1982." It consists of fifty-seven typed pages, including seven pages of notes but lacking a bibliography and an index, and improves only modestly on the existing German literature.

57. I checked the *Encyclopedia Britannica Online*. Conring is mentioned exactly once in Burns and Goldie, *Cambridge History of Political Thought, 1450–1700* (1991), 90, in Donald Kelley's essay "Law," where it is pointed out that Conring considered Roman law the "measure of positive law," with a reference to Wolf, "Hermann Conring" (1963). The most important exception is the chapter "The Final Breach with Roman Law and Traditions" in Gross, *Empire and Sovereignty* (1975), 255–92, the best available survey of Conring's significance in English hitherto.

58. See the notes to chapter 2, below.

59. "For this I am obliged to be responsible: if I get myself tangled up, if there is vanity and faultiness in my reasonings that I do not perceive or that I am not capable of perceiving when pointed out to me. For faults often escape our eyes; but infirmity of judgment consists in not being able to perceive them when another reveals them to us. Knowledge and truth can lodge in us without judgment, and judgment also without them; indeed the recognition of ignorance is one of the fairest and surest testimonies of judgment that I find." Montaigne, "Of Books" (1986), 297.

CHAPTER TWO

1. Kelley, *Foundations of Modern Historical Scholarship* (1970); Oakley, *Natural Law, Conciliarism, and Consent* (1984); Oakley, *Politics and Eternity* (1999); Pocock, *Machiavellian Moment* (1975); Skinner, *Foundations of Modern Political Thought* (1978); Tierney, *Religion, Law, and the Growth of Constitutional Thought* (1982); and Tierney, *Idea of Natural Rights* (1997).

2. Brunner, *Land und Herrschaft* (1965), in English *Land and Lordship* (1992); Dreitzel, *Protestantischer Absolutismus* (1970); Dreitzel, *Monarchiebegriffe in der Fürstengesellschaft* (1991); Habermas, *Strukturwandel der Öffentlichkeit* (1962), in English *Structural Transformation of the Public Sphere* (1989); Koselleck, *Kritik und Krise* (1959), in English *Critique and Crisis* (1988); Oestreich, *Geist und Gestalt des frühmodernen Staates* (1969), in English *Neostoicism and the Early Modern State* (1982); Stolleis, *Reichspublizistik und Policeywissenschaft* (1988); and Stolleis, *Staat und Staatsräson* (1990).

3. Chittolini, Molho, and Schiera, *Origini dello stato* (1994), also available in English translation with somewhat different contents as Kirshner, *Origins of the State in Italy* (1995); Prodi, *Il sovrano pontefice* (1982), in English *Papal Prince* (1987); Prodi, *Sacramento del potere* (1992); and Quaglioni, *Limiti della sovranità* (1992).

4. For good studies of early modern French and Spanish political thought, one is still well advised to turn to works written by Anglophone authors like Keohane, *Philosophy and the State in France* (1980); Salmon, *Renaissance and Revolt* (1987); Giesey, *Cérémonial et puissance souveraine* (1987); Major, *From Renaissance Monarchy to Absolute Monarchy* (1994); Hamilton, *Political Thought in Sixteenth-Century Spain* (1963); and Pagden, *Spanish Imperialism* (1990). For some noteworthy exceptions, see Secrétan, *Privilèges* (1990); Genet, *L'état moderne* (1990), one in a series of conference proceedings edited by the same author; Zarka, *Raison et déraison d'état* (1994); Zarka, *Hobbes* (1995); Senellart, *Arts de gouverner*

(1995); Fernández-Santamaría, *Reason of State* (1983); and Mate and Niewöhner, *Spaniens Beitrag* (1994).

5. Among the most impressive products are the detailed histories of key concepts in political language assembled by Brunner, Conze, and Koselleck, *Geschichtliche Grundbegriffe* (1972–92); the survey by Skinner, *Foundations of Modern Political Thought* (1978); the handbook by Burns and Goldie, *Cambridge History of Political Thought, 1450–1700* (1991); and the series of volumes on the origin of the modern state published by Oxford University Press under the auspices of the European Science Foundation: Blockmans and Genet, *Origins of the Modern State* (1995–2000). Also worth mentioning are scholarly journals that pay special attention to the history of political thought, such as *Pensiero politico* (1968–), *Zeitschrift für historische Forschung* (1974–), and *History of Political Thought* (1980–).

6. For some remarks on "medieval wholeness" or "medieval universalism," see Ullmann, *History of Political Thought* (1970), 16–18; and the skeptical reflections on that passage by Burns, *Cambridge History of Medieval Political Thought* (1988), 2. For a classic exposition of the misrepresentations that result from projecting modern distinctions between state and society, public and private affairs, or law and politics onto medieval history, see Brunner, *Land and Lordship* (1992), esp. 95–138.

7. Skinner, "Meaning and Understanding" (1969), reprinted in Tully, *Meaning and Context* (1988), 29–67.

8. The boundary between state and church and that between law and morals are similarly problematic. For a neat investigation of a closely related problem, see Konrad Repgen, "What Is a 'Religious War'?" (1987).

9. Marsiglio of Padua, *Defensor Pacis* (1980); Locke, *Two Treatises of Government* (1988). The glosses of Accursius are available only in manuscripts and early modern prints. For the most part, the works of Bartolus must also be consulted in manuscripts and early modern editions such as the one of his *Opera* (1570–71) used here. For a rare exception, see Quaglioni, *Politica e diritto* (1983). The many volumes of the *Tractatus universi iuris* (1584–86) are a veritable mountain range of untranslated sources that few have attempted to scale.

10. More than a half-century ago, Gilmore, *Argument from Roman Law* (1941), already stated the need for more attention to the role of the jurists in the history of European political thought as clearly as could be desired.

11. For fundamental studies with a broad perspective on the whole of European history, illustrating both the strength of the boundary between law and politics and the difficulties in trying to cross it, see Wieacker, *Privatrechtsgeschichte der Neuzeit* (1967), in English *History of Private Law* (1995); Bellomo, *L'Europa del diritto comune* (1991), in English *Common Legal Past of Europe* (1995); and Berman, *Law and Revolution* (1983). For major scholarly studies illustrating the same point, but with a sharper focus on the late medieval and early modern period, see Canning, *Political Thought of Baldus* (1987); Maclean, *Interpretation and Meaning* (1992); Wells, *Law and Citizenship* (1994); Maffei, *Inizi dell' umanesimo giuridico* (1956); Mazzacane, *Scienza, logica e ideologia* (1971); Cavallar, *Francesco Guicciardini, giurista* (1991); Grossi, *Il dominio e le cose* (1992); Kisch, *Erasmus und die Jurisprudenz* (1960); Trusen, *Anfänge des gelehrten Rechts* (1962); Hammerstein, *Jus und Historie* (1972); Willoweit, *Rechtsgrundlagen der Territorialgewalt* (1975); and Troje, *Humanistische Jurisprudenz* (1993). For a particularly instructive collection of papers, see Schnur, *Die Rolle der Juristen* (1986).

12. See Ullmann, *Medieval Papalism* (1949); Tierney, *Foundations of the Conciliar Theory* (1955); Oakley, *Natural Law, Conciliarism, and Consent* (1984); and Post, *Studies in Medieval Legal Thought* (1964). The interest these scholars share in bridging the divide between law and politics should not be confused with consensus on how to bridge it; see Oakley, "Celestial Hierarchies Revisited" (1973).

13. Outside the history of political thought, the work of Paul Oskar Kristeller and Heiko Oberman has extended early modern questions far back into the Middle Ages. See Kristeller, *Renaissance Thought and Its Sources* (1979); and Oberman, *Werden und Wertung der Reformation* (1977), in English *Masters of the Reformation* (1981). Cary Nederman has been especially active in drawing medieval subjects to modernists' attention; see his articles "Nature, Sin, and the Origins of Society" (1988), "Freedom, Community, and Function" (1992), and "Meaning of Aristotelianism" (1996).

14. John of Salisbury, *Policraticus* (1990); John Quidort of Paris, *On Royal and Papal Power* (1974); William of Ockham, *Short Discourse* (1992). See also the valuable translation of selections from Ockham's *Dialogus* (1992).

15. See above, note 5, and cf. Burns, *Cambridge History of Medieval Political Thought* (1988). For two particularly interesting attempts to cross the boundary in question, see Oakley, *Omnipotence, Covenant, and Order* (1984); and Black, *Guilds and Civil Society* (1984).

16. Thus, for example, Pennington, *The Prince and the Law* (1993), 276–84, and esp. 8: "Jean Bodin (1529/30–1596) exaggerated the novelty of his analysis of political power, and historians have exaggerated the novelty of his exaggeration. That Bodin stressed his originality is forgivable; that is an author's prerogative. That historians have accepted his contention without careful scrutiny is less understandable."

17. Franklin, *Jean Bodin and the Sixteenth-Century Revolution* (1963), 17, for example, while acknowledging the creativity of jurists like Bartolus in bringing Roman law to bear on the "pattern of territorial communities that was emerging in the later middle ages," concludes that "the creative achievement of medieval jurisprudence depended upon a pair of premises which it had never attempted to establish scientifically: the assumption, first, that the Roman Law is intrinsically perfect; and second, that the Roman Law as it was taught to medieval students was identical with the law of Rome as it was understood by Justinian. Neither of these premises, of course, could survive a critical appraisal. And both, as I shall now attempt to show, were fatally undermined by new methods of interpretation which developed in the sixteenth century." Note the implication that modern views were "scientifically established." Similar, though often less circumspectly formulated, tributes to modernity are legion in every area of scholarship. For a particularly influential study, see Blumenberg, *Die Legitimität der Neuzeit* (1973–76), in English *Legitimacy of the Modern Age* (1983).

18. On Orientalism proper, see Said's now classic *Orientalism* (1979).

19. Empire used to be a neglected category in the study of early modern political thought, as Ferdinand Seibt, for example, complained in *Karl IV* (1978), 376–81. That may be changing. See Yates, *Astraea* (1975); Headley, "Habsburg World Empire" (1975); Headley, *Emperor and His Chancellor* (1983); Bosbach, *Monarchia universalis* (1988); Nederman, "Humanism and Empire" (1993); Pagden, *Lords of All the World* (1995); Muldoon, *Empire and Order* (1999); and Armitage, *Theories of Empire* (1998). Even so, the Holy Roman Empire as such has profited relatively little from this trend.

20. A noteworthy exception has long been made for the thought of Johannes Althusius, whose ideas about popular sovereignty have received a disproportionate share of the

attention owed to early modern German theorists of law and politics ever since Gierke, *Johannes Althusius* (1902), made him familiar, and even more so since Gierke's book was translated into English as *Development of Political Theory* (1939). A more recent, but increasingly important, exception concerns Pufendorf. See, e.g., Hont, "Language of Sociability and Commerce" (1987); Palladini, *Samuel Pufendorf discepolo di Hobbes* (1990); Dufour, "Pufendorf" (1991); and Doering, *Pufendorf Studien* (1992).

21. A point well made in the classic study by Figgis, *Studies of Political Thought* (1916).

22. As has been argued, among others, by Krieger, *German Idea of Freedom* (1957).

23. For welcome expressions of interest in German political thought, see Tuck, *Philosophy and Government* (1992), xiv, 120–31; and Franklin, "Sovereignty and the Mixed Constitution" (1991). For important studies other than those already mentioned, see Barraclough, *Origins of Modern Germany* (1947), old but in some ways unsurpassed; Vann and Rowan, *Old Reich* (1974); Aretin, *Das Alte Reich* (1993–97); Dickmann, *Der Westfälische Frieden* (1977); and Press, *Das Alte Reich* (1997). See also Angermeier, *Die Reichsreform* (1984); Schubert, *Die deutschen Reichstage* (1966); Walker, *German Home Towns* (1971); Gross, *Empire and Sovereignty* (1975); Bireley, *Religion and Politics* (1981); Maier, *Deutsche Staats- und Verwaltungslehre* (1980); Bernd Roeck, *Reichssystem und Reichsherkommen* (1984); and Weber, *Prudentia Gubernatoria* (1992).

24. Unless otherwise indicated, the following information is taken from the old, but still standard, biography by Ernst von Moeller, *Hermann Conring, der Vorkämpfer des deutschen Rechts* (1915); the excellent catalog published by Herberger and Stolleis, *Hermann Conring* (1981), on the occasion of an exhibition and conference that took place at the Herzog August Bibliothek in Wolfenbüttel to commemorate the three-hundredth anniversary of Conring's death; and an exceptionally informative article by Kundert, "Conring als Professor" (1983). For briefer accounts of Conring's life, see Wolf, "Hermann Conring" (1963), first published in 1939 and revised in 1944, 1951, and 1963; Willoweit, "Hermann Conring" (1977), reprinted with some changes as Willoweit, "Hermann Conring" (1995); and Stolleis, "Die Einheit der Wissenschaften" (1983). In the absence of a satisfactory biography, Schmid, "Vita Hermanni Conringii," in *Opera*, 1:xix–xxiv, is still surprisingly useful.

25. Ritter, *Deutsche Geschichte* (1889–1908), 1:12.

26. Herberger and Stolleis, 69–70. On Conring's relations to East Frisia, see Cassens and Schmidt, *Hermann Conring* (1982); and Schmidt, "Hermann Conring und Ostfriesland" (1983). On East Frisia more generally, see Deeters, *Kleine Geschichte Ostfrieslands* (1985); and Reimers, *Ostfriesland* (1968); or the nineteenth-century standard by Perizonius, *Geschichte Ostfrieslands* (1868–69).

27. On Emden, see Pettegree, *Emden and the Dutch Revolt* (1992); and Schilling, "Sündenzucht und frühneuzeitliche Sozialdisziplinierung" (1989). Kingdon, "International Calvinism" (1995), is especially lucid.

28. See Stayer, "Radical Reformation" (1995); and Haude, *In the Shadow of "Savage Wolves"* (2000).

29. Wolf, "Hermann Conring" (1963), 222–23.

30. Moeller, 4–5.

31. I am grateful to Helene Baumann for tracking down biographical information about Conring's teachers.

32. Moeller, 5–14.

33. I am unaware of any study devoted to Johannes Caselius other than the old work

by Koldewey, *Geschichte der klassischen Philologie* (1895). On Lipsius, see Oestreich, *Antiker Geist und moderner Staat* (1989); and Stolleis, "Lipsius-Rezeption" (1987); on Scaliger, see Grafton, *Joseph Scaliger* (1983–93); on Heinsius, see Becker-Cantarino, *Daniel Heinsius* (1978); and Meter, *Literary Theories of Daniel Heinsius* (1984). On the culture of late humanism in central Europe, see Evans, *Rudolf II and His World* (1973); and Kaufmann, *Court, Cloister, and City* (1995).

34. On the University of Helmstedt, see Baumgart, "Gründung der Universität Helmstedt" (1978); Baumgart and Pitz, *Statuten der Universität Helmstedt* (1963); Wallmann, "Helmstedter Theologie" (1983); Behse, *Die juristische Fakultät* (1920); and Triebs, *Die medizinische Fakultät* (1995). Very useful is also Kundert, *Katalog der Helmstedter juristischen Disputationen* (1984), which contains an informative opening section with detailed information about the university's history and organization. Less reliable, but rich in detail and well illustrated is the catalog of the exhibition *Academia Julia: Die Universität Helmstedt, 1576–1810,* published on occasion of the world exhibition in Hannover in 2000 in two separate volumes by Ahrens, *Die alte Universität* (2000); and Volkmann, *Die Universität Helmstedt* (2000).

35. Wallmann, "Helmstedter Theologie," 38–39; Herberger and Stolleis, 21.

36. Kundert, "Conring als Professor," 399–412.

37. Wallmann, "Helmstedter Theologie," 38–39.

38. On Aristotelianism in Germany, see Dreitzel, *Protestantischer Absolutismus* (1970); and Petersen, *Geschichte der aristotelischen Philosophie* (1921). On Aristotelianism in Conring's thought, see Dreitzel, "Aristoteles' Politik" (1986). On humanism more generally, see Kristeller, *Renaissance Thought and Its Sources* (1979); and Rabil, *Renaissance Humanism* (1988).

39. Conring, *Disputatio de origine formarum* (1630). On its relationship to Calixt's theology, see Mager, "Hermann Conring als theologischer Schriftsteller" (1983), 57–59.

40. On Calixt, the standard work remains the old study by Henke, *Georg Calixtus* (1853–60). See also Bottigheimer, *Zwischen Polemik und Irenik* (1996); Mager, *Georg Calixts theologische Ethik* (1969); and Schüssler, *Georg Calixt* (1961).

41. Wallmann, "Helmstedter Theologie," 39–53. For background see Steinmetz, *Bible in the Sixteenth Century* (1990); and Reventlow, Sparn, and Woodbridge, *Historische Kritik* (1988).

42. Cf. Schlee, *Der Streit des Daniel Hofmann über das Verhältnis der Philosophie zur Theologie* (1862); and Mager, "Lutherische Theologie und aristotelische Philosophie" (1975).

43. Conring, *Animadversiones politicae in Nicolai Machiavelli librum De principe* (1661); cf. Stolleis, "Machiavellismus und Staatsräson" (1983); Dreitzel, "Hermann Conring und die politische Wissenschaft" (1983).

44. Conring, *De origine iuris Germanici commentarius historicus* (1643), translated as *Der Ursprung des deutschen Rechts* by Hoffmann-Meckenstock and Stolleis (1994). On the connection of the writing of this work to the controversy sparked by Calixt, see Moeller, 67–74; and Luig, "Conring, das deutsche Recht und die Rechtsgeschichte" (1983).

45. See Mager, "Hermann Conring als theologischer Schriftsteller" (1983), 57–58, 63–64, 76, 79–83.

46. Kundert, "Conring als Professor," 399–400.

47. On Leiden, see Lunsing-Scheuvleer, Herman, and Meyjes, *Leiden University in the Seventeenth Century* (1975); and for vivid details, Grafton, *Joseph Scaliger* (1983–93), 2:72–93.

48. On Vossius, see Rademaker, *Life and Work of Gerardus Joannes Vossius* (1981); and Wickenden, *G. J. Vossius* (1993). On Barlaeus, see Blok, *Caspar Barlaeus* (1976); and Horst, *Inventaire* (1978).

49. See Heesakkers, "Foundation and Early Development of the Athenaeum" (1982); and Amsterdam University, *Humanists and Humanism in Amsterdam* (1973).

50. *De arabibus latinisque philosophis hypomnemata* (1627), *De primis philosophis* (1627), and *De scriptoribus ecclesiasticis et obiter quibusdam philologicis* (1628); see Moeller, 23; Herberger and Stolleis, 24.

51. On the three disputations he published in Leiden, see below, p. 61. During the same years, he edited two works in the fields of medicine and natural philosophy: *De fractura cranii*, by Berengario da Carpi (1629), and *Observationum et paradoxorum chymiatricorum libri duo*, by Billich (1631).

52. Moeller, 22, mentions three other teachers with whom Conring was, or may have been, in contact during his years in Leiden: Petrus Cunaeus (or Peter von der Cun, 1586–1638), best known for his *De republica Hebraeorum* (1617); Gilbert Jacchaeus (or Gilbert Jack, 1585–1628), who wrote *Institutiones physicae* (1619); and Franco Burgersdicius (or Franco Burgersdijck, 1590–1635), who wrote widely on natural, moral, and political philosophy and especially on logic. Burgersdicius published a synopsis as well as a detailed textbook of logic that turned out to be unusually successful and was often reprinted; see his *Institutionum logicarum synopsis* (1632) and *Institutionum logicarum libri duo* (1632). Conring dedicated his *Theses variae de morali prudentia* of 1629 to Burgersdicius. We know nothing about his relationship to Cunaeus and Jacchaeus.

53. Aristotle, *Politicorum libri octo* (1621). In 1637 Conring published the Latin translation of the *Politics* by Obertus Giphanius with a preface that throws important light on his gloomy assessment of Germany's condition after the Peace of Prague ("Praefatio in politicam Aristotelis," in *Opera*, 1:117–28); in 1656 he published the *Politics* again, this time in the Latin translation of Petrus Victorius with the Greek text of Heinsius and with a much-expanded introduction and philological observations of his own—one of the few occasions on which Conring practiced textual criticism of this kind; see Moeller, 64, 102–3. *Opera*, 3:491–723, reproduces the edition of 1656; for the introduction ("Hermanni Conringii introductio in Politica Aristotelis"), see *Opera*, 3:457–90. Moeller, 64, seems to suggest that Conring published another version of Giphanius's translation, without preface or introduction, as early 1635. I have not been able to verify that such an edition existed.

54. *Disputatio physica de calido innato* (1627); cf. *De calido innato sive igne animali* (1647). Conring's correspondence on this subject with Severino is described by Trevisani, "Medizinisch-wissenschaftliche Beziehungen" (1983).

55. *Disputatio de origine formarum* (1630). He was going to return to the subject at length in his *Introductio in naturalem philosophiam* (1638); cf. Moeller, 45–46.

56. Moeller, 23–24. Grotius's *De iure belli ac pacis libri tres* has been published in many different editions. I am going to rely on the edition by James Brown Scott, trans. Francis W. Kelsey (1913–25).

57. For brief and incisive treatments of Grotius, see Hofmann, "Hugo Grotius" (1995); and Tuck, "Grotius and Selden" (1991). See also Tuck, *Philosophy and Government* (1992), 154–201. Tuck places welcome emphasis on the originality and importance of Grotius for the development of European political thought.

58. Compare, for example, the portrayal by Tuck, "Grotius and Selden," 499–529, with the remarks of Dreitzel, "Hermann Conring und die politische Wissenschaft" (1983), 152.

59. See Grotius, "De veritate religionis christianae, cum annotationibus Hermanni Conringii," in *Opera*, 5:1–105. Conring's annotations were not published during his lifetime. On their transmission in two manuscripts, one of which was owned by Thomasius, and their first publication by Johann Christoph Koecher in his edition of Grotius, *De veritate religionis christianae* (1726–27), see the remarks by Goebel in *Opera*, 5:a2–b. Conring's annotations have never been studied in any detail; see Wallmann, "Helmstedter Theologie," 35; Mager, "Hermann Conring als theologischer Schriftsteller," 56.

60. For an undated and unpublished letter from Conring to Grotius, see Herberger, "Die ungedruckten Briefe Hermann Conrings" (1983), 520. For two published letters from Grotius to Conring, see Ammermann, "Die gedruckten Briefe Conrings" (1983), 456.

61. Grotius, *De iure belli ac pacis*, bk. 2, chap. 4 (trans. Kelsey, 2:220–30), was decisive for the understanding of prescription advanced in *Discursus novus*, chaps. 18, 19, 20, 25; see below, pp. 113–15. Conring mentioned Grotius's *Liber de antiquitate reipublicae Batavicae* (1610) in chapter 8 and his *Apologeticus eorum qui Hollandiae . . . praefuerunt* (1622) in chapter 40. It is probably fair to say that the *Discursus novus* owed its greatest intellectual debt to Grotius.

62. See Raabe, "Die Bibliotheca Conringiana" (1983), 431, listing the authors who contributed the largest number of books to Conring's library. The list is led by Calixt with 44, Erasmus with 29, Luther with 28, and Grotius with 24. Conring owned 18 books by Aristotle, 17 by Galen, and 13 by Cicero.

63. "Id siquidem nemo temere inficiabitur, Duumviros hosce [i.e., Conring and Grotius] non uni civitati, non suae nationi tantum, sed toti Europae, eruditionis suae gloria splendidissimum intulisse decus, et utrumque simili fere aemulatione et clementia a summis orbis Regibus expetitum cultumque, immo pari gloria in suo quemque genere novos disciplinarum fontes ita aperuisse, ut posteri viam semel tentatam facillimo negotio ulterius investigare et feliciter perficere possint." *Opera*, 5:a2.

64. Moeller, 28. It is uncertain whether this offer arrived before or after the letter from Calixt containing an offer of employment in Helmstedt, on which see immediately below. Herberger and Stolleis, 24, suggest that it arrived before the letter from Calixt.

65. It is printed and translated into German in Herberger and Stolleis, 28–29; cf. Moeller, 26–30.

66. Wallmann, "Helmstedter Theologie," 38.

67. The ceremony and the relevant documents are detailed by Moeller, 33–4. It is worth adding that the terms of the appointment gave both Conring and his employer the right to part on six months notice.

68. Moeller, 33.

69. Ibid., 34–35.

70. See Dietrich, "Jacobus Lampadius" (1958); Stolleis, *Reichspublizistik und Policeywissenschaft* (1988), 163–64.

71. Lampadius, *De iurisdictione, iuribus principum et statuum imperii* (1620). On the different titles under which this work circulated, see below, note 98.

72. Jam enim tunc, ut aliarum rerumpublicarum, ita et hujus aliqua mihi, in Batavis

comparata, quidem notitia fuerat, sed levior; qualis nempe ad familiares vitae civilis congressus videbatur satis homini, artem medicam facienti ac naturalis praecipue philosophiae sectanti culturam. *Opera,* 2:25.

73. Lehmann, *Chronica der freyen Reichs Statt Speyr* (1612).

74. "Cum autem forte fortuna incidisset in manus meas Christophori Lehmanni, neutiquam ex titulo aestimandum, sed reapse incomparabile opus, illius diligente lectione coepi demum Imperii rerum formam, a primis incunabilis ad nostra usque productam tempora, animo comprehendere." *Opera,* 2:25.

75. The shift from *iurisdictio* in the title Lampadius had given his work via *constitutio* to *respublica* in the titles given by Conring reflects, in a small way, his contribution to the shift from medieval to modern concepts of political order.

76. "Et vero isthac occasione, ex frequentibus de republica sermonibus [cum Lampadio], incensus est in me ardor, Imperii statum omnem penitius cognoscendi. . . . Hac occasione [ad communis Imperii accuratiorem peritiam manuducendi academicam nostram juventutem] autem a me saepius (frequenter enim repetere illam institutionem, studium juvandae nostrae adolescentiae et commodi publici amor me adegit) libellus ille fuit illustratus." *Opera,* 2:25–26.

77. *Aristotelis laudatio* (1633). For the entire episode, see the detailed account in Moeller, 35–43; cf. Mager, "Hermann Conring als theologischer Schriftsteller," 63–64.

78. For the broader issue, see Ginzburg, *Il nicodemismo* (1970); and Zagorin, *Ways of Lying* (1990).

79. Conring, *Disputatio medica de scorbuto* (1634); cf. the three dissertations on scurvy by Conring's students: *Disputatio medica de scorbuto,* resp. Krüger (1638), *Disputatio medica inauguralis de scorbuto,* resp. Gieseler (1644), and *Disputatio medica inauguralis de scorbuto,* resp. Behrens (1659).

80. According to the statutes, there should have been three professors. But the third was not appointed until 1652. Kundert, "Conring als Professor," 400.

81. Moeller, 48.

82. For details on Stucke, see Herberger and Stolleis, 91–92.

83. It is in good repair, adorned by a plaque commemorating Conring flatteringly but inaccurately as "prof.[essor] theol.[ogiae], jur.[is], med.[icinae] et philos.[ophiae]." Conring was professor of natural philosophy, medicine, and politics, but neither of theology nor of law. Next to his plaque is a similar one commemorating Hermann von der Hardt, a later occupant of the building and a professor at the University of Helmstedt best remembered for his studies of Hebrew and Syriac and an important collection of documents relating to the Council of Constance, *Magnum oecumenicum Constantiense Concilium* (1697–1700).

84. For information about Hermann Conring's wife, father-in-law, children, and possessions, Herberger and Stolleis, 89–95, is the best source of information. Moeller, 1–5, 49–50, is good on Conring's parents and siblings but otherwise sketchy.

85. Conring, *Introductio in naturalem philosophiam* (1638). For a summary, see Moeller, 43–46.

86. See Rosner, "Hermann Conring als Arzt" (1983); cf. Rosner, "Die Bedeutung Hermann Conrings" (1969); and Marx, "Zur Erinnerung der ärztlichen Wirksamkeit Hermann Conrings" (1873).

87. See French, *Harvey's Natural Philosophy* (1994); Bylebyl, *William Harvey and His Age* (1979); and Lindeboom, "Reception of Harvey's Theory" (1957).

88. For a listing of these exercises and the individual respondents, see "Gedruckte Werke," 539–41, nos. 35–38, 42–43, 49–52.

89. Conring, *De habitus corporum Germanicorum antiqui ac novi causis dissertatio* (1645); cf. Rosner, "Hermann Conring als Arzt," 98–103.

90. *De hermetica Aegyptiorum vetere et Paracelsicorum nova medicina* (1648). On Paracelsus and Paracelsian medicine, there is a growing body of literature; see Debus, *Chemical Philosophy* (1977), and by the same author, *French Paracelsians* (1991).

91. *De hermetica medicina libri duo* (1669); see the "Benevolo Lectori" on unnumbered pages 11–22 of the front matter.

92. See Cohn, "Ludwig XIV." (1870); Fasolt, "From Helmstedt via Mainz to Paris" (1989).

93. *Introductio in universam artem medicam* (1654).

94. On the authorship of the *Discursus novus* see below, chapter 3.

95. The *Introductio* was reprinted in Helmstedt in 1687 and in Halle in 1726; "Gedruckte Werke," 550, nos. 136a and 136b; cf. Rosner, "Hermann Conring als Arzt," 93–98.

96. Among the minor medical works, see the preface "De doctrina pathologica" in his edition of *Observationum medicarum centuriae tres posthumae*, by Salmuth (1648), 3–16. For his editions, see the *Tractatus . . . de curatione pestiferorum apostematum*, by Capelluti (1642); and his edition of the *Libri chirurgici*, by Fienus (1649). For the dissertations, see "Gedruckte Werke," for the years 1637–50.

97. Conring, *Disputatio politica de mutationibus rerumpublicarum*, resp. Engelbrecht (1635). For dissertations published until 1643, see "Gedruckte Werke," 537–42.

98. The first of these editions was printed by Jean Maire in Leiden under the title *De republica Romano-Germanica* (1634), in a pocket format deliberately similar to Elsevier's popular guides to the states of the world. *De republica Romano-Germanica* is the title that appears on the title page and the running heads. But the same work is also known under the title *Tractatus de constitutione imperii Romano-Germanici*, which appears on a separate engraved title page. In 1640 Conring had the *De republica Romano-Germanica* reprinted in the same small format that Maire had used in 1634, but by Rixner in Helmstedt and without the engraved title page (not listed in "Gedruckte Werke"). In 1642 Maire produced a third edition in Leiden, again with a separate title page, under the title *De republica Romano-Germanica* (not listed in "Gedruckte Werke"). In 1671, finally, Conring published a revised edition with his own commentary on the text that was published by Müller in Helmstedt and reprinted in *Opera*, 2:22–237. The commentary is substantial and often critical, but except in his lectures he never managed to carry it beyond book 3, chapter 7. For the remainder, see Goebel's edition of Conring's *Discursus ad Lampadium posterior*, published from a manuscript in *Opera*, 2:238–466.

99. See Moeller, 103.

100. Conring, ed., *De moribus Germanorum*, by Tacitus (1635); cf. Etter, *Tacitus in der Geistesgeschichte* (1966); Schellhase, *Tacitus in Renaissance Political Thought* (1976); and more recently Burke, "Tacitism, Scepticism, and Reason of State" (1991); and Luce and Woodman, *Tacitus and the Tacitean Tradition* (1993).

101. For a detailed analysis of the "Praefatio de historiarum, Germanorum inprimis, studiis," see Fasolt, "Conring on History" (1987); cf. Hammerstein, "Die Historie bei Conring" (1983). For Conring's reaffirmation of the principles first enunciated in 1635, see the preface to his third edition of *De moribus Germanorum* (1678), in *Opera*, 5:253–57.

102. Nullius voluminis atque hujus morosa mihi et plena taedii conscriptio fuit hactenus. *Opera*, 3:281.

103. "Praefatio in politicam Aristotelis" (1637).

104. *De origine iuris Germanici commentarius historicus* (1643). For a recent German translation with an excellent introduction, see Conring, *Der Ursprung des deutschen Rechts* (1994).

105. Among those who have said a little more are Stintzing, "Hermann Conring" (1884); Moeller, 74–92; Lenz, "Hermann Conring und die deutsche Staatslehre" (1926); Kossert, *Conrings rechtsgeschichtliches Verdienst* (1939); Gross, *Empire and Sovereignty* (1975), 255–92; Luig, "Conring, das deutsche Recht und die Rechtsgeschichte" (1983); Stolleis, *Reichspublizistik und Policeywissenschaft* (1988), 231–33; and Stolleis, "Hermann Conring und die Begründung der deutschen Rechtsgeschichte" (1994).

106. Stobbe, *Hermann Conring, der Begründer der deutschen Rechtsgeschichte* (1870); Moeller, *Hermann Conring, der Vorkämpfer des deutschen Rechts* (1915).

107. For the Lotharian legend and Conring's place in its history, see, e.g., Moeller, 67–74; Luig, "Conring, das deutsche Recht und die Rechtsgeschichte" (1983); and especially the concise statement by Michael Stolleis, "Hermann Conring und die Begründung der deutschen Rechtsgeschichte" (1994), 257–61.

108. See Wieacker, *Privatrechtsgeschichte der Neuzeit* (1967), in English *History of Private Law* (1995), pt. 3, "Der Usus modernus und der Abschluss der praktischen Rezeption"; cf. Coing, "Bartolus und der usus modernus" (1962).

109. Herberger and Stolleis, 47, call it Conring's "staatsrechtliche Hauptschrift," but apart from the dated and superficial analysis by Knoll, *Conring als Historiker* (1889), 46–92, there are only scattered remarks in Moeller, 94–99; Wolf, "Hermann Conring" (1963), 238–41; and Mazzacane, "Conring, Baronio e la storia" (1983), 269–70. Lang, *Staat und Souveränität* (1970), whom one might have expected to treat the *De Germanorum imperio Romano* in some detail, excluded it from consideration altogether—a casualty of conceptual limits imposed by legal history. Seifert, "Conring und die 'Ottonische Legende,'" in Seifert, *Der Rückzug der biblischen Prophetie* (1990), 165–86, is by far the most interesting and thoughtful treatment to date.

110. See Goez, *Translatio Imperii* (1958); and Folz, *L'idée d'empire en Occident* (1953), in English *Concept of Empire* (1969).

111. Conring, *De finibus imperii Germanici* (1654).

112. On the meaning of the term *res publica* in Conring's writings and the translation of *res publica* as "state," see the introduction to my edition and translation of the *Discursus novus* (forthcoming). Cf. Mager, "Republik" (1984); Koenigsberger, *Republiken und Republikanismus* (1988); Skinner, "The State" (1989); Koselleck et al., "Staat und Souveränität" (1990); and the old piece by Dowdal, "The Word 'State'" (1923).

113. See Arno Seifert, "Conring und die 'Ottonische Legende,'" in Seifert, *Der Rückzug der biblischen Prophetie* (1990), 165–86; Willoweit, "Kaiser, Reich und Reichsstände" (1983); and Knoll, *Conring als Historiker* (1889), 46–92. Cf. Mazzacane, "Hermann Conring e la storia" (1982); and Mazzacane, "Conring, Baronio e la storia" (1983).

114. Felberg, *Conrings Anteil am politischen Leben* (1931), 26.

115. Goldschlag, *Beiträge zur politischen und publizistischen Thätigkeit* (1884), 8–17; Droste, "Hermann Conring und Schweden" (1999), 348–49.

116. Williams, *Descartes* (1978), 23–24.

117. On Conring's relations with East Frisia, see Schmidt, "Hermann Conring und Ostfriesland" (1983).

118. Droste, "Hermann Conring und Schweden" (1999), 355.

119. The circumstances of Conring's appointment to the chair in politics are best described by Kundert, "Conring als Professor," 402–4. His preference for Cellarius over Aristotle is mentioned ibid., 409.

120. In Gross Twülpstedt, the place where he was going to be buried; see Herberger and Stolleis, 89–90.

121. Naturam et constitutionem Reipublicae seu Imperii Romano-Germanici, as the terms of his new appointment put it; Kundert, "Conring als Professor," 403.

122. Conring's absences from the university are surveyed by Kundert, ibid., 408–9.

123. Since Goebel decided to limit his edition of Conring's works to historical, legal, and political writings, the shift in Conring's interest away from medicine can be documented by comparing the number of works produced by Conring overall (historical, legal, political, theological, medical, and natural scientific) with the number of works included in the *Opera* (only historical, legal, and political) and noting the difference. "Gedruckte Werke," 536–46, lists a total of 96 works published during the two decades from 1630 to 1649. But only 32, exactly one-third, made it into the *Opera,* indicating how much more attention Conring paid to medicine and natural philosophy during those years. For the following two decades, from 1650 to 1669, "Gedruckte Werke," 547–61, lists 128 works, of which 73, well over half, made it into the *Opera,* indicating Conring's increased attention to history and politics. If one adds the 22 works that Goebel was the first to publish in 1730, almost all of which are likely to have been written in the two decades after 1650, the total number of works written from 1650 to 1669 would rise to 150, and the number of works included in the *Opera* to 95, or almost two-thirds. For the last decade of Conring's life, "Gedruckte Werke," 561–64, lists only 29 works, 18 of which appear in the *Opera.* Conring's energies, though clearly waning, were still focused on matters historical and political.

124. I count 29 medical dissertations for the years 1651 to 1681, as compared to 30 for the years from 1637 to 1650, or an average of less than 1 per year after 1650, as compared to more than 2 per year before 1650. The numbers are not meant to be precise, but they give a fair impression of orders of magnitude.

125. *Theses miscellaneae de civili prudentia,* resp. Ottendorf (1650); *Theses miscellaneae excerptae ex cap. 1 et 2 libri De civili prudentia,* resp. Dassel (1651); *Theses miscellaneae excerptae ex cap. 3,* resp. Pogwisch (1651); *Theses miscellaneae excerptae ex cap. 4,* resp. Wickeden (1651); *Theses miscellaneae excerptae ex cap. 5,* resp. Dresinck (1651). The various *Theses miscellaneae excerptae* were not reprinted in the *Opera* as such. But compare the parallel in the first five chapters (out of a total of fourteen) of *De civili prudentia* in *Opera,* 3:282–306.

126. *Dissertatio de ratione status,* resp. Voss (1651). See Stolleis, "Machiavellismus und Staatsräson" (1983).

127. *De civili prudentia liber unus* (1662).

128. Irenaeus Eubulus (i.e., Hermann Conring), *Pro pace perpetua Protestantibus danda* (1648).

129. *De pace perpetua* (1657), reprinted in 1677 as *De pace civili,* a small but interesting change of words.

130. Conring, ed., *Via regia*, by Witzel (1650); and Conring, ed., *De sacris nostri temporis controversiis*, by Georg Cassander and Georg Witzel (1659); cf. Mager, "Hermann Conring als theologischer Schriftsteller," 76.

131. Locke, *Letter concerning Toleration* (1983).

132. *De electione Urbani IIX et Innocentii X* (1651); *Fundamentorum fidei pontificiae concussio* (1654); *Defensio ecclesiae Protestantium* (1654).

133. *Vindiciae pacificationis Osnabruccensis et Monasteriensis* (1653), published under the pseudonym Ludovicus de Montesperato; also published as *Rettung des Osnabrückischen und Münsterischen Friedens* (1653?).

134. *Animadversiones in Christopheri Haunoldi . . . libellum* (1654); *Examen libelli a Vito Erbermanno . . . oppositi* (1654); *Responsio ad Valerianum Magnum* (1654); *Responsio altera pro sua Concussione fundamentorum fidei pontificiae* (1655). *Epistola de electione Alexandri VII* (1655); and *Glossa ordinaria ad litteras circulares Alexandri papae septimi* (1655), also published in German as *Nothwendige Anmerckungen auff Pabst Alexanders des Siebenden Kreisz Schreiben* (1656). For more details, see Wallmann, "Helmstedter Theologie," 49 n. 38.

135. *De purgatorio animadversiones in Ioannem Mulmannum* (1651).

136. *De finibus imperii Germanici libri duo* (1654).

137. See *Opera*, 1:vii and 6:373. "Gedruckte Werke," 550 no. 135, lists the edition by Martin in Lyon as the main one, but Goebel's list of "Scripta, quae auctor pro suis non agnovit nec heredes agnoscunt," *Opera*, 1:xxxvii–xxxviii, makes it clear that Conring regarded the Lyon edition as an unauthorized reprint.

138. It was reprinted in Frankfurt by Ellinger in 1680, and again in Frankfurt by Heinich in 1693; see "Gedruckte Werke," 550. On Leopold I's interest in this work, see Goebel's remarks in *Opera*, 1:vii–ix, and the letters cited there.

139. *De finibus imperii Germanici liber tertius* (1681). Goebel included the material of this "third book" in the footnotes to his edition of the *De finibus* in *Opera*, 1:114–485, and marked them with the siglum "C.A.E.," i.e., "Conringii annotationes editae." They are not to be confused either with Goebel's own notes (identified by the siglum "Göbel") or with the notes that Goebel took from Conring's lecture manuscript (identified by the siglum "C.A.M.," i.e., "Conringii annotationes manuscriptae"). They are especially not to be confused with the "fourth book" of notes on the *De finibus* that was published anonymously and that Goebel reprinted in *Opera*, 1:463–85. On Goebel's handling of the text of the *De finibus* and the various annotations, see *Opera*, 1:vii–ix.

140. "De statu Europae, ac inprimis Germanici imperii," in *Opera*, 6:658–868.

141. See below, p. 89.

142. Kundert, "Conring als Professor," 410.

143. Kundert, *Katalog der Helmstedter juristischen Disputationen*, 37.

144. See Schrohe, *Johann Christian von Boineburg* (1926); Ultsch, *Johann Christian von Boineburg* (1936); Saring, "Boineburg" (1955); Reitzel, "Leibniz, Boineburg und Johann Philipp von Schönborn" (1961); and now especially Peterse, "Johann Christian von Boineburg und die Mainzer Irenik" (2000), with further references. I am grateful to Hans Peterse for furnishing me access to his copies of the pieces by Schrohe and Reitzel, neither of which I was able to find in the United States.

145. Ammermann, "Die gedruckten Briefe Conrings" (1983), lists about 350 printed letters between Boineburg and Conring. Herberger, "Die ungedruckten Briefe Conrings" (1983), lists about 250 unprinted ones. Most of the printed letters can be found in Gruber, *Commercii epistolici Leibnitiani . . . tomus prodromus* (1745).

146. On Schönborn, the old biography by Mentz, *Johann Philipp von Schönborn* (1896–99), has never been superseded, but see von Pöllnitz, "Johann Philipp von Schönborn" (1963); and Jürgensmeier, *Johann Philipp von Schönborn* (1977).

147. On the role of the arch-chancellor, see Mathy, "Über das Mainzer Erzkanzleramt" (1965); and Aretin, *Das Alte Reich* (1993–97), 2:116–30. See also the old study by Seeliger, *Erzkanzler und Reichskanzleien* (1889). For a brief introduction to the constitution of the Holy Roman Empire in English, see Gross, "Holy Roman Empire in Modern Times" (1974).

148. See Mager, "Hermann Conring als theologischer Schriftsteller"; Dunin-Borkowski, "Aus der Briefmappe eines berühmten Konvertiten" (1922–23); and Peterse, "Johann Christian von Boineburg und die Mainzer Irenik" (2000).

149. Krappmann, *Johann Philipp von Schönborn und das Leibnizsche Consilium Aegyptiacum* (1931).

150. Herberger, "Die ungedruckten Briefe Hermann Conrings," 474–500, lists well over eight hundred letters from Conring to Duke August. Cf. Herzog August Bibliothek, *Sammler, Fürst, Gelehrter* (1979).

151. *Assertio iuris Moguntini in coronandis regibus Romanorum* (1655).

152. Conring contributed *Castigatio libelli cui titulus Anticonringiana defensio iuris Coloniensis* (1656); and *Iteratarum vindiciarum iuris coronandi pro archidioecesi Coloniensi examen* (1656). The whole body of texts outlining the positions and responses of both Mainz and Cologne was conveniently assembled by Goebel in *Opera,* 1:614–811. But note that Goebel's introduction, *Opera,* 1:x–xii, is misinformed on the authorship of some of these writings and does not present them in chronological order.

153. For details, see Becker, "Diplomatik und Rechtsgeschichte" (1983), 341–43; and Wallner, *Krönungsstreit zwischen Kurköln und Kurmainz* (1967); cf. Felberg, *Conrings Anteil am politischen Leben* (1931), 32–45.

154. *Vicariatus imperii Palatinus defensus* (1658); cf. Felberg, *Conrings Anteil am politischen Leben* (1931), 46–59.

155. For Conring's work on behalf of France, see Felberg, *Conrings Anteil am politischen Leben* (1931), 69–85; Kunisch, "Hermann Conrings mächtepolitisches Weltbild" (1983); and especially the unpublished dissertation by Wardemann, "Hermann Conrings Gutachtertätigkeit" (1981), a very useful, though not always reliable, study of Conring's activity as an observer and participant in the political affairs of the day with a scope extending far beyond his dealings with France. As far as I can tell, Wardemann's dissertation has gone unnoticed in the literature on Hermann Conring. I am grateful to Albrecht von Arnswaldt for alerting me to its existence.

156. *Animadversiones politicae in Nicolai Machiavelli librum De principe* (1661); cf. Fasolt, "From Helmstedt via Mainz to Paris" (1989).

157. Cohn, "Ludwig XIV." (1870).

158. Duchhardt, "Et Germani eligunt et Germanus eligendus" (1980).

159. See above, note 91.

160. "Consilium de maris mediterranei dominio," in *Opera,* 1:989–1008. This was not published during Conring's lifetime. Goebel proudly noted that, to the best of his knowledge, he was the first to have discovered it; see his remarks in *Opera,* 1:xvi. For a paraphrase, see Fasolt, "From Helmstedt via Mainz to Paris" (1989).

161. "Bedenken zu der holländischen Triple-alliance."

162. Scheel, "Hermann Conring als historisch-politischer Ratgeber" (1983).

163. *Gründlicher Bericht von der landesfürstlichen ertzbischöfflichen Hoch- und Gerechtigkeit über die Stadt Bremen* (1652).

164. *De iustitia armorum Suecicorum* (1655), published under the pseudonym Cyriacus Thrasymachus, also in German as *Epistola oder Sendschreiben, des Cyriaci Thrasymachi, von der gerechten Kriegs-Armatur der Cron Schweden wieder die Cron Polen* (1655); *Brevis ac praeliminaris enarratio* (1656). On the Swedish connection, see Goldschlag, *Beiträge zur politischen und publizistischen Thätigkeit* (1884), 17–65; Kunisch, "Hermann Conrings mächtepolitisches Weltbild" (1983), 244–46; and above all Droste, "Hermann Conring und Schweden" (1999).

165. Conring, ed., *De controversiis Suecopolonicis*, by Mithobius (1656); Conring, ed., *Polonia*, by Simon Starovolski (1656).

166. "Ohnmassgebliches Bedencken von stets-waehrender Erhaltung der neuen Erb-Monarchie des hoechstloeblichen Koenigreichs Dennemarck," in *Opera*, 2:953–66. See Kunisch, "Hermann Conrings mächtepolitisches Weltbild," 251–54.

167. "Bericht, wie es mit dem Rechte der Engelländer Fischereyen ... bewandt," in *Opera*, 2:917–32; "Ohnmassgeblicher Vorschlag von Auffnahm Ihro Königlichen Majestäten zu Dennemarck und Norwegen Königreichen und anderen Ländern," in *Opera*, 2:932–52.

168. *Censura diplomatis quod Ludovico imperatori fert acceptum coenobium Lindaviense* (1672). See Becker, "Diplomatik und Rechtsgeschichte" (1983), 346–48; cf. Meyer von Knonau, "Das bellum diplomaticum Lindaviense" (1871).

169. Becker, "Diplomatik und Rechtsgeschichte," 343–46; cf. Junkers, *Der Streit zwischen Kurstaat und Stadt Köln* (1935); and Kisky, "Die Akten der Abteilung 'Köln contra Köln'" (1914). Goebel was well informed about the existence of Conring's *Deductio Coloniensis* and did his best to obtain it not only from the city of Cologne but also from acquaintances who he was certain had copies, but he failed miserably, "no matter how hard I tried and how often I begged" (*omni licet adhibita diligentia et precibus*); see *Opera*, 1:xxxviii, no. 24. It was perhaps his biggest failure, and it is testimony both to the importance of Conring's memorandum and to its political sensitivity as late as the 1730s.

170. For a concise summary, see Herberger and Stolleis, 60–63; cf. Felberg, *Conrings Anteil am politischen Leben* (1931), 63–64, 68, 77–78.

171. Though the rulers of Sweden repeatedly promised Conring considerable payments, they never seem to have made good on their promises; see Droste, "Hermann Conring und Schweden" (1999), 346 n. 36, 350.

172. Herberger and Stolleis, 60.

173. Felberg, *Conrings Anteil am politischen Leben*, 77–78.

174. See, for example, Stobbe, *Hermann Conring* (1870), 18–23; Bresslau, "Hermann Conring" (1876), 450; Goldschlag, *Beiträge zur politischen und publizistischen Thätigkeit*, 42; Knoll, *Conring als Historiker* (1889), 39–45.

175. Moeller, 110–11.

176. Wolf, "Hermann Conring," 239–44.

177. For an unusually judicious account of Conring's activity as a political adviser, see Droste, "Hermann Conring und Schweden" (1999).

178. Conring, ed., *Princeps*, by Machiavelli (1660); *Animadversiones politicae in Nicolai Machiavelli librum De principe* (1661). See Stolleis, "Machiavellismus und Staatsräson" (1983). In *Opera*, 2:973–1092, Conring's commentary is printed in the form of extended footnotes to his edition of the Latin text of the *Prince*.

179. *De civili prudentia liber unus* (1662). See Dreitzel, "Hermann Conring und die politische Wissenschaft" (1983); and Dreitzel, "Aristoteles' Politik" (1986).

180. *Propolitica sive brevis introductio in civilem philosophiam* (1663).

181. *Dissertatio de comitiis imperii,* resp. Engelbrecht (1666); *Dissertatio de praecipuis negotiis in comitiis,* resp. Becker (1666); *Dissertatio de officialibus imperii,* resp. Burgstorff (1669).

182. *De constitutione episcoporum Germaniae,* resp. Blume (1647). Conring's dissertations on the empire thus fall into two clearly demarcated periods: the 1640s and the 1660s; cf. Willoweit, "Kaiser, Reich und Reichsstände" (1983).

183. Conring, ed., *De republica Romano-Germanica,* by Lampadius (1671).

184. *Exercitationes academicae de republica imperii Germanici* (1674). The ten dissertations included in this work were reprinted by Goebel. Conring's introduction was not.

185. *Thesaurus rerumpublicarum,* ed. Oldenburger (1675).

186. *Admonitio de Thesauro rerumpublicarum* (1675).

187. *Exercitatio historico-politica de notitia singularis alicuius reipublicae,* in *Opera,* 4:1–43; and *Examen rerumpublicarum potiorum totius orbis,* in *Opera,* 4:47–520.

188. See Seifert, "Conring und die Begründung der Staatenkunde" (1983); Zehrfeld, *Hermann Conrings Staatenkunde* (1926); cf. Felsing, *Statistik als Methode* (1930).

189. *De finibus imperii Germanici liber tertius* (1681).

190. *Ex politicis dissertatio academica de senatu liberarum rerum-publicarum,* resp. Holste (1681).

191. On Conring's estate, see Herberger and Stolleis, 89–90; on his library, see Raabe, "Die Bibliotheca Conringiana" (1983), esp. 418–19. Raabe identifies 4,622 books, bound in 3,264 volumes. Considerably larger were the libraries of Benedikt Carpzow (15,515 volumes) and Jakob Thomasius (8,441), but Pufendorf's was smaller (1,697); cf. *Catalogus bibliothecae Conringianae* (1694).

192. One of the six daughters surviving to adulthood is known to have predeceased him. Three are known to have survived him. The dates of death for the remaining two are not known; see Herberger and Stolleis, 89.

CHAPTER THREE

1. *Discursus novus,* chap. 52. Since the pagination differs from one version of the text to another and the chapters of the *Discursus novus* are mostly short, I refer to chapters rather than pages. For a brief analysis of the argument of the *Discursus novus* with further references to the literature, see Fasolt, "Question of Right" (1997). For an interesting contemporary parallel, see Ullmann, "Reflections on the Medieval Empire" (1964), 97–98:

> Of course, it is true that emperorship added nothing to actual royal powers, and yet at once the question arises why then the Germans from Otto I throughout the medieval period were so anxious to receive the crown? Merely for the sake of some dignity? Should one really assume that this constituted such a lure that every one of them embarked on costly Italian campaigns, which involved years of absence from Germany, which made the establishment of orderly government in Germany an excruciatingly difficult task, which entailed so much loss in men and material—and all this just for the sake of an imperial dignity?

2. The literature on the issue is huge. For an initial approach, see Folz, *Concept of Empire* (1969); Lübke-Wolf, "Die Beutung der Lehre von den vier Weltreichen" (1984); Neddermeyer, *Mittelalter in der deutschen Historiographie* (1988); and Seifert, *Rückzug der biblischen Prophetie* (1990).

3. More precisely, Lampadius began with the year 3212 from the creation of the world, the year in which he calculated Rome to have been founded, 2,370 years before his own time; see Conring's edition of Lampadius's work under the title *De republica Romano-Germanica* (1671), pt. 2, par. 1, in *Opera*, 2:50.

4. See Bireley, *Religion and Politics* (1981); and Bosbach, *Monarchia universalis* (1988); cf. Headley, *Emperor and His Chancellor* (1983). Pagden, *Lords of All the World* (1995), has little to say about Germany.

5. Conring had already expressed his unhappiness about the publication of the *Discursus novus* to Johannes Schwartzkopf, the chancellor of Brunswick-Wolfenbüttel, in a letter of November 1642; Moeller, 76. In his preface to *De Germanorum imperio Romano*, in *Opera*, 1:27, dated December 1643, however, he stated that he obtained a copy of the *Discursus novus* "six months" ago, about the middle of 1643. That suggests that he heard about the *Discursus novus* in the fall of 1642 but did not actually see a copy until the summer of 1643.

6. "Nihilo tamen minus inventus est superiore anno, qui libellum istum meo nomine evulgaret, titulo praescripto sane insolente, *Discursus novi de Imperatore* [sic]; credo, quo pelliceret emptorem, et hedera suspenderetur vino alias minus vendibili: utque lateret fucus, et suum et loci sui nomen dissimulavit typographus, corollariis aliisque praesectis. Id scriptum cum ante hos sex menses in manus meas incideret, obstupui sane, eo rediisse mores, ut quis tantum facinus ausus me vivo. Maxime dolui, quod suum locique sui nomen subticente typographo, libellus raram adeo prae se ferens frontem, hac tempestate sequiorem facile suspicionem movere, et notam famae meae possit inurere. Graviter profecto momordit me haec injuria; praesertim quum exemplo forte careat, nec pro merito queat vindicari. Neque vero ego aliud restituendae in integrum existimationi meae (illam enim laesam crudo isto ac supposititio foetu non possum non credere) remedium potui excogitare, quam si ipsemet argumentum illud sumerem pertractandum. Ita ego coactus sum horas, quas proximis hisce septimanis potui ordinario labori suffurari, alienis illis studiis impendere." Conring, "Benevolo Lectori," *Opera*, 1:27.

7. "Scripta, quae auctor pro suis non agnovit nec heredes agnoscunt," *Opera*, 1:xxxvii–xxxviii. "Gedruckte Werke," 540 no. 48, similarly notes that Conring denied being the author of the *Discursus novus*.

8. References to the *Discursus novus*, where they can be found at all, are cursory, for example, in Moeller, 94–95. The closely related *Exercitatio de imperatore Romano Germanico* (1641), on which see below, is briefly summarized, but not analyzed, by Knoll, *Conring als Historiker* (1889), 24–26; and Willoweit, "Kaiser, Reich und Reichsstände" (1983), 324–25.

9. In 1674 he called it "altera mearum Exercitationum, quae est *de Imperatore Romano Germanico*." *Exercitationes academicae* (1674), p. 9 of the unpaginated front matter. He referred to it again as "disputationem meam" in the lectures on Lampadius that were posthumously published by Goebel; see his "Discursus ad Lampadium posterior," *Opera*, 2:239.

10. "Exercitatio de imperatore Romano Germanico," in *Exercitationes academicae* (1674), 32–72.

11. *Opera*, 1:528–42.

12. "De imperatore Romano Germanico discursus historico-politicus," in *De imperii Germanici republica acroamata sex* (1655), 275–309.

13. The evidence for this history consists mostly of the title pages of the various printings that will be mentioned below, the results of a close comparison of the texts in question, the preface to Conring's *De Germanorum imperio Romano*, *Opera*, 1:26–27, and the preface to his *Exercitationes academicae* (1674), esp. pp. 9–11 of the unpaginated front matter. The latter is a particularly valuable source of information for Conring's attitude to the dissertations written by his students, but it was unfortunately not reprinted in the *Opera*.

14. Only so far as we can tell, because we do not know enough about the development of Conring's thought from the time when he first began to devote himself to the study of the empire in 1632, through the beginning of his lectures on the empire in about 1634, to the appearance of his first dissertations about the empire in 1641; see Moeller, 64–65; and Kundert, "Conring als Professor" (1983), 403.

15. Bogislaus Otho von Hoym was one of Conring's less distinguished students. We know about him only that he belonged to an old noble family with an ancestral seat near Quedlinburg. See *Neue deutsche Biographie*, *Allgemeine deutsche Biographie*, and *Deutsches biographisches Archiv*, s.v. "Hoym," where several other and more distinguished members of the family are mentioned.

16. The following account draws heavily on Kundert, *Katalog der Helmstedter juristischen Disputationen* (1984), esp. 44–67; and Schubart-Fikentscher, *Untersuchungen zur Autorschaft von Dissertationen* (1970).

17. I am grateful to Anders Winroth and Ed Sandifer for sharing their understanding of corollaries with me.

18. The full title reads, *Theses Variae De morali prudentia quas Praeside D. Francone Burgerselicio* [sic], *Academiae Lugdunensis Philosopho ad diem Decembris 1629. ventilavit Hermannus Conringius. Viris dignitate & virtute Reverendis Hermanno Conringio Et M. Joanni Conringio Illi patri suo & Nordanae ecclesiae: huic fratri & Ultrajectinae ecclesiae Pastori; Viro quoque praestantissimo doctissimoque Andreae Kinderlingio Philos. Magistro, fautori benevolo; Charissimis sibi capitibus Theses hasce ex more dedicare voluit Hermannus Conringius*, A. & R. *Opera*, 6:335.

19. *De habitus corporum Germanicorum antiqui ac novi causis dissertatio* (1645); *Dissertatio ad legem primam Codicis Theodosiani*, *De studiis liberalibus urbis Romae et Constantinopolis* (1655); "Dissertatio de republica imperii Germanici communi, Lampadio praemissa," in Conring, ed., *De republica Romano-Germanica*, by Lampadius (1671); "Exercitatio historico-politica de notitia singularis alicuius reipublicae," in *Opera*, 4:1–43. On the latter, see Seifert, "Conring und die Begründung der Staatenkunde" (1983).

20. On the defense of the *De Germanorum imperio Romano* by Johann Christian von Boineburg, see below, pp. 110–11.

21. *Dissertatio de ratione status*, resp. Voss (1651).

22. See Stolleis, "Machiavellismus und Staatsräson" (1983), 174.

23. *Introductio in naturalem philosophiam* (1638); *Introductio in universam artem medicam* (1654); *De sanguinis generatione* (1643); *De calido innato* (1647).

24. "Ex publicis praecipue dissertationibus . . . Hermanni Conringii . . . concinnata" is Scheffer's characterization of this introduction on the title page.

25. See below, pp. 119–20.

26. The full title is *Exercitatio de Imperatore Romano Germanico quam Ex discursibus*

praecipue Viri Clarissimi, Excellentissimi atque Experientissimi Hermanni Conringii Philosoph.[iae] ac Med.[icinae] D.[octoris] hujusque in illustri Iulia Academia Professoris celeberrimi, Fautoris ac Praeceptoris plurimum honorandi desumtam Eodem Praeside Examini publico submittit Bogislaus Otho ab Hoym Eq.[ues] Pomeranus. Ad diem IIX Maii. In Novo Iuleo Maiori.

27. To give two examples: the first corollary declared that "the emperor even if he is only considered as the king of Germany is chief prince of the Christian world [Imperator etiam in quantum est Rex Germanorum primarius princeps est Christiani orbis]," and the last declared that "the law of nature does not forbid taking large parts of the ocean into private possession [Neque jus naturae obstat quo minus magna Oceani pars in privatam possit redigi possessionem]."

28. The dukes of Wolfenbüttel, in their capacity as rectors of the University of Helmstedt, reserved the right to approve or disapprove the publication of any works written at their university. Since the number of such works was considerable, they had delegated the responsibility for exercising that right to the deans of the various university faculties. Each dean was expected to examine every text to be printed by a member of his faculty before permitting its publication. It thus seems likely that von Hoym's *Exercitatio* was given at least formal approval by the dean of the faculty of philosophy; see Kundert, *Katalog der Helmstedter juristischen Disputationen* (1984), 56.

29. "Biennium scilicet est, et quod excurrit, quum adolescens quidam libellum thesium de Imperatore Romano Germanico Academiae hujus examini submitteret, me praeside, ut loquuntur, defendendum. Professus ille aperte erat semetipsum auctorem scripti, nonnulla tantum meis discursibus deberi, reliqua aliunde esse desumpta." *Opera,* 1:27.

30. For pointed assessments of their value, the difficulties they present to researchers, and the reasons why they have been ignored in the past, see Wieacker's preface to Kundert, *Katalog der Helmstedter juristischen Disputationen* (1984), 11–15; Evans, "German Universities after the Thirty Years War" (1981); and Ranieri, "Juristische Literatur aus dem Ancien Régime" (1982); cf. Ranieri, *Juristische Dissertationen deutscher Universitäten* (1986).

31. The most important earlier occasion on which Conring had addressed that subject in writing was the "Praefatio de historiarum, Germanorum inprimis, studiis" in his edition of Tacitus's *De moribus Germanorum* (1635). But there he dealt with the relationship between Germany and Rome only coincidentally, because his emphasis was on the principles of historical study. For details see Fasolt, "Conring on History" (1987).

32. On the frequency of reprinted dissertations in general, see Kundert, *Katalog der Helmstedter juristischen Disputationen,* 77–85.

33. At least Conring himself believed it was the Netherlands; see his remarks in the preface to his *Exercitationes academicae* (1674), pp. 9–10 of the unpaginated front matter, cited below, note 41.

34. The *Discursus novus* has a different typeface, a different layout, and slightly fewer pages than von Hoym's *Exercitatio* (40, as compared to 44). The choice of italic type (for quotations and references) as opposed to Roman type (for the rest of the text) is not always the same. The two works also spell and capitalize a number of words differently, and not always consistently.

35. At the end of chapter 21, for example, the misprinted year "735" is corrected to "753."

36. The reference occurs at the very end of chapter 20. The question there is whether or not prescription (the Roman legal principle by which the uncontested possession of something over a certain length of time is sufficient to earn the possessor property rights

over his possession) is founded on the law of nature—an important step in Conring's argumentation. The *Exercitatio* refers to Grotius, *De iure belli ac pacis,* bk. 1, chap. 4, where Grotius actually dealt with wars of subjects against superiors. In the *Discursus novus* the reference is corrected to *De iure belli ac pacis,* bk. 2, chap. 4, "On Assumed Abandonment of Ownership and Occupation Consequent Thereon; and Wherein This Differs from Ownership by Usucapion and by Prescription." See Grotius, *De iure belli ac pacis* (1913–25), 2:220–30.

37. In chapter 23, for example, the dating of an act of King Pippin to the obviously misprinted year "71" is not corrected to "771" in the *New Discourse.*

38. The title page of the *Discursus novus* in its entirety reads: "Hermanni Conringii Discursus novus de Imperatore Romano-Germanico. Typis exscriptus 1642."

39. Kundert, *Katalog der Helmstedter juristischen Disputationen* (1984), 56–58; and Wieacker, "Zum Geleit," both insist on this point and make it well.

40. For a convenient collection of essays by Skinner and his critics on this and related methodological questions, see Tully, *Meaning and Context* (1988).

41. "Ad hoc jam ante annos hosce triginta amplius prodiit alicubi (in Batavis, quantum intellexi) in lucem altera mearum Exercitationum, quae est *de Imperatore Romano Germanico,* solius mei nomine praefixo, additaque insolente, et illa quidem bellica tempestate periculi plena, inscriptione: *Discursus novi de Imperatore.*" *Exercitationes academicae* (1674), pp. 9–10 of the unpaginated front matter.

42. Excepting the mechanical differences and typographical errors described above.

43. Conring may have suspected Jean Maire, one of the Leiden printers with whom he had begun to work during his student days in the Netherlands. Maire had printed two medical works edited by Conring while he was still in Leiden: *De fractura cranii,* by Berengario da Carpi (1629), and *Observationum et paradoxorum chymiatricorum libri duo,* by Billich (1631). In 1634 Maire also printed Conring's first edition of Lampadius's *De republica Romano-Germanica,* and he printed a third edition of the same work in 1642. As it happens, the publication of this third edition not only falls in the same year as the publication of the *Discursus novus* but is also the last known association between Maire and Conring. That may be no coincidence.

44. Actually, we do not even know that. We merely believe it. It is conceivable (and I thank Mordechai Feingold for conceiving it in private conversation) that Conring himself launched the *Discursus novus* as a means of testing how his ideas would be received, and then deliberately feigned disapproval in order to keep his role secret. There is no evidence to substantiate that possibility . . . but then that is precisely what one would expect if Conring had wanted to keep it secret. Hence the possibility can never be dismissed. But given the dangers of arguing from silence, Conring's reaction, not only in the published preface to the *De Germanorum imperio Romano,* but also in his letter to Chancellor Schwartzkopf of November 1642 (for which see above, note 5), and the changes he made in the text of the *Exercitatio de imperatore Romano Germanico* when he republished it in 1674 (on which see below, pp. 147–48) that possibility seems remote.

45. He could not respond immediately. He was very busy in 1643. He had to finish two of his most important writings, the *De sanguinis generatione et motu naturali opus novum* and the *De origine iuris Germanici commentarius historicus,* both of which were published in 1643. Only thereafter was he able to respond to the *Discursus novus;* see Moeller, 75–76.

46. Verum dum aliorum operam circumspicio et desidero, ipsemet ego, nescio qui, adigor invitus, ad suscipiendum laborem illum, ut a vitae genere ita ab animo alienum.

Neque enim declinare licuit hoc negotium, neque non invitus potui id agere, quod ab artis medicae studiis, quibus me et vitae ratio et munus Academicum adstringit, toto pene, quod ajunt, coelo remotum est. *Opera,* 1:26, from the dedication of the *De Germanorum imperio Romano* to Duke August of Brunswick-Lüneburg. In the letter "To the reader" Conring wrote similarly, "artis enim medicae negotiis occupato mihi parum profecto superest temporis adeo diversa, ut curem. . . . Caeterum ex sententia vivere non licuit mihi hoc tempore, et otio tantum medico frui, per injuriam insignem, quae tamen nescio, vel quo auctore, vel ubi illata sit." *Opera,* 1:27.

47. Moeller, 64–65; and Kundert, "Hermann Conring als Professor," 403.

48. The full title reads *De Germanorum Imperio Romano liber unus. Accessit Francisci Guicciardini Discursus de Origine Secularis potestatis in Romana Ecclesia;* cf. "Gedruckte Werke," 543 no. 66.

49. "Ad Serenissimum Principem, Dominum Augustum, Ducem Brunsvicensium et Luneburgensium, Hermanni Conringii Epistola Dedicatoria," and "Benevelo Lectori," *Opera,* 1:26–27.

50. Agit quippe de illo nomine illisque juribus Germaniae nostrae, quibus maxime illa jam aliquot seculis prae aliis Europae rebuspublicis fuit conspicua et illustris: licet eorum ratio obscurior sit, et erroribus vulgi obnoxia. *Opera,* 1:26.

51. "Neque vero, ut nomina illa in vulgus sunt cognita, ita perinde etiam quid sibi velint omnibus notum est: sed multum id hodie quidem videtur obscurum, exortis passim sententiis, quae Germanicae libertati ac dignitati queant aliquando per esse noxiae, imo jam tum haud leve dederunt detrimentum." *Opera,* 1:26.

52. "Quamquam enim ea sit hodie Germaniae miseria, ut vix sese domi suae tueatur, imo tota fere abeat in solitudinem, tantum abest, ut de amissis alibi recuperandis possit hodie cogitare: etiam tamen nunc operae est pretium, illa vetera animo repetere, ne paulatim per haec mala illorum memoria obliteretur; fortassis enim brevi aerumnis hisce finem dabit clementissimum numen, et ad priscam gloriam Germania resurget." *Opera,* 1:27.

53. "Verum dum aliorum operam circumspicio et desidero, ipsemet ego, nescio qui, adigor invitus, ad suscipiendum laborem illum, ut a vitae genere ita ab animo alienum." *Opera,* 1:26.

54. Quem nunc edo libellum, benevole Lector, ad eum conscribendum invitum me et praeter animi sententiam compulsum esse, non dissimulabo. Artis enim medicae negotiis occupato mihi parum profecto superest temporis adeo diversa, ut curem. Sed et ea est hodie Germaniae miseria, ut de illius priscis institutis ac juribus cogitare (quod, fateor, summam aliquando voluptatem mihi attulit,) non possis sine ingenti animi moerore. Hic autem affectus cum et alias perpetuo fere quemvis bonum Germaniae civem affligat, refugit profecto mens omne illud, quo sibi duplicatum iri dolorem praesentit. *Opera,* 1:27.

55. Call number 36.4 Politica. Conring's letter is glued to the back of the front cover.

56. Goebel, *Opera,* 1:vii, actually did date the publication of the *De Germanorum imperio Romano* to 1643. But that was probably because he never saw the title page of the first edition, the only place where the date of publication is given as 1644. The second edition of the *De Germanorum imperio Romano* of 1694 (the edition that Goebel reprinted) does not make any mention of 1644 as the original date of publication. But it does contain Conring's dedicatory letter to the duke of December 1643. That may have led

Goebel to believe that the *De Germanorum imperio Romano* had been published in 1643 as well.

57. The subject is defined in chap. 1, pars. 1–7, *Opera*, 1:28–29.

58. "Liber mole quidem exiguus, at argumenti neutiquam proletarius" and "libellus," in *Opera*, 1:26, 1:27.

59. *De Germanorum imperio Romano*, chap. 2, par. 3, *Opera*, 1:30. Jean Bodin, *Six livres* (1583), 189, estimated that the Roman empire covered one-thirtieth of the globe, and that the Holy Roman Empire was only a tenth the size of the Roman empire.

60. *De Germanorum imperio Romano*, chap. 3, par. 4, *Opera*, 1:31. Cf. Dante, *Monarchy* (1996).

61. *De Germanorum imperio Romano*, chap. 10, pars. 8–11, *Opera*, 1:76–77.

62. Gratian's D.63 c.33, which had been quoted, but not analyzed, in the *Discursus novus*, chap. 39. Cf. *De Germanorum imperio Romano*, chap. 10, par. 8, *Opera*, 1:76.

63. *De Germanorum imperio Romano*, chap. 6, par. 2, *Opera*, 1:43.

64. Ibid., chap. 12, par. 26, *Opera*, 1:98–99. Cf. Trithemius, *Compendium sive breviarium* (1515); Brann, *Abbot Trithemius* (1981).

65. *De Germanorum imperio Romano*, chap. 7, pars. 21–22, *Opera*, 1:58.

66. Goldast, *Monarchia* (1611–14), 3:17–21.

67. Entitled simply "P. Pithoeus Lectori Salutem," *Opera*, 1:108. On Pithou, see Carreyre, "Pithou" (1935); and Kelley, *Foundations of Modern Historical Scholarship* (1970), 241–70. Goldast's attribution of this text to Pierre Pithou was uncertain. Conring therefore found it necessary to defend his reliance on Goldast in a "New Letter to the Reader" that was posthumously published in the second edition of the *De Germanorum imperio Romano* (1694), 146–48, and reprinted in *Opera*, 1:107–8.

68. *Francisci Guicciardini Patricii Florentini Discursus de Origine potestatis secularis in Romana Ecclesia*, in *De Germanorum imperio Romano*, *Opera*, 1:107–13. On Guicciardini, see the classic study by Gilbert, *Machiavelli and Guicciardini* (1965); and Cavallar, *Francesco Guicciardini, giurista* (1991), with further references. Conring's excerpts include almost the whole of book 4, chapter 12, of the *History of Italy*. The context is Cesare Borgia's conquest of the Romagna. Both the text and the title *Discursus de Origine Secularis potestatis in Romana Ecclesia* were copied from Goldast. In the second edition of the *De Germanorum imperio Romano* (1694), Hermann Conring's son renamed this *Discursus* a *Dissertatio*. Goebel followed him in this as in other respects. For the original, see Guicciardini, *Storia d'Italia* (1971), 3:417–28.

69. The *Discursus novus* had numbered chapters (or theses) but no headings. The chapter headings of the *De Germanorum imperio Romano* are listed in the table of contents, *Opera*, 1:27–28.

70. Cf. *De Germanorum imperio Romano*, chap. 2, par. 7, *Opera*, 1:31, with *Discursus novus*, chap. 10.

71. Cf. *Discursus novus*, chaps. 39, 41, with *De Germanorum imperio Romano*, chap. 10, pars. 23–29, *Opera*, 1:80–82.

72. "Neque enim desunt, qui Romanum Imperium dudum interiisse censeant, adeoque omnes hosce titulos inanes esse arbitrentur: alii vero Imperium illud nonnisi cum hoc mundo perire posse pertendunt; et licet hodie angustis admodum terminis sit circumscriptum, superesse tamen etiamnum Germaniae atque Italiae jura integra non tantum ad recuperanda Imperii veteris amissa, verum etiam ad totum orbem terrarum

occupandum. . . . Nonnulli, utut largiantur, quae dudum amissa sunt, in illa nihil etiam juris amplius cuiquam esse, multo minus universi orbis imperium hodie ulli competere, Germaniam tamen jure optimo non in titulos tantum, verum in omnia etiam Romani Imperii jura, si quae sunt, successisse. Quae sententiae immane quantum dissident." *De Germanorum imperio Romano,* chap. 1, pars. 2–3, *Opera,* 1:28. Cf. *Discursus novus,* chaps. 3–4.

73. Cf. *De Germanorum imperio Romano,* chap. 13, pars. 3–11, *Opera,* 1:99–102, with *Discursus novus,* chap. 51.

74. "Neque enim vel jure divino arbitrario, vel jure Naturae ac Gentium, vel denique jure civili, hujusmodi quid est constitutum." *Discursus novus,* chap. 11.

75. "At cum omne jus vel aeternum sit, vel positivum, atque vel ab ipso Deo, vel ab hominibus profluxerit, nihil autem horum pro universali illo dominatu Romano valeat, quid de jure illo sit sentiendum, manifestum est." *De Germanorum imperio Romano,* chap. 3, par. 2, *Opera,* 1:31.

76. Cf., for example, the opening passages of the two works, where their rationales are established in virtually identical fashion; or *De Germanorum imperio Romano,* chap. 2, par. 1, with *Discursus novus,* chaps. 5–6, where the same textual references are invoked; *De Germanorum imperio Romano,* chap. 3, par. 9, with *Discursus novus,* chap. 12; and *De Germanorum imperio Romano,* chap. 3, par. 14, with *Discursus novus,* chap. 9.

77. The title page of the disputation reads: *De Imperio Romano Germanorum Disputatio Prima, Quam Sub Praesidio Hermanni Conringii Philos.[ophiae] ac Med.[icinae] D.[octoris] hujusque Profess.[oris] publ.[ici] publice examinandam proponit Ioan Christian a Boineburg. Ad VI. Decemb.* (HelmaestadI: Typis Henningi Mulleri Acad. typ., Anno MDCXLIII); cf. "Gedruckte Werke," 542 no. 64. Note that the order of the words *imperio Romano* and *Germanorum* is reversed in the title of Boineburg's disputation. The defense of the *De Germanorum imperio Romano* was probably scheduled for two separate occasions because the work was too long for a single session.

78. Given the scarcity and brevity of this document, the corollaries are worth reproducing in full: "Corollaria. I. Modus constituendi regem, qui aliquid admistum habet haereditarij, Germaniae rebus est convenientior pure electitio. II. Privilegiorum, etiam magnorum, concessio non semper derogat quidquam summae potestati: derogat tamen interdum. III. Quod divina et naturae lege liberum est, civili lege potest definiri ad unum aliquod."

79. I am grateful to Renate Köhler and Ulrich Kopp of the Herzog August Bibliothek for confirming that only the announcement of the disputation was printed.

80. See above, p. 107.

81. Necessitati igitur obsecundans hunc libellum conscripsi, simulque, ut adolescentiae scholasticae, cui sanos de republica etiam nostra sensus a teneris instillare hercules oportet, eo rectius inservirem, per partes bis produxi in palaestram Academicam. *Opera,* 1:27.

82. More Academico bis pro hisce defendendis respondit Ioannes Christianus a Boinenburg. *De Germanorum imperio Romano* (1644), p. 7 of the unpaginated front matter. Goebel omitted that statement from its proper location in his reprint in *Opera,* 1:27, but did repeat it in his account of the publication of the *De Germanorum* in *Opera,* 1:vii, no. II.

83. In the conclusion, chap. 13, par. 27, *Opera,* 1:107.

84. Non disputabo nunc, an quadringentorum annorum possessione id quod initio

per vim et scelera peperunt sibi Pontifices nunc vere suum fecerint, praesertim quum tanto temporis spacio pauci Caesares idipsum videantur in controversiam vocasse; id certum videtur, si tot annorum praescriptione perierint nostris Regibus et Caesaribus omnia vera illa et antiqua Caesarum jura, non esse amplius quur vane jactent nonnulli nescio quod orbis aut Urbis Romae dominium, multo minus nunc esse magnis sumptibus et ingenti periculo in Italiam proficiscendum Caesaribus electis, quo a Romano Pontifice Caesaream coronam consequantur. Quin imo haud obscure hinc est dispicere, cum Orientale Imperium Romanorum per Turcam pridem sit destructum, nec Occidentalis quidquam pene supersit apud Caesares praeter nomen Imperatorium, haud injuria fortassis posse affirmari, vel Imperium Romanum funditus periisse, vel vero Papam Romanum reapse frui nunc potestate Imperatoria, si demas licentiam titulum illum usurpandi, aut in alium conferendi. *Discursus novus,* chap. 52. Apart from differences of spelling, the *Exercitatio* of 1641 says word for word the same.

85. On the Roman law of prescription and usucapion in general see Nicholas, *Introduction to Roman Law,* 120 – 30. For canon law see Helmholz, "Legal Formalism" (1994).

86. See especially *De iure belli ac pacis,* bk. 2, chap. 9, "When Sovereignty or Ownership Ceases," and bk. 2, chap. 22, "On Unjust Causes [of Wars]," trans. Kelsey, 2:310 – 19 and 2:546 – 56.

87. *De iure belli ac pacis,* bk. 2, chap. 4, trans. Kelsey, 2:220 – 30.

88. Ibid., sec. 8, 2:224.

89. Ibid., sec. 1, 2:220.

90. Conring referred repeatedly to Grotius, *De iure belli ac pacis,* bk. 2, chap. 4, in order to show that prescription was a principle of natural law. Once he referred to it explicitly, namely at the end of chapter 20 of the *Discursus novus* (in the *Exercitatio* the reference is misprinted as bk. 1, chap. 4). He referred to the same chapter again, but without acknowledging his indebtedness to Grotius, on at least three other occasions: in the last sentence of chapter 18, which is quoted almost verbatim from *De iure belli ac pacis,* bk. 2, chap. 4, sec. 11, trans. Kelsey, 2:227; in the last sentence of chapter 19, which is quoted almost verbatim from *De iure belli ac pacis,* bk. 2, chap. 4, sec. 4, trans. Kelsey, 2:222; and finally in chapter 25, where Conring relied on two quotations (one from Isocrates' *Archidamus,* 26, and one from the book of Judges 11:26) for the same purpose to which they were put in *De iure belli ac pacis,* bk. 2, chap. 4, sec. 2, trans. Kelsey, 2:220.

91. It reappears only once more after that, in chapter 43. The rest of the text speaks of *Germania* or *Regnum Germanicum.* On the history of the official title of the empire, see Weisert, "Die Reichstitel bis 1806" (1994), with further references. Weisert leaves no doubt that the proper way to refer to the empire, all popular elaborations notwithstanding, was simply "Roman empire," "Holy Empire," or "Holy Roman Empire." But cf. Nonn, "Heiliges Römisches Reich Deutscher Nation" (1982); and Hammerstein, "Das Römische am Heiligen Römischen Reich" (1983).

92. *Exercitatio de Germanici imperii civibus,* resp. Blume (1641), e.g., chaps. 6, 53.

93. See above, p. 247 n. 98. Cf. *Dissertatio de septemviris seu electoribus Germanorum regni et imperii Romani* (1644).

94. "Namque et nostris hominibus arbitror succurrendum, ne nominis illius Imperii Romani, quo nunc passim audit Germania, ancipite sensu decepti, sequius de majestate patriae suae suspicentur: et Romanorum Pontificum insolentiam retundendam, qui, ut possessionem urbis Romae, ita et jura possidendi, populo Germaniae eripere allaborant." *Opera,* 1:26 – 27.

95. *De constitutione episcoporum Germaniae* (1647); and *Exercitatio de iudiciis reipublicae Germanicae* (1647).
96. *De finibus imperii Germanici* (1654). Similarly in *De pace perpetua inter imperii Germanici ordines religione dissidentes servanda* (1657).
97. *Dissertatio de comitiis imperii Romano-Germanici* (1666); Conring, ed., *De republica Romano-Germanica*, by Lampadius (1671); *Exercitationes academicae de republica imperii Germanici* (1674).
98. Imperii urbis Romae, et eorum, quae inde pendent, jura, etsi a papa omnibus modis sint convulsa, etiamnum tamen ad Germaniam pertinere. *De Germanorum imperio Romano*, chap. 13, *Opera*, 1:99.
99. Quum nullo igitur jure excusserint Papae Caesaream vim a sese ac Urbe Roma, manifestum est, jura illa Caesarum, quibus ad Hildebrandi usque aevum fuerunt usi, utut adversum illa arietaverint Pontifices, hodieque integra subsistere. Finiam hanc disputationem verbis, quae feruntur Cyni Pistoriensis nobilissimi Jurisconsulti. *Pastores Ecclesiae in lupos rapaces sunt conversi, insatiabiles rerum temporalium et ambitione dominandi. Diversis viis illicitis nisi sunt et nituntur Imperium et imperialia usurpare. Ideo sub eorum gubernatione totus mundus positus est in maligno, et sub regimine tyrannorum. Sed sicut puto, eorum divina vindicta proxima est. Et utinam esset proximior!* *De Germanorum imperio Romano*, chap. 13, par. 27, *Opera*, 1:107, emphasis in the original. I have not been able to identify the source of the quotation.
100. See Stolleis, "Machiavellismus und Staatsräson" (1983), 183; and Lang, *Staat und Souveränität*, 3.
101. Quo scilicet eximiorum illorum juvenum ingenium et industria magis proficeret, calami proprii quasi periculum ipsos facere curavi; contentus, eos partim praeviis dissertationibus omnia sedulo docuisse, partim minus recte scripta emendasse, partim denique interpolando addidisse quae visa sunt fugisse juvenilis aetatis captum, in universum autem manu quasi duxisse eos ad exquisitiorem rerum scientiam. *Exercitationes academicae*, p. 8 of the unpaginated front matter. Note the clarity with which Conring here described his involvement in his students' dissertations: he made sure that his own lectures were accurate in the first place; he corrected mistakes in his students' dissertations that could not be left standing (*minus recte scripta*); and he made additions that he considered necessary.
102. "Supersunt sane etiamnum passim, haud falsa quidem (id enim cavi) crudum tamen quid sapientia et affectationem juvenilem: quibus proinde bonus quisque et aequus lector ignoscet, non minus atque a me in ejusmodi chartis semper est factum, et faciendum esse judicavi." *Exercitationes academicae*, p. 9 of the unpaginated front matter.
103. See above, note 72.
104. Conring was of course by no means the first to maintain this point of view. For a celebrated and much earlier parallel, see Marsiglio of Padua's *De translatione imperii* (1993), 66. For later parallels, see Luther, *An den christlichen Adel deutscher Nation* (1888), 462: "Es ist on zweyffel, das das recht Romisch reych, davon die schrifft der propheten Numeri xxiiii. und Daniel vorkundet haben, lengist vorstoret und ein end hat." Erasmus said much the same in a letter to Dukes Frederick and George of Saxony of 5 June 1517, 583: "Sed multo magis ad rem pertinet in his contemplari nomen illud imperii, quod et olim orbi sacrosanctum augustumque fuit, et nunc etiamnum multorum affectibus religiosum ac venerabile est cum nihil fere supersit praeter inanem magni nominis umbram, quam foedis initiis in mundum irrepserit."

105. Igitur si imperii Romani voce intelligas vastam aliquam rempublicam, cujus jura ad urbem illam pertineant, ut factum olim, dudum desiit Romanum imperium omne. Si vero ad nominis illius majestatem tuendam sufficit unius urbis regimen, durat Romanum imperium hodieque. *De Germanorum imperio Romano,* chap. 11, par. 12, *Opera,* 1:89.

106. In *De Germanorum imperio Romano,* chap. 11, pars. 13–14, *Opera,* 1:89–90.

107. "Enimvero quae de Babylone visa sunt sanctissimo Joanni *Apocal. XVII. et XVIII.* ea ad septicollem hanc urbem pertinere, pene dixerim sole esse clarius." *De Germanorum imperio Romano,* chap. 11, par. 13, *Opera,* 1:89.

108. Nemo porro est qui nesciat, papam Romanum eo nomine, quasi urbi Romae id contulerit S. Petrus, jam tum per complura secula monarchiam aliquam immensam exercuisse in ecclesia Christi per omnem pene terrarum orbem, et indulgentiis, beneficiorum collationibus, dispensationibus, prostituisse sanctitatem Christianae disciplinae, subdidisse denique sibi reges et principes non vi et armis, sed religione quadam, ac tali regno suo aeternitatem polliceri. [Huc pertinet illa cantio Conradi Urspergensis: *Gaude mater nostra Roma etc. per malitiam hominum, non per tuam religionem, orbem vicisti.*] Itaque superest sane hodieque vastum aliquod Romanum imperium, sed diversae prorsus ab aliis rebuspublicis naturae, stabitque illius urbis monarchia isthaec, quamdiu supererit ipsa. [Credibile tamen est, tandem aliquando, et quidem satis forte diu ante extremum diem, urbem et imperium hoc ruiturum.] At hoc imperii genus ad Germaniam non pertinet: neque nostri instituti est, horribilem illam et sacram tyrannidem exponere. *De Germanorum imperio Romano,* chap. 11, par. 14, *Opera,* 1:90. The passages in brackets contain additions Conring made in his copy of the *De Germanorum imperio Romano.* They were first published in the second edition of 1694.

109. Conring's reasons for arguing that prescription had deprived the Romans of any rights to the western parts of the empire by the time of Charlemagne at the latest are discussed at length in *Discursus novus,* chaps. 18–20, 24–25, and in *De Germanorum imperio Romano,* chap. 5, *Opera,* 1:43–51.

110. See *De Germanorum imperio Romano,* chap. 13, par. 25, *Opera,* 1:106.

111. "Caeterum tempore Ottonis M.[agni] qui praeterpropter 100. annis vixit post Carolum M.[agnum] ipsius felicitate regnum Germaniae, quod tum regnum Francorum dictum, alterno [*sic*] foedere jungebatur regno Italiae et imperio romano, quod ostensum a me in libro de imperio romano germanico. Quibus liber iste non est in manibus, legant disputationem meam de imperio germanico, quae quasi est compendium ejus rei." "Discursus ad Lampadium posterior," *Opera,* 2:239. Taken by itself, "disputatio mea de imperio germanico" is not unequivocal. It could refer to other works, for example, the "Dissertatio de republica imperii Germanici communi, Lampadio praemissa," in Conring, ed., *De republica Romano-Germanica,* by Lampadius (1671). But only the *Exercitatio de imperatore Romano Germanico* could plausibly be considered a "compendium" of the *De Germanorum imperio Romano.*

112. Namque et nostris hominibus arbitror succurrendum, ne nominis illius Imperii Romani, quo nunc passim audit Germania, ancipite sensu decepti, sequius de majestate patriae suae suspicentur: et Romanorum Pontificum insolentiam retundendam, qui, ut possessionem urbis Romae, ita et jura possidendi, populo Germaniae eripere allaborant. Quamquam enim ea sit hodie Germaniae miseria, ut vix sese domi suae tueatur, imo tota fere abeat in solitudinem, tantum abest, ut de amissis alibi recuperandis possit hodie cogitare: etiam tamen nunc operae est pretium, illa vetera animo repetere, ne paulatim per

haec mala illorum memoria obliteretur; fortassis enim brevi aerumnis hisce finem dabit clementissimum numen, et ad priscam gloriam Germania resurget. *Opera,* 1:26–27.

113. See above, note 7.

114. For details, see above, pp. 84–88; cf. Goldschlag, *Beiträge zur politischen und publizistischen Thätigkeit* (1884); Felberg, *Conrings Anteil am politischen Leben* (1931).

115. Nam et in plerisque circa statum Germaniae mecum consentiebat, et sua scripta longe diversum a reliqua turba genium prae se ferentia, promte communicabat. In quibus, etsi multa sat libere posita erant, non obscure tamen apparebat, non parum ipsum dissimulasse declinandis potentiorum offensis, aut ne infulsorum hominum clamores in se irritaret. *Opera,* 1:xxvi.

116. "De Hermanno Conringio ejusque scriptis doctorum virorum judicia et testimonia." *Opera* 1:xxv–xxxvi.

117. Hippolithus a Lapide, *Dissertatio de ratione status* (1640). The date of publication is uncertain, but 1640 seems most likely.

118. See Dickmann, *Der Westfälische Frieden* (1977), 137–42; Stolleis, *Reichspublizistik und Policeywissenschaft* (1988), 203–7.

119. Quamvis videlicet haud improbem Platonis consilium, reipublicae leges non esse vulgo examini exponendas: non tamen illud ad quasvis promiscue leges pertinet, sed duntaxat illas quarum censuram non admittit publica civilis societatis tranquillitas. *Exercitationes academicae,* pp. 7–8 of the unpaginated front matter.

120. Momigliano, "Historicism Revisited" (1977), 370. Taylor, *Sources of the Self* (1989), offers ontological reasons why it has to be so.

121. See Vann and Rowan, *Old Reich* (1974); Aretin, *Das Alte Reich* (1993–97); Vann, *Making of a State* (1984); Boyer and Kirshner, *Politics and Society* (1986).

122. Stolleis, *Reichspublizistik und Policeywissenschaft* (1988).

123. Grimmelshausen, *Simplicius Simplicissimus* (1964).

124. They complained that "über den Religionsfrieden . . . viel mehr und allerlei disputationes und Fragen fürgebracht und etliche resolutive, etliche problematice defendirt werden, ja es ist sogar dahin gekommen, dass man nicht allein in scholis öffentlich in cathedra davon profitiert, sondern auch ein jeder Student, der nur ein Prob seiner Scientz erzeigen will, aber in keiner Fürsten Archiv gesehen noch in einigen negotiis publicis gebraucht gewesen, gleich eine disputation de pace religionis et prophana, juribus Imperatoris, Imperii statuum, de Aurea Bulla und anderen constitutionibus Imperii zu Papier bringen und in offenen Druck geben tut, wie denn alle Buchläden von solchen Scriptis voll." Quoted from Dickmann, *Der Westfälische Frieden* (1977), 16.

125. Good information about Conring's identification with the university, his desire to protect its integrity, and the means he thought appropriate to that end can be found in Conring, *Pietas Academiae Juliae* (1668), which finally broke the silence the university had observed for many years in the polemics over Calixt's theology.

126. Martin Luther, "Epistola Lutheriana ad Leonem decimum" (1897), 43. The word here translated as "morals" is *mores* in the Latin. It could also be translated as "customs" or "conduct" or as "merely human laws."

127. Oberman, *Luther* (1982), in English *Luther* (1989).

128. Locke's *Letter concerning Toleration* is the classic statement.

129. For different perspectives on these themes, see, e.g., Elias, *Über den Prozess der Zivilisation* (1939); Koselleck, *Kritik und Krise* (1959); Macpherson, *Political Theory of Possessive Individualism* (1962); and Moore, *First European Revolution* (2000).

130. Etenim cum non liceat non in vos peccare, minimum omnium peccaturum me judicavi, si ea dicerem, quae quisque vestrum etiam sine amore, sine odio, probare hactenus et laudare qua privatim, qua publice solitus est. *Aristotelis laudatio* (1633), in *Opera*, 5:727.

131. Habermas, *Strukturwandel der Öffentlichkeit* (1962).

132. Is this not the fundamental point of Wittgenstein's *Tractatus Logico-Philosophicus* (1922)? And did it not survive his changes of mind in *Philosophical Investigations* (1953)?

133. Sacer scilicet morbus opinio est: mundus tamen hic nulla perinde re quam hac ipsa regitur. *Opera*, 5:262. The double entendre of "sacer" is impossible to capture in English.

134. The motto can be found beneath a portrait engraved in 1666 and reproduced on the frontispiece of the first volume of the *Opera*.

135. Cf. "Gedruckte Werke," 550 no. 134. On the title page, the year of publication is 1655. The frontispiece preceding the title page has 1654. A moderate, but not negligible, research effort, involving several hours of leafing through both standard and recondite monographs, handbooks, and bibliographies on the history of printing in early modern France, as well as the consultation of several librarians, left me without any useful information on the anonymous *societas* that claimed to have printed the *Acroamata sex*. The imprint may be fictitious.

136. In the *Acroamata sex* these were printed in the chronological order in which they were first published. They are (1) pp. 1–23: *Exercitatio de Germanici imperii civibus*, resp. Blume (1641), dealing not with "citizens," but with the estates represented in the imperial diet; (2) pp. 25–76: *Exercitatio de urbibus Germanicis*, resp. Bode (1641); (3) pp. 77–96: *Exercitatio de ducibus et comitibus imperii Germanici*, resp. Struve (1643); (4) pp. 97–120: *Dissertatio de septemviris seu electoribus Germanorum regni et imperii Romani*, resp. Pape (1644); (5) pp. 121–96: *De constitutione episcoporum Germaniae*, resp. Blume (1647); and (6) pp. 197–274: *Exercitatio de iudiciis reipublicae Germanicae*, resp. Burgkstorff (1647). The printers of the *Acroamata sex*, like those of the *Discursus novus*, omitted words like *Exercitatio* and *Dissertatio*, along with references to respondents, from the titles, presumably for similar reasons.

137. On pp. 275–309.

138. To be more precise, *Acroamata sex*, 275–76, up to the words "sive iure," is taken from *Discursus novus*, chaps. 1–4 and the first sentence of chap. 5; *Acroamata sex*, 276–89, from the words "Totum enim terrarum orbem" to the words "saepius iam memorata," is taken from *De Germanorum imperio Romano*, chaps. 2–5, replacing chaps. 6–23 of the *Discursus novus*; the rest, that is, *Acroamata sex*, 289–309, starting with the words "Hec vero cum ita se habeant," is taken from *Discursus novus*, chaps. 24–56. The printers also removed the chapter numbering and changed the text in other small ways.

139. "Qui liber [i.e., the *De imperii Germanici republica acroamata sex*] cum in Galliam Italiam imo et Hispaniam ac Britanniam penetraverit, passim ipsimet orbi persuasum est jamdudum, mihi auctori isthaec omnia deberi." *Exercitationes academicae*, p. 10 of the unpaginated front matter.

140. Caeterum quia hae Exercitationes non in totum sunt meae, passus sum eas hactenus vagari, earumque singulas huc illuc spargi, omni quasi cura illarum seposita, jam tum praesertim circa vere propria satis occupatus. Ast nunc mutare istum animum non una de caussa sum coactus. Observavi videlicet, libellos istos Disputationum, sine discrimine omnes, a quammultis praeclare doctis viris passim, non in Germania duntaxat

nostra sed etiam alibi, mihi uni acceptos referri, idque non dissimulari etiam editis scriptis. . . . Accedit, quod benignis praestantium virorum judiciis ac praeconiis persuasum sit in ipsum vulgus, contineri hisce Exercitationibus multa utilia, quae ab alio tamen nemine sint dicta ac proinde alibi nusquam invenire sit; ex quo illarum lectio passim desideratur, ipsis tamen raro comparentibus. Haec sane aliaque nonnulla ad curas secundas horum libellorum me quamvis neutiquam otio abundantem, tandem revocaverunt. Nec vero fas fuit visum, eorum abjicere omnem prope amorem, quorum pars saltim maxima reapse mihi debebatur: multo minus, postquam hominum quasi communi consensu, etsi erroneo, in unius mei nomen sunt pridem adoptata. Cumque injuria non levis et bono publico et singulatim mihi hactenus fuerit illata, cum perquam mendosis editionibus tum mutationibus inconsultis, saltim imposterum illam avertere, (quia quod factum est nequit infectum reddi) etiam officii mei et existimationis tuendae, esse judicavi. *Exercitationes academicae,* pp. 9–11 of the unpaginated front matter.

141. *Dissertatio de praecipuis negotiis in comitiis,* resp. Becker (1666); *Dissertatio de comitiis,* resp. Engelbrecht (1666); *Dissertatio de officialibus,* resp. Burgstorff (1669).

142. "Et sane initio quidem unum hoc consilium fuit, omnia non nisi in pristinam integritatem restituta edere, uno tamen volumine comprehensa; dum post longum autem temporis intervallum relego cuncta, statim observavi, quamplura correctione indigere, alicubi et augmentum aliquod esse necessarium. Eoque in recensione utrumque deinceps etiam egi; mutavi, inquam, tantum non infinities si quae visa fuerunt minus commodis verbis dicta (ab assertionibus enim ipsis primis vix semel iterumque discessi) etiam interpolando varia passim et frequenter addidi, ita tamen, ut ad plenam tractationem argumenti cujuslibet multa adhuc deesse neutiquam velim diffiteri." *Exercitationes academicae,* pp. 11–12 of the unpaginated front matter.

143. See Conring's remarks in *Exercitationes academicae,* pp. 12–14 of the unpaginated front matter.

144. This was unfortunately omitted from the *Opera.*

145. Id certum *haud forte injuria* videtur; si tot annorum praescriptione perierint nostris Regibus et Caesaribus, omnia vera illa et antiqua Caesarum jura (*quod tamen neutiquam admitti potest*) non esse amplius, quur vane jactent. . . . *Exercitatio de imperatore Romano Germanico,* chap. 52. The words in italics were added in 1674.

146. See Goebel's remarks in his preface to *Opera,* 1:vii, no. II.

147. It seems likely that at least some of those notes were made during Conring's rereading of the *Exercitatio de imperatore Romano Germanico* of 1641 in preparation for its republication in the *Exercitationes* of 1674.

148. *De Germanorum imperio Romano liber unus. Ex autographo b.[eati] auctoris auctus* (1694). "Gedruckte Werke," 543 no. 66b.

149. *Opera,* 1:26–107. Note that Goebel's reprint confuses matters by using the title of the work that was published in 1644 (*De Germanorum imperio Romano*) but dating it to the year 1643. "Gedruckte Werke," 542 no. 64a, also confuses matters by suggesting that Goebel's reprint consisted of Boineburg's *De imperio Romano Germanorum disputatio prima.* Of Boineburg's dissertation, we only have the printed announcement, on which see above, p. 110. The confusion in "Gedruckte Werke" is perhaps due to the fact that Goebel dated his version of the *De Germanorum imperio Romano* to 1643. "Gedruckte Werke," 543 no. 66a, is also mistaken in listing the *De Germanorum imperio Romano* as reprinted in *De imperii Germanici republica acroamata sex* (1655), 1–144. The text reprinted in the *Acroamata sex* is only a part of the *De Germanorum imperio Romano,* namely, chaps. 2–5, and

that part is found on pp. 275–309. It is conceivable that there exists a variant edition of the *Acroamata sex* that did indeed print the whole of the *De Germanorum imperio Romano* on the first 144 pages; but I have not seen such an edition.

150. "Index autorum et monumentorum," 195–96 [i.e., 165–66], reprinted by Goebel, *Opera*, 1:113–14. The "Index rerum" consists of five unnumbered leaves at the end of the book. Goebel did not reprint that index, presumably because he compiled his own subject index for all of Conring's works in volume seven of the *Opera*.

151. On 146–48 (*Opera*, 1:107–8); cf. above, note 67.

152. *Vid.* or *Add.* in the Latin.

153. Thus, for example, chap. 9, par. 5, on p. 67, which mentions in passing a question about the nature of Charlemagne's empire; chap. 10, par. 22, on p. 91, commenting briefly on a statement of Georg Calixt on the western church; and chap. 13, par. 26, on pp. 143–44, which contains a number of references designed to substantiate the point that the kings of Germany never acquiesced in the usurpation of imperial rights that Conring believed the papacy to have been guilty of practicing since the times of Pope Gregory VII.

154. "Enimvero quae de Babylone visa sunt sanctissimo Joanni *Apocal. XVII. et XVIII.* ea ad septicollem hanc urbem pertinere, pene dixerim sole esse clarius." *De Germanorum imperio Romano*, chap. 11, par. 13, *Opera*, 1:89.

155. Credibile tamen est, tandem aliquando, et quidem satis forte diu ante extremum diem, urbem et imperium hoc ruiturum. *De Germanorum imperio Romano*, chap. 11, par. 14, *Opera*, 1:90.

156. Koselleck, "Vergangene Zukunft der frühen Neuzeit" (1979).

157. In *Opera*, 1:v–vii, Goebel describes the scope of his edition and the series of steps he took in order to complete it. For some of the difficulties he encountered, see his remarks in *Opera*, 1:xvi–xvii, 1:xxxviii.

158. *Exercitatio de imperatore Romano Germanico*, in *Opera*, 1:528–42.

159. *Tractatus Logico-Philosophicus* (1922), 6.522.

160. Thomas Hobbes, *Leviathan* (1994), chap. 16, sec. 4, 101.

161. Et meae sunt igitur Exercitationes illae, et meae non sunt. *Exercitationes academicae*, p. 9 of the unpaginated front matter.

CHAPTER FOUR

1. Readers interested in the full text of the *Discursus novus* are referred to my edition and translation (forthcoming).

2. For contemporary studies of medieval German history, see Todd, *Early Germans* (1992); Fried, *Der Weg in die Geschichte* (1994); Reuter, *Germany in the Early Middle Ages* (1991); Fuhrmann, *Germany in the High Middle Ages* (1986); Haverkamp, *Medieval Germany* (1992); Leuschner, *Germany in the Late Middle Ages* (1980); Keller, *Zwischen regionaler Begrenzung und universalem Horizont* (1986); Moraw, *Von offener Verfassung zu gestalteter Verdichtung* (1985); and Du Boulay, *Germany in the Later Middle Ages* (1983). Bryce, *Holy Roman Empire* (1904); and Barraclough, *The Origins of Modern Germany* (1947), are still worth reading. For ideas of empire, see Goez, *Translatio Imperii* (1958); Folz, *Concept of Empire* (1969); Duverger, *Le concept d'empire* (1980); Pagden, *Lords of All the World* (1995); and Armitage, *Theories of Empire* (1998).

3. *Discursus novus*, chaps. 1–4.

4. See Bartolus's commentary on *Digest* 49.15.24, s.v. "hostes," *Opera*, 6:228r, col. a, no. 7, a passage we shall consider in detail below.

5. Luke 2:1 (KJV). The *locus classicus* for the description of the Roman emperor as "lord of the world" is the so-called Rhodian law, *Digest* 14.2.9, ed. Mommsen, 221. Originally written in Greek, it refers to the emperor as τοῦ κόσμου κύριος, literally "lord of the cosmos," translated into Latin as *dominus mundi*. It may be worth adding that experts in canon law were, if anything, even less equivocal about the emperor's universal power than experts in Roman law (though of course they had different ideas about his relationship to the church). The ordinary gloss on Gratian's *Decretum* D.1 c.12, s.v. "quod nulli," for example, calls the emperor *princeps totius mundi*, and the gloss on Pope Innocent III's famous decretal *Venerabilem* (*Liber Extra* 1.6.34) describes the Roman empire as *regimen mundi*. For details, see Calasso, *I glossatori e la teoria della sovranità* (1957), 42–47; Muldoon, "Extra ecclesiam non est imperium" (1966); and Muldoon, *Empire and Order* (1999).

6. What exactly those thinkers may have meant by calling the emperor "lord of the world" is one of those particular questions about the history of medieval Europe that we cannot pursue any further. We shall have a lot more to say about Bartolus, however.

7. Yates, *Astraea* (1975), 3.

8. At the very end of the sixteenth century, the *Consultationes Saxonicae* still maintained that "Bartoli auctoritas supremo habetur in actu practico; contra ipsum velle concedere aut contrarium defendere perquam est temerarium." Quoted from Stintzing and Landsberg, *Geschichte der deutschen Rechtswissenschaft* (1880–1910), 1:112. Troje, *Humanistische Jurisprudenz* (1993), has argued that the "Italian manner" (*mos italicus*) of interpreting Roman law along lines laid down by Bartolus and his "Bartolist" followers remained important much longer than is commonly believed. Cf. Riccobono, "*Mos italicus e mos gallicus*" (1935); Willoweit, *Rechtsgrundlagen der Territorialgewalt* (1975), 17–32; Kelley, "Civil Science Italian Style" (1979).

9. See above, pp. 61–62, 113–14.

10. The passage in which Grotius refers to Bartolus is worth quoting to highlight the similarities to Conring: "Vix adderem stultum esse titulum quem quidam tribuunt Imperatori Romano, quasi ipse etiam in remotissimos et incognitos hactenus populos jus imperandi habeat, nisi Iurisconsultorum diu princeps habitus Bartolus haereticum ausus esset pronuntiare qui id negat; nimirum quia et Imperator interdum se mundi dominum vocet, et in sacris litteris imperium illud, quod Romaniam posteriores scriptores vocant, appelletur τῆς οἰκουμένης nomine: qualia sunt et illa: 'Orbem jam totum victor Romanus habebat,' multaque similia per complexionem, aut excessum, aut excellentiam dicta: quippe cum et in iisdem sacris litteris sola Iudaea saepe veniat nomine τῆς οἰκουμένης, quo sensu accipiendum dictum vetus Iudaeorum, medio telluris sitam urbem Hierosolyma, id est in medio Iudaeae, sicut in medio Graeciae Delphi similiter dicti orbis umbilicus." *De iure belli ac pacis*, bk. 2, chap. 22, sec. 13, ed. Scott, 1:387. Among his sources Grotius identified the Rhodian law in *Digest* 14.2.9, Bartolus's commentary on *Digest* 49.15.24, and the Gospel of Luke 2:1. The other relevant passage is taken from Petronius, *Satyricon*, 119. For the parallel in the *Discursus novus*, see immediately below.

11. He used the same list of authorities that he had found in Grotius again in the first edition of the *De Germanorum imperio Romano*, chap. 2, pp. 3–4, adding references to Cicero, Claudian, and the council of Chalcedon, but not acknowledging his indebtedness to Grotius. It was only an addition to the text in the second, posthumous edition of

the *De Germanorum imperio Romano* of 1694, chap. 2, par. 1, *Opera,* 1:29, that finally referred readers to Grotius, as well as to a parallel passage in bk. 6, chap. 10 of William Barclay *De regno et regali potestate* (1600), 449.

12. Neque enim desunt nonnulli, magni nominis viri, qui totum terrarum orbem Romanis olim paruisse, vel certe parere debuisse profiteantur. Usque adeo enim verum id esse, ut alios nunc taceam, credidit olim magnum illud Iurisconsultorum lumen Bartolus, ut non dubitaverit adversam sententiam haereseos postulare. Fundamentum autem opinionis hujus peti solet partim ex illis Lucae Evangelistae verbis; *Exijt edictum a Caesare Augusto, ut totus orbis censeretur:* ubi οἰκουμένης voce ambitus Imperij Romani circumscribitur: partim ex corpore juris Iustinianeo, ubi persaepe Imperatori *orbis* dominium tribuitur; partim denique ex ijs, quae apud alios scriptores legas; quale est Petronij illud: *Orbem jam totum victor Romanus habebat.* Et Dionysij Halicarnassei *lib.* I. Cap. 3. *Romanorum civitas imperat per cunctas terrae plagas, quae quidem inaccessae non sunt, sed habitantur ab hominibus. Discursus novus,* chaps. 5–6, emphasis in the original. Conring mentions the same authorities as Grotius, except that he adds Dionysius of Halicarnassus, *Roman Antiquities,* 1.3, to the list and fails to identify the relevant passages in Bartolus's writings (the commentary on *Digest* 49.15.24) and Roman law (*Digest* 14.2.9). That makes it possible to rule out another famous attack on Bartolus as the immediate source from which Conring drew his statement of the common wisdom, namely, Jean Bodin's declaration in bk. 1, chap. 9 of his *Six livres de la république* (1583), 189, that "Bartol a laissé par escrit, que tous ceux-là sont heretiques, qui ne croyent pas que l'Empereur soit seigneur de tout le monde: ce qui ne merite point de response: veu que les Empereurs de Rome ne furent iamais seigneurs de la trentieme partie de la terre: et que l'Empire d'Allemagne n'est pas la dixieme partie de l'Empire des Romains." In the margin Bodin refers to Bartolus's commentary on *Digest* 49.15.24 and the Rhodian law. For the same reason, Conring is unlikely to have drawn on William Barclay's attack on Bartolus in bk. 6, chap. 10, of his *De regno et regali potestate* (1600), 449.

13. Principio autem sciendum est, quid olim florentibus Romanorum rebus ad Romanum Imperium pertinuerit, sive reapse, sive jure. *Discursus novus,* chap. 5.

14. Broadly speaking, Conring thus aligned himself with the so-called French manner (*mos gallicus*) of interpreting Roman law, developed in the sixteenth century by Guillaume Budé, Andrea Alciato, Jacques Cujas, and others opposing the "Italian manner" (*mos italicus*) of Bartolus and his followers; see Maffei, *Inizi dell' umanesimo giuridico* (1956); Kisch, *Humanismus und Jurisprudenz* (1955); Franklin, *Jean Bodin and the Sixteenth-Century Revolution* (1963); Kelley, *Foundations of Modern Historical Scholarship* (1970); and Kelley, "Civil Science in the French Manner" (1981).

15. *Discursus novus,* chaps. 7–10.

16. "Nec vero illa adducta ex Evangelio, aut quae in eam sententiam in libris juris Romani habentur, vel alibi leguntur, id quod Bartolus vult, evincunt; subesse enim quandam αὔξησιν etiam ipsis Sacris literis non infrequentem, per se liquet, jamque tum a doctissimis est viris animadversum." *Discursus novus,* chap. 10. Conring was again following the precedent of Grotius, *De iure belli ac pacis,* bk. 2, chap. 22, sec. 13, ed. Scott, 1:387, according to whom statements about the universality of the Roman empire, like biblical references to Judea as the *oecumene,* needed to be interpreted "per complexionem, aut excessum, aut excellentiam."

17. *Discursus novus,* chaps. 11–13.

18. "Non tantum vero totus orbis paruit nunquam Romanis, sed ne quidem ad illos jus aliquod imperij in totum orbem pertinuit. Neque enim vel jure divino arbitrario, vel

jure Naturae ac Gentium, vel denique jure civili, hujusmodi quid est constitutum." *Discursus novus,* chap. 11. Note the different analysis offered in the *De Germanorum imperio Romano,* above, p. 109.

19. "Sane de jure divino arbitrario hinc patet, quoniam tale jus divinum nullibi legitur in sacris voluminibus, nec traditione ad nos devenit, quo uno tamen modo arbitraria Dei instituta nobis innotescunt." *Discursus novus,* chap. 11. Actually he did not consider the case of the Bible as obvious as all that: he found it necessary to address biblical passages that had for a long time been thought to identify the Roman empire with the last of four universal monarchies; but he postponed the matter until a much later point where he rejected it as a misinterpretation of the Bible; see *Discursus novus,* chap. 54 and below, pp. 163–64.

20. "Tale item jus Naturae aut gentium nemo hominum ex principiis natura notis hactenus probavit vel probare conatus est, nec probari videtur posse: non aliunde tamen jus Naturae solet probari." *Discursus novus,* chap. 11. Given the difficulties inherent in defining the content of natural law, this was not an unreasonable bit of fudging.

21. Iure porro civili urbis Romae non potuisse Romanis jus aliquod competere in terrarum orbem vel puero liquet. Qui enim totum terrarum orbem obliget, quod unus populus sua in urbe constituit? *Discursus novus,* chap. 11.

22. The relationship between civil law and natural law is considered in *Institutes* 1.2, ed. Mommsen, 1, and in *Digest* 1.1, ed. Mommsen, 29. It is famously complicated by sharply conflicting definitions of natural law and by the existence of a third kind of law, the *ius gentium* or law of nations. For an introduction to varying understandings of those terms, see Nicholas, *Introduction to Roman Law* (1962), 54–59; Carlyle, "The Political Theory of the Roman Lawyers" (1903), 1:33–79; Weigand, *Naturrechtslehre* (1967); and Reibstein, *Völkerrecht* (1958–63).

23. It is worth noting for future reference that Conring did not directly address the question of why, then, the Roman emperor did refer to himself as *dominus mundi.*

24. *Discursus novus,* chaps. 14–25.

25. Ibid., chaps. 14–19.

26. Ibid., chaps. 20–23.

27. Ibid., chaps. 24–25.

28. Ibid., chaps. 26–28.

29. Ibid., chaps. 29–41.

30. Ibid., chap. 29.

31. Ibid., chaps. 30, 39.

32. Ibid., chaps. 31–41.

33. "Ac prius quidem vel illo uno potest abunde refelli quod et Germania et Langobardicum regnum comitia sua de rebus maximis ad rempublicam pertinentibus omni tempore instituerit, egerit quoque res maximas non impetrato consensu vel Papae vel aliorum Imperii istius civium." *Discursus novus,* chap. 40. The anachronism in Conring's own argument here deserves to be noted. In the tenth and eleventh centuries, there surely were assemblies of imperial and royal vassals. But assemblies of estates that might have exercised a formal constitutional role along the lines that Conring here envisioned would not come into being until much later.

34. *Discursus novus,* chap. 40. Cf. Cavina, "*Imperator Romanorum triplici corona coronatur*" (1991).

35. *Discursus novus,* chap. 41.

36. Ibid., chaps. 42–44.

37. "Haec vero omnia cum longe sint certissima, nihil est, quur non aperte tandem pronunciemus; *neque Germaniam neque Langobardicum Italiae regnum vere partes esse Romani Imperii, sed respublicas ab illo distinctas, adeoque nec Imperatorem, in quantum est Imperator, esse vel Germanici vel Langobardici regni caput aut magistratum, sed quatenus idem simul Rex est.*" *Discursus novus*, chap. 42, emphasis in the original.

38. Ibid., chaps. 45–47.

39. Ibid., chaps. 48–51.

40. Ibid., chap. 51.

41. *Discursus novus*, chaps. 53–56.

42. Quomodo totum illud de non nisi quatuor magnis futuris monarchiis seu Imperiis mundi, plus habet famae quam veri. Ibid., chap. 54.

43. This is the main point at which Conring's historical perspective conflicts with prophetic interpretations of the Bible; see Reeves, *Influence of Prophecy in the Later Middle Ages* (1969); Seifert, *Rückzug der biblischen Prophetie* (1990).

44. "Antichristi certe tempora excepta demum interitum Romani Imperii, communis omnium primae aetatis Christianorum fuit sententia. De ipsius autem Urbis Romae extremo excidio accipienda videntur omnino illa quae c. 18. Apocalyps. leguntur." *Discursus novus*, chap. 54. There is a marked difference between Conring's unequivocal rejection of the prophecy of Daniel and the hesitant language in which he accepts the predictions of the New Testament without saying precisely what those predictions amounted to, much less how they could be reconciled with his rejection of the prophecy of Daniel. His answer was much clearer in *De Germanorum imperio Romano*, on which see above, pp. 122–23.

45. "Eo argumenti genere usos quidem perquam multos, a Lotharii Caesaris usque temporibus ad nostram hanc aetatem, eos qui Romani juris doctrinam professi sunt; quorum nonnullis pene persuasum est, omnia omnino illa competere hodieque Caesaribus nostris, quae olim Iustiniano imo Augusto Imperatori convenerunt." *Discursus novus*, chap. 55.

46. "Verum haec quidem doctrina apta est concitandis bellis, movendis tumultibus, evertendae reipublicae. Si enim omnia ad illam faciem Augustaei aevi sunt componenda, non haec tantum nostra Germania sed pene totus orbis erit commovendus. Est autem tota illa colligendi ratio frivola, ne quid dicam gravius. Nulla certe illi vis inest, nisi pro confesso et certo sumas: populum Caesaremque Romanum nihil potuisse jure amittere, aut vero omne quod in corpore illo Legum Romanarum reperitur id ex jure naturae venire adeoque aeternae esse veritatis. Quae omnia longe sunt falsissima. . . . Stultum vero est omnem qui in nomen aut aliquo modo succedit in locum, eundem etiam in jura quae ante aliquot centum aut mille annos obtinuerunt, succedere. Non minus sane hoc ineptum est quam illud nonullorum commentum Carolo V. jus fuisse ad occupandos Americanos, eo quod esset Imperator adeoque dominus orbis." *Discursus novus*, chap. 55. Conring still spoke of Charles's pretended right "to occupy the Americans," as opposed to "America," a usage nicely reflecting the transition from a time when political power was power over people to a time when it was power over a territory.

47. *Discursus novus*, chap. 56.

48. "Itaque quum dignitas haec et προεδρία non tam a Caesareo titulo quam ab ipsa amplitudine Imperii veniat, et vero Germanicum regnum in quieta ejus honoris possessione hactenus fuerit, manifestum est, etiam si tollas omne Caesareum nomen, jus tamen

suum Germanico regno permansurum integrum." *Discursus novus,* chap. 56. But note that this could only increase the bitterness with which Conring witnessed the destruction brought upon Germany by the Thirty Years War; see his "Praefatio in politicam Aristotelis" (1637).

49. Even historians with such obvious sympathy for the idea of universal lordship as Frances Yates, *Astraea* (1975), 1–28, have treated it as a mystical idea, yielding the ground almost without resistance to the untested notion that ideas like sovereignty and the distinction between the public and the private sphere are any less mystical than universal lordship.

50. Among recent scholars who have been brave enough to deal with such questions are Quaglioni, *Politica e diritto* (1983); Cavallar, Degenring, and Kirshner, *Grammar of Signs* (1994); Kirshner, "Civitas sibi faciat civem" (1973); Canning, *Political Thought of Baldus* (1987); and Walther, "Wasser in Stadt und Contado" (1992). For an indispensable old study, see Woolf, *Bartolus of Sassoferrato* (1912); for a reliable introduction, see Calasso, "Bartolo da Sassoferrato" (1965); for an excellent collection of articles, see *Bartolo da Sassoferrato* (1962); and for the transmission of Bartolus's writings, see Casamassima, *Iter Germanicum* (1971); and García y García, *Iter Hispanicum* (1973).

51. The other three volumes are the *Institutes* (or *Institutions*), the *Code,* and the *Novels.* See Engelmann, *Wiedergeburt der Rechtskultur* (1938); Koschaker, *Europa und das Römische Recht* (1966); Kuttner, "Revival of Jurisprudence" (1982); Berman, *Law and Revolution* (1983); Robinson, Fergus, and Gordon, *European Legal History* (2000); and Bellomo, *L'Europa del diritto comune* (1991), in English *Common Legal Past of Europe* (1995).

52. "Ulpianus libro primo institutionum: Hostes sunt, quibus bellum publice populus Romanus decrevit vel ipsi populo Romano: ceteri latrunculi vel praedones appellantur. et ideo qui a latronibus captus est, servus latronum non est, nec postliminium illi necessarium est: ab hostibus autem captus, ut puta a Germanis et Parthis, et servus est hostium et postliminio statum pristinum recuperat." *Digest* 49.15.24, ed. Mommsen, 887. Cf. Honoré, *Ulpian* (1982).

53. For more information about these and other basic terms of Roman law, see Berger, *Encyclopedic Dictionary* (1953), s.v. "hostis," "latro," and "praedo"; Nicholas, *Introduction to Roman Law* (1962); and Buckland, *Textbook of Roman Law* (1963).

54. *Possessions* is here taken in the strict sense of the term, referring to things you possess in fact, as distinguished from property, to which you have a legal title of ownership. Berger, *Encyclopedic Dictionary* (1953), s.v. "postliminium" and "servus."

55. On the significance of the last, see Pennington, *The Prince and the Law* (1993), 165–201; on violence and enmity more broadly, see Brunner, *Land und Herrschaft* (1965), in English *Land and Lordship* (1992); Bossy, *Disputes and Settlements* (1983); and Althoff, *Spielregeln der Politik* (1997); on conflicts between church and state in the first half of the fourteenth century, see Miethke and Bühler, *Kaiser und Papst im Konflikt* (1988); Strayer, *Reign of Philip the Fair* (1980); Denton, *Robert Winchelsey* (1980); and the classic studies by Scholz, *Die Publizistik zur Zeit Philipps des Schönen* (1903); and Rivière, *Le problème de l'église et de l'état* (1926).

56. Vos debetis scire, quod duo sunt genera gentium principaliter: primo populus Romanus, secundo populi extranei. Bartolus on *Digest* 49.15.24, s.v. "hostes," *Opera,* 6:228r, col. a, no. 2.

57. "Glossa dicit, hic accipitur pro toto Imperio Romano." Bartolus on *Digest* 49.15.24, s.v. "hostes," *Opera,* 6:228r, col. a, no. 3. For more on the gloss, see Landsberg,

Die Glosse des Accursius (1883); Genzmer, "Die iustinianische Kodifikation und die Glossatoren" (1934–35); and Weimar, "Die legistische Literatur" (1973).

58. Sed diceres tu, cum modicae gentes sint quae Romano Imperio obediant, ergo videtur quod sit parvus populus Romanus. Bartolus on *Digest* 49.15.24, s.v. "hostes," *Opera,* 6:228r, col. a, no. 3.

59. Respondeo quaedam sunt gentes, quae Imperio Romano obediunt, et istae sine dubio sunt de populo Romano. Quaedam sunt, quae non obediunt Romano Imperio in totum, sed in aliquibus obediunt, ut quia vivunt secundum legem populi Romani et Imperatorem Romanorum esse dominum omnium fatentur, ut sunt civitates Tusciae, Lombardiae, et similes, et istae etiam sunt de populo Romano. Nam cum populus Romanus in eis exerceat iurisdictionem in aliquo articulo, totam iurisdictionem retinet. Bartolus on *Digest* 49.15.24, s.v. "hostes," *Opera,* 6:228r, col. a, nos. 3–4. Note that according to this passage, the city-states of Tuscany and Lombardy regarded the emperor as "lord of all" (*dominum omnium*).

60. Quidam sunt populi, qui nullo modo obediunt Principi, nec istis legibus vivunt, et hoc dicunt se facere ex privilegio Imperatoris, et isti similiter sunt de populo Romano, ut faciunt Veneti. Nam cum illam libertatem ipsi habere se dicant ab Imperio Romano et privilegio quodammodo precario teneant ab eo, et posset privilegium illud revocare, quando vellet, cum ei liceat mutare voluntatem suam. Bartolus on *Digest* 49.15.24, s.v. "hostes," *Opera,* 6:228r, col. a, no. 4.

61. I am not going to enter into the details of what Bartolus taught about the Donation of Constantine. See, e.g., Woolf, *Bartolus of Sassoferrato* (1912), 94–100; Maffei, *La donazione di Costantino* (1964); and Riesenberg, *Inalienability of Sovereignty* (1956).

62. Quidam sunt populi, qui non obediunt Principi, tamen asserunt se habere libertatem ab ipso ex contractu aliquo, ut provinciae, quae tenentur ab ecclesia Romana quae fuerunt donatae ab Imperatore Constantino ecclesiae Romanae, posito pro constanti, quod donatio tenuerit, quodque revocari non possit, adhuc dico istos de populo Romano esse. Nam ecclesia Romana exercet illas in terras iurisdictionem, quae erat Imperio Romano, et istud fatentur: non ergo desinunt esse de populo Romano, sed administratio istarum provinciarum est alteri concessa. Vide in simili, Iurisdictio in clericos est concessa totaliter Papae, desinunt ne propter hoc clerici esse cives Romani? Certe non, quod apparet: quia retinent ius succedendi. Bartolus on *Digest* 49.15.24, s.v. "hostes," *Opera,* 6:228r, col. a, nos. 4–5.

63. On the close relationship between Roman and canon law, see, e.g., Kuttner, "Papst Honorius III. und das Studium des Zivilrechts" (1952); Trusen, *Anfänge des gelehrten Rechts* (1962), 1–33.

64. Et idem dico de istis alijs Regibus et principibus qui negant se esse subditos Regi Romanorum, ut Rex Franciae, Angliae, et similes. Si enim fatentur ipsum esse dominum universalem, licet ab illo universali dominio se subtrahant ex privilegio, vel ex praescriptione, vel consimili, non desinunt esse cives Romani, propter ea quae dicta sunt. Et secundum hoc quasi omnes gentes, quae obediunt Sanctae matri Ecclesiae sunt de populo Romano. Et forte si quis diceret dominum Imperatorem non esse dominum, et monarcham totius orbis, esset haereticus: quia diceret contra determinationem ecclesiae, contra textum Sancti Evangelij, dum dicit, Exivit edictum a Caesare Augusto ut describeretur universus orbis, ut habes Luc. ij. c. Ita etiam recognovit Christus Imperatorem, ut dominum. Bartolus on *Digest* 49.15.24, s.v. "hostes," *Opera,* 6:228r, col. a, nos. 6–7. I am taking "forte" to go with "si quis diceret." If it is taken to go with "esset haereticus,"

Bartolus's claim would be more mildly put but no less telling. Note the difference between "deny that they are subject to the king of the Romans" and "remove themselves from the emperor's universal lordship."

65. Tamar Herzog's study *Defining Nations* (2003) demonstrates the importance of this distinction for understanding citizenship in early modern Europe with the methods of a social and legal historian.

66. "Secundo dixi, quod alij populi sunt extranei, et sunt populi extranei proprie, qui non fatentur Imperatorem Romanum esse dominum universalem, ut Graeci, qui non credunt Imperatorem Romanum esse dominum universalem, sed dicunt Imperatorem Constantinopolitanum esse dominum totius mundi. Item Tartari, qui dicunt Grantchan, esse dominum universalem. Et Sarraceni, qui dicunt dominum eorum esse dominum totius mundi. Idem in Iudaeis. Verum inter istos est differentia. Nam quidam ex istis sunt nobis foederati, ut erant Graeci nobis foederati, contra Turcas. Quidam sunt, cum quibus habemus pacem, ut Tartari. Nam mercatores nostri vadunt ad illos, et illi ad nostros. Quidam cum quibus non habemus pacem, nec guerram, nec aliquid facere, ut cum illis de India. Quidam sunt cum quibus habemus guerram indictam, ut cum Sarracenis, et hodie cum Turcis: sed modicum ad nos de illis, qui foris sunt." Bartolus on *Digest* 49.15.24, s.v. "hostes," *Opera*, 6:228r, col. a, no. 8.

67. Cecil Woolf thought that it was "one of the most interesting and important passages in his works." See his *Bartolus of Sassoferrato* (1912), 25–28. Woolf knew that Grotius had rejected this passage, and he pointed out that Bodin had rejected it as well.

68. This is a common interpretation of Bartolus, precisely because it does seem more logical. It appears to go back to Ercole, *Impero e papato* (1911). A more recent example is furnished by Skinner, *Foundations of Modern Political Thought* (1978), 1:10, according to whom Bartolus "proceeds without hesitation to open up an entirely new perspective on the conventional analysis of *merum Imperium:* he insists that the *de facto* situation is one which the law and thus the Emperor must now be prepared to accept." Similarly Canning, *Political Thought of Baldus* (1987), 93–97; and Canning, *History of Medieval Political Thought* (1996), 168–69. The chief weakness of this line of analysis is that it leaves no alternative but to deny the legitimacy of the emperor's universal lordship.

69. Some historians believe that none are to be expected. Pennington, *The Prince and the Law* (1970), 197, for example, charges that "exasperated historians who have looked for unity in his thought have expected a defense of Roman power from a civilian. We should not impose our paradoxes on him. Anyone who has read the previous pages of this book should understand that Bartolus simply adhered to traditional doctrines of the *ius commune* that he could not ignore." But that seems unduly defeatist. That historians have not been able to find coherence in Bartolus's thought does not prove that no such coherence existed, much less that Bartolus did not believe it to exist.

70. *Code* 1.1.1, ed. Krüger, 5.

71. Aut verbum regit, hic positum intelligitur prout de iure est, et tunc de iure regit omnes populos, et sic relativum ponitur declarative, quos scilicet omnes. Et hoc puto fuisse de mente Imperatoris. Aut vis intelligere prout est de facto, et tunc, quia quidam de facto non obediunt, et sic talis qualitas non competit omnibus de genere, tunc relativum ponitur restrictive. Bartolus on *Code* 1.1.1, s.v. "Cunctos populos," *Opera*, 7:3v, col. a, no. 1. See Woolf, *Bartolus of Sassoferrato* (1912), 21–22.

72. There is an interesting parallel in *Institutes,* proem 1: "Omnes vero populi legibus iam a nobis vel promulgatis vel compositis reguntur." This simply says that "all peoples

are ruled by laws that we have either promulgated or collected." It thus seems to furnish evidence in support of the emperor's claim to universality. The translation of *Justinian's Institutes* by Birks and McLeod (1987), 33, however, renders this as follows: "However, it is by the laws which we have already managed to enact and collect that all *our* peoples are ruled," emphasis added. Birks and McLeod may well be right to deny the presence of any claims to universality by translating *omnes populi* not as "all peoples" but as "all our peoples." But their translation requires a specific interpretation. That interpretation is precisely what was at issue between Conring and Bartolus.

73. I agree with the line of thinking taken by David, "Le contenu de l'hégémonie impériale" (1962), who draws on Bartolus's tract on tyranny to argue that the emperor retained legal rights over the Italian cities. Keen, "Political Thought of the Fourteenth-Century Civilians" (1965), 115, maintains similarly that "whatever the limits of the emperors' *de facto* authority, the empire was still coterminous with Christendom. It embraced all who were part of the *populus Romanus,* and that, as John of Legnano explained, meant all who obeyed mother church, the whole *res publica Christiana.* That it was in this sense that Bartolus too used the phrase is clear from his statement that a man who is banished from a city, though he loses all his rights as a citizen, does not lose his rights under the *ius civile,* the law of the empire." Skinner, *Foundations of Modern Political Thought* (1978), 1:10, considers this misleading because it underestimates the significance of the independence that Bartolus granted to the Italian city-states.

74. There is a large and controversial literature on the meaning of these phrases; for some authors they signal early declarations of sovereignty, whereas others find them doing no damage to the universal power of the emperor at all. I offer my own interpretation on the following pages. Readers who are interested in sampling conflicting positions should compare Woolf, *Bartolus of Sassoferrato* (1912), 107–12, 154–62; Mochi Onory, *Fonti canonistiche* (1951), 227–33, 271–88; Calasso, *I glossatori e la teoria della sovranità* (1957); David, "Le contenu de l'hégémonie impériale" (1962); Baszkiewicz, "Quelques remarques sur la conception de dominium mundi" (1962); Post, *Studies in Medieval Legal Thought* (1964), 434–93; Keen, "Political Thought of the Fourteenth-Century Civilians" (1965); Skinner, *Foundations of Modern Political Thought* (1978), 1:9–12; and Canning, *Political Thought of Baldus* (1987), 93–97.

75. Early modern humanists were adamant that this etymology was false. See Gothofredus's standard gloss on the title of *Digest* 2, *De Jurisdictione,* in *Corpus Iuris Civilis in quatuor partes distinctum* (1688), 35 n. a: "Fallitur Accursius hoc titulo dum notat a ditione Iurisdictionem esse, cum sit a jure dicundo." For them, there was a fundamental distinction between exercising power (*ditio*) and pronouncing law (*dicere ius*). For Bartolus, not so. This casts a bright light on the difference between medieval and modern views of power. But since *ditio* and *dicere* are themselves related by etymology, it is not clear at all which is the better view.

76. This is probably a misprint. I have not been able to determine exactly what Bartolus was referring to. Perhaps it was the gloss on *Digest* 2.1.1, perhaps *Digest* 1.21.1.

77. Iurisdictio dividitur in imperium, et iurisdictionem. Et imperium dividitur in merum et mistum imperium. . . . Nunc venio ad materiam, et pro eius declaratione quaero, quid sit iurisdictio in genere sumpta? Respondeo iurisdictio est potestas de iure publico introducta, etc. ut notat glossa in l. i. supra eodem et ibi plene dixi. Secundo quaero, unde dicatur iurisdictio? Dicit glossa hic quod dicitur a ditione, quod est potestas, et iuris, quasi iuris potestas. Quod autem ditio sit idem quod potestas, probatur in

prooemio Inst. ibi, nostrae ditioni, etc. et C. de libe. et eo. liber. l. ii. Tertio quaero utrum imperium merum et mixtum comprehendantur sub hoc genere, quod est iurisdictio. Quidam dicunt quod non per hanc legem. Ponuntur enim hic, ut species separatae, iurisdictio ab imperio. Glossa tenet contrarium, et bene, ut probatur supra tit. ii. l. i. ubi merum imperium appellat iurisdictionem, et in corpore et defen. civi. §. iusiurandum in fi. et hic dum dicit, quod etiam potestas appellatur. Nam potestas et iurisdictio idem sunt, ut dixi, et est potestas iuris, ergo est iurisdictio. Idem de mero et misto imperio, per hunc textum qui dicit, cui etiam iurisdictio inest sicut genus inest speciei suae, ut l. si quid earum §. interemptum. de leg. iii. et ibi no. . . . Videamus ergo quid sit imperium simpliciter sumptum? Respondeo imperium est iurisdictio quae officio iudicis nobili expeditur, hoc quod dico iurisdictio opponitur in diffinitione tanquam genus. Sequitur, quae officio nobili expeditur hoc ponitur ad differentiam iurisdictionis quae expeditur iudicis officio mercenario, quod hoc sit verum probatur in auth. de defen. civi. §. Iusiurandum in fi. Bartolus on *Digest* 2.1.3, s.v. "imperium," *Opera,* 1:48r, col. a, nos. 2–5. Technically, Bartolus calls the office noble, not the judge.

78. For more on the "mercenary" judge see Willoweit, *Rechtsgrundlagen der Territorialgewalt* (1975), 19–21.

79. "Merum imperium, est iurisdictio, quae officio iudicis nobili, vel per accusationem exercetur, publicam utilitatem respiciens. . . . Mistum imperium est, quod officio iudicis nobili exercetur privatam respiciens utilitatem. . . . Iurisdictio simplex est, quae officio iudicis mercenario expeditur, privatam utilitatem respiciens." Bartolus on *Digest* 2, "Diffinitiones et declarationes iurisdictionum," *Opera,* 1:45v, col. a. "Merum imperium est iurisdictio quae officio iudicis nobili expeditur, vel per accusationem, publicam utilitatem respiciens principaliter. . . . Hoc dixi ad differentiam misti imperij, quod principaliter respicit privatam utilitatem." Bartolus on *Digest* 2.1.3, s.v. "imperium," *Opera,* 1:48r, col. b, no. 6.

80. "Et dividitur [merum imperium] secundum Bar. in sex gradus, ut in hac figura patet intuenti, licet Ias. ponat tamen quatuor gradus et melius, quia secundum eundem maius, et magnum constituunt tantum unum gradum: et parvum, et minus constituunt tantum unum. Maximum, est condere legem, secundum Bar. et alios in d. l. imperium." Bartolus on *Digest* 2, "Diffinitiones et declarationes iurisdictionum," *Opera,* 1:45v, col. a, with reference to *Digest* 2.1.3. Bartolus explicitly rejected the identification of *merum imperium* with the ability to inflict punishment, on the grounds that *merum imperium* included the power to make laws: "Iac. de Are. fuit ille qui primo incepit ponere diffinitionem, et dicebat sic. Merum imperium est iurisdictio severioris ultionis inferendae, publicam utilitatem respiciens. Haec diffinitio non placet. Nam constat quod condere legem est meri imperij." Bartolus on *Digest* 2.1.3, s.v. "imperium," *Opera,* 1:48r, col. b, no. 6. In many editions of Bartolus's works, guidance to the various species and subspecies of *iurisdictio* is supplied in two ways: first, there is a section at the beginning of the commentary on the second book of the *Digest* that is compiled from different passages in Bartolus's writings and treats all varieties of jurisdiction in systematic order. Second, many editions also contain an illustration in which the different species and subspecies of jurisdiction are represented as branches on a "tree of jurisdiction." Neither of these, however, were produced by Bartolus himself; see "Arbor iurisdictionum" and "Diffinitiones et declarationes iurisdictionum" in *Opera,* 1:45r-v; and appendix C in Woolf, *Bartolus of Sassoferrato* (1912), 405–7.

81. For all of these meanings see Berger, *Encyclopedic Dictionary* (1953), s.v. "imperium."

82. Ibid., s.v. "iurisdictio."

83. Ibid., s.v. "imperium." Berger adds: "The juristic sources do not agree as to the attribution of certain magisterial acts of jurisdictional character (*restitutio in integrum, missiones,* appointment of guardians) to *imperium* or *iurisdictio*. The confusion is doubtless the result of alterations of the texts or misunderstanding on the part of Justinian compilers for whom older distinctions lost their practical significance."

84. Ibid., s.v. "imperium merum." Berger adds, disarmingly, that "the origin of this distinction is somewhat obscure."

85. For more about the meaning of *imperium* in antiquity, see Lintott, "What Was the 'Imperium Romanum'?" (1981); Richardson, "Imperium Romanum" (1991); and Brunt, "Laus Imperii" (1990).

86. On medieval Aristotelianism in general, see Kretzmann, Kenny, and Pinborg, *Cambridge History of Later Medieval Philosophy* (1982); for its impact on the study of Roman law, see Meijers, "L'université d'Orléans" (1959).

87. See above, note 80. In antiquity *imperium* was "subject only to three limitations: in the first place, though each [of two magistrates of equal rank] had full power, each was subject to the veto of the other; in the second place, they held office only for a year; and lastly, their power might be limited by legislation." Nicholas, *Introduction to Roman Law* (1962), 3. Note the ingenious Roman system of having two officials with identical powers, as opposed to the modern separation of different powers. Both limit the exercise of political power by checks and balances, but the mechanism is completely different.

88. New, of course, only by comparison with the views of ancient jurists, not those of Bartolus's immediate predecessors. The present discussion deals in no way with the medieval origin of Bartolus's ideas and says nothing about his originality or lack thereof. On medieval views of *imperium* and *iurisdictio* preceding Bartolus, Calasso, *I glossatori e la teoria della sovranità* (1957), is outstanding. See also Gilmore, *Argument from Roman Law* (1941); Cortese, *La norma giuridica* (1962–64); and Costa, *Iurisdictio* (1969), esp. 96–184, on jurisdiction, with special attention to Bartolus at 161–64.

89. Hobbes, *Leviathan* (1994), chap. 29, "Of Those Things That Weaken or Tend to the Dissolution of a Commonwealth," 210–19, turning his attention first to "want of absolute power."

90. Berger, *Encyclopedic Dictionary* (1953), s.v. "dominium"; cf. Nicholas, *Introduction to Roman Law* (1962), 153–57.

91. For two good accounts of the meaning of lordship and *dominium* in the Middle Ages, see Tellenbach, *Libertas* (1936), in English *Church, State, and Christian Society* (1959), esp. 1–37 on "fundamental principles"; and Brunner, *Land and Lordship* (1992), esp. 139–52 on territory and 200–211 on lordship.

92. A classic study is Meynial, "Notes sur la formation de la théorie du domaine divisé" (1908). For more recent work, see Willoweit, "Dominium und Proprietas" (1974); Grossi, "'Gradus in dominio'" (1985); and Grossi, *Il dominio e le cose* (1992).

93. Sicut ergo dominium cohaeret personae domini: tamen est in re, ita iurisdictio cohaeret officio, et personae eius qui habet officium: tamen est in territorio, et sic non est qualitas territorij, sed magis personae. Et ista aequiparatio de iurisdictione ad dominium probatur sic. Princeps habet omnem iurisdictionem, ut supra de const. prin. l.

1. et ex hoc dicitur dominus mundi, ut infra ad l. Rho. de iactu. l. deprecatio. Sicut quilibet iudex dicitur princeps civitatis, vel territorij cui praeest: ut infra de excu. tut. l. spadonem §. si civitatis, rectae [sic] potest dici dominus totius illius territorij universaliter considerati, sicut de principe pluries dixi, et maxime in prima constitutione huius libri. Bartolus on *Digest* 2.1.1, s.v. "ius dicentis," *Opera*, 1:47r, col. a, no. 15.

94. Ex hoc sequitur pulchra consequentia, et vera quod si princeps, vel alius concederet tibi universaliter unum territorium, videtur tibi concedere universaliter iurisdictionem, quia sicut ille qui concedit rem singularem, dicitur dominium rei singularis concedere, ut l. si ita. in fi. de contrah. emp. ita ille qui concedit universale territorium videtur concedere iurisdictionem, quae est idem quod dominium alicuius rei particularis. Bartolus on *Digest* 2.1.1, s.v. "ius dicentis," *Opera*, 1:47r, cols. a–b, no. 16. I have translated this rather conservatively. The Latin "ille qui concedit universale territorium videtur concedere iurisdictionem, quae est idem quod dominium alicuius rei particularis" could easily be translated as "he who gives you a territory as a whole gives you the jurisdiction over it as well because jurisdiction is the same as *dominium* over some particular thing."

95. Omnem rei publicae nostrae sanctionem iam esse purgatam et compositam . . . *Digest,* constitution *Omnem,* ed. Mommsen, 10.

96. Note the distinction between two types of *dominium:* "*dominium* of universal jurisdiction" and "*dominium* over individual things." They are different, but both are clearly identified as *dominium.*

97. Querit glossa super verbo sanctionem, nunquid secundum quod Imperator dicitur habere dominium universalis iurisdictionis, ita et particularium rerum? Quae quaestio fuit antiquitus agitata inter Martinum et Bulgarum. Et primo videtur quod secundum quod ille est dominus universalium, ita et sic particularium rerum, ut est text. in l. deprecatio. ad l. Rho. de Iac. et l. bene a Zenone in prin. C. de quadriennii praescriptione. . . . In contrarium facit, quia dominium insolidum penes duos esse non potest, ut l. si ut certo. §. si duobus vehiculum. infra commo. Sed ego video quod dominia rerum sunt singulorum, ut insti. de re divi. §. singulorum. Ergo non principis. Praeterea, rei vendicatio datur domino, ut infra. de rei vendi. l. in rem actio. Sed ego video, quod singulares homines possunt res vendicare, ut l. i. de rei ven. et sic sunt domini. Si ipsi sunt domini, ergo non princeps. Quid dicendum? Glossa hic determinat pro opinione Bulgari quod Imperator non sit dominus particularium rerum. Bartolus on *Omnem, Opera,* 1:4r, col. a, no. 3.

98. Omnia principis esse intellegantur. *Code* 7.37.3.1a.

99. Cf. Gilmore, *Argument from Roman Law* (1941), 15–44; and Pennington, *The Prince and the Law,* 15–37.

100. Respondetur quod ratione protectionis et iurisdictionis Imperator dicitur dominus mundi, quia tenetur totum mundum defendere, et protegere, et sic appositio verbi nostrae, potest referri ad dominium et tunc non refertur ad Principem. Interdum ratione protectionis, et tunc refert, ut hic. Item probatur, quia ego video, quod ratione protectionis vel administrationis, dicitur quis esse dominus, ut l. interdum §. qui tutelam infra de furtis et l. qui fundum §. si tutor infra pro emptore. Bartolus on *Omnem, Opera,* 1:4r, col. a, no. 3.

101. See Willoweit, *Rechtsgrundlagen der Territorialgewalt* (1975), 25 and n. 34, arguing against Woolf, *Bartolus of Sassoferrato* (1912), 23; and against Quaritsch, *Staat und Souveränität* (1970), 87: "Nunmehr aber fragt Bartolus nach der Natur der kaiserlichen

Gewalt, und er beschreibt sie gerade nicht mit dem Begriff der *iurisdictio*, sondern gelangt zu dem Ergebnis, der Kaiser werde '*dominus mundi*' genannt '*ratione protectionis, vel administrationis.*' Der Inhalt dieses Schutzes hat nichts mit der Jurisdiktionsgewalt gemein."

102. Ex hoc nota modum pronunciandi et exequendi, quando petitur universitas rerum, quod licet iudex pronunciet gregem esse meum, tamen restitutio fiet mihi detractis capitibus alienis. Pro hoc ego sum consuetus dicere in prima constitutione huius libri, ut cum Imperator sit dominus totius mundi. Et glossae dicunt eum dominum quo ad protectionem: quia cum alij sint domini singulariter, plures non poterunt esse domini in solidum. Ego quod Imperator est dominus totius mundi vere. Nec obstat, quod alij sunt domini particulariter, quia mundus est universitas quaedam: unde potest quis habere dictam universitatem, licet singulae res non sint suae. Unde si alius teneret mundum, ipse Imperator posset vendicare. Bartolus on *Digest* 6.1.1, s.v. "per hanc autem actionem," *Opera*, 1:172r, col. b, nos. 1–2.

103. Principum placita animo ius condendi facta, habent vim legis generalis: nisi sint facta ad certas personas, quia tunc personas non egrediuntur. Bartolus on *Digest* 1.4.1, s.v. "quod principi," *Opera*, 1:21r, col. b.

104. "Sic quaero nunquid legem concedendo possit simpliciter auferre dominium rei meae, sine aliqua causa? Et dico quod non, ut dicit Inn. in c. quae in ecclesiarum, extra de const. in c. quia plerique, de immu. eccle." Bartolus on *Omnem, Opera*, 1:4r, col. b, no. 4. The reference is to two constitutions of Pope Innocent III, *Liber Extra* 1.2.7 and 3.49.8; see Friedberg, *Corpus Iuris Canonici* (1879–81), 2:9, 2:656–57.

105. No. quod omnia sunt Principis quo ad iurisdictionem et universale dominium, sed non quantum ad particulare. Bartolus on *Code* 11.50.2, s.v. "coloni," *Opera*, 9:41v, col. a, no. 2.

106. For a good summary see Costa, *Iurisdictio* (1969), 194–98.

107. See above, note 93.

108. Sunt populi extranei proprie, qui non fatentur Imperatorem Romanum esse dominum universalem. Bartolus on *Digest* 49.15.24, s.v. "hostes," *Opera*, 6:228r, col. a, no. 8.

109. The literature on Bartolus often insists on the importance of the distinction between matters of fact and matters of right without considering the distinction between different, but equally legitimate, levels of jurisdiction; see, e.g., Skinner, *Foundations of Modern Political Thought* (1978), 1:10; and Canning, *History of Medieval Political Thought* (1996), 168–69. But if it were true that the freedom of the Italian city states was purely *de facto*, Bartolus would have had no conceptual foundation to distinguish their government from tyranny (or to maintain that the emperor was truly *dominus mundi*). Yet he clearly did believe that there was such a foundation. The Italian city-states (at least those who were not governed by tyrants) had a title that was entirely *de iure*. The possibility of such a title turned on a distinction between jurisdiction over a part of the world and jurisdiction over the whole of the world that is impossible to reduce to the distinction between matters of fact and matters of law.

110. Nota quod etiam Imperator invocavit nomen domini, et sic fuit Christianus ut dixi supra in prin. constitutione. Et ex hoc sequitur, quod si non fuisset Christianus non potuisset esse Imperator, nec haberet temporalem iurisdictionem. Bartolus on *Digest* 1, *Rubrica, Opera*, 1:5v, col. a, no. 1.

111. Imperium et ecclesia processerunt a Deo, tanquam a causa efficiente. Bartolus on *Deo auctore, Opera*, 1:3v, col. b, no. 14.

112. This is a cursory statement of an argument developed to far-reaching effect by Whitehead, *Science and the Modern World* (1925), in an attempt to elaborate the rationality of a non-Cartesian metaphysics taking its beginnings, not from substances (whether intellectual or material), but from relationships.

113. See above, note 94.

114. David, "Le contenu de l'hégémonie impériale" (1962), 207.

115. For a classic account by a medieval theologian see Aquinas, *Treatise on Law* (1993). For influential views taken by medievalists, see Carlyle and Carlyle, *History of Mediaeval Political Theory* (1903–36), 5:441–74, 6:503–26; Kern, "Recht und Verfassung im Mittelalter" (1919); or the same author's *Gottesgnadentum und Widerstandsrecht* (1914), in English *Kingship and Law in the Middle Ages* (1939); Vinogradoff, "Sources of the Law" (1928); Tellenbach, *Church, State, and Christian Society* (1959), 1–37; Brunner, *Land and Lordship* (1992), 114–24; Kuttner, "Sur les origines du terme 'droit positif'" (1936); Gaudemet, "'Ius' et 'Leges'" (1950); Gagnér, *Studien zur Ideengeschichte der Gesetzgebung* (1960); Genzmer, *Mittelalterliches Rechtsdenken* (1961); and d'Entrèves, *Natural Law* (1951). For the lively debate concerning the origin of subjective rights, see Villey, "Les origines de la notion de droit subjectif" (1953–54); Tuck, *Natural Rights Theories* (1979); McGrade, "Ockham and the Birth of Individual Rights" (1980); Coing, "Zur Geschichte des Begriffs 'Subjektives Recht'" (1982); Tierney, *Idea of Natural Rights* (1997); and Helmholz, *Fundamental Human Rights in Medieval Law* (2001).

116. Hobbes, *Leviathan* (1994), chap. 14, sec. 3, 79–80.

117. "Quid ergo est dominium? Responde, est ius de re corporali perfecte disponendi, nisi lege prohibeatur." Bartolus on *Digest* 41.2.17, s.v. "differentia," *Opera*, 5:92v, col. a. "Iurisdictio est potestas de iure publico introducta." Bartolus on *Digest* 2.1.3, s.v. "imperium," *Opera*, 1:48r, col. a, no. 3. Note the circular relationship between *lex, ius,* and *iurisdictio*. *Ius* is limited by *lex* in the first passage but is said to be the source of *iurisdictio* in the second, and we have already seen that legislation is the highest function of *iurisdictio*; see above, note 80.

118. Bartolus furnishes a good example for an elementary difference in the logical foundations of medieval and modern ways of thinking about politics, law, and history. That difference ought to be easy to state precisely for someone with an adequate grasp of formal logic as it has developed since Frege recognized the logical significance of names, and Wittgenstein that of the difference between saying and showing. I regret that not having such a grasp compels me to resort to language that is only suggestive where it ought to be lucid. For more about the name in medieval Christianity, see Bartlett, *Making of Europe* (1993), 250–55.

119. The best treatments of Bodin remain those of Julian Franklin; see his *Jean Bodin and the Sixteenth-Century Revolution* (1963), *Jean Bodin and the Rise of Absolutist Theory* (1973), and, for a briefer account, "Sovereignty and the Mixed Constitution" (1991). Cf. Quaglioni, *Limiti della sovranità* (1992).

120. Cum alijs multis magistratibus geritur Imperium Germanicum, tum unus summus illi praeest. *Discursus novus,* chap. 1.

121. "Enimvero non est Caesari nostro quidquam potestatis in liberas respublicas, sed ratione αὐτονομίας etiam parva respublica libera, qualis est Rhegusina exempli gratia, non minus sua habet plena majestatis jura quam aliqua magna." *Discursus novus,* chap. 56.

122. Conring, *De finibus imperii Germanici* (1654).

123. For some sense of the range of possibilities, see Hinsley, *Sovereignty* (1986); Franklin, *Jean Bodin and the Rise of Absolutist Theory* (1973); Quaritsch, *Staat und Souveränität* (1970); and Schmitt, *Political Theology* (1985).

124. Julian Franklin disagrees. For him, Jean Bodin had it wrong when he considered indivisibility to be the hallmark of sovereignty. See his remarks in Bodin, *On Sovereignty* (1992), xiii, and his arguments in *Jean Bodin and the Rise of Absolutist Theory* (1973). From the perspective adopted here, however, Bodin was quite right to insist on the indivisibility of sovereignty. Not to have done so would have been tantamount to conceding victory to Bartolus. Nor is it entirely clear that the distinction between separate branches of government in the constitution of the United States of America (which Franklin is concerned to reconcile with sovereignty) does in fact amount to a division of sovereignty.

125. Rousseau, *Social Contract* (1968), bk. 1, chap. 7, pp. 62–63, states this principle with unusual clarity: "The sovereign, bearing only one single and identical aspect, is in the position of a private person making a contract with himself, which shows that there neither is, nor can be, any kind of fundamental law binding on the people as a body, not even the social contract itself."

126. "The people or the aristocracy (*seigneurs*) of a commonwealth can purely and simply give someone absolute and perpetual power to dispose of all possessions, persons, and the entire state at his pleasure, and then to leave it to anyone he pleases, just as a proprietor can make a pure and simple gift of his goods for no other reason than his generosity. This is a true gift because it carries no further conditions, being complete and accomplished all at once, whereas gifts that carry obligations and conditions are not authentic gifts. And so sovereignty given to a prince subject to obligations and conditions is properly not sovereignty or absolute power." Bodin, *On Sovereignty* (1992), bk. 1, chap. 8, pp. 7–8.

127. For a classic statement. see Carlyle, *History of Mediaeval Political Theory* (1903–36), 5:457–74, esp. 471: "The authority of the prince was then, in the political system, as well as in the theory of the Middle Ages, founded upon law and limited by law. It is here that we find the foundation of that contractual principle which was sometimes expressed and always implied in mediaeval political theory. The obligations of the prince and the people were mutual obligations, and these obligations were expressed in the law."

128. Bodin, *On Sovereignty* (1992), bk. 1, chap. 8, p. 6.

129. As indeed he was; see the beginning of his tract "On the Tyrant" (1986), 7.

130. Hence Bodin's notion that the true mark of the tyrant is not his relationship to law but his lack of respect for property; see Bodin, *On Sovereignty* (1992), bk. 1, chap. 8, pp. 38–42. That is about as good a definition of tyranny as can be expected under modern circumstances. It goes without saying that tyrants do not respect natural law either, but that is a different matter; cf. Fasolt, "Visions of Order" (1995), 46–50.

131. Bodin, *On Sovereignty* (1992), bk. 1, chap. 8, pp. 13–14, 35, 38–42. That has made it difficult for scholars to explain precisely how modern theories of natural law differ from their medieval precursors. See the incisive remarks by Tuck, *Philosophy and Government* (1992), xiv–xv, that in spite of superficial similarities and contrary to a scholarly opinion of long standing, early modern ideas of natural law do in fact amount to a "profound break with the scholastics." Clarity here can only come from more attention to the voluntarist tradition that stands at the center of Francis Oakley's work; see his *Omnipotence, Covenant, and Order* (1984), and especially *Politics and Eternity* (1999).

132. Mill, *On Liberty* (1974), 69.

133. For an example of the use of "private," see his declaration that certain types of war can be declared by private persons: "Hoc praemisso videamus qui possunt indicere bellum, et quis est indicti belli effectus, et hoc videamus inter nos. Respondeo quod quoddam est bellum, quod potest indici a quolibet privato, ut pro defensione suae rei, vel pro recuperatione incontinenti potest facere adunationem gentium, et pugnare cum aliis iuste." Bartolus on *Digest* 49.15.24, s.v. "hostes," *Opera*, 6:228r, col. a, no. 9. "Public," as we have seen, was part and parcel of his definition of *iurisdictio* itself: "Iurisdictio est potestas de iure publico introducta." Bartolus on *Digest* 2.1.3, s.v. "imperium," *Opera*, 1:48r, col. a, no. 2.

134. *Digest*, constitution *Deo auctore*, ed. Mommsen, 8.

135. *Code* 1.1, ed. Krüger, 1–12.

136. See Wieacker, "Ratio scripta" (1944).

137. Ut eleganter Celsus definit, ius est ars boni et aequi. Cuius merito quis nos sacerdotes appellet: iustitiam namque colimus et boni et aequi notitiam profitemur, aequum ab iniquo separantes, licitum ab illicito discernentes, bonos non solum metu poenarum, verum etiam praemiorum quoque exhortatione efficere cupientes, veram nisi fallor philosophiam, non simulatam affectantes. *Digest* 1.1.1, ed. Mommsen, 29.

138. See above, note 110.

139. *Discursus novus*, chap. 10.

140. For a clear statement of Conring's views on these issues, see the preface to his *De hermetica medicina* (1669), pp. 11–21 of the unpaginated front matter. On the metaphysical difficulties in which his methodological assumptions involved him, see Fasolt, "Conring on History" (1987).

141. *Discursus novus*, chap. 54.

142. Costa, *Iurisdictio*, 164, arrives at essentially the same conclusion: "Bartolo rappresenta così il massimo sforzo di 'aggiornamento' della tradizione; 'oltre' di lui si apriva la storia di un linguaggio, a poco a poco, diverso."

143. Kuhn, *Structure of Scientific Revolutions* (1970). For a collection of detailed critical investigations into the questions raised by Kuhn, see Lakatos and Musgrave, *Criticism and the Growth of Knowledge* (1970).

144. See, e.g., LaCapra, *Rethinking Intellectual History* (1983); Skinner, *Return of Grand Theory* (1985); and Toews, "Intellectual History after the Linguistic Turn" (1987).

145. Wittgenstein, *Culture and Value* (1980), 1e.

146. *Discursus novus*, chap. 5.

147. Ibid.

148. Ibid., chap. 11; cf. above, note 21.

149. Ibid., chap. 55; cf. above, note 46.

CHAPTER FIVE

1. The kind of guessing that Skinner, "Limits of Historical Explanations" (1966), described with particular clarity.

2. Manuductrix igitur severiorum scientiarum est historia, tantumque parit delectationis quantum scientiae atque artes quaelibet largiuntur. Sed hanc ejus voluptatem atque hunc illius fructum percipere non est cujusvis. Tantum enim iis id concessum est, qui communes leges atque praecepta universalia aut ipsimet suopte ingenio norunt construere

ex singularibus eventis, aut vero a magistris hactenus ea didicerunt, ut ad absolutam omnibus numeris rerum scientiam nil praeter experimenta postuletur. *Opera,* 5:258. For more on Conring's views on the relationship between history and political science, see Fasolt, "Conring on History" (1987).

3. Ipsemet ego nonnulla quidem paulo aliter scripta malim: sed fortassis haud fas est, juvenilem laborem omnem exactioris aetatis trutina expendere, et singulis temporibus suus aliquis naevus relinquendus est, modo non nimium dedecoret: ac proinde non est cur quidquam mutem. *Opera,* 5:278.

4. Savigny, *Geschichte des römischen Rechts* (1815–31); cf. Stobbe, *Hermann Conring, der Begründer der deutschen Rechtsgeschichte* (1870), 14; Knoll, *Conring als Historiker* (1889), 44; Whitman, *Legacy of Roman Law* (1990).

5. From the opening paragraph of Pollock and Maitland, *History of English Law* (1898), 1:1. Maitland goes on, "but, as we rend it, we may watch the whence and whither of a few of the severed and ravelling threads which have been making a pattern too large for any man's eye." Cf. the use to which this is put by Berman, *Law and Revolution* (1983), 49.

6. For good examples of historians pushing the boundary back into the Middle Ages, see Oberman, *Werden und Wertung der Reformation* (1977); Kristeller, *Renaissance Thought and Its Sources* (1979); and Skinner, *Foundations of Modern Political Thought* (1978). For historians pulling it still further in the same direction, see Southern, *Making of the Middle Ages* (1953); Tierney, *Religion, Law, and the Growth of Constitutional Thought* (1982); and Berman, *Law and Revolution* (1983). For examples of medieval history written in a genuinely modern key, see Bartlett, *Making of Europe* (1993); and Moore, *First European Revolution* (2000). Hassinger, *Das Werden des neuzeitlichen Europa* (1959), was among the first to propose the existence of an early modern period of European history between the Middle Ages and modern history. By now that idea has gained wide currency; see Brady, Oberman, and Tracy, *Handbook of European History* (1994–95).

7. They could also be made about the differences between the nations. Unlike the boundary between the Middle Ages and modernity, the differences between nations do not divide different ages but contemporary bodies politic. But very much like the boundary between the Middle Ages and modernity, they are differences made, not given. Hence they are equally impossible to grasp by histories mistaking them for fact.

8. For a good example of a contemporary postcolonial historian struggling with precisely this difficulty in the history of India, see Chakrabarty, *Provincializing Europe* (2000).

Works Cited

The following list is divided into primary sources and secondary literature. English translations of works written in foreign languages are listed with the originals. Conring's works are listed as they were first published. If they were included in the seven-volume edition of his *Opera* by Johann Wilhelm Goebel in Brunswick in 1730 (reprinted in Aalen in 1970–73), I have added a reference to that effect. Works edited by Conring are listed under his name and grouped following his own works. *Beiträge* refers to *Hermann Conring, 1606–1681: Beiträge zu Leben und Werk,* ed. Michael Stolleis (Berlin: Duncker und Humblot, 1983). "Resp." refers to "respondents" defending dissertations written under Conring's guidance in public academic exercises. "Praeses" refers to the presiding examiner at such an exercise.

PRIMARY SOURCES

Accursius. *Glossa in Codicem.* Venice: Baptista de Tortis, 1488. Reprint, Turin: Ex officina Erasmiana, 1968.

Aquinas, Thomas. *The Treatise on Law: Being "Summa Theologiae" I–II, QQ. 90 through 97.* Ed. and trans. Robert J. Henle. Notre Dame, IN: University of Notre Dame Press, 1993.

Aristotle. *Politicorum libri octo. Cum perpetua Danielis Heinsii in omnes libros paraphrasi.* Ed. Daniel Heinsius. Leiden: Ex officina Elzeviriana, 1621.

Barclay, William. *De regno et regali potestate adversus Buchananum, Brutum, Boucherium et reliquos monarchomachos libri sex.* Paris: Chardière, 1600.

Bartolus of Sassoferrato. *Opera.* 12 vols. in 10. Venice: Apud Iuntas, 1570–71.

———. "Tractatus de tyranno." In *Politica e diritto nel Trecento italiano,* ed. Diego Quaglioni, 171–213. Florence: Olschki, 1983. In English "On the Tyrant," trans. Julius Kirshner, in *University of Chicago Readings in Western Civilization,* vol. 5, *The Renaissance,* ed. Eric Cochrane and Julius Kirshner (Chicago: University of Chicago Press, 1986), 7–30.

Baumgart, Peter, and Ernst Pitz, eds. *Die Statuten der Universität Helmstedt.* Göttingen: Vandenhoeck und Ruprecht, 1963.
Bodin, Jean. *On Sovereignty: Four Chapters from Six Books of the Commonwealth.* Trans. Julian H. Franklin. Cambridge: Cambridge University Press, 1992.
———. *Les six livres de la république.* Paris: Iacques du Puys, 1576. In English *The Six Bookes of a Commonweale,* trans. Richard Knolles (London: Bishop, 1606); rev. ed., revised by Kenneth D. McRae (Cambridge: Harvard University Press, 1962).
———. *Les six livres de la république.* Paris: Iacques du Puis, 1583. Reprint, Aalen: Scientia, 1977.
Burgersdicius, Franco. *Institutionum logicarum libri duo.* Leiden: Commelinus, 1632.
———. *Institutionum logicarum synopsis sive rudimenta logica.* Leiden: Commelinus, 1632.
Catalogus bibliothecae Conringianae variis in omni genere doctrinae eximiisque libris refertae. Helmstedt: Hamm, 1694.
Code. See Justinian, *Codex Iustinianus.*
Conring, Hermann. *Admonitio de Thesauro rerumpublicarum totius orbis quadripartito Genevae hoc anno publicato.* Helmstedt: H. D. Müller, 1675. Reprint, *Opera,* 4:44–47.
———. *Animadversiones in Christopheri Haunoldi . . . libellum Concussioni fundamentorum fidei pontificiae oppositum.* Helmstedt: H. Müller, 1654.
———. *Animadversiones politicae in Nicolai Machiavelli librum De principe.* Helmstedt: H. Müller, 1661. Reprint, *Opera,* 2:973–1092.
———. "Annotationes in Hugo Grotius, *De veritate religionis christianae.*" In *Opera,* 5:1–105.
———. *Aristotelis laudatio.* Helmstedt: Lucius, 1633. Reprint, *Opera,* 5:726–61.
———. *Assertio iuris Moguntini in coronandis regibus Romanorum.* Frankfurt: Serlin und Fickwirth, 1655. Reprint, *Opera,* 1:695–709.
———. "Bedenken zu der holländischen Triple-Alliance." Herzog August Bibliothek, Wolfenbüttel, MS 90.4 Extrav., fol. 226r–28v, n.d.
———. "Bericht, wie es mit dem Rechte der Engelländer Fischereyen, auff der norwegischen und issländischen See eigentlich bewandt." In *Opera,* 2:917–32.
———. *Brevis ac praeliminaris enarratio causarum, ob quas . . . Carolus Gustavus . . . coactus est regem Poloniae bello adoriri.* Helmstedt: H. Müller, 1656.
———. *Castigatio libelli cui titulus Anticonringiana defensio iuris Coloniensis in coronandis Romanorum regibus.* Frankfurt: Serlin und Fickwirth, 1656. Reprint, *Opera,* 1:794–811.
———. *Censura diplomatis quod Ludovico imperatori fert acceptum coenobium Lindaviense.* Helmstedt: H. Müller, 1672. Reprint, *Opera,* 2:567–698.
———. "Consilium de maris mediterranei dominio et commerciis regi christianissimo vindicandis." In *Opera,* 1:989–1008.
———. *De calido innato sive igne animali liber unus.* Helmstedt: H. Müller, 1647.
———. *De civili prudentia liber unus.* Helmstedt: H. Müller, 1662. Reprint, *Opera,* 3:280–421.
———. *De constitutione episcoporum Germaniae.* Resp. H. J. Blume. Helmstedt: H. Müller, 1647. Reprint, *Opera,* 2:699–755.
———. *Defensio ecclesiae Protestantium adversus duo Pontificiorum argumenta.* Helmstedt: H. Müller, 1654.
———. *De finibus imperii Germanici. Editio nova.* 3 vols. Frankfurt: Ellinger, 1680–81.
———. *De finibus imperii Germanici libri duo, quibus iura finium a primo imperii exordio ad*

haec nostra usque tempora propugnantur. Helmstedt: H. Müller, 1654. Reprint, *Opera*, 1:114–485.

———. *De finibus imperii Germanici liber tertius.* Helmstedt: J. Müller, 1681. Reprinted in footnotes marked C.A.E. in *Opera*, 1:114–485.

———. *De Germanorum imperio Romano liber unus.* Helmstedt: H. Müller, 1644. Reprint, *Opera*, 1:26–107.

———. *De Germanorum imperio Romano liber unus. Ex autographo b.[eati] auctoris auctus.* Ed. Hermann Johann Conring. 2d ed. Helmstedt: Hamm, 1694. Reprint, *Opera*, 1:26–107.

———. *De habitus corporum Germanicorum antiqui ac novi causis dissertatio.* Helmstedt: H. Müller, 1645. Reprint, *Opera*, 5:222–53.

———. *De hermetica Aegyptiorum vetere et Paracelsicorum nova medicina liber unus.* Helmstedt: H. Müller, 1648.

———. *De hermetica medicina libri duo.* 2d ed. Helmstedt: H. Müller, 1669.

———. "De imperatore Romano Germanico discursus historico-politicus." In *De imperii Germanici republica acroamata sex historico-politica*, 275–309. Embrun: Apud Societatem, 1655. Called "Tractatus de imperatore Romano Germanico" on the title page. Amalgamated from *Discursus novus de imperatore Romano-Germanico* (1642) and *De Germanorum imperio Romano* (1644).

———. *De imperii Germanici republica acroamata sex historico-politica.* Embrun: Apud Societatem, 1655. 1654 on the frontispiece.

———. *De imperio Romano Germanorum disputatio prima.* Resp. J. C. von Boineburg. Helmstedt: H. Müller, 1643.

———. [Cyriacus Thrasymachus, pseud.]. *De iustitia armorum Suecicorum in Polonos, perque ea liberata a magno periculo Germania.* N.p., 1655. Reprint, *Opera*, 5:1084–96.

———. *De origine iuris Germanici commentarius historicus.* Helmstedt: H. Müller, 1643. Reprint, *Opera*, 6:77–202. In German *Der Ursprung des deutschen Rechts*, trans. Ilse Hoffmann-Meckenstock and Michael Stolleis (Frankfurt: Insel Verlag, 1994).

———. *De pace civili inter imperii ordines religione dissidentes perpetuo conservanda libri duo.* 2d ed. Helmstedt: J. Müller, 1677. Reprint, *Opera*, 2:467–566.

———. *De pace perpetua inter imperii Germanici ordines religione dissidentes perpetuo conservanda libri duo.* Helmstedt: H. Müller, 1657. Reprint, *Opera*, 2:467–566.

———. *De purgatorio animadversiones in Ioannem Mulmannum Iesuitam.* Helmstedt: H. Müller, 1651.

———. *De sanguinis generatione et motu naturali opus novum.* Helmstedt: H. Müller, 1643.

———. "De statu Europae, ac inprimis Germanici imperii, tempore conclusae ac confectae pacificationis Osnabrugensis et Monasteriensis." In *Opera*, 6:658–868.

———. "Discursus ad Lampadium posterior ex manuscripto." In *Opera*, 2:238–466.

———. *Discursus novus de imperatore Romano-Germanico.* N.p., 1642. Reprint, with revisions, in *Opera*, 1:528–42. Forthcoming in English as *New Discourse on the Roman-German Emperor*, ed. and trans. Constantin Fasolt (Tempe: Medieval and Renaissance Texts and Studies).

———. *Disputatio de origine formarum.* Resp. Hermann Conring. Leiden: Patius, 1630.

———. *Disputatio medica de scorbuto.* Praeses Johann Wolf. Resp. Hermann Conring. Helmstedt: Lucius, 1634.

———. *Disputatio medica de scorbuto.* Resp. L. Krüger. Helmstedt: Lucius, 1638.

———. *Disputatio medica inauguralis de scorbuto.* Resp. J. G. Behrens. Helmstedt: Calixt, 1659.

———. *Disputatio medica inauguralis de scorbuto.* Resp. L. Gieseler. Helmstedt: H. Müller, 1644.

———. *Disputatio physica de calido innato.* Resp. Hermann Conring. Leiden: Patius, 1627.

———. *Disputatio politica de mutationibus rerumpublicarum.* Resp. C. W. Engelbrecht. Helmstedt: Lucius, 1635. Reprint, *Opera*, 3:1034–46.

———. *Dissertatio ad legem primam Codicis Theodosiani, De studiis liberalibus urbis Romae et Constantinopolis.* Helmstedt: H. Müller, 1655. Reprint, *Opera*, 6:1–27.

———. *Dissertatio de comitiis imperii Romano-Germanici.* Resp. A. H. Engelbrecht. Helmstedt: H. Müller, 1666. Reprint, *Opera*, 2:789–818.

———. *Dissertatio de officialibus imperii Romano-Germanici.* Resp. C. F. von Burgstorff. Helmstedt: H. Müller, 1669. Reprint, *Opera*, 2:766–77.

———. *Dissertatio de praecipuis negotiis in comitiis imperii Germanici olim et hodienum tractari solitis.* Resp. J. C. Becker. Helmstedt: H. Müller, 1666. Reprint, *Opera*, 2:818–39.

———. *Dissertatio de ratione status.* Resp. H. Voss. Helmstedt: H. Müller, 1651. Reprint, *Opera*, 4:549–80.

———. "Dissertatio de republica imperii Germanici communi, Lampadio praemissa." In *De republica Romano-Germanica*, by Jacob Lampadius, ed. Hermann Conring. Helmstedt: H. Müller, 1671. Reprint, *Opera*, 2:5–22.

———. *Dissertatio de septemviris seu electoribus Germanorum regni et imperii Romani.* Resp. H. W. Pape. Helmstedt: H. Müller, 1644. Reprint, *Opera*, 2:777–89.

———. *Epistola de electione Alexandri VII papae opposita appendici Examinis Erbermanniani.* Helmstedt: H. Müller, 1655. Reprint, *Opera*, 5:632–42.

———. [Cyriacus Thrasymachus, pseud.]. *Epistola oder Sendschreiben, des Cyriaci Thrasymachi, von der gerechten Kriegs-Armatur der Cron Schweden wieder die Cron Polen, und von dem dadurch aus grosser Gefahr erretteten Teutschlande.* N.p., 1655.

———. *Examen libelli a Vito Erbermanno . . . Concussioni fundamentorum fidei pontificiae oppositi.* Helmstedt: H. Müller, 1654.

———. "Examen rerumpublicarum potiorum totius orbis." In *Opera*, 4:47–520.

———. *Exercitatio de ducibus et comitibus imperii Germanici.* Resp. G. A. Struve. Helmstedt: H. Müller, 1643. Reprint, *Opera*, 2:755–65.

———. *Exercitatio de Germanici imperii civibus.* Resp. C. W. Blume. Helmstedt: H. Müller, 1641. Reprint, *Opera*, 1:516–28.

———. *Exercitatio de imperatore Romano Germanico.* Resp. Bogislaus Otho von Hoym. Helmstedt: H. Müller, 1641. Reprint, with revisions, in *Opera*, 1:528–42.

———. "Exercitatio de imperatore Romano Germanico." In *Exercitationes academicae de republica imperii Germanici*, 32–72. Helmstedt: J. Müller, 1674. Reprint, *Opera*, 1:528–42.

———. *Exercitatio de iudiciis reipublicae Germanicae.* Resp. C. U. von Burgkstorff. Helmstedt: H. Müller, 1647. Reprint, *Opera*, 2:864–99.

———. *Exercitatio de urbibus Germanicis.* Resp. G. Bode. Helmstedt: H. Müller, 1641. Reprint, *Opera*, 1:485–516.

———. "Exercitatio historico-politica de notitia singularis alicuius reipublicae." In *Opera*, 4:1–43.

———. *Exercitationes academicae de republica imperii Germanici.* Helmstedt: J. Müller, 1674.

———. *Ex politicis dissertatio academica de senatu liberarum rerum-publicarum.* Resp. F. Holste. Helmstedt: H. D. Müller, 1681. Reprint, *Opera,* 3:797–816.

———. *Fundamentorum fidei pontificiae concussio.* Helmstedt: H. Müller, 1654.

———. *Glossa ordinaria ad litteras circulares Alexandri papae septimi.* N.p., 1655.

———. *Gründlicher Bericht von der landesfürstlichen ertzbischöfflichen Hoch- und Gerechtigkeit über die Stadt Bremen.* N.p., 1652. Reprint, *Opera,* 1:844–984.

———. *Introductio in naturalem philosophiam et naturalium institutionum liber primus.* Helmstedt: H. Müller, 1638.

———. "Introductio in Politica Aristotelis." In *Aristotelis Politicorum libri superstites,* ed. Hermann Conring. Helmstedt: H. Müller, 1656. Reprint, *Opera,* 3:457–90.

———. *Introductio in universam artem medicam singulasque eius partes.* Resp. S. Scheffer. Helmstedt: H. Müller, 1654.

———. *In universam artem medicam singulasque eius partes introductio.* Ed. Günther Christoph Schelhammer. 2d ed. Helmstedt: Hamm, 1687.

———. *Iteratarum vindiciarum iuris coronandi pro archidioecesi Coloniensi examen.* Frankfurt, 1656. Reprint, *Opera,* 1:765–85.

———. *Nothwendige Anmerckungen auff Pabst Alexanders des Siebenden Kreisz Schreiben.* N.p., 1656.

———. "Ohnmassgeblicher Vorschlag von Auffnahm Ihro Königlichen Majestäten zu Dennemarck und Norwegen Königreichen und anderen Ländern, vermittelst dreyen grossen Fisch-Handlungen." In *Opera,* 2:932–52.

———. "Ohnmassgebliches Bedencken von stets-waehrender Erhaltung der neuen Erb-Monarchie des hoechstloeblichen Koenigreichs Dennemarck." In *Opera,* 2:953–66.

———. *Opera.* Ed. Johann Wilhelm Goebel. 7 vols. Brunswick: Meyer, 1730. Reprint, Aalen: Scientia, 1970–73.

———. *Pietas Academiae Juliae programmate publico prorectoris et senatus academici adversus improbas et iniquas calumnias cum aliorum quorundam tum D. A. Strauchii asserta.* Helmstedt: H. Müller, 1668.

———. "Praefatio de doctrina pathologica." In *Observationum medicarum centuriae tres posthumae,* by Philipp Salmuth, ed. Hermann Conring, 3–16. Brunswick: Duncker, 1648.

———. "Praefatio de historiarum, Germanorum inprimis, studiis." In *De moribus Germanorum,* by Tacitus, ed. Hermann Conring. Helmstedt: Lucius, 1635. Reprint, *Opera,* 5:253–78.

———. "Praefatio in politicam Aristotelis." In *Politicorum libri octo,* by Aristotle, ed. Hermann Conring. Helmstedt: Lucius, 1637. Reprint, *Opera,* 1:117–28.

———. [Irenaeus Eubulus, pseud.]. *Pro pace perpetua Protestantibus danda consultatio catholica.* Frideburgi: Apud Germanum Patientem, 1648. Reprint, *Opera,* 2:472–90.

———. *Propolitica sive brevis introductio in civilem philosophiam.* Helmstedt: H. Müller, 1663.

———. *Responsio ad Valerianum Magnum . . . pro sua Concussione fundamentorum fidei pontificiae.* Helmstedt: H. Müller, 1654.

———. *Responsio altera pro sua Concussione fundamentorum fidei pontificiae ad Valeriani Magni . . . epistolam.* Helmstedt: H. Müller, 1655.

———. *Rettung des Osnabrückischen und Münsterischen Friedens wieder Bapst Innocentii X. Nulliteths Erklärung.* N.p., n.d. [1653?].

———. *Thesauri rerumpublicarum pars prima—quarta*. Ed. Philipp Andreas Oldenburger. 4 vols. Geneva: S. de Tournes, 1675.
———. *Theses miscellaneae de civili prudentia*. Resp. H. Ottendorf. Helmstedt: H. Müller, 1650. Reprint, *Opera*, 277–80.
———. *Theses miscellaneae excerptae ex cap. 1 et 2 libri De civili prudentia*. Resp. G. von Dassel. Helmstedt: H. Müller, 1651.
———. *Theses miscellaneae excerptae ex cap. 3 libri De civili prudentia*. Resp. B. von Pogwisch. Helmstedt: H. Müller, 1651.
———. *Theses miscellaneae excerptae ex cap. 4 libri De civili prudentia*. Resp. T. H. von Wickeden. Helmstedt: H. Müller, 1651.
———. *Theses miscellaneae excerptae ex cap. 5 libri De civili prudentia*. Resp. H. Dresinck. Helmstedt: H. Müller, 1651.
———. *Theses variae de morali prudentia*. Praeses Franco Burgersdicius. Resp. Hermann Conring. Leiden: Patius, 1629. Reprint, *Opera*, 6:335–37.
———. *Der Ursprung des deutschen Rechts*. Trans. Ilse Hoffmann-Meckenstock and Michael Stolleis. Frankfurt: Insel, 1994.
———. *Vicariatus imperii Palatinus defensus*. N.p., 1658. Reprint, *Opera*, 1:811–36.
———. [Ludovicus de Montesperato, pseud.]. *Vindiciae pacificationis Osnabruccensis et Monasteriensis, a declaratione nullitatis articulorum arrogantiae pontificum temerariae praeiudicialium, impudenter satis et audacter attentata ab Innocentio Papa X*. London: J. de Valetz, 1653.
Conring, Hermann, ed. *De controversiis Suecopolonicis sive de iure quod in Sueciam regi, ad Livoniam regno Poloniae, nullum competit . . . dissertatio*, by Hector Johannes Mithobius. Helmstedt: H. Müller, 1656. Reprint, *Opera*, 5:1060–83.
———. *De electione Urbani IIX et Innocentii X pontificum commentarii historici duo*, by an unnamed author. Trans. Franz-Heinrich Witzendorff. Helmstedt: H. Müller, 1651. Reprint, *Opera*, 5:664–725.
———. *De fractura cranii*, by Jacopo Berengario da Carpi. Leiden: Maire, 1629.
———. *De moribus Germanorum*, by Tacitus. Helmstedt: Lucius, 1635. Reprint, *Opera*, 5:253–355.
———. *De republica Romano-Germanica*, by Jacob Lampadius, with annotations by Hermann Conring. Helmstedt: H. Müller, 1671. Reprint, *Opera*, 2:22–237.
———. *De sacris nostri temporis controversiis libri duo*, by Georg Cassander and Georg Witzel. Helmstedt: H. Müller, 1659.
———. *Libri chirurgici duodecim de praecipuis artis chirurgicae controversiis*, by Thomas Fienus. Frankfurt: Goez, 1649.
———. *Observationum et paradoxorum chymiatricorum libri duo*, by Anton Günther Billich. Leiden: Maire, 1631.
———. *Observationum medicarum centuriae tres posthumae*, by Philipp Salmuth. Brunswick: Duncker, 1648.
———. *Politicorum libri octo*, by Aristotle. Trans. Obertus Giphanius. Helmstedt: Lucius, 1637.
———. *Politicorum libri superstites*, by Aristotle. Ed. Daniel Heinsius. Trans. Petrus Victorius. Helmstedt: H. Müller, 1656. Reprint, *Opera*, 3:491–723.
———. *Polonia*, by Simon Starovolski. Wolfenbüttel: Buno, 1656. Reprint, *Opera*, 6:523–54.

———. *Princeps*, by Niccolò Machiavelli. Based on the translation by Sylvester Telio. Helmstedt: H. Müller, 1660. Reprint, *Opera*, 2:973–1092.

———. *Tractatus . . . de curatione pestiferorum apostematum*, by Rolando Capelluti. Frankfurt: Zunner, 1642.

———. *Tractatus de republica Romano-Germanica*, by Jacob Lampadius. Leiden: Maire, 1634. Called *Tractatus de constitutione imperii Romano-Germanici* on a separate, engraved title page.

———. *Tractatus de republica Romano-Germanica*, by Jacob Lampadius. 2d ed. Helmstedt: Rixner, 1640.

———. *Tractatus de republica Romano-Germanica*, by Jacob Lampadius. 3d ed. Leiden: Maire, 1642.

———. *Via regia sive de controversis religionis capitibus conciliandis sententia*, by Georg Witzel. Helmstedt: H. Müller, 1650.

Corpus Iuris Canonici. See Friedberg.

Corpus Iuris Civilis. See Justinian.

Cunaeus, Petrus. *De republica Hebraeorum libri tres*. Leiden: Apud Ludovicum Elzevirium, 1617.

Dante Alighieri. *Monarchy*. Trans. Prue Shaw. Cambridge: Cambridge University Press, 1996.

Digest. See Justinian, *Digesta*.

Dionysius of Halicarnassus. *The Roman Antiquities of Dionysius of Halicarnassus*. Trans. Earnest Cary. 7 vols. Cambridge: Harvard University Press, 1937–50.

Erasmus. Letter to Dukes Frederick and George of Saxony, Antwerp, 5 June 1517. In *Opus Epistolarum Desiderii Erasmi Roterdami*, ed. Percy S. Allen, 1:578–86. Oxford: Clarendon Press, 1906. In English in *Correspondence of Erasmus: Letters 446 to 593, 1516 to 1517*, trans. Roger A. B. Mynors and Douglas F. S. Thomson, 373–83 (Toronto: University of Toronto Press, 1977).

Friedberg, Emil Albert, ed. *Corpus Iuris Canonici*. 2 vols. Leipzig: Tauchnitz, 1879–81.

Goldast von Haiminsfeld, Melchior. *Monarchia S.[acri] Romani Imperii, sive tractatus de iurisdictione imperiali seu regia et pontificia seu sacerdotali*. 3 vols. Hanau: Biermann, 1611–14.

Gratian. *Decretum Magistri Gratiani*. Ed. Emil A. Friedberg. *Corpus Iuris Canonici*, 1. Leipzig: Tauchnitz, 1879.

Gregory IX. *Liber Extra*. Ed. Emil A. Friedberg. *Corpus Iuris Canonici*, 2:1–928. Leipzig: Tauchnitz, 1881.

Grimmelshausen, Hans Jacob Christoffel von. *Simplicius Simplicissimus*. Trans. Hellmuth Weissenborn and Lesley Macdonald. London: Calder, 1964.

Grotius, Hugo. *Apologeticus eorum qui Hollandiae Westfrisiaeque et vicinis quibusdam nationibus ex legibus praefuerunt ante mutationem quae evenit anno MDCXVIII*. Paris: Buon, 1622.

———. *De iure belli ac pacis libri tres*. Ed. James Brown Scott. Trans. Francis W. Kelsey. 2 vols. Washington, DC: Carnegie Institution, 1913–25.

———. *De veritate religionis christianae*. Ed. Johann Christoph Koecher. 2 vols. Jena: Bailliar, 1726–27.

———. "De veritate religionis christianae, cum annotationibus Hermanni Conringii." In *Opera*, 5:1–105.

———. *Liber de antiquitate reipublicae Batavicae*. Leiden: Ex officina Plantiniana Raphelengij, 1610.
Gruber, Johann Daniel, ed. *Commercii epistolici Leibnitiani . . . tomus prodromus, qui totus est Boineburgicus*. 2 vols. Hannover: Apud fratres Schmidios, 1745.
Guicciardini, Francesco. *Storia d'Italia*. Ed. Silvana Seidel Menchi. 3 vols. Turin: Einaudi, 1971.
Hardt, Hermann von der. *Magnum oecumenicum Constantiense Concilium de universali Ecclesiae reformatione, unione, et fide*. 6 vols. Frankfurt: Genschius, 1697–1700.
Hippolithus a Lapide [Bogislaus Philipp von Chemnitz]. *Dissertatio de ratione status in imperio nostro Romano-Germanico*. N.p., 1640.
Hobbes, Thomas. *Leviathan*. Ed. Edwin Curley. Indianapolis: Hackett, 1994.
Institutes. See Justinian, *Institutiones*.
Jacchaeus, Gilbert. *Institutiones physicae*. 3d ed. Jena: Weidnerus, Boetnerus, 1619.
John of Salisbury. *Policraticus: Of the Frivolities of Courtiers and the Footprints of Philosophers*. Trans. Cary J. Nederman. Cambridge: Cambridge University Press, 1990.
John Quidort of Paris. *On Royal and Papal Power*. Trans. Arthur P. Monahan. New York: Columbia University Press, 1974.
Justinian. *Codex Iustinianus*. Ed. Paul Krüger. *Corpus Iuris Civilis*, 2. Berlin: Weidmann, 1877. Reprint, Berlin: Weidmann, 1967.
———. *Corpus Iuris Civilis in quatuor partes distinctum*. Ed. Dionysius Gothofredus. Frankfurt: Wustius, 1688.
———. *Digesta*. Ed. Theodor Mommsen. In *Corpus Iuris Civilis*, 1. Berlin: Weidmann, 1872. Reprint, Berlin: Weidmann, 1973. In English *The Digest of Justinian*, translation edited by Alan Watson, 4 vols. (Philadelphia: University of Pennsylvania Press, 1985).
———. *Digestum vetus*. 3 vols. Lyon: Apud Hugonem a Porta, 1550.
———. *Institutiones*. Ed. Paul Krüger. In *Corpus Iuris Civilis*, 1. Berlin: Weidmann, 1872. Reprint, Berlin: Weidmann, 1973. In English *Justinian's Institutes*, trans. Peter Birks and Grant McLeod (Ithaca, NY: Cornell University Press, 1987).
———. *Novellae*. Ed. Rudolf Schoell and Wilhelm Kroll. *Corpus Iuris Civilis*, 3. Berlin: Weidmann, 1895. Reprint, Berlin: Weidmann, 1972.
Lampadius, Jacob. *De iurisdictione, iuribus principum et statuum imperii*. Heidelberg: Geyder, 1620.
Lehmann, Christoph. *Chronica der freyen Reichs Statt Speyr*. Frankfurt: Hoffmann, 1612.
Liber Extra. See Gregory IX.
Locke, John. *A Letter concerning Toleration*. Ed. James Tully. Indianapolis: Hackett, 1983.
———. *Two Treatises of Government*. Ed. Peter Laslett. Cambridge: Cambridge University Press, 1988.
Luther, Martin. *An den christlichen Adel deutscher Nation von des christlichen Standes Besserung*. In *Werke: Kritische Gesammtausgabe*, 6:404–69. Weimar: Böhlau, 1888. In English *An Appeal to the Ruling Class of German Nationality as to the Amelioration of the State of Christendom*, in *Martin Luther: Selections from His Writings*, ed. John Dillenberger, 403–85 (New York: Doubleday, 1961).
———. "Epistola Lutheriana ad Leonem decimum summum pontificem." In *Werke: Kritische Gesammtausgabe*, 7:42–49. Weimar: Böhlau, 1897. In English "Letter to Pope Leo X," in *University of Chicago Readings in Western Civilization*, vol. 5, *The Renaissance*, ed. Eric Cochrane and Julius Kirshner, 325–33 (Chicago: University of Chicago Press, 1986).

Marsiglio of Padua. *Defensor minor.* In *Writings on the Empire,* trans. Cary J. Nederman. Cambridge: Cambridge University Press, 1993.

———. *De translatione imperii.* In *Writings on the Empire,* trans. Cary J. Nederman. Cambridge: Cambridge University Press, 1993.

Montaigne, Michel. "Of Books." Trans. Donald M. Frame. In *University of Chicago Readings in Western Civilization,* vol. 5, *The Renaissance,* ed. Eric Cochrane and Julius Kirshner, 296–308. Chicago: University of Chicago Press, 1986.

Novels. See Justinian, *Novellae.*

Ockham, William of. *Dialogus: Auszüge zur politischen Theorie.* Trans. Jürgen Miethke. Darmstadt: Wissenschaftliche Buchgesellschaft, 1992.

———. *A Short Discourse on the Tyrannical Government over Things Divine and Human, but Especially over the Empire and Those Subject to the Empire Usurped by Some Who Are Called Highest Pontiffs.* Trans. John Kilcullen and Arthur Stephen McGrade. Cambridge: Cambridge University Press, 1992.

Petronius. Trans. Michael Heseltine. Rev. by Eric H. Warmington. Cambridge: Harvard University Press, 1987.

Quaglioni, Diego. *Politica e diritto nel Trecento italiano: Il "De tyranno" di Bartolo da Sassoferrato, 1314–1357. Con l'edizione critica dei trattati "De Guelphis et Gebellinis," "De regimine civitatis" e "De tyranno."* Florence: Olschki, 1983.

Schmid, Melchior. "Vita Hermanni Conringii." In *Opera,* 1:xix–xxiv.

Seckler-Hudson, Catheryn. *Federal Textbook on Citizenship: Our Constitution and Government.* Rev. ed. Washington, DC: U.S. Government Printing Office, 1978.

Sophocles. *Oedipus the King, Oedipus at Colonus, Antigone.* Trans. David Grene. 2d ed. Chicago: University of Chicago Press, 1991.

Tractatus universi iuris, duce, et auspice Gregorio XIII pontifice maximo in unum congesti. 18 vols. in 25. Venice: Zilettus, 1584–86.

Trithemius, Johannes. *Compendium sive breviarium primi voluminis Annalium sive historiarum de origine regum et gentis Francorum.* Mainz: Schöffer, 1515.

SECONDARY SOURCES

Ahrens, Sabine. *Die alte Universität: Aus der Geschichte der Academia Julia zu Helmstedt.* Wolfenbüttel: Roco-Druck, 2000.

Allen, John William. *A History of Political Thought in the Sixteenth Century.* London: Methuen, 1928.

Allgemeine deutsche Biographie. Ed. Historische Commission bei der Königlichen Akademie der Wissenschaften. 56 vols. Leipzig: Duncker und Humblot, 1875–1912.

Althoff, Gerd. *Spielregeln der Politik im Mittelalter: Kommunikation in Frieden und Fehde.* Darmstadt: Wissenschaftliche Buchgesellschaft, 1997.

Ammermann, Monika. "Die gedruckten Briefe Conrings und die Brieftypologie des 17. Jahrhunderts." In *Beiträge,* 437–63.

Amsterdam University. *Humanists and Humanism in Amsterdam: Catalogue of an Exhibition in the Trippenhuis, Amsterdam, Aug. 20–25.* Amsterdam: The University, 1973.

Anderson, Benedict. *Imagined Communities: Reflections on the Origin and Spread of Nationalism.* 2d ed. New York: Verso, 1991.

Angermeier, Heinz. *Die Reichsreform, 1410–1555: Die Staatsproblematik in Deutschland zwischen Mittelalter und Gegenwart.* Munich: Beck, 1984.

Ankersmit, Frank R. *Narrative Logic: A Semantic Analysis of the Historian's Language.* The Hague: Nijhoff, 1983.
Appleby, Joyce Oldham, Lynn Avery Hunt, and Margaret C. Jacob. *Telling the Truth about History.* New York: Norton, 1994.
Aretin, Karl Otmar Freiherr von. *Das Alte Reich, 1648–1806.* 3 vols. Stuttgart: Klett-Cotta, 1993–97.
Armitage, David, ed. *Theories of Empire, 1450–1800.* Aldershot: Ashgate, 1998.
Austin, John Langshaw. *How to Do Things with Words.* 1955. Ed. J. O. Urmson and Marina Sbisà. 2d ed. Cambridge: Harvard University Press, 1975.
Ball, Terence, James Farr, and Russell Hanson, eds. *Political Innovation and Conceptual Change.* Cambridge: Cambridge University Press, 1989.
Baron, Hans. *The Crisis of the Italian Renaissance: Civic Humanism and Republican Liberty in an Age of Classicism and Tyranny.* 2d ed. Princeton, NJ: Princeton University Press, 1966.
Barraclough, Geoffrey. *Main Trends in History.* Ed. Michael Burns. Expanded ed. New York: Holmes and Meier, 1991.
———. *The Origins of Modern Germany.* Rev. ed. Oxford: Blackwell, 1947.
Bartlett, Robert. *The Making of Europe: Conquest, Colonization, and Cultural Change, 950–1350.* Princeton, NJ: Princeton University Press, 1993.
Bartolo da Sassoferrato: Studi e documenti per il VI centenario. Ed. Università degli studi di Perugia. 2 vols. Milan: Giuffrè, 1962.
Baszkiewicz, Jan. "Quelques remarques sur la conception de dominium mundi dans l'oeuvre de Bartolus." In *Bartolo da Sassoferrato: Studi e documenti per il VI centenario,* 2:7–25. Milan: Giuffrè, 1962.
Baumgart, Peter. "Die Gründung der Universität Helmstedt." In *Beiträge zu Problemen deutscher Universitätsgründungen der frühen Neuzeit,* ed. Peter Baumgart and Notker Hammerstein, 217–41. Nendeln: KTO Press, 1978.
Becker, Hans-Jürgen. "Diplomatik und Rechtsgeschichte: Conrings Tätigkeit in den Bella Diplomatica um das Recht der Königskrönung, um die Reichsfreiheit der Stadt Köln und um die Jurisdiktion über die Stadt Lindau." In *Beiträge,* 335–53.
Becker-Cantarino, Barbara. *Daniel Heinsius.* Boston: Twayne, 1978.
Behse, Arthur. *Die juristische Fakultät der Universität Helmstedt im Zeitalter des Naturrechts.* Wolfenbüttel: Zwissler, 1920.
Bellomo, Manlio. *L'Europa del diritto comune.* 5th ed. Rome: Cigno Galilei Edizioni di Arte e Scienze, 1991. In English *The Common Legal Past of Europe, 1000–1800,* trans. Lydia G. Cochrane (Washington, DC: Catholic University of America Press, 1995).
Benson, Robert L., and Giles Constable, eds. *Renaissance and Renewal in the Twelfth Century.* Cambridge: Harvard University Press, 1982.
Berger, Adolf. *Encyclopedic Dictionary of Roman Law.* Philadelphia: American Philosophical Society, 1953.
Bergson, Henri. *Essai sur les données immédiates de la conscience.* Paris: Alcan, 1889. In English *Time and Free Will: An Essay on the Immediate Data of Consciousness,* trans. Frank L. Pogson (New York: Macmillan, 1910).
Berlin, Isaiah. *Vico and Herder.* New York: Viking, 1976.
Berman, Harold J. *Law and Revolution: The Formation of the Western Legal Tradition.* Cambridge: Harvard University Press, 1983.

Bireley, Robert. *Religion and Politics in the Age of the Counterreformation: Emperor Ferdinand II, William Lamormaini, S.J., and the Formation of Imperial Policy.* Chapel Hill: University of North Carolina Press, 1981.
Black, Antony. *Guilds and Civil Society in European Political Thought from the Twelfth Century to the Present.* Ithaca, NY: Cornell University Press, 1984.
Bloch, Marc. *The Historian's Craft.* Trans. Peter Putnam. New York: Knopf, 1953.
Blockmans, Wim, and Jean-Philippe Genet, eds. *The Origins of the Modern State in Europe, Twelfth to Eighteenth Centuries.* 7 vols. Oxford: Clarendon Press, 1995–2000.
Blok, Frans Felix. *Caspar Barlaeus: From the Correspondence of a Melancholic.* Trans. H. S. Lake and D. A. S. Reid. Assen: Van Gorcum, 1976.
Blumenberg, Hans. *Die Legitimität der Neuzeit.* 2d ed. 3 vols. Frankfurt: Suhrkamp, 1973–76. In English *The Legitimacy of the Modern Age,* trans. Robert M. Wallace (Cambridge: MIT Press, 1983).
Bonnell, Victoria E., and Lynn Avery Hunt, eds. *Beyond the Cultural Turn: New Directions in the Study of Society and Culture.* Berkeley: University of California Press, 1999.
Bonney, Richard, ed. *Economic Systems and State Finance.* Oxford: Clarendon Press, 1995.
Bosbach, Franz. *Monarchia universalis: Ein politischer Leitbegriff der frühen Neuzeit.* Göttingen: Vandenhoeck und Ruprecht, 1988.
Bossy, John, ed. *Disputes and Settlements: Law and Human Relations in the West.* Cambridge: Cambridge University Press, 1983.
Bottigheimer, Christoph. *Zwischen Polemik und Irenik: Die Theologie der einen Kirche bei Georg Calixt.* Münster: Lit, 1996.
Boyer, John, and Julius Kirshner, eds. *Politics and Society in the Holy Roman Empire, 1500–1806.* Chicago: University of Chicago Press, 1986.
Brady, Thomas A., Jr., Heiko A. Oberman, and James D. Tracy, eds. *Handbook of European History, 1400–1600: Late Middle Ages, Renaissance, and Reformation.* 2 vols. Leiden: Brill, 1994–95.
Brann, Noel L. *The Abbot Trithemius, 1462–1516: The Renaissance of Monastic Humanism.* Leiden: Brill, 1981.
Breisach, Ernst. *Historiography: Ancient, Medieval, and Modern.* 2d ed. Chicago: University of Chicago Press, 1994.
Bresslau, Harry. "Hermann Conring." *Allgemeine Deutsche Biographie* 4 (1876): 446–51.
Brunner, Otto. *Land und Herrschaft: Grundfragen der territorialen Verfassungsgeschichte Österreichs im Mittelalter.* 5th ed. Vienna: Rohrer, 1965. In English *Land and Lordship: Structures of Governance in Medieval Austria,* trans. Howard Kaminsky and James Van Horn Melton (Philadelphia: University of Pennsylvania Press, 1992).
Brunner, Otto, Werner Conze, and Reinhart Koselleck, eds. *Geschichtliche Grundbegriffe: Historisches Lexikon zur politisch-sozialen Sprache in Deutschland.* 7 vols. Stuttgart: Klett, 1972–92.
Brunt, Peter A. "'Laus Imperii.'" In *Roman Imperial Themes,* by Peter A. Brunt, 288–323. Oxford: Clarendon Press, 1990.
Bryce, James. *The Holy Roman Empire.* Rev. ed. New York: Macmillan, 1904. Reprint, New York: Schocken Books, 1961.
Buckland, William Warwick. *A Textbook of Roman Law from Augustus to Justinian.* 3d ed., rev. by Peter Stein. Cambridge: Cambridge University Press, 1963.
Burckhardt, Jacob. *Die Kultur der Renaissance in Italien.* 1860. Ed. Horst Günther.

Frankfurt am Main: Deutscher Klassiker Verlag, 1989. In English *The Civilization of the Renaissance in Italy*, trans. Samuel George Chetwynd Middlemore (Harmondsworth: Penguin Books, 1990).

Burke, Peter. "Tacitism, Scepticism, and Reason of State." In *Cambridge History of Political Thought, 1450–1700*, ed. James H. Burns and Mark Goldie, 479–98. Cambridge: Cambridge University Press, 1991.

———. *Vico*. Oxford: Oxford University Press, 1985.

Burns, James H. Introduction to *Cambridge History of Medieval Political Thought, c. 350–c. 1450*, ed. James H. Burns, 1–8. Cambridge: Cambridge University Press, 1988.

Burns, James H., ed. *Cambridge History of Medieval Political Thought, c. 350–c. 1450*. Cambridge: Cambridge University Press, 1988.

Burns, James H., and Mark Goldie, eds. *Cambridge History of Political Thought, 1450–1700*. Cambridge: Cambridge University Press, 1991.

Bylebyl, Jerome J., ed. *William Harvey and His Age: The Professional and Social Context of the Discovery of the Circulation*. Baltimore: Johns Hopkins University Press, 1979.

Calasso, Francesco. "Bartolo da Sassoferrato." In *Dizionario biografico degli Italiani*, 6:5–34. Rome: Istituto della Enciclopedia Italiana, 1960–. Vol. 6 published in 1965.

———. *I glossatori e la teoria della sovranità*. 3d ed. Milan: Giuffrè, 1957.

Canning, Joseph. *A History of Medieval Political Thought, 300–1450*. London: Routledge, 1996.

———. *The Political Thought of Baldus de Ubaldis*. Cambridge: Cambridge University Press, 1987.

Cantor, Norman F. *Inventing the Middle Ages: The Lives, Works, and Ideas of the Great Medievalists of the Twentieth Century*. New York: W. Morrow, 1991.

Carlyle, Alexander J. "The Political Theory of the Roman Lawyers." In *A History of Mediaeval Political Theory in the West*, by Robert W. Carlyle and Alexander J. Carlyle, 1:33–79. Edinburgh: Blackwood, 1903.

Carlyle, Robert W., and Alexander J. Carlyle. *A History of Mediaeval Political Theory in the West*. 6 vols. Edinburgh: Blackwood, 1903–36.

Carr, Edward Hallett. *What Is History?* London: Macmillan, 1961.

Carreyre, Jean. "Pithou." In *Dictionnnaire de théologie catholique*, ed. Alfred Vacant and Eugène Mangenot, 12:2233–38. Paris: Letouzey et Ané, 1903–50. Vol. 12 published in 1935.

Casamassima, Emanuele. *Iter Germanicum*. Vol. 1 of *Codices operum Bartoli a Saxoferrato recensiti*. Florence: Olschki, 1971.

Cassens, Johann-Tönjes, and Heinrich Schmidt. *Hermann Conring, 1606–1681: Ein ostfriesischer Gelehrter von europäischem Rang*. Norden: Soltau, 1982.

Cavallar, Osvaldo. *Francesco Guicciardini, giurista: I ricordi degli onorari*. Milan: Giuffrè, 1991.

Cavallar, Osvaldo, Susanne Degenring, and Julius Kirshner. *A Grammar of Signs: Bartolo da Sassoferrato's Tract on Insignia and Coats of Arms*. Berkeley, CA: Robbins Collection, 1994.

Cavina, Marco. *"Imperator Romanorum triplici corona coronatur": Studi sull'incoronazione imperiale nella scienza giuridica fra Tre e Cinquecento*. Milan: Giuffrè, 1991.

Chakrabarty, Dipesh. *Provincializing Europe: Postcolonial Thought and Historical Difference*. Princeton, NJ: Princeton University Press, 2000.

Chickering, Roger. *Karl Lamprecht: A German Academic Life, 1856–1915.* Atlantic Highlands, NJ: Humanities Press, 1993.
Chittolini, Giorgio, Anthony Molho, and Pierangelo Schiera, eds. *Origini dello stato: Processi di formazione statale in Italia fra medioevo ed età moderna.* Bologna: Il Mulino, 1994. In English, with somewhat different contents, *The Origins of the State in Italy, 1300–1600,* ed. Julius Kirshner (Chicago: University of Chicago Press, 1995.)
Cochrane, Eric. *Historians and Historiography in the Italian Renaissance.* Chicago: University of Chicago Press, 1981.
Cohn, Gustav. "Ludwig XIV. als Beschützer der Gelehrten." *Historische Zeitschrift* 23 (1870): 1–16.
Coing, Helmut. "Bartolus und der usus modernus pandectarum in Deutschland." In *Bartolo da Sassoferrato: Studi e documenti per il VI centenario,* 1:23–45. Milan: Giuffrè, 1962. Reprinted in *Gesammelte Aufsätze zu Rechtsgeschichte, Rechtsphilosophie und Zivilrecht, 1947–1975,* ed. Dieter Simon, 1:277–96 (Frankfurt: Klostermann, 1982).
———. "Zur Geschichte des Begriffs 'Subjektives Recht.'" In *Gesammelte Aufsätze zu Rechtsgeschichte, Rechtsphilosophie und Zivilrecht, 1947–1975,* ed. Dieter Simon, 1:241–62. Frankfurt: Klostermann, 1982.
Collingwood, Robin George. *The Idea of History.* Ed. Jan van der Dussen. Rev. ed. Oxford: Clarendon Press, 1994.
Cortese, Ennio. *La norma giuridica: Spunti teorici nel diritto comune classico.* 2 vols. Milan: Giuffrè, 1962–64.
Costa, Pietro. *Iurisdictio: Semantica del potere politico nella pubblicistica medievale, 1100–1433.* Milan: Giuffrè, 1969.
Courtenay, William J. "Nominalism and Late Medieval Religion." In *The Pursuit of Holiness in Late Medieval and Renaissance Religion,* ed. Charles Trinkaus and Heiko Oberman, 26–59. Leiden: Brill, 1974.
Danto, Arthur C. *Narration and Knowledge: Including the Integral Text of Analytical Philosophy of History.* New York: Columbia University Press, 1985.
David, Marcel. "Le contenu de l'hégémonie impériale dans la doctrine de Bartole." In *Bartolo da Sassoferrato: Studi e documenti per il VI centenario,* 2:199–216. Milan: Giuffrè, 1962.
Debus, Allen G. *The Chemical Philosophy: Paracelsian Science and Medicine in the Sixteenth and Seventeenth Centuries.* 2 vols. New York: Science History Publications, 1977.
———. *The French Paracelsians: The Chemical Challenge to Medical and Scientific Tradition in Early Modern France.* Cambridge: Cambridge University Press, 1991.
Deeters, Walter. *Kleine Geschichte Ostfrieslands.* Leer: Schuster, 1985.
Denton, Jeffrey H. *Robert Winchelsey and the Crown, 1294–1313: A Study in the Defense of Ecclesiastical Liberty.* Cambridge: Cambridge University Press, 1980.
d'Entrèves, Alexander Passerin. *Natural Law: An Introduction to Legal Philosophy.* London: Hutchinson, 1951.
Deutsches biographisches Archiv. Ed. Bernhard Fabian. Munich: Saur, 1982–84.
Dickmann, Fritz. *Der Westfälische Frieden.* 4th ed., rev. by Konrad Repgen. Münster: Aschendorff, 1977.
Dietrich, Richard. "Jacobus Lampadius: Seine Bedeutung für die deutsche Verfassungsgeschichte und Staatstheorie." In *Forschungen zu Staat und Verfassung: Festgabe für Fritz Hartung,* ed. Richard Dietrich and Gerhard Oestreich, 163–85. Berlin: Duncker und Humblot, 1958.

Dilthey, Wilhelm. *Weltanschauung und Analyse des Menschen seit Renaissance und Reformation*. Leipzig: Teubner, 1914.

Doering, Detlef. *Pufendorf Studien: Beiträge zur Biographie Samuel von Pufendorfs und seiner Entwicklung als Historiker und theologischer Schriftsteller*. Berlin: Duncker und Humblot, 1992.

Dowdal, H. C. "The Word 'State.'" *Law Quarterly Review* 39 (1923): 98–125.

Dreitzel, Horst. "Aristoteles' Politik im Denken Hermann Conrings." In *Categorie del reale e storiographia: Aspetti di continuità e trasformazione nell' Europa moderna*, ed. F. Fagiani and G. Valera, 33–59. Milan: Franco Angeli, 1986.

———. "Hermann Conring und die politische Wissenschaft seiner Zeit." In *Beiträge*, 135–72.

———. *Monarchiebegriffe in der Fürstengesellschaft: Semantik und Theorie der Einherrschaft in Deutschland von der Reformation bis zum Vormärz*. 2 vols. Cologne: Böhlau, 1991.

———. *Protestantischer Absolutismus und absoluter Staat: Die "Politica" des Henning Arnisaeus, ca. 1575–1636*. Wiesbaden: Steiner, 1970.

Droste, Heiko. "Hermann Conring und Schweden: Eine vielschichtige Beziehung." *Ius Commune* 26 (1999): 337–62.

Droysen, Johann Gustav. *Historik: Rekonstruktion der ersten vollständigen Fassung der Vorlesungen (1857), Grundriss der Historik in der ersten handschriftlichen (1857/1858) und in der letzten gedruckten Fassung (1882)*. Ed. Peter Leyh. Stuttgart–Bad Cannstatt: Frommann-Holzboog, 1977. In English *Outline of the Principles of History*, trans. E. Benjamin Andrews (Boston: Ginn, 1893).

Du Boulay, Francis Robin Houssemayne. *Germany in the Later Middle Ages*. New York: St. Martin's, 1983.

Duchhardt, Heinz. "Et Germani eligunt et Germanus eligendus: Die Zulassung ausländischer Fürsten zum Kaiseramt im Jus Publicum des 17./18. Jahrhunderts." *Zeitschrift der Savigny-Stiftung für Rechtsgeschichte, Germanistische Abteilung* 97 (1980): 232–53.

Dufour, Alfred. "Pufendorf." In *Cambridge History of Political Thought, 1450–1700*, ed. James H. Burns and Mark Goldie, 561–88. Cambridge: Cambridge University Press, 1991.

Dunin-Borkowski, Stanislaus von. "Aus der Briefmappe eines berühmten Konvertiten des 17. Jahrhunderts." *Stimmen der Zeit* 10 (1922–23): 132–47.

Duverger, Maurice, ed. *Le concept d'empire*. Paris: Presses Universitaires de France, 1980.

Elias, Norbert. *Über den Prozess der Zivilisation: Soziogenetische und psychogenetische Untersuchungen*. 2 vols. Basel: Haus zum Falken, 1939. In English *The Civilizing Process*, trans. Edmund Jephcott (Oxford: Blackwell, 1994).

Engelmann, Woldemar. *Die Wiedergeburt der Rechtskultur in Italien durch die wissenschaftliche Lehre*. Leipzig: Koehler, 1938.

Ercole, Francesco. *Impero e papato nel diritto pubblico italiano del Rinascimento sec. XIV–XV*. Bologna: Presso la R. Deputazione di storia patria, 1911.

Etter, Else-Lilly. *Tacitus in der Geistesgeschichte des 16. und 17. Jahrhunderts*. Basel: Helbing und Lichtenhahn, 1966.

Evans, Robert John Weston. "German Universities after the Thirty Years War." *History of Universities* 1 (1981): 169–90.

———. *Rudolf II and His World: A Study in Intellectual History, 1576–1612*. Oxford: Clarendon Press, 1973.

Fasolt, Constantin. "Conring on History." In *Supplementum Festivum: Studies in Honor of*

Paul Oskar Kristeller, ed. James Hankins, John Monfasani, and Frederick Purnell, 563–87. Binghamton, NY: Medieval and Renaissance Texts and Studies, 1987.

———. "From Helmstedt via Mainz to Paris: Hermann Conring and Hugues de Lionne." In *Proceedings of the Annual Meeting of the Western Society for French History,* vol. 16, ed. Gordon C. Bond, 126–34. Auburn, AL: Western Society for French History, 1989.

———. "A Question of Right: Hermann Conring's *New Discourse on the Roman-German Emperor.*" *Sixteenth Century Journal* 28 (1997): 739–58.

———. "Sovereignty and Heresy." In *Infinite Boundaries: Order, Disorder, and Reorder in Early Modern German Culture,* ed. Max Reinhart, 381–91. Kirksville, MO: Sixteenth Century Essays and Studies, 1998.

———. "Visions of Order in the Canonists and Civilians." In *Handbook of European History, 1400–1600,* ed. Thomas A. Brady Jr., Heiko Oberman, and James Tracy, 2:31–59. Leiden: Brill, 1995.

Felberg, Paul. *Conrings Anteil am politischen Leben seiner Zeit.* Trier: Paulinus, 1931.

Felsing, Ferdinand. *Die Statistik als Methode der politischen Ökonomie im 17. und 18. Jahrhundert.* Borna: Noske, 1930.

Fernández-Santamaría, J. A. *Reason of State and Statecraft in Spanish Political Thought, 1595–1640.* Lanham, MD: University Press of America, 1983.

Feyerabend, Paul. "Progress in Philosophy, the Sciences, and the Arts." In *Farewell to Reason,* by Paul Feyerabend, 143–61. New York: Verso, 1987.

Figgis, John Neville. *Studies of Political Thought from Gerson to Grotius, 1414–1625.* 2d ed. Cambridge: Cambridge University Press, 1916.

Folz, Robert. *L'idée d'empire en Occident du Ve au XIVe siècle.* Paris: Aubier, 1953. In English *The Concept of Empire in Western Europe from the Fifth to the Fourteenth Century,* trans. Sheila Ann Ogilvie (London: Edward Arnold, 1969).

Foucault, Michel. *Les mots et les choses: Une archéologie des sciences humaines.* Paris: Gallimard, 1966. In English *The Order of Things: An Archaeology of the Human Sciences* (New York: Pantheon Books, 1971).

Franklin, Julian H. *Jean Bodin and the Rise of Absolutist Theory.* Cambridge: Cambridge University Press, 1973.

———. *Jean Bodin and the Sixteenth-Century Revolution in the Methodology of Law and History.* New York: Columbia University Press, 1963.

———. "Sovereignty and the Mixed Constitution: Bodin and His Critics." In *Cambridge History of Political Thought, 1450–1700,* ed. James H. Burns and Mark Goldie, 298–328. Cambridge: Cambridge University Press, 1991.

Freedman, Paul, and Gabrielle Spiegel. "Medievalisms Old and New: The Rediscovery of Alterity in North American Medieval Studies." *American Historical Review* 103 (1998): 677–704.

French, Roger Kenneth. *William Harvey's Natural Philosophy.* Cambridge: Cambridge University Press, 1994.

Fried, Johannes. *Der Weg in die Geschichte: Die Ursprünge Deutschlands bis 1024.* Berlin: Propyläen Verlag, 1994.

Fueter, Eduard. *Geschichte der neueren Historiographie.* Munich: Oldenbourg, 1911.

Fuhrmann, Horst. *Germany in the High Middle Ages, c. 1050–1200.* Trans. Timothy Reuter. Cambridge: Cambridge University Press, 1986.

Gadamer, Hans Georg. *Wahrheit und Methode: Grundzüge einer philosophischen Hermeneutik.*

3d ed. Tübingen: Mohr, 1972. In English *Truth and Method*, trans. and rev. by Joel Weinsheimer and Donald G. Marshall, 2d rev. ed. (New York: Crossroad, 1989).

Gagnér, Sten. *Studien zur Ideengeschichte der Gesetzgebung*. Uppsala: Almqvist och Wiksell, 1960.

García y García, Antonio. *Iter Hispanicum*. Vol. 2 of *Codices operum Bartoli a Saxoferrato recensiti*. Florence: Olschki, 1973.

Gaudemet, Jean. "'Ius' et 'Leges.'" *Iura* 1 (1950): 223–52.

Gellner, Ernest. *Nations and Nationalism*. Ithaca, NY: Cornell University Press, 1983.

Genet, Jean-Philippe, ed. *L'état moderne, genèse: Bilans et perspectives*. Paris: Editions du Centre National de la Recherche Scientifique, 1990.

Genzmer, Erich. "Die iustinianische Kodifikation und die Glossatoren." In *Atti del congresso internazionale di diritto Romano: Bologna e Roma, xvii–xxvii aprile MCMXXXIII*, 1:345–430. Pavia: Fusi, 1934–35.

———. *Mittelalterliches Rechtsdenken*. Hamburg: Stiftung Europa-Kolleg, 1961.

Gierke, Otto Friedrich von. *Johannes Althusius und die Entwicklung der naturrechtlichen Staatstheorien: Zugleich ein Beitrag zur Geschichte der Rechtssystematik*. 2d ed. Breslau: M. und M. Marcus, 1902. In English *The Development of Political Theory*, trans. Bernard Freyd (New York: Norton, 1939).

Giesey, Ralph E. *Cérémonial et puissance souveraine: France, XVe–XVIIe siècles*. Paris: Colin, 1987.

Gilbert, Felix. *Machiavelli and Guicciardini: Politics and History in Sixteenth-Century Florence*. Princeton, NJ: Princeton University Press, 1965.

Gilmore, Myron P. *Argument from Roman Law in Political Thought, 1200–1600*. Cambridge: Harvard University Press, 1941.

Ginzburg, Carlo. *Il nicodemismo: Simulazione e dissimulazione religiosa nell'Europa del '500*. Torino: Einaudi, 1970.

Goez, Werner. *Translatio Imperii: Ein Beitrag zur Geschichte des Geschichtsdenkens und der politischen Theorien im Mittelalter und in der frühen Neuzeit*. Tübingen: Mohr, 1958.

Goldschlag, Nathan. *Beiträge zur politischen und publizistischen Thätigkeit Herman [sic] Conrings*. Berlin: Winser, 1884.

Grafton, Anthony. *Defenders of the Text: The Traditions of Scholarship in an Age of Science, 1450–1800*. Cambridge: Harvard University Press, 1991.

———. "Humanism and Political Theory." In *Cambridge History of Political Thought, 1450–1700*, ed. James H. Burns and Mark Goldie, 9–29. Cambridge: Cambridge University Press, 1991.

———. *Joseph Scaliger: A Study in the History of Classical Scholarship*. 2 vols. Oxford: Clarendon Press, 1983–93.

Gross, Hanns. *Empire and Sovereignty: A History of the Public Law Literature in the Holy Roman Empire, 1599–1804*. Chicago: University of Chicago Press, 1975.

———. "The Holy Roman Empire in Modern Times: Constitutional Reality and Legal Theory." In *The Old Reich: Essays on German Political Institutions, 1495–1806*, ed. James A. Vann and Steven W. Rowan, 1–29. Brussels: Librairie Encyclopédique, 1974.

Grossi, Paolo. *Il dominio e le cose: Percezioni medievali e moderne dei diritti reali*. Milan: Giuffrè, 1992.

———. "'Gradus in dominio': Zasius e la teorica del dominio diviso." *Quaderni fiorentini per la storia del pensiero giuridico moderno* 14 (1985): 373–99.

Habermas, Jürgen. *Strukturwandel der Öffentlichkeit: Untersuchungen zu einer Kategorie der*

bürgerlichen Gesellschaft. Neuwied: Luchterhand, 1962. In English *The Structural Transformation of the Public Sphere: An Inquiry into a Category of Bourgeois Society*, trans. Thomas Burger (Cambridge: MIT Press, 1989).
Hale, John Rigby. *War and Society in Renaissance Europe, 1450–1620*. Baltimore: Johns Hopkins University Press, 1986.
Hamilton, Bernice. *Political Thought in Sixteenth-Century Spain: A Study of the Political Ideas of Vitoria, De Soto, Suarez, and Molina*. Oxford: Clarendon Press, 1963.
Hammerstein, Notker. "Die Historie bei Conring." In *Beiträge*, 217–36.

———. *Jus und Historie: Ein Beitrag zur Geschichte des historischen Denkens an deutschen Universitäten im späten 17. und 18. Jahrhundert*. Göttingen: Vandenhoeck und Ruprecht, 1972.

———. "Das Römische am Heiligen Römischen Reich Deutscher Nation in der Lehre der Reichs-Publicisten." *Zeitschrift der Savigny-Stiftung für Rechtsgeschichte, Germanistische Abteilung* 100 (1983): 119–44.
Hankins, James. "The Baron Thesis after 40 Years." *Journal of the History of Ideas* 56 (1995): 309–38.
Hankins, James, John Monfasani, and Frederick Purnell Jr., eds. *Supplementum Festivum: Studies in Honor of Paul Oskar Kristeller*. Binghamton, NY: Medieval and Renaissance Texts and Studies, 1987.
Haskins, Charles Homer. *The Renaissance of the Twelfth Century*. Cambridge: Harvard University Press, 1927.
Hassinger, Erich. *Empirisch-rationaler Historismus: Seine Ausbildung in der Literatur Westeuropas von Guicciardini bis Saint-Evremond*. Bern: Francke, 1978.

———. *Das Werden des neuzeitlichen Europa, 1300–1600*. Brunswick: Westermann, 1959.
Haude, Sigrun. *In the Shadow of "Savage Wolves": Anabaptist Münster and the German Reformation during the 1530s*. Boston: Humanities Press, 2000.
Haverkamp, Alfred. *Medieval Germany, 1056–1273*. Trans. Helga Braun and Richard Mortimer. 2d ed. Oxford: Oxford University Press, 1992.
Headley, John M. *The Emperor and His Chancellor: A Study of the Imperial Chancellery under Gattinara*. Cambridge: Cambridge University Press, 1983.

———. "The Habsburg World Empire and the Revival of Ghibellinism." *Medieval and Renaissance Studies* 7 (1975): 93–127.
Heesakkers, C. L. "Foundation and Early Development of the Athenaeum Illustre at Amsterdam." *Lias* 9 (1982): 3–18.
Heidegger, Martin. *Sein und Zeit: Erste Hälfte*. Halle: Niemeyer, 1927. In English *Being and Time: A Translation of Sein und Zeit*, trans. Joan Stambaugh (Albany: State University of New York Press, 1996).

———. "Wissenschaft und Besinnung." In *Vorträge und Aufsätze*, by Martin Heidegger, 41–66. Pfullingen: Neske, 1954.
Helmholz, Richard H. *Fundamental Human Rights in Medieval Law*. Chicago: Law School of the University of Chicago, 2001.

———. "Legal Formalism, Substantive Policy, and the Creation of a Canon Law of Prescription." In *Prescriptive Formality and Normative Rationality in Modern Legal Systems: Festschrift for Robert S. Summers*, ed. Werner Krawietz, Neil MacCormick, and Georg Henrik von Wright, 265–83. Berlin: Duncker und Humblot, 1994.
Hempel, Carl Gustav. "The Function of General Laws in History." *Journal of Philosophy* 39 (1942): 35–48.

Henke, Ernst Ludwig Theodor. *Georg Calixtus und seine Zeit.* 2 vols. Halle: Buchhandlung des Waisenhauses, 1853–60.
Herberger, Patricia. "Die ungedruckten Briefe Hermann Conrings." In *Beiträge,* 471–534.
Herberger, Patricia, and Michael Stolleis. *Hermann Conring, 1606–1681: Ein Gelehrter der Universität Helmstedt.* Wolfenbüttel: Herzog August Bibliothek, 1981.
Herzog August Bibliothek. *Sammler, Fürst, Gelehrter: Herzog August zu Braunschweig und Lüneburg, 1579–1666.* Brunswick: Limbach, 1979.
Herzog, Tamar. *Defining Nations: Immigrants and Citizens in Early Modern Spain and Spanish America.* New Haven, CT: Yale University Press, 2003.
Hinsley, Francis Harry. *Sovereignty.* 2d ed. Cambridge: Cambridge University Press, 1986.
Hobart, Michael E., and Zachary S. Schiffman. *Information Ages: Literacy, Numeracy, and the Computer Revolution.* Baltimore: Johns Hopkins University Press, 1998.
Hoelscher, Lucian. *Die Entdeckung der Zukunft.* Frankfurt: Fischer, 1999.
Hoffmann, Philip T., and Kathryn Norberg, eds. *Fiscal Crises, Liberty, and Representative Government, 1450–1789.* Stanford, CA: Stanford University Press, 1994.
Hofmann, Hasso. "Hugo Grotius." In *Staatsdenker in der frühen Neuzeit,* 3d ed., ed. Michael Stolleis, 52–77. Munich: Beck, 1995.
Honoré, Tony. *Ulpian.* Oxford: Clarendon Press, 1982.
Hont, Istvan. "The Language of Sociability and Commerce: Samuel Pufendorf and the Theoretical Foundations of the 'Four-Stages Theory.'" In *The Languages of Political Theory in Early-Modern Europe,* ed. Anthony Pagden, 253–76. Cambridge: Cambridge University Press, 1987.
Horst, Koert van der. *Inventaire de la correspondance de Caspar Barlaeus, 1602–1648.* Assen: Van Gorcum, 1978.
Hughes, H. Stuart. *History as Art and as Science: Twin Vistas on the Past.* New York: Harper and Row, 1964.
Hunt, Lynn, ed. *The New Cultural History.* Berkeley: University of California Press, 1989.
Huppert, George. *The Idea of Perfect History: Historical Erudition and Historical Philosophy in Renaissance France.* Urbana: University of Illinois Press, 1970.
Iggers, Georg G. *The German Conception of History: The National Tradition of Historical Thought from Herder to the Present.* Rev. ed. Middletown, CT: Wesleyan University Press, 1983.
———. *New Directions in European Historiography.* Rev. ed. Middletown, CT: Wesleyan University Press, 1984.
Jenkins, Keith, ed. *The Postmodern History Reader.* London: Routledge, 1997.
Joachimsen, Paul. *Geschichtsauffassung und Geschichtsschreibung in Deutschland unter dem Einfluss des Humanismus.* Leipzig: Teubner, 1910.
Junkers, Karl. *Der Streit zwischen Kurstaat und Stadt Köln am Vorabend des Holländischen Krieges, 1667–1672.* Düsseldorf: Nolte, 1935.
Jürgensmeier, Friedhelm. *Johann Philipp von Schönborn, 1605–1673, und die Römische Kurie: Ein Beitrag zur Kirchengeschichte des 17. Jahrhunderts.* Mainz: Gesellschaft für Mittelrheinische Kirchengeschichte, 1977.
Kaufmann, Thomas DaCosta. *Court, Cloister, and City: The Art and Culture of Central Europe, 1450–1800.* Chicago: University of Chicago Press, 1995.
———. *The Mastery of Nature: Aspects of Art, Science, and Humanism in the Renaissance.* Princeton, NJ: Princeton University Press, 1993.

Keen, Maurice H. "The Political Thought of the Fourteenth-Century Civilians." In *Trends in Medieval Political Thought,* ed. Beryl Smalley, 105–26. Oxford: Blackwell, 1965.

Keller, Hagen. *Zwischen regionaler Begrenzung und universalem Horizont: Deutschland im Imperium der Salier und Staufer, 1024 bis 1250.* Berlin: Propyläen Verlag, 1986.

Kelley, Donald R. "Civil Science in the Renaissance: Jurisprudence in the French Manner." *History of European Ideas* 2 (1981): 261–76.

———. "Civil Science in the Renaissance: Jurisprudence Italian Style." *Historical Journal* 22 (1979): 777–94.

———. *Foundations of Modern Historical Scholarship: Language, Law, and History in the French Renaissance.* New York: Columbia University Press, 1970.

———. "Law." In *Cambridge History of Political Thought, 1450–1700,* ed. James H. Burns and Mark Goldie, 66–94. Cambridge: Cambridge University Press, 1991.

Kelley, Donald R., and David Harris Sacks, eds. *The Historical Imagination in Early Modern Britain: History, Rhetoric, and Fiction, 1500–1800.* Cambridge: Cambridge University Press, 1997.

Kelly, William Ashford. *Hermann Conring, 1606–1681: A Study in Versatility.* East Linton, Scotland: Cat's Whiskers Press, 1993.

Kelly, William Ashford, and Michael Stolleis. "Hermann Conring: Gedruckte Werke, 1627–1751." In *Beiträge,* 535–72.

Keohane, Nannerl O. *Philosophy and the State in France: The Renaissance to the Enlightenment.* Princeton, NJ: Princeton University Press, 1980.

Kern, Fritz. *Gottesgnadentum und Widerstandsrecht im früheren Mittelalter: Zur Entwicklungsgeschichte der Monarchie.* Leipzig: Koehler, 1914. In English *Kingship and Law in the Middle Ages,* trans. Stanley B. Chrimes, 2 vols. (Oxford: Blackwell, 1939).

———. "Recht und Verfassung im Mittelalter." *Historische Zeitschrift* 120 (1919): 1–79.

Kingdon, Robert M. "International Calvinism." In *Handbook of European History, 1400–1600,* ed. Thomas A. Brady Jr., Heiko A. Oberman, and James D. Tracy, 2:229–47. Leiden: Brill, 1995.

Kirshner, Julius. "'Civitas sibi faciat civem': Bartolus of Sassoferrato's Doctrine on the Making of a Citizen." *Speculum* 48 (1973): 694–713.

Kirshner, Julius, ed. *The Origins of the State in Italy, 1300–1600.* Chicago: University of Chicago Press, 1995.

Kisch, Guido. *Erasmus und die Jurisprudenz seiner Zeit: Studien zum humanistischen Rechtsdenken.* Basel: Helbing und Lichtenhahn, 1960.

———. *Humanismus und Jurisprudenz: Der Kampf zwischen mos italicus und mos gallicus an der Universität Basel.* Basel: Helbing und Lichtenhahn, 1955.

Kisky, Wilhelm. "Die Akten der Abteilung 'Köln contra Köln': Verhältnis der Stadt zum Erzbischof." *Mitteilungen aus dem Stadtarchiv von Köln* 34 (1914): 118–23.

Klempt, Adalbert. *Die Säkularisierung der universalhistorischen Auffassung.* Göttingen: Musterschmidt, 1960.

Knoll, Robert. *Hermann Conring als Historiker.* Rostock: Universitäts-Buchdruckerei von Adler's Erben, 1889.

Koenigsberger, Helmut G., ed. *Republiken und Republikanismus im Europa der frühen Neuzeit.* Munich: Oldenbourg, 1988.

Kolakowski, Leszek. *Main Currents of Marxism: Its Rise, Growth, and Dissolution.* Trans. Paul S. Falla. 3 vols. Oxford: Oxford University Press, 1978.

Koldewey, Friedrich. *Geschichte der klassischen Philologie auf der Universität Helmstedt.* Brunswick: Vieweg, 1895.
Koschaker, Paul. *Europa und das Römische Recht.* 4th ed. Munich: Beck, 1966.
Koselleck, Reinhart. *Kritik und Krise: Eine Studie zur Pathogenese der bürgerlichen Welt.* Freiburg: Alber, 1959. Trans. into English by an uncredited translator as *Critique and Crisis: Enlightenment and the Pathogenesis of Modern Society* (Cambridge: MIT Press, 1988).
———. *Vergangene Zukunft: Zur Semantik geschichtlicher Zeiten.* Frankfurt: Suhrkamp, 1979. In English *Futures Past: On the Semantics of Historical Time,* trans. Keith Tribe (Cambridge: MIT Press, 1985).
———. "Vergangene Zukunft der frühen Neuzeit." In *Vergangene Zukunft: Zur Semantik geschichtlicher Zeiten,* by Reinhart Koselleck, 17–37. Frankfurt am Main: Suhrkamp, 1979. In English "Modernity and the Planes of History," in *Futures Past: On the Semantics of Historical Time,* trans. Keith Tribe, 3–20 (Cambridge: MIT Press, 1985).
Koselleck, Reinhart, Werner Conze, Görg Haverkate, Diethelm Klippel, and Hans Boldt. "Staat und Souveränität." In *Geschichtliche Grundbegriffe: Historisches Lexikon zur politisch-sozialen Sprache in Deutschland,* ed. Otto Brunner, Werner Conze, and Reinhart Koselleck, 6:1–154. Stuttgart: Klett, 1990.
Koselleck, Reinhart, Wolfgang J. Mommsen, and Jörn Rüsen, eds. *Objektivität und Parteilichkeit in der Geschichtswissenschaft.* Munich: Deutscher Taschenbuch Verlag, 1977.
Kossert, Karl. *Hermann Conrings rechtsgeschichtliches Verdienst.* Cologne: Orthen, 1939.
Kouri, Erkki I., and Tom Scott, eds. *Politics and Society in Reformation Europe: Essays for Sir Geoffrey Elton on His Sixty-Fifth Birthday.* New York: St. Martin's Press, 1987.
Koyré, Alexandre. *From the Closed World to the Infinite Universe.* Baltimore: Johns Hopkins University Press, 1968.
Krappmann, Friedrich Josef. *Johann Philipp von Schönborn und das Leibnizsche Consilium Aegyptiacum: Ein Beitrag zur Politik der letzten Jahre des Kurfürsten.* Würzburg: Bayerische Julius-Maximilians-Universität, 1931.
Kretzmann, Norman, Anthony Kenny, and Jan Pinborg, eds. *Cambridge History of Later Medieval Philosophy: From the Rediscovery of Aristotle to the Disintegration of Scholasticism, 1100–1600.* Cambridge: Cambridge University Press, 1982.
Krieger, Leonard. *The German Idea of Freedom: History of a Political Tradition from the Reformation to 1871.* Chicago: University of Chicago Press, 1957.
Kristeller, Paul Oskar. "The Humanist Movement." In *Renaissance Thought and Its Sources,* by Paul Oskar Kristeller, ed. Michael Mooney, 21–32. New York: Columbia University Press, 1979.
———. *Renaissance Thought: The Classic, Scholastic, and Humanistic Strains.* New York: Harper and Row, 1961.
Kuhn, Thomas S. *The Essential Tension: Selected Studies in Scientific Tradition and Change.* Chicago: University of Chicago Press, 1977.
———. *The Structure of Scientific Revolutions.* 2d ed. Chicago: University of Chicago Press, 1970.
Kundert, Werner. "Hermann Conring als Professor der Universität Helmstedt." In *Beiträge,* 399–412.
———. *Katalog der Helmstedter juristischen Disputationen, Programme und Reden, 1574–1810.* Wiesbaden: Harrassowitz, 1984.
Kunisch, Johannes. "Hermann Conrings mächtepolitisches Weltbild." In *Beiträge,* 237–54.

Kuttner, Stephan. "Papst Honorius III. und das Studium des Zivilrechts." In *Festschrift für Martin Wolff: Beiträge zum Zivilrecht und internationalen Privatrecht,* ed. Ernst von Caemmerer, Walter Hallstein, F. A. Mann, and Ludwig Raiser, 79–101. Tübingen: Mohr, 1952.

———. "The Revival of Jurisprudence." In *Renaissance and Renewal in the Twelfth Century,* ed. Robert L. Benson and Giles Constable, 299–323. Cambridge: Harvard University Press, 1982.

———. "Sur les origines du terme 'droit positif.'" *Revue d'histoire de droit français et étranger* 15 (1936): 728–40.

LaCapra, Dominick. *Rethinking Intellectual History: Texts, Contexts, Language.* Ithaca, NY: Cornell University Press, 1983.

LaCapra, Dominick, and Steven L. Kaplan, eds. *Modern European Intellectual History: Reappraisals and New Perspectives.* Ithaca, NY: Cornell University Press, 1982.

Lakatos, Imre, and Alan Musgrave, eds. *Criticism and the Growth of Knowledge.* Cambridge: Cambridge University Press, 1970.

Landsberg, Ernst. *Die Glosse des Accursius und ihre Lehre vom Eigenthum: Rechts- und dogmengeschichtliche Untersuchung.* Leipzig: Brockhaus, 1883.

Lang, Walter. *Staat und Souveränität bei Hermann Conring.* Augsburg: Blasaditsch, 1970.

Lenz, Georg. "Hermann Conring und die deutsche Staatslehre des 17. Jahrhunderts." *Zeitschrift für die gesamte Staatswissenschaft* 81 (1926): 128–53.

Leuschner, Joachim. *Germany in the Late Middle Ages.* Trans. Sabine MacCormack. New York: North-Holland Publishing Co., 1980.

Levine, Joseph M. *Humanism and History: Origins of Modern English Historiography.* Ithaca, NY: Cornell University Press, 1987.

Levy, Fred Jacob. *Tudor Historical Thought.* San Marino, CA: Huntington Library, 1967.

Lilla, Mark. *G. B. Vico: The Making of an Anti-Modern.* Cambridge: Harvard University Press, 1993.

Lindeboom, Gerrit A. "The Reception in Holland of Harvey's Theory of the Circulation of the Blood." *Janus* 46 (1957): 183–200.

Lintott, Andrew. "What Was the 'Imperium Romanum'?" *Greece and Rome* 28 (1981): 53–67.

Logan, George M. "Substance and Form in Renaissance Humanism." *Journal of Medieval and Renaissance Studies* 7 (1977): 1–34.

Long, Pamela O. "Humanism and Science." In *Renaissance Humanism: Foundations, Forms, and Legacy,* ed. Albert A. Rabil Jr., 3:486–512. Philadelphia: University of Pennsylvania Press, 1988.

Löwith, Karl. *Meaning in History: The Theological Implications of the Philosophy of History.* Chicago: University of Chicago Press, 1949.

Lübke-Wolf, Gertraude. "Die Bedeutung der Lehre von den vier Weltreichen für das Staatsrecht des römisch-deutschen Reiches." *Der Staat* 23 (1984): 369–89.

Luce, T. James, and Anthony J. Woodman, eds. *Tacitus and the Tacitean Tradition.* Princeton, NJ: Princeton University Press, 1993.

Luig, Klaus. "Conring, das deutsche Recht und die Rechtsgeschichte." In *Beiträge,* 355–95.

Lunsing-Scheuvleer, Theodoor Herman, and Guillaume Henri Marie Posthumus Meyjes, eds. *Leiden University in the Seventeenth Century: An Exchange of Learning.* Leiden: Brill, 1975.

Lyon, Bryce. "Henri Pirenne and the Origins of *Annales* History." *Annals of Scholarship* 1 (1980): 69–84.
Maclean, Ian. *Interpretation and Meaning in the Renaissance: The Case of Law.* Cambridge: Cambridge University Press, 1992.
Macpherson, Crawford Brough. *The Political Theory of Possessive Individualism.* Oxford: Oxford University Press, 1962.
Maffei, Domenico. *La donazione di Costantino nei giuristi medievali.* Milan: Giuffrè, 1964.
———. *Gli inizi dell' umanesimo giuridico.* Milan: Giuffrè, 1956.
Mager, Inge. *Georg Calixts theologische Ethik und ihre Nachwirkungen.* Göttingen: Vandenhoeck und Ruprecht, 1969.
———. "Hermann Conring als theologischer Schriftsteller, insbesondere in seinem Verhältnis zu Georg Calixt." In *Beiträge,* 55–84.
———. "Lutherische Theologie und aristotelische Philosophie an der Universität Helmstedt im 16. Jahrhundert." *Jahrbuch der Gesellschaft für niedersächsische Kirchengeschichte* 73 (1975): 83–98.
Mager, Wolfgang. "Republik." In *Geschichtliche Grundbegriffe: Historisches Lexikon zur politisch-sozialen Sprache in Deutschland,* ed. Otto Brunner, Werner Conze, and Reinhart Koselleck, 5:549–651. Stuttgart: Klett, 1984.
Maier, Hans. *Die ältere deutsche Staats- und Verwaltungslehre.* 2d ed. Munich: Beck, 1980.
Major, J. Russell. *From Renaissance Monarchy to Absolute Monarchy: French Kings, Nobles, and Estates.* Baltimore: Johns Hopkins University Press, 1994.
Mandelbaum, Maurice. *The Anatomy of Historical Knowledge.* Baltimore: Johns Hopkins University Press, 1977.
Martines, Lauro. *Power and Imagination: City-States in Renaissance Italy.* New York: Knopf, 1979.
Marx, Karl Friedrich Heinrich. "Zur Erinnerung der ärztlichen Wirksamkeit Hermann Conrings." In *Abhandlungen der Königlichen Gesellschaft der Wissenschaften zu Göttingen, Physikalische Classe* 18 (1873): 3–51.
Mate, Reyes, and Friedrich Niewöhner, eds. *Spaniens Beitrag zum politischen Denken in Europa um 1600.* Wiesbaden: Harrassowitz, 1994.
Mathy, H. "Über das Mainzer Erzkanzleramt in der Neuzeit: Stand und Aufgaben der Forschung." *Geschichtliche Landeskunde* 2 (1965): 109–49.
Mattingly, Garrett. *Renaissance Diplomacy.* Boston: Houghton Mifflin, 1955.
Mazzacane, Aldo. "Conring, Baronio e la storia della costituzione germanica." In *Beiträge,* 255–70.
———. "Hermann Conring e la storia della costituzione germanica." In *Diritto e potere nella storia Europea: Atti in onore di Bruno Paradisi,* 567–610. Florence: Olschki, 1982.
———. *Scienza, logica e ideologia nella giurisprudenza Tedesca del secolo XVI.* Milan: Giuffrè, 1971.
McGrade, Arthur S. "Ockham and the Birth of Individual Rights." In *Authority and Power: Studies on Medieval Law and Government,* ed. Brian Tierney and Peter Linehan, 149–65. Cambridge: Cambridge University Press, 1980.
Meijers, Eduard M. "L'université d'Orléans au XIIIe siècle." In *Etudes d'histoire du droit,* by Eduard M. Meijers, ed. Robert Feenstra and H. W. D. Fischer, 3:3–148. Leiden: Universitaire Pers Leiden, 1959.
Meinecke, Friedrich. *Die Entstehung des Historismus.* 2 vols. Berlin: R. Oldenbourg, 1936. In English *Historism,* trans. J. E. Anderson (New York: Herder and Herder, 1972).

Mentz, Georg. *Johann Philipp von Schönborn, Kurfürst von Mainz, Bischof von Würzburg und Worms, 1605–1673: Ein Beitrag zur Geschichte des siebzehnten Jahrhunderts.* 2 vols. Jena: Fischer, 1896–99.

Mesnard, Pierre. *L'essor de la philosophie politique au XVIe siècle.* Paris: Boivin et Cie., 1936.

Meter, Jan Hendrik. *The Literary Theories of Daniel Heinsius: A Study of the Development and Background of His Views on Literary Theory and Criticism during the Period from 1602 to 1612.* Assen: Van Gorcum, 1984.

Meyer von Knonau, Gerold. "Das bellum diplomaticum Lindaviense." *Historische Zeitschrift* 26 (1871): 75–130.

Meynial, Edouard. "Notes sur la formation de la théorie du domaine divisé (domaine direct et domaine utile) du XIe au XIVe siècle." In *Mélanges Fitting*, 2:409–61. Montpellier: Laros et Tenin, 1908.

Miethke, Jürgen, and Arnold Bühler. *Kaiser und Papst im Konflikt: Zum Verhältnis von Staat und Kirche im späten Mittelalter.* Düsseldorf: Schwann, 1988.

Mill, John Stuart. *On Liberty.* Ed. Gertrude Himmelfarb. Harmondsworth: Penguin Books, 1974.

Mink, Louis O. *Historical Understanding.* Ed. Brian Fay, Eugene O. Golob, and Richard T. Vann. Ithaca, NY: Cornell University Press, 1987.

Mochi Onory, Sergio. *Fonti canonistiche dell'idea moderna dello stato: Imperium spirituale, iurisdictio divisa, sovranità.* Milan: Vita e pensiero, 1951.

Moeller, Bernd. "The German Humanists and the Beginnings of the Reformation." In *Imperial Cities and the Reformation*, by Bernd Moeller, trans. H. C. Erik Midelfort and Mark U. Edwards Jr., 19–38. Philadelphia: Fortress Press, 1972.

Moeller, Ernst von. *Hermann Conring, der Vorkämpfer des deutschen Rechts, 1606–1681.* Hannover: Geibel, 1915.

Momigliano, Arnaldo. "Historicism Revisited." In *Essays in Ancient and Modern Historiography*, by Arnaldo Momigliano, 365–73. Middletown, CT: Wesleyan University Press, 1977.

Mommsen, Theodor E. "Petrarch's Conception of the 'Dark Ages.'" In *Medieval and Renaissance Studies*, by Theodor E. Mommsen, ed. Eugene F. Rice, 106–29. Ithaca, NY: Cornell University Press, 1959.

Moore, Robert Ian. *The First European Revolution, c. 970–1215.* Oxford: Blackwell, 2000.

———. *The Formation of a Persecuting Society: Power and Deviance in Western Europe, 950–1250.* Oxford: Blackwell, 1987.

Moraw, Peter. *Von offener Verfassung zu gestalteter Verdichtung: Das Reich im späten Mittelalter, 1250 bis 1490.* Berlin: Propyläen Verlag, 1985.

Muhlack, Ulrich. *Geschichtswissenschaft im Humanismus und in der Aufklärung: Die Vorgeschichte des Historismus.* Munich: Beck, 1991.

Muldoon, James. *Empire and Order: The Concept of Empire, 800–1800.* New York: St. Martin's Press, 1999.

———. "Extra ecclesiam non est imperium: The Canonists and the Legitimacy of Secular Power." *Studia Gratiana* 9 (1966): 551–80.

Nabokov, Vladimir V. *Ada, or Ardor: A Family Chronicle.* New York: McGraw-Hill, 1969.

Nauert, Charles. "Humanism as Method: Roots of Conflict with the Scholastics." *Sixteenth Century Journal* 29 (1998): 427–38.

———. "Renaissance Humanism: An Emergent Consensus and Its Critics." *Indiana Social Studies Quarterly* 33 (1980): 5–20.

Neddermeyer, Uwe. *Das Mittelalter in der deutschen Historiographie vom 15. bis zum 18. Jahrhundert: Geschichtsgliederung und Epochenverständnis in der frühen Neuzeit.* Cologne: Böhlau, 1988.

Nederman, Cary J. "Freedom, Community, and Function: Communitarian Lessons of Medieval Political Theory." *American Political Science Review* 86 (1992): 977–86.

———. "Humanism and Empire: Aeneas Sylvius Piccolomini, Cicero, and the Imperial Ideal." *Historical Journal* 36 (1993): 499–515.

———. "The Meaning of Aristotelianism in Medieval Moral and Political Thought." *Journal of the History of Ideas* 57 (1996): 563–85.

———. "Nature, Sin, and the Origins of Society: The Ciceronian Tradition in Medieval Political Thought." *Journal of the History of Ideas* 49 (1988): 3–26.

Neue deutsche Biographie. Ed. Historische Kommission bei der Bayerischen Akademie der Wissenschaften. Berlin: Duncker und Humblot, 1953–.

Nicholas, Barry. *An Introduction to Roman Law.* Oxford: Clarendon Press, 1962.

Nonn, Ulrich. "Heiliges Römisches Reich Deutscher Nation: Zum Nationenbegriff im 15. Jahrhundert." *Zeitschrift für historische Forschung* 9 (1982): 129–42.

Novick, Peter. *That Noble Dream: The "Objectivity Question" and the American Historical Profession.* Cambridge: Cambridge University Press, 1988.

Oakley, Francis. "The Absolute and Ordained Power of God and King in the Sixteenth and Seventeenth Centuries: Philosophy, Science, Politics, and Law." *Journal of the History of Ideas* 59 (1998): 669–90.

———. "The Absolute and Ordained Power of God in Sixteenth- and Seventeenth-Century Theology." *Journal of the History of Ideas* 59 (1998): 437–61.

———. "Celestial Hierarchies Revisited: Walter Ullmann's Vision of Medieval Politics." *Past and Present* 60 (1973): 3–48.

———. "Christian Theology and the Newtonian Science: The Rise of the Concept of the Laws of Nature." *Church History* 30 (1961): 433–57.

———. *Natural Law, Conciliarism, and Consent in the Late Middle Ages.* London: Variorum Reprints, 1984.

———. *Omnipotence, Covenant, and Order: An Excursion in the History of Ideas from Abelard to Leibniz.* Ithaca, NY: Cornell University Press, 1984.

———. *Politics and Eternity: Studies in the History of Medieval and Early-Modern Political Thought.* Leiden: Brill, 1999.

Oberman, Heiko A. *Luther: Mensch zwischen Gott und Teufel.* Berlin: Severin und Siedler, 1982. In English *Luther: Man between God and the Devil,* trans. Eileen Walliser-Schwarzbart (New Haven, CT: Yale University Press, 1989).

———. "*Via Antiqua* and *Via Moderna:* Late Medieval Prolegomena to Early Reformation Thought." *Journal of the History of Ideas* 48 (1987): 23–40.

———. *Werden und Wertung der Reformation.* Tübingen: Mohr, 1977. Rev. and abridged in English as *Masters of the Reformation: The Emergence of a New Intellectual Climate in Europe,* trans. Dennis Martin (Cambridge: Cambridge University Press, 1981).

Oestreich, Gerhard. *Antiker Geist und moderner Staat bei Justus Lipsius 1546–1606: Der Neustoizismus als politische Bewegung.* Ed. Nicolette Mout. Göttingen: Vandenhoeck und Ruprecht, 1989.

———. *Geist und Gestalt des frühmodernen Staates: Ausgewählte Aufsätze.* Berlin: Duncker und Humblot, 1969. In English *Neostoicism and the Early Modern State,* ed. Brigitta Oestreich and Helmut G. Koenigsberger, trans. David McLintock (Cambridge: Cambridge University Press, 1982).

Pagden, Anthony, *Lords of All the World: Ideologies of Empire in Spain, Britain, and France, c. 1500–c. 1800.* New Haven, CT: Yale University Press, 1995.

———. *Spanish Imperialism and the Political Imagination: Studies in European and Spanish-American Social and Political Theory, 1513–1830.* New Haven, CT: Yale University Press, 1990.

Pagden, Anthony, ed. *The Languages of Political Theory in Early-Modern Europe.* Cambridge: Cambridge University Press, 1987.

Palladini, Fiammetta. *Samuel Pufendorf discepolo di Hobbes: Per una reinterpretazione del giusnaturalismo moderno.* Bologna: Il Mulino, 1990.

Parker, Geoffrey. *The Military Revolution: Military Innovation and the Rise of the West, 1500–1800.* Cambridge: Cambridge University Press, 1988.

Pennington, Kenneth. *The Prince and the Law, 1200–1600: Sovereignty and Rights in the Western Legal Tradition.* Berkeley: University of California Press, 1993.

Perizonius, H. F. W. *Geschichte Ostfrieslands.* 4 vols. Weener: Risius, 1868–69. Reprint, Leer: Schuster, 1974.

Peterse, Hans. "Johann Christian von Boineburg und die Mainzer Irenik des 17. Jahrhunderts." In *Union, Konversion, Toleranz: Dimensionen der Annäherung zwischen den christlichen Konfessionen im 17. und 18. Jahrhundert,* ed. Heinz Duchhardt and Gerhard May, 105–18. Mainz: von Zabern, 2000.

Petersen, Peter. *Geschichte der aristotelischen Philosophie im protestantischen Deutschland.* Leipzig: Meiner, 1921.

Pettegree, Andrew. *Emden and the Dutch Revolt: Exile and the Development of Reformed Protestantism.* Oxford: Clarendon Press, 1992.

Pocock, John Greville Agard. *The Ancient Constitution and the Feudal Law: A Study of English Historical Thought in the Seventeenth Century.* Rev. ed. Cambridge: Cambridge University Press, 1987.

———. *The Machiavellian Moment: Florentine Political Thought and the Atlantic Republican Tradition.* Princeton, NJ: Princeton University Press, 1975.

Pöllnitz, G. Freiherr von. "Johann Philipp von Schönborn." *Nassauische Lebensbilder* 2 (1963): 91–108.

Pollock, Frederick, and Frederic William Maitland. *The History of English Law before the Time of Edward I.* 2d ed. 2 vols. Cambridge: Cambridge University Press, 1898.

Post, Gaines. *Studies in Medieval Legal Thought: Public Law and the State, 1100–1322.* Princeton, NJ: Princeton University Press, 1964.

Press, Volker. *Das Alte Reich: Ausgewählte Aufsätze.* Ed. Johannes Kunisch. Berlin: Duncker und Humblot, 1997.

Preston, Joseph H. "Was There an Historical Revolution?" *Journal of the History of Ideas* 38 (1977): 353–64.

Prodi, Paolo. *Il sacramento del potere: Il giuramento politico nella storia costituzionale dell'Occidente.* Bologna: Il Mulino, 1992.

———. *Il sovrano pontefice, un corpo e due anime: La monarchia papale nella prima età moderna.* Bologna: Il Mulino, 1982. In English *The Papal Prince, One Body and Two Souls: The Papal Monarchy in Early Modern Europe,* trans. Susan Haskins (Cambridge: Cambridge University Press, 1987).

Quaglioni, Diego. *I limiti della sovranità: Il pensiero di Jean Bodin nella cultura politica e giuridica dell'età moderna.* Padua: Cedam, 1992.

Quaritsch, Helmut. *Staat und Souveränität,* Vol. 1, *Die Grundlagen.* Frankfurt: Athenäum, 1970.

Raabe, Paul. "Die Bibliotheca Conringiana: Beschreibung einer Gelehrtenbibliothek des 17. Jahrhunderts." In *Beiträge*, 413–34.
Rabil, Albert A., Jr., ed. *Renaissance Humanism: Foundations, Forms, and Legacy*. 3 vols. Philadelphia: University of Pennsylvania Press, 1988.
Rademaker, Cornelis Simon Maria. *Life and Work of Gerardus Joannes Vossius, 1577–1649*. Assen: Van Gorcum, 1981.
Ranieri, Filippo. "Juristische Literatur aus dem Ancien Régime und historische Literatursoziologie." In *Aspekte europäischer Rechtsgeschichte: Festgabe für Helmut Coing zum 70. Geburtstag*, ed. Christoph Bergfeld et al., 293–322. Frankfurt: Klostermann, 1982.
Ranieri, Filippo, ed. *Juristische Dissertationen deutscher Universitäten, 17.–18. Jahrhundert: Dokumentation zusammengestellt von einer Arbeitsgruppe unter der Leitung von Filippo Ranieri*. Frankfurt: Klostermann, 1986.
Ranum, Orest. *Artisans of Glory: Writers and Historical Thought in Seventeenth-Century France*. Chapel Hill: University of North Carolina Press, 1980.
Reeves, Marjorie. *The Influence of Prophecy in the Later Middle Ages: A Study in Joachimism*. Oxford: Oxford University Press, 1969.
Reibstein, Ernst. *Völkerrecht: Eine Geschichte seiner Ideen in Lehre und Praxis*. 2 vols. Freiburg: Alber, 1958–63.
Reimers, Heinrich. *Ostfriesland bis zum Aussterben seines Fürstenhauses*. 2d ed. Wiesbaden: Sandig, 1968.
Reitzel, Adam Michael. "Leibniz, Boineburg und Johann Philipp von Schönborn in der Mainzer Rechts- und Reichsgeschichte: Ein Beitrag zur Europapolitik." *Mainzer Almanach* (1961): 5–27.
Repgen, Konrad. "What Is a 'Religious War'?" In *Politics and Society in Reformation Europe: Essays for Sir Geoffrey Elton on His Sixty-Fifth Birthday*, ed. Erkki I. Kouri and Tom Scott, 311–28. New York: St. Martin's Press, 1987.
Reuter, Timothy. *Germany in the Early Middle Ages, 800–1056*. London: Longman, 1991.
Reventlow, Henning, Walter Sparn, and John D. Woodbridge, eds. *Historische Kritik und biblischer Kanon in der deutschen Aufklärung*. Wiesbaden: Harrassowitz, 1988.
Riccobono, Salvatore. "*Mos italicus* e *mos gallicus* nella interpretazione del corpus iuris civilis." In *Acta congressus iuridici internationalis VII saeculo a decretalibus Gregorii IX et XIV a codice Iustiniano promulgatis, Romae, 12–17 Novembris 1934*, 2:377–98. Rome: Libraria pontificii instituti utriusque iuris, 1935.
Richardson, John S. "'Imperium Romanum': Empire and the Language of Power." *Journal of Roman Studies* 81 (1991): 1–9.
Rickert, Heinrich. *Die Grenzen der naturwissenschaftlichen Begriffsbildung*. Tübingen: J. C. B. Mohr, 1902. In English *The Limits of Concept Formation in Natural Science: A Logical Introduction to the Historical Sciences*, abr. ed., trans. Guy Oakes (Cambridge: Cambridge University Press, 1986).
———. *Kulturwissenschaft und Naturwissenschaft*. 5th ed. Tübingen: J. C. B. Mohr, 1926.
Ricoeur, Paul. *Temps et récit*. 3 vols. Paris: Seuil, 1983–85. In English *Time and Narrative*, trans. Kathleen McLaughlin and David Pellauer, 3 vols. (Chicago: University of Chicago Press, 1984–88).
Riesenberg, Peter. *Inalienability of Sovereignty in Medieval Political Thought*. New York: Columbia University Press, 1956.
Ritter, Moriz. *Deutsche Geschichte im Zeitalter der Gegenreformation und des Dreissigjährigen Krieges, 1555–1648*. 3 vols. Stuttgart: Cotta, 1889–1908.

Rivière, Jean. *Le problème de l'église et de l'état au temps de Philippe le Bel.* Louvain: Spicilegium sacrum Lovaniense, 1926.
Robinson, O. F., T. D. Fergus, and William M. Gordon. *European Legal History: Sources and Institutions.* 3d ed. London: Butterworths, 2000.
Roeck, Bernd. *Reichssystem und Reichsherkommen: Die Diskussion über die Staatlichkeit des Reiches in der politischen Publizistik des 17. und 18. Jahrhunderts.* Wiesbaden: Steiner, 1984.
Rorty, Richard. *Philosophy and the Mirror of Nature.* Princeton, NJ: Princeton University Press, 1980.
Rosenthal, Bernard, and Paul E. Szarmach, eds. *Medievalism in American Culture: Papers of the Eighteenth Annual Conference of the Center for Medieval and Early Renaissance Studies.* Binghamton: Center for Medieval and Early Renaissance Studies, State University of New York at Binghamton, 1989.
Rosner, Edwin. "Die Bedeutung Hermann Conrings in der Geschichte der Medizin." *Medizinhistorisches Journal* 4 (1969): 287–304.
———. "Hermann Conring als Arzt und als Gegner Hohenheims." In *Beiträge,* 87–120.
Rousseau, Jean-Jacques. *The Social Contract.* Trans. Maurice Cranston. Harmondsworth: Penguin Books, 1968.
Rüsen, Jörn. *Grundzüge einer Historik.* 3 vols. Göttingen: Vandenhoeck und Ruprecht, 1983.
Said, Eward W. *Orientalism.* New York: Vintage Books, 1979.
Salmon, John Hearsey McMillan. *Renaissance and Revolt: Essays in the Intellectual and Social History of Early Modern France.* Cambridge: Cambridge University Press, 1987.
Saring, Hans. "Boineburg, Johann Christian Frhr. v." *Neue Deutsche Biographie* 2 (1955): 424–25.
Savigny, Friedrich Karl von. *Geschichte des römischen Rechts im Mittelalter.* 6 vols. Heidelberg: Mohr, 1815–31.
Scheel, Günter. "Hermann Conring als historisch-politischer Ratgeber der Herzöge von Braunschweig und Lüneburg." In *Beiträge,* 271–301.
Schellhase, Kenneth Charles. *Tacitus in Renaissance Political Thought.* Chicago: University of Chicago Press, 1976.
Schiffman, Zachary S. *On the Threshold of Modernity: Relativism in the French Renaissance.* Baltimore: Johns Hopkins University Press, 1991.
———. "Renaissance Historicism Reconsidered." *History and Theory* 24 (1985): 170–82.
Schilling, Heinz. "Sündenzucht und frühneuzeitliche Sozialdisziplinierung: Die calvinistische presbyteriale Kirchenzucht in Emden vom 16. bis 19. Jahrhundert." In *Stände und Gesellschaft im Alten Reich,* ed. Georg Schmidt, 265–302. Stuttgart: Steiner, 1989.
Schlee, Ernst. *Der Streit des Daniel Hofmann über das Verhältnis der Philosophie zur Theologie.* Marburg: Elwert, 1862.
Schmidt, Heinrich. "Hermann Conring und Ostfriesland." In *Beiträge,* 303–17.
Schmitt, Carl. *Politische Theologie: Vier Kapitel zur Lehre von der Souveränität.* Leipzig: Duncker und Humblot, 1934. In English *Political Theology: Four Chapters on the Concept of Sovereignty,* trans. George Schwab (Cambridge: MIT Press, 1985).
Schnur, Roman, ed. *Die Rolle der Juristen bei der Entstehung des modernen Staates.* Berlin: Duncker und Humblot, 1986.
Scholz, Richard. *Die Publizistik zur Zeit Philipps des Schönen und Bonifaz' VIII.* Stuttgart: Enke, 1903.

Schrohe, Heinrich. *Johann Christian von Boineburg, Kurmainzer Oberhofmarschall*. Mainz: Falk und Söhne, 1926.
Schubart-Fikentscher, Gertrud. *Untersuchungen zur Autorschaft von Dissertationen im Zeitalter der Aufklärung*. Berlin: Akademie Verlag, 1970.
Schubert, Friedrich Hermann. *Die deutschen Reichstage in der Staatslehre der frühen Neuzeit*. Göttingen: Vandenhoeck und Ruprecht, 1966.
Schüssler, Hermann. *Georg Calixt: Theologie und Kirchenpolitik: Eine Studie zur Ökumenizität des Luthertums*. Wiesbaden: Steiner, 1961.
Secrétan, Catherine. *Les privilèges, berçeau de la liberté: La révolte des Pays-Bas. Aux sources de la pensée politique moderne, 1566–1619*. Paris: Vrin, 1990.
Seeliger, Gerhard. *Erzkanzler und Reichskanzleien: Ein Beitrag zur Geschichte des Deutschen Reiches*. Innsbruck: Wagner, 1889.
Seibt, Ferdinand. *Karl IV.: Ein Kaiser in Europa, 1346–1378*. Munich: Süddeutscher Verlag, 1978.
Seifert, Arno. *Cognitio Historica: Die Geschichte als Namengeberin der frühneuzeitlichen Empirie*. Berlin: Duncker und Humblot, 1976.
———. "Conring und die Begründung der Staatenkunde." In *Beiträge*, 201–14.
———. *Der Rückzug der biblischen Prophetie von der neueren Geschichte: Studien zur Geschichte der Reichstheologie des frühneuzeitlichen deutschen Protestantismus*. Cologne: Böhlau, 1990.
Seigel, Jerrold E. "'Civic Humanism' or Ciceronian Rhetoric? The Culture of Petrarch and Bruni." *Past and Present* 34 (1966): 3–48.
Senellart, Michel. *Les arts de gouverner: Du regimen médiéval au concept de gouvernement*. Paris: Seuil, 1995.
Skinner, Quentin. *The Foundations of Modern Political Thought*. 2 vols. Cambridge: Cambridge University Press, 1978.
———. "The Limits of Historical Explanations." *Philosophy* 41 (1966): 199–215.
———. "Meaning and Understanding in the History of Ideas." *History and Theory* 8 (1969): 3–53. Reprinted in *Meaning and Context: Quentin Skinner and His Critics*, ed. James Tully, 29–67 (Princeton, NJ: Princeton University Press, 1988).
———. "The State." In *Political Innovation and Conceptual Change*, ed. Terence Ball, James Farr, and Russell Hanson, 90–131. Cambridge: Cambridge University Press, 1989.
Skinner, Quentin, ed. *The Return of Grand Theory in the Human Sciences*. Cambridge: Cambridge University Press, 1985.
Smalley, Beryl, ed. *Trends in Medieval Political Thought*. Oxford: Blackwell, 1965.
Southern, Richard W. *The Making of the Middle Ages*. New Haven, CT: Yale University Press, 1953.
Spitz, Lewis W. "Humanism and the Protestant Reformation." In *Renaissance Humanism: Foundations, Forms, and Legacy*, ed. Albert A. Rabil Jr., 3:380–411. Philadelphia: University of Pennsylvania Press, 1988.
Stayer, James M. "The Radical Reformation." In *Handbook of European History, 1400–1600*, ed. Thomas A. Brady Jr., Heiko A. Oberman, and James D. Tracy, 2:249–82. Leiden: Brill, 1995.
Steinmetz, David. *The Bible in the Sixteenth Century*. Durham, NC: Duke University Press, 1990.
Stintzing, Roderich von. "Hermann Conring." In *Geschichte der deutschen Rechtswis-

senschaft, by Roderich von Stintzing and Ernst Landsberg, vol. 1, pt. 2, 165–88. Munich: Oldenbourg, 1884.
Stintzing, Roderich von, and Ernst Landsberg. *Geschichte der deutschen Rechtswissenschaft*. 3 vols. Munich: Oldenbourg, 1880–1910.
Stobbe, Otto. *Hermann Conring, der Begründer der deutschen Rechtsgeschichte*. Berlin: Hertz, 1870.
Stolleis, Michael. "Die Einheit der Wissenschaften: Hermann Conring, 1606–1681." In *Beiträge*, 11–31.
———. "Hermann Conring und die Begründung der deutschen Rechtsgeschichte." In *Der Ursprung des deutschen Rechts*, by Hermann Conring, 253–68. Frankfurt: Insel Verlag, 1994.
———. "Lipsius-Rezeption in der politisch-juristischen Literatur des 17. Jahrhunderts in Deutschland." *Der Staat* 27 (1987): 1–30.
———. "Machiavellismus und Staatsräson: Ein Beitrag zu Conrings politischem Denken." In *Beiträge*, 173–99.
———. *Pecunia Nervus Rerum: Zur Staatsfinanzierung in der frühen Neuzeit*. Frankfurt: Klostermann, 1983.
———. *Reichspublizistik und Policeywissenschaft, 1600–1800*. Vol. 1 of *Geschichte des öffentlichen Rechts in Deutschland*. Munich: Beck, 1988.
———. *Staat und Staatsräson in der frühen Neuzeit: Studien zur Geschichte des öffentlichen Rechts*. Frankfurt: Suhrkamp, 1990.
Stolleis, Michael, ed. *Hermann Conring, 1606–1681: Beiträge zu Leben und Werk*. Berlin: Duncker und Humblot, 1983.
———. *Staatsdenker im 17. und 18. Jahrhundert: Reichspublizistik, Politik, Naturrecht*. Frankfurt: Metzner, 1977.
———. *Staatsdenker in der frühen Neuzeit*. 3d ed. Munich: Beck, 1995.
Stone, Lawrence. "The Revival of Narrative: Reflections on a New Old History." *Past and Present* 85 (1979): 3–24.
Strauss, Leo. *Natural Right and History*. Chicago: University of Chicago Press, 1953.
Strayer, Joseph R. *The Reign of Philip the Fair*. Princeton, NJ: Princeton University Press, 1980.
Taylor, Charles. *Sources of the Self: The Making of the Modern Identity*. Cambridge: Harvard University Press, 1989.
Tellenbach, Gerd. *Libertas: Kirche und Weltordnung im Zeitalter des Investiturstreites*. Stuttgart: Kohlhammer, 1936. In English *Church, State, and Christian Society at the Time of the Investiture Controversy*, trans. Ralph F. Bennett (London: Blackwell and Mott, 1959).
Tierney, Brian. *Foundations of the Conciliar Theory: The Contribution of the Medieval Canonists from Gratian to the Great Schism*. Cambridge: Cambridge University Press, 1955. Rev. ed., Leiden: Brill, 1998.
———. *The Idea of Natural Rights: Studies on Natural Rights, Natural Law, and Church Law, 1150–1625*. Atlanta: Scholars Press, 1997.
———. *Origins of Papal Infallibility, 1150–1350: A Study on the Concepts of Infallibility, Sovereignty, and Tradition in the Middle Ages*. Leiden: Brill, 1972.
———. *Religion, Law, and the Growth of Constitutional Thought, 1150–1650*. Cambridge: Cambridge University Press, 1982.
Todd, Malcolm. *The Early Germans*. Oxford: Blackwell, 1992.

Toews, John E. "Intellectual History after the Linguistic Turn: The Autonomy of Meaning and the Irreducibility of Experience." *American Historical Review* 92 (1987): 879–907.

Toulmin, Stephen E., and June Goodfield. *The Discovery of Time.* New York: Harper and Row, 1965.

Tracy, James. "Humanism and the Reformation." In *Reformation Europe: A Guide to Research,* ed. Steven Ozment, 33–57. St. Louis: Center for Reformation Research, 1982.

Trevisani, Francesco. "Medizinisch-wissenschaftliche Beziehungen zwischen Italien und Deutschland im 17. Jahrhundert: Eine unbekannte Korrespondenz zwischen H. Conring und M. A. Severino." In *Beiträge,* 121–31.

Triebs, Michaela. *Die medizinische Fakultät der Universität Helmstedt, 1576–1810: Eine Studie zu ihrer Geschichte unter besonderer Berücksichtigung der Promotions- und Übungsdisputationen.* Wiesbaden: Harrassowitz, 1995.

Trinkaus, Charles E., and Heiko A. Oberman, eds. *The Pursuit of Holiness in Late Medieval and Renaissance Religion.* Leiden: Brill, 1974.

Troje, Hans Erich. *Humanistische Jurisprudenz: Studien zur europäischen Rechtswissenschaft unter dem Einfluss des Humanismus.* Goldbach: Keip, 1993.

Trusen, Winfried. *Die Anfänge des gelehrten Rechts in Deutschland: Ein Beitrag zur Geschichte der Frührezeption.* Wiesbaden: Steiner, 1962.

Tuck, Richard. "Grotius and Selden." In *Cambridge History of Political Thought, 1450–1700,* ed. James H. Burns and Mark Goldie, 499–529. Cambridge: Cambridge University Press, 1991.

———. *Natural Rights Theories: Their Origin and Development.* Cambridge: Cambridge University Press, 1979.

———. *Philosophy and Government, 1572–1651.* Cambridge: Cambridge University Press, 1992.

Tully, James, ed. *Meaning and Context: Quentin Skinner and His Critics.* Princeton, NJ: Princeton University Press, 1988.

Ullmann, Walter. *A History of Political Thought: The Middle Ages.* Rev. ed. Harmondsworth: Penguin Books, 1970.

———. *Medieval Papalism: The Political Theories of the Medieval Canonists.* London: Methuen, 1949.

———. "Reflections on the Medieval Empire." *Transactions of the Royal Historical Society,* 5th ser., 14 (1964): 89–108.

Ultsch, Eva. *Johann Christian von Boineburg: Ein Beitrag zur Geistesgeschichte des 17. Jahrhunderts.* Würzburg: Becker, 1936.

Van Engen, John, ed. *The Past and Future of Medieval Studies.* Notre Dame, IN: University of Notre Dame Press, 1994.

Vann, James A. *The Making of a State: Württemberg, 1593–1793.* Ithaca, NY: Cornell University Press, 1984.

Vann, James A., and Steven W. Rowan, eds. *The Old Reich: Essays on German Political Institutions, 1495–1806.* Brussels: Librairie Encyclopédique, 1974.

Villey, Michel. "Les origines de la notion de droit subjectif." *Archives de philosophie du droit* 2 (1953–54): 163–87.

Vinogradoff, Paul. "Sources of the Law: Right and Law." In *The Collected Papers of Paul Vinogradoff,* 2:465–78. Oxford: Clarendon Press, 1928.

Voegelin, Eric. *The New Science of Politics: An Introduction.* Chicago: University of Chicago Press, 1952.

Volkmann, Rolf. *Die Universität Helmstedt, 1576–1810, im internationalen Netzwerk: Ihre wissenschaftlichen Beziehungen zum europäischen Ausland und zu Nordamerika.* Wolfenbüttel: Roco-Druck, 2000.

Walker, Mack. *German Home Towns: Community, State, and General Estate, 1648–1871.* Ithaca, NY: Cornell University Press, 1971.

Wallmann, Johannes. "Helmstedter Theologie in Conrings Zeit." In *Beiträge,* 35–53.

Wallner, Günter. *Der Krönungsstreit zwischen Kurköln und Kurmainz, 1653–1657.* Mainz: Ditters Bürodienst, 1967.

Walsh, William H. *Philosophy of History: An Introduction.* Rev. ed. New York: Harper, 1967.

Walther, Helmut G. "Wasser in Stadt und Contado: Perugias Sorge um Wasser und der Flusstraktat 'Tyberiadis' des Perusiner Juristen Bartolus von Sassoferrato." In *Mensch und Natur im Mittelalter,* ed. Albert Zimmermann, 882–97. Berlin: De Gruyter, 1992.

Wardemann, Hartmut. "Hermann Conrings Gutachtertätigkeit für das Frankreich Ludwigs XIV." Ph.D. dissertation, Ludwig-Maximilians-Universität, Munich, 1981.

Weber, Wolfgang. *Prudentia Gubernatoria: Studien zur Herrschaftslehre in der deutschen politischen Wissenschaft des 17. Jahrhunderts.* Tübingen: Niemeyer, 1992.

Weigand, Rudolf. *Die Naturrechtslehre der Legisten und Dekretisten von Irnerius bis Accursius und von Gratian bis Johannes Teutonicus.* Munich: Hueber, 1967.

Weimar, Peter. "Die legistische Literatur der Glossatorenzeit." In *Handbuch der Quellen und Literatur der neueren europäischen Privatrechtsgeschichte,* ed. Helmut Coing, 1:129–260. Munich: Beck, 1973.

Weisert, Hermann. "Die Reichstitel bis 1806." *Archiv für Diplomatik* 40 (1994): 441–513.

Weiss, Roberto. *The Renaissance Discovery of Classical Antiquity.* 2d ed. Oxford: Blackwell, 1988.

Wells, Charlotte C. *Law and Citizenship in Early Modern France.* Baltimore: Johns Hopkins University Press, 1994.

White, Hayden. *The Content of the Form: Narrative Discourse and Historical Representation.* Baltimore: Johns Hopkins University Press, 1987.

———. *Metahistory: The Historical Imagination in Nineteenth-Century Europe.* Baltimore: Johns Hopkins University Press, 1975.

Whitehead, Alfred N. *Science and the Modern World.* 1925. Reprint, New York: Free Press, 1967.

Whitman, James Q. *The Legacy of Roman Law in the German Romantic Era: Historical Vision and Legal Change.* Princeton, NJ: Princeton University Press, 1990.

Wickenden, Nicholas. *G. J. Vossius and the Humanist Concept of History.* Assen: Van Gorcum, 1993.

Wieacker, Franz. *Privatrechtsgeschichte der Neuzeit: Unter besonderer Berücksichtigung der deutschen Entwicklung.* 2d ed. Göttingen: Vandenhoeck und Ruprecht, 1967. In English *History of Private Law in Europe with Particular Reference to Germany,* trans. Tony Weir (Oxford: Clarendon Press, 1995).

———. "Ratio scripta: Das römische Recht und die abendländische Rechtswissenschaft." In *Vom römischen Recht: Wirklichkeit und Überlieferung,* by Franz Wieacker, 195–283. Leipzig: Koehler und Amelang, 1944.

———. "Zum Geleit." In *Katalog der Helmstedter juristischen Disputationen, Programme und Reden, 1574–1810,* by Werner Kundert, 11–15. Wiesbaden: Harrassowitz, 1984.

Williams, Bernard. *Descartes: The Project of Pure Inquiry.* Harmondsworth: Penguin Books, 1978.

Willoweit, Dietmar. "Dominium und Proprietas: Zur Entwicklung des Eigentumbegriffs in der mittelalterlichen und neuzeitlichen Rechtswissenschaft." *Historisches Jahrbuch* 94 (1974): 131–56.

———. "Hermann Conring." In *Staatsdenker im 17. und 18. Jahrhundert: Reichspublizistik, Politik, Naturrecht,* ed. Michael Stolleis, 129–47. Frankfurt: Metzner, 1977.

———. "Hermann Conring." In *Staatsdenker in der frühen Neuzeit,* 3d ed., ed. Michael Stolleis, 129–47. Munich: Beck, 1995.

———. "Kaiser, Reich und Reichsstände bei Hermann Conring." In *Beiträge,* 321–34.

———. *Rechtsgrundlagen der Territorialgewalt: Landesobrigkeit, Herrschaftsrechte und Territorium in der Rechtswissenschaft der Neuzeit.* Cologne: Böhlau, 1975.

Windelband, Wilhelm. *Geschichte und Naturwissenschaft.* Strassburg: Heitz, 1894.

Witt, Ronald G. "The Humanist Movement." In *Handbook of European History, 1400–1600,* ed. Thomas A. Brady Jr., Heiko A. Oberman, and James D. Tracy, 2:93–125. Leiden: Brill, 1995.

———. *In the Footsteps of the Ancients: The Origins of Humanism from Lovato to Bruni.* Leiden: Brill, 2000.

Witt, Ronald G., John M. Najemy, Craig Kallendorf, and Werner Gundersheimer. "AHR Forum: Hans Baron's Renaissance Humanism." *American Historical Review* 101 (1996): 107–44.

Wittgenstein, Ludwig. *Culture and Value.* Ed. Georg Henrik von Wright. Trans. Peter Winch. Chicago: University of Chicago Press, 1980.

———. *Philosophical Investigations.* German and English. Trans. Gertrude Elizabeth Margaret Anscombe. Oxford: Blackwell, 1953.

———. *Tractatus Logico-Philosophicus.* German and English. Trans. Charles K. Ogden and Frank P. Ramsey. London: Routledge and Kegan Paul, 1922.

Wolf, Erik. "Hermann Conring, 1606–1681." In *Grosse Rechtsdenker der deutschen Geistesgeschichte,* by Erik Wolf, 4th ed., 220–52. Tübingen: Mohr, 1963.

Woolf, Cecil N. Sidney. *Bartolus of Sassoferrato: His Position in the History of Medieval Political Thought.* Cambridge: Cambridge University Press, 1912.

Worstbrock, Franz Josef, ed. *Krieg und Frieden im Horizont des Renaissancehumanismus.* Weinheim: VCH, 1986.

Yates, Frances A. *Astraea: The Imperial Theme in the Sixteenth Century.* London: Routledge and Kegan Paul, 1975.

Zagorin, Perez. *Ways of Lying: Dissimulation, Persecution, and Conformity in Early Modern Europe.* Cambridge: Harvard University Press, 1990.

Zarka, Yves Charles. *Hobbes et la pensée politique moderne.* Paris: Presses Universitaires de France, 1995.

Zarka, Yves Charles, ed. *Raison et déraison d'état: Théoriciens et théories de la raison d'état aux XVIe et XVIIe siècles.* Paris: Presses Universitaires de France, 1994.

Zehrfeld, Reinold. *Hermann Conrings (1606–1681) Staatenkunde: Ihre Bedeutung für die Geschichte der Statistik unter besonderer Berücksichtigung der Conringschen Bevölkerungslehre.* Berlin: De Gruyter, 1926.

Index

absence. *See* history, and absence
Accursius, 48, 275n. 75
America, 25, 26, 164; United States of, 7, 35, 42
anachronism. *See* history, and anachronism
Annales, 35
Antichrist, 18, 122, 271n. 44
antiquity. *See* Conring, and antiquity; history, and antiquity
Apocalypse, 122–23, 148–49, 163–64
Aristotelianism, 23, 33, 54–57, 61, 183
Aristotle, 9, 23; *Politics,* 61, 72–73, 79, 88. *See also* Conring, and Aristotle
Arminians, 60–61, 63–64
Augsburg Confession, 63
August, duke of Brunswick-Wolfenbüttel and Lüneburg, 54, 68–69, 78, 84, 106, 125
Augustine, Saint, 9, 29
Augustus, Emperor, 18, 75, 164. *See also* Luke, Gospel of
authenticity. *See* history, and authenticity
authority. *See* history, and authority
authorship, 43, 44, 104–5, 111–12, 150–53, 205–7; in dissertations, 71–72, 94–99, 145–46, 153. *See also* Conring, and authorship; dissertations
autonomy. *See* history, and autonomy; sovereignty

Babylon, 18, 122
Barclay, William, 269nn. 11, 12
Barlaeus, Caspar, 60–62, 64, 128
Baron, Hans, 33–34
Bartolus of Sassoferrato, 43–44, 45, 48–49, 165–99, 203–13, 216; and antiquity, 169, 181–85; and Conring, 117, 157–58, 176–77, 207–15; and context, 177–78, 189, 195–97, 204–6; on *dominium,* property, and lordship, 185–92, 198, 203–4; and facts, 169–73, 175–77, 208–9, 279n. 109; on foreign people, 169, 173, 176, 193–94; on French and English monarchies, 171–72, 174, 177, 192–96, 203–4; fundamental assumptions of, 183–84, 195–99, 203–14; and heresy, 156–58, 167, 171–72, 174, 185, 192–95, 208, 209–12; and hierarchy, 195–99, 204–7; and history, 204–7; on *imperium,* 178–85; on Italian city-states, 169–71, 174, 177, 181, 192–94, 204, 279n. 109; on jurisdiction, 178–81, 183–99; on legislation, 181, 184, 191–92; on noble and hired judges, 179–80; and obedience, 169–73, 184, 192–99, 200–202; on the prince, 186, 197–98; and public and private spheres, 178–80, 185–92, 198, 202–4; and *rei vindicatio,* 188–89, 190–91, 204; on the Roman church, 170–73; on the Roman empire, 167–99, 203–13; and Roman law, 175–77, 204–6; on the Roman people, 169–73; and *sibi princeps,* 177; and sovereignty, 192–93, 202–4; on territorial rule, 186–87, 193, 196–98, 203–4; and tyranny, 177, 184, 194, 201, 279n. 109; on universal empire, 156–58, 171–78, 192–95, 202–4, 208. *See also* *dominium*; *imperium*; jurisdiction; law; Roman empire; Roman law; universal empire
Bible, 21, 23, 56–58, 108–9, 156–59, 163–64. *See also* Apocalypse; Luke, Gospel of

317

Bodin, Jean, 25, 48–49, 200–202, 220, 234n. 2, 241nn. 16–17, 259n. 59, 269n. 12
Bogislaus Philipp of Chemnitz, 130
Boineburg, Johann Christian von, 82–86, 110–11
Brunner, Otto, 46, 240nn. 5, 6
Brunswick-Wolfenbüttel, dukes of, 54, 63–65, 68, 84, 87, 89, 256n. 28
Bulgarus, 188–89
Burckhardt, Jacob, 30, 31, 42
Burgersdicius, Franco, 61, 96, 244n. 52

Calixt, Georg, 56–59, 62, 63, 67, 74; on the consensus of antiquity, 56–58, 83
Calov, Abraham, 58
Calvin, Jean, 24
Calvinism, 50–52, 60
Caselius, Johannes, 53, 54, 55, 56, 57, 59
Cassander, Georg, 80
Catholic Church, 122, 148–49, 172–73, 204–5
Catholicism, 18–19, 56, 60, 80–81, 83–84, 93, 133–34
Cellarius, Balthasar, 79
Charlemagne, Emperor, 75, 108, 109, 113, 156, 160–61, 224
Charles IV, Emperor, 115
Charles IV, duke of Lorraine, 85
Charles V, Emperor, 115, 164
Charles X, king of Sweden, 87
Chittolini, Giorgio, 46
Christian church, 122, 171–73, 193–94
Christianity, 18–19, 23, 56–58, 75, 137, 172, 193, 195, 204–6, 230–31
Christina, queen of Sweden, 69, 77–78, 87
chronological Orientalism, 49, 219, 227–28
Cicero, 22, 62
Ciceronians, 33
Cino of Pistoia, 117–18
citizenship, 7, 21, 143, 226, 228; Roman, 76, 160–61, 162, 167–73. *See also* history, and politics; sovereignty; state
Code, of Justinian, 192, 205; 1.1.1 (*Cunctos populos*), 175–76, 205; 6.7.2, 178; 7.37.3 (*Bene a Zenone*), 188. *See also* Roman law
Colbert, Jean Baptiste, 71, 85
Collingwood, R. G., 37
Cologne (city), 86–87
Cologne, archbishop of, 84–85, 87
Conring, Galatea, born Copin (mother), 51
Conring, Hermann, 30, 40–45, 50–89, 141–43, 223–27; and academic freedom, 55, 60, 63–64, 67, 119, 134–35; and antiquity, 53, 57, 71, 72, 75, 92–93, 157–60, 206–7; on the Apocalypse, 122–23, 148–49; and Aristotle, 55–56, 61, 62, 67, 73, 79, 88, 219–20; and authority, 67, 95, 104–5, 119–21, 126, 129–30, 137–40, 143, 150–53, 206–7, 212, 219, 224–26; and authorship, 80, 93–94, 96–100, 103–5, 124–25, 126–28, 145–46, 150–53; and Barlaeus, 60–62, 63–64; and Bartolus, 166–67, 176–77, 199–200, 207–14, 215; and Boineburg, 82–86, 110–11; and Calixt, 56–59, 62, 63, 67, 74; character of, 52, 64, 85, 87–88, 128–32, 138–43, 225–26; childhood, 50–54; and codification, 75; and Cologne, 87; and conscience, 63–64, 135, 138–40, 142–43, 214, 224, 226; and the consensus of antiquity, 56–58, 83; and context, 58, 132–43, 150–54, 209–15, 228, 230; and death of, 89; and Descartes, 78, 142; and diplomatics, 41, 86; and dissertations, 69, 70, 71, 72, 73, 93–106, 110–11, 119–20, 130, 134–35, 144–47, 149–50, 152–53; dissertations on the Holy Roman Empire, 88–89, 144–47; and dissimulation, 64, 67, 128–32, 140; earliest writings, 53; edition of the works of, 67, 70, 88, 89, 94, 149–50, 226, 249n. 123; education of, 52–53, 54–62, 68; and facts, 123–24, 158–59, 165–66, 176–77, 206–9, 212–14, 217, 223; family of, 51–52, 68–69, 79, 89; as founder of German legal history, 62, 74, 224; and Germany, 41–42, 63–65, 70–71, 75–77, 81, 106, 115–17, 125–26, 156–64; and Grotius, 60, 61–62, 113–14, 157; and heresy, 57, 109, 207–15, 225–26; and the historical revolt, 53, 65–67, 125–26, 207–18, 223–26; inaugural address of, 67, 128, 139–40; income and estate of, 68, 69, 78, 79, 87, 89; influence of, 77, 79, 82, 84–88, 145–46; and Lampadius, 65–67, 72, 73, 88–89, 93, 247n. 98; on law, 109, 113–15; lectures on the Holy Roman Empire, 72, 73, 79, 88, 111, 124–25, 132–33, 144–47; lectures on politics, 72–73, 78, 79, 80, 88; and Leibniz, 84; letter to Barlaeus, 63–64; library of, 62, 89, 253n. 191; literature about, 42–43, 77, 87, 131, 142, 226; and Luther, 50–52, 135–41, 142; and Machiavelli, 58, 85, 88, 207, 220; main factors in intellectual background of, 52, 54–62, 65–67, 132–41;

and Mainz, 84–85, 251n. 152; medical writings, 70–72, 79, 98–99, 249nn. 123, 124; motto of, 142; and nationalist historiography, 77, 131; on opinion, 141–42; and Palatine Vicariate, 85; on the papacy, 57, 76, 81, 109, 117, 122–23, 125–26; and Paracelsus, 71, 79; and the Peace of Westphalia, 80–82; pedagogical principles of, 111, 119–21; as physician, 63, 66, 68, 77, 78, 79, 87, 135; and the plague, 52, 58; as political adviser, 77, 78, 84–88, 89; political writings, 61, 73, 75–77, 79–82, 85, 88–89, 249n. 123; portrait of, 142; and prescription, 113–15, 117, 123, 124, 163, 200; as professor of medicine, 68, 70–72, 78, 79; as professor of natural philosophy, 65, 67, 68, 69–70; as professor of politics, 78–79, 80–82, 88; as professor of rhetoric, 65; and public and private spheres, 69, 118–19, 128–30, 135, 138–40, 141–43, 225; and Pufendorf, 129; and religious freedom, 60, 63–64, 67; religious writings, 80–81; reputation of, 68, 79–80, 85, 86, 89, 93, 105–6, 129–30, 135, 145–46; on the Roman empire, 65–67, 75–77, 81–82, 92–93, 106–9, 115–17, 122–23, 125–26, 132–33, 147–49, 156–64; on Roman law, 74–75, 77, 113–15, 159–60, 209–14; and scurvy, 68; service to Brunswick-Wolfenbüttel, 86, 89; service to Denmark, 86, 87; service to France, 85–86, 87; service to Sweden, 77–78, 86; significance of, 41–42, 142–43, 215–17, 223–26; and sovereignty, 75, 76–77, 162, 199–204; and the state, 66–67, 75–77, 82, 113–15, 155, 164, 199–200; and statistics, 60, 72–73, 82, 88–89, 97; teachers of, 55–58, 60–61; and the Thirty Years War, 54, 58–59, 63, 65, 93, 137–41; titles of, 68, 77, 78, 87; and the University of Helmstedt, 52, 53–59, 63, 77–79, 82, 97, 134–35; and the University of Leiden, 56, 59–62, 64–65; wedding of, 68–69; what he really thought, 103–5, 118, 125–26, 130, 141–43, 150–53. *See also* history; Roman empire; sovereignty; state; universal empire

Conring, Hermann, works: *Acroamata sex historico-politica*, 144–45, 146, 147, 148, 149–50; *Animadversiones politicae in Nicolai Machiavelli librum De principe*, 85; *Aristotelis laudatio*, 67, 128, 139–40; *Assertio iuris Moguntini*, 84–85; *Censura diplomatis quod Ludovico imperatori fert acceptum coenobium Lindaviense*, 86; *De calido innato*, 61, 71; *De civili prudentia*, 61, 73, 80, 88, 201, 223; *Deductio Coloniensis*, 87, 252n. 169; *De finibus imperii Germanici*, 76, 81–82, 116, 250n. 139; *De habitus corporum Germanicorum antiqui ac novi causis*, 70–71, 97; *De hermetica medicina*, 71, 79; *De imperii Germanici republica acroamata sex historico-politica*, 144–45, 146, 147, 148, 149–50; *De origine formarum*, 56, 61; *De origine iuris Germanici*, 58, 74–75, 77; *De ratione status*, 80, 98; *De sanguinis generatione et motu naturali*, 70, 98–99; *De statu Europae*, 82, 87; *Discursus ad Lampadium posterior*, 88–89, 124–25; *Dissertatio ad legem primam Codicis Theodosiani*, 97; *Dissertatio de republica imperii Germanici communi*, 97; *Exercitatio historico-politica de notitia singularis alicuius reipublicae*, 97; *Exercitationes academicae de republica imperii Germanici*, 89, 145–47; *Introductio in naturalem philosophiam*, 69–70, 71, 98; *In universam artem medicam singulasque eius partes introductio*, 71–72, 98; *Opera*, 67, 70, 88, 89, 94, 149–50, 226, 249n. 123; *Propolitica*, 88; *Theses variae de morali prudentia*, 61, 96; *Vicariatus imperii Palatinus defensus*, 85; ed. Aristotle, *Politics*, 72–73, 79, 88; ed. Lampadius, *De republica Romano-Germanica*, 67, 73, 88–89, 247n. 98; ed. Machiavelli, *The Prince*, 88; ed. Tacitus, *Germania*, 73, 223. *See also* dissertations; Exercise on the Roman German Emperor; New Discourse on the Roman-German Emperor; The Roman Empire of the Germans

Conring, Hermann (father), 51
Conring, Hermann Johannes (son), 148
Conring, Johannes (brother), 52, 53
Conring, Johannes (grandfather), 51
Conring, Maria, born Meiners (grandmother), 51
conscience. *See* Conring, and conscience; history, and conscience
Constance, Council of, 157
Constantinople, 170, 173
context. *See* history, and context
contract, 48, 159, 170, 201–2
corollaries, 95, 99, 101, 107, 110, 126
Corpus doctrinae Julium, 63
Corpus Iuris, 48, 74, 158, 167, 177, 205–7.
See also Roman law
Counter-Reformation, 18, 60, 93

crisis, xx–xxi, 35–37, 216–17
Crusades, 231–32
Cunaeus, Petrus, 244n. 52
Cunctos populos, 175–76, 205. See also Roman law; universal empire

Daniel, book of, 163–64, 207
Dante, 107, 117
Dark Ages, 19, 26, 166
David, Marcel, 197, 275n. 73
De Germanorum imperio Romano. See *The Roman Empire of the Germans*
Denmark, 86, 87
Deo auctore, 205, 279n. 111. See also Roman law; universal empire
Descartes, René, 9–10, 78, 142
Diephold, Rudolf, 55, 57
Digest, of Justinian, 167, 187, 194; *Deo auctore*, 195, 205, 279n. 111; *Omnem*, 186, 187–92; 1.1.1, 282n. 137; 1.4.1, 186; 2.1.1, 178, 186, 197; 2.1.3, 178–79; 6.1.1, 188, 190–91; 6.1.23, 188; 13.6.5, 188; 14.2.9 (Rhodian law), 156–58, 186, 188, 206; 18.1.25, 187; 27.1.15, 186; 32.1.47, 179; 49.15.24, 167–73. See also Roman law
Dilthey, Wilhelm, 42
Dionysius of Halicarnassus, 157–58
diplomatics. See Conring, and diplomatics
Discursus novus de imperatore Romano-Germanico. See *New Discourse on the Roman-German Emperor*
dissertations, 94–99, 100, 152–53; and books, 101–2, 152–53; and corollaries, 95; criticized at diet of Regensburg, 134–35; as evidence for intellectual history, 100; inaugural, 95; nature and purpose of, 94–96, 101–2, 152–53; and oral performance, 96; and plagiarism, 96; as textbooks, 98; variety of, 95. See also Conring, and dissertations
dominium, 185–204; in antiquity, 185; in Bartolus, 185–99, 203–4; as defense and protection, 189–91; divisibility and indivisibility, 185, 188–89, 190–91, 203–4; and jurisdiction, 185–92, 197–99; and lordship, 186–87; and property, 186, 187–89, 198, 203–4; and *rei vindicatio*, 188–89, 190–91, 204; and territory, 186–87, 198; of universal jurisdiction, 188–89, 192, 278n. 96. See also jurisdiction; property; sovereignty; universal empire
dominium mundi, dominium universale, dominus mundi, dominus universalis, dominus universalium. See universal empire

dominium universalis iurisdictionis, 188, 192. See also universal empire
dominus et monarcha totius orbis, 172, 175. See also universal empire
dominus totius mundi vere, 190–91, 192, 279n. 102. See also universal empire
Donation of Constantine, 170–71
Donation of Otto the Great, 107
Dreitzel, Horst, 46
Droysen, Johann Gustav, 42

early modern political thought, 17–25, 45, 62, 199–203, 223–25, 229–30; in Germany, 42, 49–50, 92–93; study of, 46–50, 229–30
East Frisia, 50–51, 78, 87
Emden, 50
empire. See *imperium*; Roman empire; universal empire
Encyclopedia Britannica, 42
Engelbrecht, Arnold, 63, 64–65, 69
England, 25, 42, 49, 85, 145, 156, 160, 161. See also Bartolus, on French and English monarchies
Enlightenment, xiv, 32, 41, 49, 57, 132, 142–43
Enno Ludwig, count of East Frisia, 50
Erasmus, Desiderius, 62, 236n. 20, 262n. 104
Erbermann, Vitus, 57
evidence. See history, and evidence
Exercise on the Roman German Emperor, 94–128, 134–35, 143, 147–49, 156–64; authenticity of, 124–25, 126–27, 152–53; author of, 99–100, 112, 119–21, 126–27; changes made by Conring, 147–48; conclusion, 112–13, 118, 147–48; importance of, 100–101; and the *New Discourse on the Roman-German Emperor*, 94, 101–5, 126–27; as property, 127; publication of, 94, 99; and *The Roman Empire of the Germans*, 124–25, 147–48. See also Conring, and dissertations; Conring, on the Roman empire; *New Discourse on the Roman-German Emperor*; *The Roman Empire of the Germans*

facts. See history, and facts
Ferdinand II, Emperor, 93
Ferdinand III, Emperor, 50
fiction. See history, and fiction
Foucault, Michel, 37, 38
four world monarchies, theory of, 18, 19–20, 93, 163–64, 207. See also history, and periodization

France, 25, 42, 49, 81, 83–87, 145, 156, 160, 161. *See also* Bartolus, on French and English monarchies
Franklin, Julian, 241n. 17, 280n. 119, 281n. 124
Frederick III, Emperor, 115
Frederick III, king of Denmark, 86
freedom. *See* history, and liberty
Friedrich Wilhelm, Great Elector, of Brandenburg, 81

Gadamer, Hans Georg, 37, 38
Galen, 62
Germany, 41–42, 49–50, 66. *See also* Conring, and Germany; Holy Roman Empire; Roman empire
Giphanius, Obertus, 73, 244n. 53
gloss: on Roman law, 47–48; on *dominium*, 188, 189–91; on jurisdiction, 178–79, 275n. 75; on the Roman people, 169. *See also* Bartolus; Roman law
God, law of, 109, 157, 198, 205–7; and the Roman empire, 195, 197; and truth, 205–7, 211–12, 230–31. *See also* law; universal empire
Goebel, Johann Wilhelm, 62, 82, 89, 129; as editor of Conring's *Opera*, 67, 70, 88, 149, 226, 249n. 123, 250n. 139, 251nn. 152, 160, 252n. 169, 258n. 56, 260n. 82, 267n. 157; and the *New Discourse on the Roman-German Emperor*, 94, 127, 149
Goldast, Melchior, 108
Göttingen, University of, 54, 82, 89
Gran, Nicolaus, 55, 57
Greece, 18, 173, 176. *See also* Roman empire, eastern
Gregory VII, Pope, 57, 117, 156, 163, 224
Gross Twülpstedt, 89, 249n. 120
Grotius, Hugo, 48, 59, 60; on Charlemagne, 113; and Conring, 61–62, 101, 113–14, 157; as founder of international law, 62; on prescription and time, 113–14
Guicciardini, Francesco, 48, 108

Habermas, Jürgen, 46, 238n. 44
Harvey, William, 70
Heidegger, Martin, xxi, 37, 38, 216
Heidmann, Christoph, 55, 78
Heinsius, Daniel, 53, 60–61, 73, 88
Helmstedt (city), 58, 65, 67–68, 69, 79
Helmstedt, University of, 54–55, 58–59, 63, 65, 68, 78, 82, 256n. 28; and intellectual freedom, 55, 63–64, 67, 134–35.

See also Conring, and the University of Helmstedt
Henry IV, Emperor, 57, 156, 163
Henry VII, Emperor, 115, 168
heresy. *See* history, and heresy
Hermes Trismegistus, 71
Herodotus, 29, 31
hierarchy, 197–99, 202–4. *See also* universal empire
Hildebrand. *See* Gregory VII, Pope
Hildebrandine heresy, 57, 109
Hippolithus a Lapide, 130
historical civility, 165–66, 214, 225
historical perspective, 19–22, 32–33, 41–42, 45, 223–25, 231–32
historical revolt, xiv, 16–25, 27, 29–30, 41, 195, 216; in Conring, 43, 53, 65–67, 125–26, 209–17, 223–26; and prescription, 114–15. *See also* history
historicism, 30–31
history, xiii–xxi, 3–45, 89–91, 154, 165–67, 207–18, 219–32; and absence, 5, 7–8, 10–11, 12–13; and absurdity, xxi, 25, 37, 164, 191; and anachronism, 6, 11, 13–15, 17, 90, 132–33, 155, 206, 227–28; and antiquity, 17–25, 29, 31, 228; and authenticity, 44, 104–5, 111, 150–53; and authority, xiv, 10, 16–22, 25, 33–34, 39, 151–53, 156–57, 224–26; and autonomy, xvi–xviii, 9–10, 13–15, 21, 224, 228, 230; and bias, xv–xvi, xviii–xix, 3, 26–27, 219, 231; and boundaries in space and time, 4, 7, 10–12, 14–16, 26–29, 47–50, 75–77, 81, 139–41, 154, 199–200, 227–30; condition of, today, ix, xiii–xxi, 16, 27–29, 30–33, 35–39, 46–50, 90–91, 216–17, 226–30; and conscience, 8–10, 24–25, 27–28, 136–41, 229; and context, ix, 6, 11–12, 29–30, 32–33, 39, 44, 92, 154, 209–15, 217–18, 221–22, 227, 230; and crisis, xx–xxi, 35–37, 216–17; definition of, xiii, 3, 231; and evidence, xvii–xviii, 5–6, 10, 12–13, 14, 20–21, 25, 26, 28–29, 36, 39, 40, 44–45, 90–91, 206–7, 214, 221–23, 224, 227, 231; and facts, 131–32, 158–59, 166–67, 176–77, 206–9, 211–13, 223–24; and fear, xix–xx, 5, 23–25, 28, 225; and fiction, 15, 36; as a form of knowledge, xiii–xx, 3, 4–6, 13–16, 21, 22–24, 26–27, 30–31, 40, 219–23, 230–32; as a form of self-assertion, xiii–xiv, 12–25, 30–31, 222–26, 230–32; founding principle of, 4, 6, 7, 12; fundamental

history (*continued*)
  assumptions of, ix, xvi–xviii, 4–16, 32–39, 219–23, 227, 230–32; in Germany, 41–42, 66; harm done by, 3–4, 26–29, 31–32, 35–36, 39, 231–32; and heresy, 22, 23–24, 25, 27, 207–15, 225–26; and illocutionary acts, 15–16, 102–3, 127–28, 151–52, 222; and immutability, 5, 7–8, 10–11, 12–13; and incommensurability, 44, 212–13, 215–18, 221; and irony, 27; lack of self-understanding of, 22–29, 32–33, 35–36, 39–40, 131–32, 165–67, 214, 227, 230–31; and liberty, xiii–xiv, xvi–xviii, 7–8, 20–22, 31, 66, 215–17, 230; limits of, xviii, xxi, 39–41, 43–45, 47–50, 89–91, 150–54, 165–67, 206–18, 219–32; and modernity, xvi–xviii, 8–10, 13, 16–29, 32–39, 46–50, 200–4, 215–18, 224–32; and moral judgment, 131–32; and nature, xvi–xviii, 8–10, 20, 28, 32, 199, 206–7, 223–24, 231; and objectivity, xv–xvi, xviii–xix, 9, 15–16, 21–22, 25, 26–29, 30–31, 35–37, 39, 221–22, 230–31; and the past, ix, xxi, 4–16, 26, 27–29, 30, 36, 42, 165–67, 227–31; and periodization, 18–20, 26–27, 48–49, 227–28; and philosophy, 37–39; and politics, xiii–xxi, 6–10, 13–15, 30–31, 35–36, 47–50, 66–67, 224–26, 228–32; as practice, xvi, xxi, 12, 15, 45, 231; and the present, 4–16, 27–29, 223–24, 231; as a profession, ix, xiii, xv–xvi, xviii–xix, 4, 19–20, 26–27, 31, 34–35, 40, 226–27; and progress, xiv, xviii, 7, 22, 23, 143, 215–16; and projection, 221–22, 227–28; and public and private spheres, 15, 35–36, 137–38, 142–43, 151–52, 202–4; and reality, 12–13, 20–21, 206–7; and reason, 8–9, 32, 40, 213, 222, 227–28, 231; and religion, xiv, xvi–xviii, 16–20, 47, 49, 230–32; and responsibility, xvi–xviii, 22–25, 31, 36, 131–32, 214; and revolution, xiv, 16, 21–25, 29, 31, 75, 208–9, 215–16, 224, 226; and rhetoric, 17–18, 214, 224; as ritual, 230–32; and science, xiv, xvi–xviii, 8–9, 10, 11, 20, 42, 231; seductive power of, ix, xiv, 23–24, 32–33, 38, 39, 40, 65–67, 165–67, 216–17, 225–26, 230–31; and sovereignty, 7–8, 13–14, 24, 25, 26, 42, 113–14, 199–200, 202; and the state, 66, 113–15, 199–200, 228–31; and subjectivity, 9–10, 15–16, 28–29, 35–37, 45, 90–91, 132–41, 215–17, 227; as technology, xiii, xiv, xvii; and theory, xix–xxi, 15, 36–39, 40, 44–45, 231; and three-dimensional perspective, 20–21; and time, ix, 4–16, 26–29, 35–39, 113–15, 199–200, 206–7, 215–17, 221–23, 226–32; two sides of, 14–16, 27–29, 35–36; and understanding, 3, 13, 26–27, 31, 40, 43–45, 46–50, 92, 102–5, 150–54, 165–67, 209–15, 217, 219–32; varieties of, xv, xviii, xx, 30–31, 33–35, 36–37, 90–91; and violence, xviii, 3, 24, 26–29, 31–32, 34, 39, 41–42, 113–14, 207, 231–32; and writing, 6, 13, 20–21, 24, 29, 206–7. *See also* Bartolus; Conring; historical revolt
Hobbes, Thomas, 24, 42, 49–50, 152, 184, 199, 201, 207, 219–20
Holy Roman Empire, 16–19, 26, 42, 47, 49–50, 83, 90–92; constitution of, 67, 83, 88; coronations, 83, 85, 109, 112, 115, 156, 162; jurisdiction of, 67, 93; title of, 67, 26¹n. 91; vitality of, 42, 132–33. *See also* Conring, on the Roman empire; Roman empire; universal empire
Hornejus, Konrad, 56–57, 67, 128
Hoym, Bogislaus Otho von, 94, 99, 100, 105, 111, 119–21
humanism, 17–27, 33–34, 54–56, 59–60, 73, 74, 157, 166

illocutionary acts. *See* locutionary contents and illocutionary acts
immutability. *See* history, and immutability
imperator, 177, 181–83. *See also imperium;* Roman empire; universal empire
imperium, 177–85, 192–95; in antiquity, 181–83; as criminal jurisdiction, 180; *imperium merum et mixtum*, 178–79, 180, 182; as jurisdiction, 67, 93, 179–80, 183–84; as legislation, 180, 181; and obedience, 169–73, 184, 192–95, 200–202; as power to command, 181–83; redefined by Bartolus, 183–84; as universal lordship, 192–95. *See also dominium;* jurisdiction; Roman empire; sovereignty; universal empire
incommensurability. *See* history, and incommensurability
Innocent X, Pope, 81
Institutes, of Justinian, preface to, 178, 274n. 72; 2.1.11, 188. *See also* Roman law
intention. *See* history, and understanding; locutionary contents and illocutionary acts

Italian city-states. *See* Bartolus, on Italian city-states
Italy, 29, 48–49, 74–75, 145, 160–64, 168. *See also* Roman empire
iurisdictio. *See* jurisdiction
ius, 198–99, 201. *See also* jurisdiction; law

Jacchaeus, Gilbert, 244n. 52
John of Salisbury, 49
John Quidort of Paris, 49
Juliane, regent of East Frisia, 78, 87
Julius, duke of Brunswick-Wolfenbüttel, 63
jurisdiction, 67, 93, 178–95, 197–99, 200–201, 246n. 75, 279n. 109; in antiquity, 181–83; civil, 180; criminal, 180; definition, 178–79; from *ditio*, 178–79, 275n. 75; genus and species, 180, 183–84; and the gloss, 178–79, 275n. 75; *iurisdictio in genere sumpta*, 180; *iurisdictio simplex*, 180; and *ius*, 198–99, 201; and legislation, 180, 181; *potestas de iure publico introducta*, 178–80; and the prince, 25, 186–87, 193, 197–98; universal, 188–89, 192. *See also* Bartolus; *dominium; imperium;* Roman empire; sovereignty; universal empire
Justinian, Emperor, 167, 183, 205. See also *Code; Digest; Institutes; Novels;* Roman law

Kelley, Donald, 46
Kinderling, Andreas, 59–60
knowledge. *See* history, as a form of knowledge
Koselleck, Reinhart, 35–36, 37, 46, 237n. 22
Kristeller, Paul Oskar, 33, 241n. 13
Kuhn, Thomas, 37, 39, 208–9

Lampadius, Jacob, 65, 119; and Conring, 65–67, 72, 105–6, 116; on the Roman empire, 65–66, 67, 93
Lamprecht, Karl, 34
law, 7–9, 47–48, 109, 228–29; canon, 33, 48, 198, 230; civil, 159, 214; codification, 75; and contract, 48, 159, 170, 201–2; divine, 109, 159, 195, 205–6; eternal, 109; human, 109, 159–60; international, 62, 77, 113; moral, 8–9, 20, 36, 47, 58, 61, 136, 229; of nations, 270n. 22; natural, 8–9, 20, 25, 32, 61, 109, 114–15, 159, 164, 198, 202, 211, 214, 229; positive, 9, 20, 25, 61, 109, 113, 114, 138, 159–60, 164, 229; and reason, 61, 109, 114, 159, 164, 198, 202, 204–6, 229; and rights, 113–15, 198–99, 230; and

sovereignty, 7–8, 9–10, 201–2; and time, 7–9, 109, 113–15, 228–29. *See also* jurisdiction; Roman law; sovereignty
laws of nature, 8–9, 206, 230. *See also* history, and science
legislation, 180–81, 184, 191–92, 200–202. *See also* jurisdiction; sovereignty
Lehmann, Christoph, 66
Leibniz, Gottfried Wilhelm, 84, 121
Leiden, University of, 53, 54, 59–60, 62, 64–65, 68
Leo X, Pope, 136
Leopold I, Emperor, 81
liberty. *See* history, and liberty
Lindau (city and convent), 86
Lionne, Hugues de, 85
Lipsius, Justus, 24, 53, 59
literature. *See* history, and fiction
Locke, John, 24, 48, 49, 50, 81, 202–3, 215
locutionary contents and illocutionary acts, 15–16, 102–3, 127–28, 151–52, 222. *See also* history, and understanding
lordship. *See dominium;* universal empire
Lorraine, duchy of, 85, 128
Lothar II, Emperor, 74, 164
Lotharian legend, 74, 164
Louis XIV, king of France, 81, 85
Luke, Gospel of, 156–58, 172, 174, 204–5
Lüneburg. *See* Brunswick-Wolfenbüttel
Luther, Martin, 24, 26, 49, 62, 142, 153, 207, 236n. 20, 262n. 104; and Conring, 135–41, 142
Lutheranism, 50–52, 54, 56–58, 60, 63, 83, 133

Mabillon, Jean, 86
Machiavelli, Niccolò, 24, 42, 50, 58, 85, 88, 207
Magni, Valerianus, 57
Magnus, Hibbe, 53
Mainz, archbishop of, 83–85
Mainz, archbishopric of, 83
Maire, Jean, 247n. 98, 257n. 43
Maitland, Frederic William, 227
Marsiglio of Padua, 41, 47, 262n. 104
Martini, Cornelius, 54, 55, 56, 57
Martinus, 188–89
Mazarin, Cardinal, 85, 133
meaning. *See* history, and understanding; locutionary contents and illocutionary acts
medievalists, 20, 27, 227–28

medieval universalism, 17, 18–22, 25, 42, 43–44, 47, 93, 195–207. *See also* Middle Ages; universal empire
Meinecke, Friedrich, 42
Melanchthon, Philipp, 24, 54, 57, 74
Mesander, Hermann, 53
Middle Ages, 18, 19, 20, 22–23, 26–27, 47, 48–49, 227–29
Mill, John Stuart, 203
Mithobius, Hector Johannes, 86
modernity. *See* history, and modernity
Momigliano, Arnaldo, 41, 131–32
Montaigne, Michel de, 44
Monumenta Germaniae Historica, 42
morality, 8–9, 35–36, 47, 58, 61, 131–32, 136–40, 142. *See also* history, and conscience; law, natural
Mulmann, Johannes, 81

Napoleon, 26, 28, 42
naturalization, 7
natural law. *See* law, natural
nature. *See* history, and nature; law, natural
New Discourse on the Roman-German Emperor, 40–41, 43–45, 50, 92–94, 101–6, 149–50, 156–64, 223–24; argument of, 92–93, 123–24, 156–64, 214, 223–24; authenticity of, 94, 105, 124–25, 126–27, 153; author of, 99–100, 112, 126–28, 151–52; and the Bible, 156–58, 159, 163–64; on Charlemagne, 160–61; conclusion, 112–13, 118–19, 123–24, 147–48, 163; on divine law, 159; and the *Exercise on the Roman German Emperor,* 94, 101–2, 103–5, 124–25, 126–27, 147, 149–50; forgotten, 94, 149–50; on Germany, 92–93, 115, 156, 161–62, 164; and Grotius, 62, 113–15, 157; the hybrid version, 94, 144–45, 153; logic of, 158, 207–15, 223–24, 225–26; on natural law, 114–15, 159, 164; on the Ottonian Empire, 161–62, 163; on the papacy, 115, 123–24, 162–63; popularity of, 94, 144–45; on prescription, 115, 123, 163; as property, 127; publication of, 92, 105; on the question of fact, 158–59; on the question of right, 158–60; rejected by Conring, 93–94, 103–5, 126–27, 130, 135, 149–50; on the Roman empire, 92–93, 112–13, 115, 123–24, 156–63; and *The Roman Empire of the Germans* (differences), 93–94, 107–9, 112, 116–18, 118–19, 123–24, 127–28, 147–48; and *The Roman Empire of the Germans* (similarities), 109–12, 124–25, 127–28, 145; on Roman law, 159–60, 164, 214; significance of, 94, 103–4, 123–24, 135, 149–51, 151–53, 215, 225–26; and sovereignty, 162, 200; on the triple crown, 162; on universal empire, 112–13, 123–24, 156–58, 159–60, 163–64. *See also* Conring, on the Roman empire; *Exercise on the Roman German Emperor; The Roman Empire of the Germans*
Nietzsche, Friedrich, 37–38, 216
Norden, 50–53
Novels, of Justinian, 15.1.1, 179. *See also* Roman law

Oakley, Francis, 46, 48, 237n. 26
Oberman, Heiko, 241n. 13
objectivity. *See* history, and objectivity
Oestreich, Gerhard, 46
Oldenbarnevelt, Johan van, 60
Oldenburger, Philipp, 89
Oldewelt, Johann, 53
Omnem, 187–92. *See also* Roman law; universal empire
Orientalism, chronological, 49, 219, 227–28
Otto the Great, 161–62, 163, 164, 224
Overbeck, Mathias van, 59, 62

papacy, 16–17, 19, 26, 41, 57, 81; and the Roman empire, 75–76, 92–93, 109, 112, 115, 117, 125–26, 148–49, 156, 162–63; as tyranny, 122–23, 148–49. *See also* medieval universalism
Paracelsus, 71, 79
past, ix, xxi, 4–16, 26, 30, 36; absence and immutability of, 5, 7–8, 10–11, 12–13; stateless, 27–29, 42, 165–67, 227–31. *See also* history
Paul, Saint, 23
Peace of Westphalia, 80–82, 132, 141
Pennington, Kenneth, 241n. 16, 274n. 69
periodization. *See* history, and modernity; history, and periodization; Middle Ages
Petrarch, Francesco, 216
Petronius, 157–58
philosophy. *See* history, and philosophy; history, and theory
Pithou, Pierre, 108, 148
plagiarism. *See* authorship, in dissertations; dissertations
Plato, 67, 130

Pocock, J. G. A., 46
politics. *See* history, and politics
Post, Gaines, 48
postliminium, 168
prescription. *See* Conring, and prescription
present, 4–16, 27–29, 223–24, 231. *See also* history, and modernity
primary literature. *See* history, and evidence
prince, 25, 186–87, 193, 197–98. *See also* jurisdiction; sovereignty
Prodi, Paolo, 46
progress, xiv, xviii, 7, 22, 23, 143, 215–16
property, 48, 185–92, 198, 202–4. *See also dominium*
Protestantism, 17–18, 19, 50–52, 54–64, 80–81, 132–34
public and private. *See* history, and public and private spheres
Pufendorf, Samuel, 129

Ranke, Leopold von, xviii, xix–xx, 27, 30, 31, 42
ratio scripta, 205
reason, 8–9, 32, 40, 61, 142, 198, 202, 204–6, 213, 222, 227–28; and faith, 61, 67, 159; and law, 61, 109, 114, 159, 164, 198, 229; of state, 33, 80, 98, 130. *See also* history; law
Reformation, 17–18, 22, 25, 48–50, 135–38, 142–43, 215. *See also* historical revolt
rei vindicatio, 188–89, 190–91, 204
Renaissance, 22, 25, 48, 59, 215. *See also* historical revolt
responsibility. *See* history, and responsibility
revolution. *See* historical revolt; history, and revolution
rhetoric. *See* history, and rhetoric
Rhodian law, 156–58, 186, 188, 206. *See also* Roman law; universal empire
Ricoeur, Paul, 37
Roman empire, 16–17, 18–19, 115–16, 167–68, 181–83; borders of, 75–77, 81, 160, 169; divine foundation of, 195; eastern, 17, 112, 160–61, 173; as evil empire, 122–23, 148–49; as German-Italian state, 93, 108–9, 121; as mere title, 108; as minimum empire, 123; as myth, 27–29, 115–16, 165–67, 174–75, 228–30; size of, 107, 169; as universal empire, 108, 121–22. *See also* Bartolus; Holy Roman Empire; *imperium*; jurisdiction; Roman law; universal empire

Roman Empire of the Germans, The, 75–77, 93–94, 106–12, 116–28, 144, 148–49; and the *Acroamata sex*, 144; and the Apocalypse, 122–23, 148–49; author of, 94, 97, 111–12; conclusion, 117–18, 123, 124, 127–28, 147–48; as a dissertation, 82–83, 97, 110–11; on Germany, 109–10, 116–18; and Guicciardini, 108; on law, 109; letter of dedication, 106–7, 125–26; letter to the reader, 92–93, 106–7; and the *New Discourse on the Roman-German Emperor* (differences), 107–9, 112, 116–18, 118–19, 123–24, 127–28, 147–48; and the *New Discourse on the Roman-German Emperor* (similarities), 109–12, 124–25, 127–28, 145; on the papacy, 117–18, 122–24, 148–49; and Pithou, 108, 148; on prescription, 117, 124; publication of, 106–7, 111; the revised edition, 148–49; on the Roman empire, 108–9, 116–18, 121–22, 123, 124; significance of, 75–77, 127–28, 135, 140–41, 143; structure of, 108, 145; subject of, 106. *See also* Conring, on the Roman empire; *Exercise on the Roman German Emperor*; *New Discourse on the Roman-German Emperor*
Roman law, 8–9, 21, 23, 26; authority of, in Germany, 74–75; on enemies of Rome, 167–68; as *ratio scripta*, 205; on *rei vindicatio*, 188–89, 190–91, 204; universality of, 156–58, 205–6. *See also* Bartolus, and Roman law; *Code*; Conring, on Roman law; *Corpus Iuris*; *Digest*; *dominium*; gloss on Roman law; *imperium*; *Institutes*; jurisdiction; law; *Novels*; Roman empire
Romans (Saint Paul's letter), 205
Romanticism, 28, 228
Rome (city), 53, 75–76, 115, 121, 156–64, 214
Rorty, Richard, 37
Rostock, University of, 51
Rousseau, Jean-Jacques, 203, 281n. 125

Savigny, Friedrich Karl von, 226
Scaliger, Joseph Justus, 53, 59
Scheffer, Sebastian, 72, 98
scholasticism, 17–18, 33, 57, 183
Schönborn, Johann Philipp von, 83
Schrader, Christoph, 59, 60, 65, 67
Schwartzkopf, Johannes, 78, 254n. 5
science. *See* history, and nature; history, and science

Scientific Revolution, 17–18
self-assertion. *See* history, as a form of self-assertion
Sennert, Daniel, 78
Sigismund, Emperor, 115, 157
Skinner, Quentin, 46, 47, 49, 102, 274n. 68, 275n. 73, 282n. 1
sources. *See* history, and evidence
sovereignty, 7–8, 13–14, 24, 25, 26, 28, 48, 137–38, 199–204; absolute and unconditional, 201; and borders in space and time, 7, 113–14, 199–200, 202; in Conring, 75, 76–77, 84, 162, 199–200, 203–4; in Germany, 40–41; indivisibility of, 200, 202–3; and law, 7–8, 9–10, 48, 201–2; and obedience, 200–202; and the prince, 25, 186–87, 193, 197–98; and tyranny, 25, 201. *See also* history, as a form of self-assertion; history, and sovereignty; jurisdiction
Spain, 60, 145
Starovolski, Simon, 86
state, 47, 48, 49–50, 90, 143, 228–31. *See also* Conring, and the state; history, and the state; sovereignty
stateless past. *See* past, stateless
statistics. *See* Conring, and statistics
Stolleis, Michael, 41, 46
Stucke, Anna Maria, 68–69
Stucke, Johann, 68–69, 77
subject and subjectivity. *See* history, and subjectivity; sovereignty
Sweden, 55, 69, 77–78, 83, 86

Tacitus, 21, 23, 29, 71, 73
Taylor, Charles, 38, 215, 237n. 24, 264n. 120
Telio, Sylvester, 88
theory. *See* history, and theory
Thirty Years War. *See* Conring, and the Thirty Years War
Thomas Aquinas, Saint, 23
Thomasius, Christian, 245n. 59
Thucydides, 29, 134
Tierney, Brian, 46, 48
time. *See* history, and time
Trithemius, Johannes, 107–8
Troeltsch, Ernst, 42

Ullmann, Walter, 48, 240n. 6, 253n. 1
Ulpian, 167–68
unconsciousness. *See* history, lack of self-understanding of
understanding. *See* history, and understanding
United Provinces, 59–60, 84
universal empire, 16–17, 93, 171–72, 192–214, 228–30; Conring versus Bartolus on, 43–44, 156–58, 165–67, 192–214, 225–26; and God, 195; and heresy, 22, 193–94, 210–11, 212, 225–26; indivisibility of, 190–91, 192, 195; limited in fact, 175–77, 194, 208–9; limited in law, 191–92, 194–95; as myth, 27–29, 165–67, 174–75, 228–30; and obedience, 169–73, 184, 192–95, 200–202; and property, 203–4; and *rei vindicatio*, 188–89, 190–91, 204; as right to universal legislation, 184, 208–9; and sovereignty, 203–4; and territorial rule, 193, 196–98. *See also dominium; imperium;* jurisdiction; medieval universalism; Roman empire

via moderna, 17–18
Vico, Giambattista, xx, 30
Victorius, Petrus, 73, 244n. 53
violence. *See* history, and violence
Voltaire, 34, 132
Voss, Heinrich, 98
Vossius, Gerhard Johannes, 60–62

Wasmuth, Matthias, 57
Weber, Max, 42
White, Hayden, 12, 37
Whitehead, Alfred North, 37, 235n. 11, 280n. 112
William of Ockham, 49
Wittenberg, University of, 51, 54, 56, 57, 78, 133
Wittgenstein, Ludwig, 40, 151, 210, 216, 238n. 50, 265n. 132, 280n. 118
Witzel, Georg, 80
Wolf, Johann, 68
Wolfenbüttel, (library), 84
writing. *See* history, and evidence; history, and writing

www.ingramcontent.com/pod-product-compliance
Lightning Source LLC
Chambersburg PA
CBHW021933290426
44108CB00012B/820